Interdisciplinary Perspectives on the
Authority of Scripture

Interdisciplinary Perspectives on the Authority of Scripture

Historical, Biblical, and Theoretical Perspectives

Edited by CARLOS R. BOVELL

Foreword by William Abraham

PICKWICK *Publications* · Eugene, Oregon

INTERDISCIPLINARY PERSPECTIVES ON THE AUTHORITY OF SCRIPTURE
Historical, Biblical, and Theoretical Perspectives

Pickwick Publications
An Imprint of Wipf and Stock Publishers
199 W. 8th Ave., Suite 3
Eugene, OR 97401

www.wipfandstock.com

isbn 13: 978-1-60899-347-5

Cataloging-in-Publication data:

Interdisciplinary perspectives on the authority of Scripture : historical, biblical, and theoretical perspectives / edited by Carlos R. Bovell

p. ; 23 cm. Includes bibliographical references.

isbn 13: 978-1-60899-347-5

1. Bible—Evidences, authority, etc. I. Title.

BS480 I5 2011

Manufactured in the U.S.A.

To Jamie, Elena, Mateo, and Luisa

May they never feel they've been "hoodwinked by a fairytale"

Contents

Foreword

William J. Abraham

Aᴛ ᴀ ʀᴇᴄᴇɴᴛ ᴀᴄᴀᴅᴇᴍɪᴄ conference where the doctrine of the inerrancy of scripture was under gentle but critical fire, an agitated participant towards the back of the room found it difficult to suppress his deep theological and spiritual distress. It was easy to sympathize with him: the doctrine of inerrancy was constitutive of his spiritual life; losing it would involve a dramatic undermining of his faith and obedience; one could see the anguish in his face and in his soul. In these circumstances it is tempting to lay low and do nothing. Perhaps one is running the risk of that threatening millstone being slung around one's neck before being cast overboard to be drowned at the bottom of the sea. However, this is but half the story. Many folk have given up the faith because of the problems related to inerrancy making it pastorally and spiritually irresponsible to be intimated by the pervasive pressure to ignore the issue or to hold back from engagement and the search for better ways of thinking about scripture. To be sure, many who have initial difficulties find their way into other versions of Christianity and stay on board. However, it is not difficult to see that even then the negative effects of inerrancy can surface in hidden ways. Witness the kind of aggressive, strident progressivism that trumpets its own unrecognized intolerance in the name of liberation and enlightenment. It is often the mirror image of the doctrine of inerrancy that is rejected; or, more aptly, the old anxieties and insecurities show up afresh in the revised edition.

In my own spiritual and theological journey, inerrancy was never a serious option. I had been introduced to scripture both at school and at church in Ireland. I can still recall the drumbeat of the diverse readings at morning assembly; I fondly remember finding the drama, say, of the book of Exodus, both repellant and attractive in a Sunday School class led by an ordinary, devout Irish farmer; and I can readily bring to mind the work of historical critics that I was exposed to in religious studies as I prepared for the regular examinations prior to university. Exposure to scripture–to its actual, messy, diverse contents–was at the core of my encounter; theoretical commitments about, say, the nature of divine inspiration, were tacit and underdeveloped. The challenge the actual contents generated were penetrating and even disturbing; they still are in my regular teaching of scripture virtually every week in my local church. Hence I can tolerate with ease homiletical readings which are superficial and silly because the content of the texts themselves are always intrinsically interesting and faith-forming. Over against this, it is an exquisite pleasure to listen to a truly great unpacking of the biblical materials by preachers, biblical scholars, and theologians. Any idea of abandoning scripture or marginalizing its place in the life of faith and the church has always been completely anathema to me.

When I was converted from atheism as a teenager, it was the figure of Christ who captured me and won my allegiance. Scripture and the incomparable hymns of Charles Wesley were the natural homeland in which he lived and had his being. My sense from the outset was that scripture was first and foremost a means of grace; it was an inexhaustible reservoir of illumination and wisdom. I was certainly interested in the debate about inspiration, revelation, and authority that swirled around the idea of scripture; in time I did a doctoral thesis on the nature of historical criticism and its application to discourse about divine action; I wrote a book on the divine inspiration of scripture; eventually I branched out to develop my own revisionist vision of canon. However, I never felt under any pressure to either accept or be intimidated by inflated theories of scripture that identified scripture with divine revelation or that required a doctrine of inerrancy to secure its pivotal place in the life of the church. Equally I did not sense any need to rail against inerrancy; if anything I found its articulation and defense a fascinating enterprise.

I have long believed that the Christian faith is best served by a really robust version of its content and practices that eschews any doctrine of inerrancy. Yet the polarization and polemic that dogs the debate about scripture seems to undercut this possibility at every turn. I find this extremely puzzling. Insofar as I have an explanation for this it would take into account the privileging of German biblical scholarship over British biblical scholarship, the legacy of the fundamentalist-modernist debate that resurfaces again and again under new labels, the drive towards ephemeral forms of certainty, and an aversion to reliability as fully adequate for the life of faith. Students in the United States, at least, seem to have little or no idea that it is possible to embrace a vision of Christianity that is deep, orthodox, spiritually satisfying, and morally responsible. Somehow, the range of options is so narrow and the polemical overtones are so pervasive that any kind of sensible, substantial form of Christianity never really gets taken seriously. I am not thinking here of some kind of wishy-washy via media that is intellectually boring and that can be had on the cheap by splitting the difference between extremes; I have in mind the kind of orthodoxy that can find a home across the great historic divisions of Christianity and that requires extensive intellectual labor to articulate. Yet even its varied exposition and defense by the indomitable and brilliant C. S. Lewis at a popular level has not created space for what is in mind. Many evangelicals readily plunder his work but deny or ignore his vision of scripture.

Much of the debate about scripture has gone round in circles because it has failed to see that scripture has played a role in the church as both a warrant for theological claims and as an indispensable means of grace that have fostered discipleship. Thus it has fallen into the domains of both epistemology and soteriology. Too often the former has been made primary; scripture has been approached first and foremost as an infallible foundation for theological claims developed under the aegis of a doctrine of divine revelation and divine inspiration. When this then collapses the soteriological function of scripture is lost; salvation has been made to hinge on a very particular range of epistemic doctrines. Beyond that the great truths of the faith as articulated in the creeds have been undercut and the church's intellectual commitments have become hopelessly unstable across space and time. It is not just an irony but a tragedy that doctrines of scripture which are intended to safeguard and foster commitment turn out to be incessantly destructive of faith. Once we grant primacy to epistemology in our understanding of Christianity— in this case an epistemology that turns scripture into a canon of truth— we become slaves to the kind of theories that can all too easily draw us away from the meaty content of the faith; or, worse still, we undermine the very content of the gospel and the great faith of the church.

It does not help that the diverse and manifold character of evangelicalism gets undermined by constant efforts to suppress its real history and to use its good name to push for one and only one vision of scripture. Thus the essentially contested character of the evangelical tradition is denied or sidelined to keep alive a supposedly high view of scripture. Even if this means suppressing the pivotal role of forms of pietism in evangelicalism, there are plenty of scholars who will pay the price and, if need be, launch their own tirades against this noble version of Christianity. Yet it is precisely evangelicals who should be leading the charge to develop healthy and intellectually illuminating doctrines of scripture. As things stand it is all too easy to report that the standard doctrine that shows up in the literature is not the best gift evangelicalism has to offer to Christianity as a whole. All too often it is the doctrine of inerrancy or a variation thereof that is held up as the jewel of the tradition.

Once we distinguish between an epistemological and soteriological vision of scripture we can make real progress on several fronts. Consider, first, how this might help in work in the epistemology of theology. We certainly need substantial visions of divine revelation in any serious epistemology of theology. It is this need that has often fuelled inflationary views of scripture. Once we see that an epistemological vision of scripture often inhibits developments in this domain then we can be released to deal with the underlying agenda with freedom and flair. We can even turn to scripture itself to mine it for fecund epistemological suggestions and insights.

Second, we can bring the whole field of soteriology and of the role of scripture in this arena into greater focus. We have barely scratched the surface here. There is plenty of talk about sin, salvation, justification, liberation, and the like, but we lack full-scale treatments that speak in a really deep way to our souls. Even then our efforts need to be integrated with the best work we can muster in ascetic theology more generally.

Permit a couple of ancillary comments before I delineate other benefits that are within reach. We can pursue these explorations in epistemology and soteriology more fruitfully once we distinguish between scholarly doctrines of scripture and the canonical doctrines that are legitimately and wisely adopted by this or that church. A doctrine of the canon of scripture is not in itself a canonical doctrine of the church in the sense of a doctrine officially, explicitly, or canonically adopted by a Christian community. It is in fact astonishing that the church in the patristic period poured much more energy into developing an official, canonical creed than it did into delineating its canon of scripture. Equally astonishing is the fact that the patristic church was perfectly happy to permit radically different options in its epistemological commitments compared to, say, its doctrine of God. Turning this on its head and insisting on the primacy of epistemology has been a hallmark of the modern and postmodern period; it has been disastrous for the spiritual welfare of the church, its ministries, and its mission.

Once we grant the distinction between a vision of the canon of scripture and the canonical commitments of the church; and once we relax about the diversity of epistemological commitments open to Christians; then we can develop a deflationary disposition even to doctrines of inerrancy. Doctrines of the inerrancy of scripture have abounded in the history of the church; they are not going to disappear any day soon. Indeed they can be developed with great sophistication and spiritual sensitivity. They can find their place in the wider debate about the epistemology of theology, which is exactly where they belong. The really deep problems arise when they are made canonical and when they are correlated with the spiritual health of believers. To be sure, there are some Christians who cannot survive if they abandon inerrancy; I would not hesitate to counsel such believers to hold to their vision of inerrancy. With the saints I believe that there is nothing more valuable than the salvation of our souls; if a person's salvation requires inerrancy, it would be imprudent to abandon inerrancy. However, it is equally folly to insist that this be true of all believers, much less that inerrancy be adopted as a canonical doctrine of the church or its teaching institutions. It is not easy to keep these kinds of distinctions in mind, but once they are grasped and internalized they are profoundly liberating.

A further, third benefit lies in store if we can find ways to get beyond doctrines of inerrancy or put them in their place in the epistemology of theology. These moves would help significantly in the quest for theological readings of scripture. We have been through a phase of biblical studies where the text has often been read by experts who take pride in their functional atheism. The real problem here is not simply the dissection of the texts into fragments and its disintegration into bits and pieces; nor is the real problem the contemporary readiness to use the text to serve this or that ideological agenda; nor is the problem the undermining of the confidence of the general reader by those who insist that only scientific or critical experts can really fathom these materials. The real problem is the inability to deal seriously with the theological and spiritual subject matter of the texts and to come to grips with them as belonging to the life of faith and to the church. Developing approaches to scripture that have real space for plumbing its spiritual and theological depths is a critical desideratum of scripture scholarship in the future. Happily, the field is opening up with the new raft of theological commentaries that are emerging. We need full-bodied, non-defensive theologies of scripture that will confirm and deepen this kind of scholarship in the future.

It is worth pursuing this topic from another angle. Much biblical scholarship is an intellectual disgrace. We have reached the point where the methods are so diverse and contradictory and the results so manifold and incoherent that a reasonable person can be forgiven for wondering if it should be taken seriously. It is certainly odd that we have intellectual disciplines named in terms of a book or even half a book; we have learned professors of Old and New Testament, of Biblical theology, of the Hebrew Bible, and so forth. So maybe the whole enterprise was botched from the beginning. However, we need not affirm this to plead that the scene taken as a whole has produced a Babel of voices that undercuts the claims to represent any kind of scientific or critical field of inquiry. We might say the same of philosophy, but philosophers have never pretended that they would provide consensus on any front; we have always known that it is a bit like looking in a dark room for a black cat that had already escaped through the window. Biblical scholarship, however, promised to throw light on scripture, the word and wisdom of God. Hence it is not at all surprising that believers take refuge in doctrines of inerrancy that provide initial if fleeting solace from the mess that biblical studies has become.

Fourth, we can hope that moving beyond inerrancy might release a flood of fresh energy to plumb the deep theological riches of the faith that lie within and without scripture. Evangelicals have been spongers when it comes to the great themes of the faith. The impulses of the mind have been much too cribbed and confined. Many feel that all we need to do is to add scripture to the latest high-powered work in analytic or post modern philosophy and all will be well. We lack the depth and existential richness of an Augustine, a Symeon, a Calvin, a Wesley, or a Dostoyesky. It would be silly to blame this on doctrines of inerrancy, but the obsession with epistemology that it makes manifest erodes immersion in the full canonical faith of the church both before and after the Great Schism. Not surprisingly the correlative forays into political theology lack nuance and depth, as rival schools reach for the slogans and platitudes of our polarized political discourse. The deep themes of creation and redemption, of glory and suffering, of sin and holiness, these need to be pursued cut free from the strictures that bedevil so much evangelical theology. In this context doctrines of inerrancy and the vast efforts expanded to keep them afloat are a distraction. The sheep of Christ deserve more from us; we can surely hope that they will be given greener pastures in which to graze.

Reference to the sheep whom Christ came to feed and save suggests a fifth and final point. Moving beyond inerrancy should foster fresh thinking and innovation in the ministry of evangelism. Many committed to inerrancy have long felt and argued that inerrancy is essential to the work of evangelism. The arguments were manifold. The mainline churches that lost inerrancy also lost the motivation for evangelism. The deep reason for this is that they lost a biblical vision of sin without which evangelism became obsolete. Something akin to these judgments was pivotal to the debate in the late twentieth century within the Southern Baptist Convention. More positively, it is thought that the doctrine of scripture in which inerrancy was embedded underwrote the constructive catechetical practice of giving new converts a Bible and urging them to use it as the foundation of their spiritual lives. These are weak arguments. As I noted earlier, inerrancy has led many to abandon the faith rather than stay with it; converts were promised what could not over time be delivered. The story of mainline decline cannot be reduced to this simplistic narrative; many mainline congregations are making significant progress in the recovery of evangelistic nerve and practice. Most important of all, proper catechetical formation needs to be far more comprehensive than any doctrine of scripture can supply. The issue before us is not that of inerrancy, infallibility, or a vision of biblical authority; what is at stake is well-rounded initiation into the great treasures of the canonical heritage of the church.

This volume should go a long way to paving the way for richer, constructive visions of scripture that should serve the church well in the days ahead. There is no quick fix; we need painstaking research that will win the hearts and minds of future theologians. The range of topics here is by no means exhaustive, but they are minimally necessary for any future work. They deserve serious and sustained attention.

Editor's Preface

Carlos R. Bovell

Late in 2007 I conceived a plan for a multi-authored work that focuses exclusively on inerrancy. The aim of the work would be to encourage conservative evangelical communities to talk more openly about the doctrine, specifically its problems and limitations, providing a great service for both those reframing evangelical conceptions of scripture's authority and those defending Warfield's classic construal.

I myself have wrestled with inerrancy's shortcomings for about fifteen years. In an early study I posed questions about the intertextual relationship between Gen 2 and the Primary History. The historical relationship I established (at least to my satisfaction) seemed to have negative ramifications for doing biblical theology.[1] In another essay, I proposed a creative, canonical reading for the book of Ruth.[2] While considering the extent to which the biblical tradents of the wisdom literature operated with a deliberate sense of canon-consciousness, I could not escape the conclusion that, on the whole, the biblical tradents, whoever they may have been, were far more interested in providing culturally and socially salient religious materials to contemporary hearers and readers than worrying about 21st century inerrantists demanding historical, geographic, and scientific accuracy.[3] I was forced early in my studies,

---

1. See C. Bovell, "Gen 3.21: The History of Israel in a Nutshell?" *Exp Tim* 115 (2004): 361–66; "Historical 'Retrojection' and the Prospect of a Pan-Biblical Theology," *Exp Tim* 115 (2004): 397–401.

2. See C. Bovell, "Symmetry, Ruth and Canon," *JSOT* 28 (2003): 189–205.

3. And this is exactly what one would expect when viewed through the lens of evolutionary psychology. Saliency, I later learned, is one of the primary factors responsible for the successful transmission of religious ideas and concepts. See C. Bovell, "If

then, to face up to what James Kugel calls "the Protestant abhorrence of intermediaries."[4] It did not take long to concede that my incessant preoccupation with inerrancy is not only anachronistic but more indicative of an emotional need for certainty than any property inherent to scripture.[5]

For observations such as the ones I describe in *Inerrancy and the Spiritual Formation of Younger Evangelicals* go beyond recognizing that all historiography is ideological and that literary works can be historical.[6] In my experience, however, inerrantists prefer, by and large, to simply leave it at that. Yet as they press on, whatever results they ultimately produce will be sure to comply fully with the inerrantist doctrine they started with. It is precisely at this juncture, however, that more searching questions are needed: *Is it academically fruitful for evangelical scholarship that inerrancy is constantly maintained during all phases of research?* Or closer to home for me: *Is it healthy for students' formative understanding of faith that they be forced to adopt inerrancy as the default bibliological position?* Although it is true that assumptions work to govern and inform all research programs, inerrancy may turn out to be too extreme a position to codify as *the* universal, evangelical starting place. On the face of it, there is something incredibly artificial about ensuring beforehand via inerrantist culture and politics that the fruits of evangelical scholarship will always support inerrancy.

If this methodological contrivance were not troubling enough, its practical outworking is enough to break a camel's back. The inerrantist communities I inhabited prided themselves on being spiritual "watchdogs" both socially and institutionally. Not a few believers reckon it their spiritual duty to police biblical scholarship for any and all threats to inerrancy. Although their intention, charitably interpreted, is to minister

Scientists Can Naturalize God, Should Philosophers Re-supernaturalize Him?" *TT* 64 (2007): 340–48.

4. See J. Kugel, "The Bible's Earliest Interpreters," *Proof* 7 (1987): 270.

5. Compare E. J Carnell: "Unless our religious convictions grow out of a divinely revealed system of truth, we shall have no means by which to be certain that *anything* is holy, not even love itself. This is probably the crucial reason why a conservative refuses to surrender his conviction that Scripture contains the only infallible rule of faith and practice." See Carnell, "Conservatives and Liberals Do Not Need Each Other," *Christianity Today*, May 21,1965, repr. in E. J. Carnell, *The Case for Biblical Christianity: Essays on Theology, Philosophy, Ethics, Ecumenism, Fundamentalism, Separatism*, ed. R. Nash (Grand Rapids: Eerdmans, 1969), 36, italics in original.

6. C. Bovell, *Inerrancy and the Spiritual Formation of Younger Evangelicals* (Eugene, OR: Wipf and Stock, 2007).

to others by trying to help them safeguard their faith, a destructive side-effect is the painful stunting of evangelical spiritual growth, particularly for those needing space to ask honest and penetrating questions. For example, some young believers are unsettled by the inerrantist handling of critical data. Others grow leery over time of inerrantism's systemic resistance to widely accepted results of non-theological disciplines. Kent Sparks comments on the former as a believing, biblical scholar:

> In their efforts to confront the threat of liberal modernism in the church, academy, and society during the early twentieth century, fundamentalists sent their young men (and occasionally, women) to universities where they could be properly credentialed and suitably trained to understand and then refute the work of modern biblical critics. In many universities, however, fundamentalist perspectives were so academically unpalatable that it was almost impossible for a theologically conservative student to study the Bible and graduate with his or her religious views intact, as was evidenced, even then, by the many conservative graduate students who surrendered their faith during their pursuit of a doctoral credential. Many fundamentalists avoided these difficulties by majoring in the "safe" disciplines (textual criticism, Greek classics, and Near Eastern Studies) or by studying in institutions where critical issues could be avoided (especially in conservative Jewish schools and in British universities). Nevertheless, even in these more insular circumstances, it was impossible for bright, young fundamentalist students to avoid noticing that the biblical and historical evidence created, or at least seemed to create, substantial difficulties for their conservative doctrine of Scripture. As a result. . .this new generation. . .now called evangelicals—intended to use their intellectual and critical skills to prove that fundamentalism's view of the Bible was correct all along.[7]

Darrell Falk writes about the latter in his capacity *qua* believing scientist:

> People who know about astronomy, for example, will feel as though they are being asked to cast aside their understanding of this discipline if they want to follow Jesus in the context of the evangelical church. People who trust that geology is not a corrupt science will think they must make a decision between abandoning their knowledge about geology and becoming full-fledged members of Christ's body. As our young people go to college

---

7. K. Sparks, *God's Word in Human Words: An Evangelical Appropriation of Critical Biblical Scholarship* (Grand Rapids: Baker, 2009), 145–146.

and study, they will incorrectly perceive that they need to make a decision that is focused not so much on whether to pick up their cross and follow Jesus but on whether astronomy, astrophysics, nuclear physics, geology and biology are all very wrong.[8]

One need not agree with Sparks or Falk to appreciate that for some believers, inerrantism is a stumbling block. If this is the case, *something needs to be done—at least for the sake of these believers!*

For my part, that the only results acceptable to inerrantists are those reconcilable with inerrancy has proven too much to swallow.[9] In my church and seminary experiences, believers appeared all-too-ready to suddenly withhold the loving and supportive social infrastructure that comes with evangelical community from persons constructively critiquing inerrancy's explanatory adequacy. Almost without notice, an admired professor can be forced to resign, a respected church leader asked to step down, an employee inexplicably fired, or a believer dismissed as liberal or apostate. How are students supposed to integrate what they learn in school with what they learn in church if they are constantly being harassed by inerrantism's thought police?

At first, I inferred evangelical leaders must be unaware of the damaging effects of inerrantist culture else they would have afforded students various spiritual disciplines for coping with inerrancy's cultural oppressiveness. With the naiveté of an unsuspecting Socrates, I figured if evangelical leaders only knew how inerrancy leads some to debilitating fits of psycho-spiritual trauma, they would immediately change their ways, attending more closely to the spiritual dynamics of their pedagogy.[10] However, I now understand that that assumption was incalculably

8. D. Falk, *Coming to Peace with Science: Bridging the Worlds between Faith and Biology* (Downers Grove, IL: InterVarsity Press, 2004), 25.

9. A deep sense of spiritual depression had set in, deconstructing even my perception of the value of work. Compare M. Crawford, *Shop Class as Soulcraft: An Inquiry into the Value of Work* (New York: The Penguin Press, 2009), 108–9: "[T]he trappings of scholarship were used to put a scientific cover on positions arrived at otherwise. . . [P]art of my job consisted of making arguments about global warming that just happened to coincide with the positions taken by the oil companies that funded the think tank."

10. I voice my concerns in C. Bovell, *Inerrancy and the Spiritual Formation of Younger Evangelicals* (Eugene, OR: Wipf and Stock, 2007); *By Good and Necessary Consequence: A Preliminary Genealogy of Biblicist Foundationalism* (Eugene, OR: Wipf and Stock, 2009); and *Rehabilitating Inerrancy in a Culture of Fear* (Eugene, OR: Wipf and Stock, 2011). See also C. Bovell, "Two Examples of How the History of Mathematics Can Inform Theology," *Theology and Science* 8 (2010): 69–84.

wrong for not only are students seeking more credible, contemporary expressions of scripture's divine authority, evangelical leaders are, too. Whether the work already underway can remain within the pale has yet to be seen.

Accepting all of this was not easy for me. Emotionally, I simply could not process inerrancy's deep-seated, performative contradiction.[11] For whatever reason, I had adopted an attitude that held—at least when it comes to inerrancy—anything less than spiritual certainty was tantamount to unbelief. Yet at the same time, it seemed also to go without saying that if inerrantist scholarship was to be spiritually fruitful, to say nothing of academically legitimate, it had to maintain an open-ended, always-a-work-in-progress mindset, not only for biblical studies, but also for interacting with the established claims of scholarship coming from other quarters, particularly the deliverances of disciplines that have nothing to do with inerrantism in the first place.

The way some conservative authors would selectively quote critical scholars left little room for me to imagine that there could be other fruitful ways to construe an "orthodox" faith (i.e., consistent with inerrancy's *spiritual* goals) without an overarching doctrinal framework already grounded in inerrantism.[12] Even now, as I slowly move on from inerrantist evangelicalism, I marvel at the way conservative evangelical writers are virtually the only Christians still left talking about the inspiration and authority of the Bible.[13] If the faith really does live or die based on the success of inerrantism's "high" expectations for scripture, why is my little corner of inerrantist Christendom the only one insisting on defending it?[14]

11. Admitting this is a very big step toward recovering from fundamentalism, which is why to some believers works like C. Smith's *The Bible Made Impossible* (Grand Rapids: Brazos, 2011) are worth their weight in gold.

12. Noll is exactly right to say an over-commitment to inerrancy quenches the imagination: "To confuse the *distinctive* with the *essential* is to compromise the life-transforming character of Christian faith. It is also to compromise the renewal of the Christian mind." See M. Noll, *The Scandal of the Evangelical Mind* (Grand Rapids: Eerdmans, 1994), 244, italics his.

13. Compare D. Farkasfalvy, *Inspiration and Interpretation: A Theological Introduction to Scripture* (Washington, D. C.: Catholic University of America Press, 2010), 5, and W. Abraham, "Foreword," in S. Menssen and T. Sullivan, *The Agnostic Inquirer: Revelation from a Philosophical Standpoint* (Grand Rapids: Eerdmans, 2007), xiii-xiv.

14. At first, the answer seemed obvious: "Because we are the only believers left!"

Reflecting on Farkasfalvy's summary of recent developments in bibliology, I decided to peruse again the handful of multi-authored works on scripture that I have on my shelf: *Biblical Authority*; *The Authoritative Word*; *Inerrancy*; *Inerrancy and the Church*; *Errancy*; *Can the Bible Be Trusted?*; *Hermeneutics, Inerrancy and the Bible*; *Hermeneutics, Authority and Canon*; *Scripture and Truth*; *Inerrancy and Common Sense*; *The Trustworthiness of God*; *A Pathway into the Holy Scripture*; *God's Inerrant Word*; *The Infallible Word*; *Inerrancy and Hermeneutic*; and *Evangelicals and Scripture*—over 175 essays in all representing a variety of evangelical viewpoints.[15] What strikes me as most interesting is the observation that, in spite of the absolutist rhetoric surrounding some of the controversy, every inerrantist proposal presents a tentative theological construct. Scholars proffer them to the church in pious response to their reading of scripture as divine revelation.[16] On the whole, conservative believers are always looking for better and more useful ways to express,

---

But this now seems both ignorant and arrogant. Compare Noll: "In the first instance, historical study or travel throughout North America and the rest of the world should help evangelicals realize that much of what is distinctive about American evangelicalism is not essential to Christianity." See Noll, *The Scandal of the Evangelical Mind*, 243.

15. J. Rogers, ed., *Biblical Authority* (Waco, TX: Word Books, 1977); D. McKim, ed., *The Authoritative Word: Essays on the Nature of Scripture* (Grand Rapids: Eerdmans, 1983); N. Geisler, ed., *Inerrancy* (Grand Rapids: Zondervan, 1980); J. Hannah, ed., *Inerrancy and the Church* (Chicago: Moody Press, 1984); N. Geisler, ed., *Errancy* (Grand Rapids: Zondervan, 1981); E. Radmacher, ed., *Can the Bible Be Trusted?* (Wheaton, IL: Tyndale House Publishers, 1979); E. Radmacher and R. Preus, ed., *Hermeneutics, Inerrancy and the Bible: Papers from ICBI Summit II* (Grand Rapids: Zondervan, 1984); D. Carson and J. Woodbridge, ed., *Hermeneutics, Authority and Canon* (Grand Rapids: Zondervan, 1986); D. Carson and J. Woodbridge, ed., *Scripture and Truth* (Grand Rapids: Zondervan, 1983); R. Nicole and J. R. Ramsey, ed., *Inerrancy and Common Sense* (Grand Rapids: Baker, 1980); P. Helm and C. Trueman, ed., *The Trustworthiness of God: Perspectives on the Nature of Scripture* (Grand Rapids: Eerdmans, 2002); P. Satterthwaite and D. Wright, ed., *A Pathway into the Holy Scripture* (Grand Rapids: Eerdmans, 1994); J. W. Montgomery, ed., *God's Inerrant Word: An International Symposium on the Trustworthiness of Scripture* (Minneapolis, MN: Bethany Fellowship, Inc., 1974); N. Stonehouse and P. Woolley, ed., *The Infallible Word: A Symposium by Members of the Faculty of Westminster Theological Seminary* (Philadelphia: Presbyterian and Reformed Publishing Company, 1946); H. Conn, ed. *Inerrancy and Hermeneutic: A Tradition, a Challenge, a Debate* (Grand Rapids: Baker, 1988); and V. Bacote, L. Miguélez, and D. Okholm, ed., *Evangelicals and Scripture: Tradition, Authority and Hermeneutics* (Grand Rapids: InterVarsity Press, 2004).

16. Compare A. Holmes: "I see inerrancy as a second-order theological construct that is *adduced* for systematic reasons." See A. Holmes, "Ordinary Language Analysis and Theological Method," *BETS* 11 (1968): 137, italics his.

"What scripture says, God says." Ever a work in progress, a full gamut of bibliological options should remain available for believers, especially those who happen to be students.

To P. Feinberg, for example, inerrancy means "that when all facts are known, the Scriptures in their original autographs and properly interpreted will be shown to be wholly true in everything that they affirm, whether that has to do with doctrine or morality or with the social, physical, or life sciences."[17] Many understand this to have strict implications for what inerrantists can expect to find in the scholarly disciplines. To J. R. Michaels, by contrast, inerrancy means "the Bible affirms without error that truth which God intends to make known," which stipulates that "such an assertion is not subject to empirical verification or rational demonstration."[18] With such a wide range of opinions circulating among inerrantists and the discussion even now still gaining in momentum, it seems timely that the present volume should be added to the literature.

As editor, I have deliberately tried to represent diverse viewpoints from scholars working in several different fields. Each contributor was invited to discuss problems that arise as one incorporates knowledge gained from a specific area of specialization into an inerrantist framework for understanding scripture. I would like to thank the contributors for taking time out of their busy schedules to participate and for being patient with me during the long course of bringing the project to fruition. I am also grateful to the excellent staff at Pickwick Publications, not only for their commitment and genuine interest in the project but for their editorial support as they coordinated publication. May God use this collection of essays to increase evangelical awareness of the interdisciplinary perspectives involved in understanding scripture's authority.

17. P. Feinberg, "The Meaning of Inerrancy," in *Inerrancy*, ed. N. Geisler (Grand Rapids: Zondervan, 1980), 294.

18. J. R. Michaels, "Inerrancy or Verbal Inspiration? An Evangelical Dilemma," in *Inerrancy and Common Sense*, 60. According to J. Muether, Professor Michaels was forced to resign from Gordon-Conwell Theological Seminary for views presented in *Servant and Son* (John Knox Press) published the following year. See J. Muether, "Evangelicals and the Bible: A Bibliographic Postscript," in *Inerrancy and Hermeneutic*, 258.

HISTORICAL PERSPECTIVES

1

No Creed but the Bible, No Authority Without the Church

American Evangelicals and the Errors of Inerrancy

D. G. Hart

To say that evangelicalism in the United States was defined by the doctrine of inerrancy may sound like an overstatement. But when evangelicals themselves began to organize after World War II, dropping the prefix from neo-evangelicalism to become the sole claimants to the title "evangelical," they relied on inerrancy to give coherence to the institutions they founded. In fact, this doctrine was so widespread that the very academic organizations that born-again Protestants established to provide forums for fraternity and intellectual sustenance made inerrancy a criterion for membership.

Arguably, the least surprising of evangelical scholarly associations to adopt inerrancy as the standard for membership was the Evangelical Theological Society (ETS). Founded in 1949 as the academic and theological arm of the National Association of Evangelicals (NAE), begun seven years earlier, ETS was a forum for scholarship in service of the neo-evangelical movement that was beginning to take shape around institutions such as the NAE, Fuller Seminary (1947), and personalities such as Billy Graham. Indicative of the movement's leaders' aims to be as broad as possible while still rejecting the errors of Protestant liberalism (and the rejection of basic Christian beliefs owing to a loose view of

3

Scripture), ETS insisted originally on only one doctrinal affirmation for membership: "The Bible alone and the Bible in its entirety, is the Word of God written, and therefore inerrant in the autographs."[1] For an organization populated by seminary faculty and pastors, inerrancy made sense as a mechanism by which to bring together Baptists, Presbyterians, fundamentalists, Pentecostals, Wesleyans, and various other conservative Protestants while not becoming bogged down in creedal and denominational differences.

More surprising than ETS' reliance on inerrancy was the appeal of Scripture's infallibility to evangelical academics who were not in the business of theology or preaching. Even before the founding of the NAE or ETS, evangelical and fundamentalist scientists had decided in 1941 to establish the American Scientific Affiliation (ASA), a faith-based scholarly organization for those who taught and studied the natural sciences. Although this new body possessed a significant ministry component thanks to the involvement of the Moody Bible Institute, whose popular film series, "Sermons from Science," was a spur to evangelical interest in scientific investigation, ASA also enlisted evangelical scientists who desired a religious forum in which to discuss and present their academic work. The organization's original statement reflected its intention to harmonize science and Scripture:

> I believe in the whole Bible as originally given, to be the inspired word of God, the only unerring guide of faith and conduct. Since God is the Author of this Book, as well as the Creator and Sustainer of the physical world about us, I cannot conceive of discrepancies between statements in the Bible and the real facts of science.[2]

So strong was the evangelical commitment to biblical inerrancy that when evangelical historians formed their own academic association in 1959, somewhat late to the flurry of evangelical institutional proliferation, the Conference on Faith and History (CFH), they too determined to make this doctrine the criteria for the religious component of their members. These evangelical historians decided upon a statement of faith that defined an evangelical as someone who could affirm the Holy Scriptures are "the Word of God, the Christian's authoritative guide for

1. *Bulletin of the Evangelical Theological Society* 1.1 (Winter 1958) inside cover.
2. Quoted in Ronald Numbers, *The Creationists* (New York: Knopf, 1992) 159.

faith and conduct," and Jesus Christ as "the Son of God and through his atonement . . . the mediator between God and man."[3] Anyone who could affirm these doctrines was welcome to join the organization.

As cohesive as inerrancy was for evangelicals during the post-World War II era—from the laity and pastors to academics in the humanities, sciences, and theology—it would fail within a few decades to define born-again Protestantism. By 1976, the year when many evangelicals were thrilled to read that *Newsweek* magazine had designated it "the Year of the Evangelical," the movement was in the thick of the so-called "battle for the Bible." This showdown had actually been building for over a decade and by 1980 would result in a major division between evangelicals who continued to insist on inerrancy and those who believed the doctrine more the result of the fundamentalist era than the historic teaching of Christianity. What follows is a brief account of the collapse of the doctrinal consensus among evangelicals around inerrancy with an eye toward how the "battle for the Bible" became more intense and less conclusive than it should have for American Protestants because of evangelicalism's neglect of ecclesiology and confessional boundaries. The history of evangelicalism during the middle decades of the twentieth century suggests an important lesson: only in the context of a high view of the church as a confessing body that bases ordination and membership on a creed does the appropriate interpretive community exist for explaining and teaching the infallible word of God. Conversely, without that context, inerrancy functions more as a shibboleth than a binding standard that popular leaders employ with accountability only to the whims of populist parachurch organizations.

THE BATTLE FOR THE BIBLE

Although the doctrine of Scripture gave evangelicalism theological identity, less clear was whether inerrancy could supply the movement with needed intellectual vigor.[4] Some evangelical leaders sensed as much already by the 1960s. In 1965, for instance, Carl Henry assessed

3. "Proposed Constitution," *Fides et Historia* 1 (Fall 1968) 5–6.

4. The following paragraphs are adapted from D. G. Hart, *Deconstructing Evangelicalism: Conservative Protestantism in the Age of Billy Graham* (Grand Rapids: Baker, 2004) 142–48.

evangelicalism's life of the mind in his capacity as editor of *Christianity Today*. He believed conservative Protestantism's strength rested "in its high view of Scripture." But the movement was guilty of "neglecting the frontiers of formative discussion in contemporary theology . . ."[5] Some of the discussions among evangelical biblical scholars, Henry observed, were "out of touch with the frontiers of doubt in our day." Evangelicals needed to go beyond merely "retooling the past and repeating clichés." "Unless we speak to our generation in a compelling idiom, meshing the great theological concerns with current modes of thought and critical problems of the day, we shall speak only to ourselves."[6] Henry did not connect the dots, but a plausible reading of his review was that a wooden doctrine of Scripture—which even dominated evangelical faculty in the arts and sciences—prevented born-again Protestants from careful re-flection on faith and life.

Henry's former colleague at Fuller, George Ladd, registered explicit discomfort with the evangelical doctrine of Scripture in 1967 through the introduction to his book *New Testament and Criticism*. Ladd divided the conservative Protestant world between biblical scholars who were still instinctively opposed to critical scholarship, and those who tried to harmonize a commitment to fundamental doctrines while engaging with critical biblical scholarship. This division was synonymous with the growing antagonism between fundamentalists and their neo-evangelical successors. Ladd himself, as the title of his book suggested, identified with the neo-evangelical approach and he articulated their aim: "These modern successors of fundamentalism, for whom we prefer the term evangelicals, wish, in brief, to take their stand within the contemporary stream of philosophical, theological, and critical thought."[7]

Although Henry and Ladd were both part of Fuller Seminary, where the neo-evangelical project of forging a via media between evan-gelicalism and liberalism reigned, the distinction between evangelical-ism and fundamentalism was rapidly fading even as they assessed the prospects for conservative Protestantism. Indeed, a younger generation

5. Carl Henry, "American Evangelicals and Theological Dialogue," *Christianity Today*, January 15, 1965, 29, quoted in Mark Noll, *Between Faith and Criticism*, 2nd ed. (Grand Rapids: Baker, 1991) 119.

6. Henry, "American Evangelicals," quoted in Noll, *Between Faith and Criticism*, 120.

7. George E. Ladd, *The New Testament and Criticism* (Grand Rapids: Eerdmans, 1967), 11–12, quoted in Noll, *Between Faith and Criticism*, 121.

of evangelical biblical scholars was emerging who found neo-evangelicalism's third way dissatisfying precisely because the post-World War II coalition of conservatives had relied upon inerrancy as a litmus test for reliability.

The limitations of inerrancy as a doctrinal standard were nowhere more evident than at Fuller Seminary. Soon after the seminary's founding in 1947, Fuller's faculty drafted a statement of faith that included a minimal set of affirmations that followed the outline of the Westminster Confession of Faith. Eventually, Fuller faculty sensed a need for greater precision and added a statement on inerrancy. It read: "The Books which form the canon of the Old and New Testaments as originally given are plenarily inspired and free from all error in the whole and in the part. These books constitute the written Word of God, the only infallible rule of faith and practice."[8] This was an affirmation that resembled the statements of faith affirmed by evangelical scientists (ASA), theologians (ETS), and historians (CFH).

The author of that statement was Fuller faculty member Edward J. Carnell. But the longer he taught and studied, the less Carnell was convinced that inerrancy was such an easy matter or so decisive for determining orthodoxy. By the time he wrote *The Case for Orthodox Theology* in 1959, he began to express his reservations. In a chapter dedicated to "Difficulties" Carnell explored a variety of conceptions of inspiration and highlighted differences between Benjamin Warfield and James Orr. Carnell also complained that evangelicals had reached a point where they could not discuss the doctrine of Scripture openly or raise questions that emerged naturally from the phenomena of the biblical writings. In a statement that foreshadowed the assessments of Henry and Ladd, Carnell wrote that the "founding of new ideas has apparently run dry, for what was once a live issue in the church has now ossified into a theological tradition." He added, "When a gifted professor tries to interact with the critical difficulties in the text, he is charged with disaffection, if not outright heresy."[9]

Carnell's book created a significant public relations problem for Fuller Seminary, thanks to the widespread understanding of inerrancy's

8. Fuller Seminary statement quoted in Harold Lindsell, *The Battle for the Bible* (Grand Rapids: Zondervan, 1976) 107.

9. Edward John Carnell, *The Case for Orthodox Theology* (Philadelphia: Westminster, 1959) 110.

importance among the evangelical rank-and-file. George Marsden esti-
mates that the seminary needed to distribute twenty thousand brochures
that contained Fuller's statement of faith along with lists of the faculty who
affirmed it.[10] At the same time that Fuller was sending reassuring signals,
its leaders were engaged in a search to find a new president. Harold John
Ockenga had been president since the school's founding but he was also
the nationally known pastor of Park Street Congregationalist Church
in Boston and so needed to oversee the Southern California seminary
from his office in New England. Part of the desire for a new president
was to appoint someone who would reside in Pasadena. Another factor
was a perceived need by younger members of Fuller's constituency to
find an executive more sympathetic to the dilemmas that Carnell felt.
The favorite candidate was David Hubbard, an Old Testament professor at nearby Westmont College, known to have taught that the Bible
was spiritually and theologically reliable but not inerrant. Hubbard also
questioned the Mosaic authorship of the Pentateuch.[11] A key advocate
of Hubbard was Daniel Fuller, the seminary's founder's son, who had
studied theology in Europe and who had come to regard inerrancy as
a provincial expression of American evangelicalism's lack of sophistication.[12] By 1963 Fuller was a different institution. Hubbard was president and the conservative faculty who had defended inerrancy left to
work elsewhere—Wilbur Smith and Gleason Archer to teach at Trinity
Evangelical Divinity School, and Harold Lindsell to become editor at
Christianity Today. Meanwhile, Fuller's statement on Scripture changed
from an affirmation of inerrancy to a softer position: "Scripture is an
essential part and trustworthy record of this divine disclosure. All the
books of the Old and New Testaments, given by divine inspiration, are
the written Word of God, the only infallible rule of faith and practice."[13]

These changes at Fuller in the 1960s were the skirmish before the
full-scale battle for the Bible of the 1970s. Of course, what called attention to this war—perhaps even creating it—was Harold Lindsell's 1976
book, *The Battle for the Bible.* Lindsell was clearly writing to settle scores

10. See George M. Marsden, *Reforming Fundamentalism: Fuller Seminary and the New Evangelicalism* (Grand Rapids: Eerdmans, 1987) 207.

11. Marsden, *Reforming Fundamentalism,* 208.

12. For the intrigue at Fuller over inerrancy, see the fascinating account in Marsden, *Reforming Fundamentalism,* 205–18.

13. The revised Fuller statement is quoted in Lindsell, *Battle,* 116.

from his days at Fuller even though he added enough additional material to indicate that the problem was much more widespread than Fuller. He dedicated the book to former colleagues Archer, Carnell, Henry, and Smith. For good measure he lined up Ockenga, by then the president of Gordon-Conwell Theological Seminary, to write the preface. Lindsell argued that inerrancy was the "watershed" not only for evangelicalism but for orthodox Christianity. Admitting error in the Bible, he warned, ultimately resulted in "the loss of missionary outreach," quenched "missionary passion," undermined "belief in the full-orbed truth of the Bible," produced "spiritual sloth and decay," and led "to apostasy."[14] To prove this domino theory of apostasy, Lindsell explored the contemporary controversies among Missouri Synod Lutherans and Southern Baptists, where questions surrounding the authority and interpretation of Scripture were at issue. Less clear and useful for Lindsell's purposes was that neither of these denominations had ever joined the National Association of Evangelicals. In which case, were these controversies symptoms of evangelical waffling on Scripture or were they cases of tensions endemic to Lutherans and Baptists?

Lindsell soon found intellectual reinforcement from a surprising and unsolicited source. In 1979 he wrote a sequel, *The Bible in the Balance*, which appeared just two years after James Barr's book *Fundamentalism*. In each case, inerrancy was the line in the sand for evangelicalism. Lindsell believed this was a good thing, while for Barr, a reputable biblical scholar at Oxford University, inerrancy was an unscholarly attempt to put the genie of modern scholarship back in the bottle of *sola scriptura*. Barr used *evangelicalism* and *fundamentalism* interchangeably because inerrancy was crucial to each. When Lindsell read Barr's criticism of born-again Protestants for their "strange" understanding of the Bible, Lindsell was enthusiastic. "From Professor Barr's perspective it is clear that he regards biblical inerrancy as one of the major doctrinal beliefs of evangelicals," Lindsell deduced, "So it may be said that any definition of what evangelicals believe must include biblical inerrancy."[15] Thus vindicated by an Oxford don not particularly partial to evangelicalism, Lindsell had called attention to Fuller's complicity in the potential downfall of conservative Protestantism.

14. Lindsell, *Battle*, 25.
15. Harold Lindsell, *The Bible in the Balance* (Grand Rapids: Zondervan) 306.

Oddly enough, Lindsell's affirmation and defense of inerrancy generated more controversy than had Fuller's change of course a decade earlier.[16] Between 1976 and 1986 the publishers of evangelical books kept themselves busy with a series of titles that debated the merits of Lindsell's argument. Inerrantists took the lead when in 1977 they founded the International Council on Biblical Inerrancy, an organization that included Francis Schaeffer, J. I. Packer, James M. Boice, and Lindsell. In 1978 ICBI drafted *The Chicago Statement on Biblical Inerrancy*, which affirmed that the Bible is "infallible"—that is, "true and reliable in all the matters it addresses"—and "inerrant"—that is "free from all falsehood, fraud or deceit."[17] The organization also urged evangelical organizations and schools to add inerrancy clauses to their statements of faith, and explored the possibility of forming a coalition of "inerrancy seminaries" that would be doctrinally safe.[18] Finally, ICBI sponsored a number of books, five in all, which defended and promoted an inerrantist doctrine of Scripture along historical, theological, and philosophical lines.[19]

In 1979, as if publishers were not making enough money on the Bible, Jack B. Rogers and Donald K. McKim entered the fray with *The Authority and Interpretation of the Bible*. Written by two allegedly moderate evangelicals in the mainline Presbyterian Church (USA), one of whom (Rogers) taught at Fuller, this book argued that inerrancy was not the historic teaching of the Christian church but rather the creation of late-nineteenth-century Princeton theologians who combined Protestant scholasticism with the epistemology of Common Sense

16. The following paragraphs include material from D. G. Hart, "Evangelicals, Biblical Scholarship, and the Politics of the Modern American Academy," in *Evangelicals and Science in Historical Perspective*, ed. David N. Livingstone, D. G. Hart, and Mark A. Noll (New York: Oxford University Press, 1999) 306–9.

17. Reprinted in Lindsell, *Bible*, 367, 368.

18. Robert M. Price, "Inerrant the Wind: The Troubled House of North American Evangelicals," *Evangelical Quarterly* 55 (1983) 130.

19. This series included: *Inerrancy*, ed. Norman L. Geisler (Grand Rapids: Zondervan, 1979); *Biblical Errancy: Its Philosophical Roots*, ed. Norman L. Geisler (Grand Rapids: Zondervan, 1981); *Challenges to Inerrancy*, ed. Gordon Lewis and Bruce Demarest (Chicago: Moody, 1984); *Inerrancy and the Church*, ed. John Hannah (Chicago: Moody, 1984); and *Hermeneutics, Inerrancy, and the Bible*, ed. Earl Radmacher and Robert Preus (Grand Rapids: Zondervan, 1984). Another book that should be included as an ICBI project thought not formally part of this series is *The Foundations of Biblical Authority*, ed. James Montgomery Boice (Grand Rapids: Zondervan, 1978), which includes essays by the leadership of the ICBI.

Realism to formulate a "peculiar" view of Scripture unsupported by biblical teaching itself.[20]

The Rogers-McKim proposal itself became the source for debate and polemic. Robert K. Johnston, a Fuller graduate and then a professor at North Park Seminary, and William J. Abraham, professor at Southern Methodist University, attempted to build upon the shifting sands of the meaning of biblical authority, the former by looking beyond inerrancy to find other possibilities for theological unity among evangelicals, the latter by using the inadequacy of the twentieth-century doctrine of inerrancy to explore ways of understanding biblical authority culled from older expressions in the evangelical tradition.[21] From the other side of the spectrum came a review essay of Rogers and McKim (that eventually became a book) written by John Woodbridge, professor at Trinity Evangelical Divinity School, the home of Fuller inerrantists in exile. Woodbridge, displaying a familiarity with the historical record, argued that the evangelical doctrine of Scripture showed more continuity with the historic teaching of the church than the Rogers/McKim proposal. Woodbridge also turned the historicist tables on Rogers and McKim by arguing that their thesis stemmed from a source less venerable than Old Princeton, namely, Karl Barth and Neo-Orthodoxy.[22]

The battle for the Bible, consequently, turned into a historical argument about the time of the doctrine's origins. Was it the product merely of late-nineteenth-century Calvinist apologetics at Princeton Seminary under the influence of Scottish Common Sense Realism or was it the historic teaching of the Christian church? This prompted evangelical historians to enter the debates. In 1980 George Marsden took up the issue in his magisterial *Fundamentalism and American Culture*. He argued, along lines similar to Ernest R. Sandeen, that the fundamentalist doctrine of inerrancy was largely indebted to the Princeton theology and that the philosophical foundation for the militant conservative defense

20. Jack B. Rogers and Donald K. McKim, *The Authority and Interpretation of the Bible* (San Francisco, 1979) 347. For their critique of Old Princeton, see especially chs. 5–6.

21. Robert K. Johnston, *Evangelicals at an Impasse* (Atlanta: John Knox, 1979); William Abraham, *Divine Revelation and the Limits of Historical Criticism* (New York: Oxford University Press, 1982); idem, *The Coming Great Revival* (New York: Oxford University Press, 1984).

22. John D. Woodbridge, *Biblical Authority: A Critique of the Rogers/McKim Proposal* (Grand Rapids: Zondervan, 1982).

of the Bible's truthfulness in matters of history and science was Scottish Common Sense Realism.[23] Though Marsden did not really take sides in the matter,[24] his conclusions added greater weight to the Rogers/McKim thesis that inerrancy was a recent construction.

Then the Institute for the Study of American Evangelicals, newly formed, weighed in with its first conference and book, *The Bible in America*, a collection of essays that further cemented the ties between fundamentalist views about the Bible and the philosophy of the Scottish Enlightenment. In three important chapters, Marsden, Timothy P. Weber, and Grant Wacker reiterated the close affinity between fundamentalist conceptions of inspiration and inerrancy and the epistemological foundations of early modern science.[25] Finally, Mark Noll seemed to have the last word for both theologians and historians with his 1986 book, *Between Faith and Criticism*. In a masterful survey of evangelical biblical scholarship since the rise of the modern research university, Noll supplied a valuable perspective on the tensions and assumptions within American evangelicalism that contributed to its distinctive approach to and regard for the Bible. He concluded that evangelicals were firmly committed both to a high view of the Bible expressed in the idiom of inerrancy and to a scholarly outlook heavily indebted to Enlightenment epistemology.[26]

Woodbridge and D. A. Carson kept up the discussion with two collections of intelligent essays on the nature of biblical authority, *Scripture and Truth* (1983) and *Hermeneutics, Authority and Canon* (1986).[27] But

23. George M. Marsden, *Fundamentalism and American Culture: The Shaping of Twentieth-Century Evangelicalism, 1870–1925* (New York, 1980), esp. chs. 12–14, and 24.

24. John D. Woodbridge, however, did firmly believe that Marsden had taken sides. See Woodbridge, "Recent Interpretations of Biblical Authority, Part 4: Is Biblical Inerrancy a Fundamentalist Doctrine?," *Bibliotheca Sacra* 142 (1985): 292–305.

25. George Marsden, "Everyone One's Own Interpreter?: The Bible, Science, and Authority in Mid-Nineteenth-Century America"; Timothy Weber, "The Two-Edged Sword: The Fundamentalist Use of the Bible"; and Grant Wacker, "The Demise of Biblical Civilization," in *The Bible in America: Essays in Cultural History*, ed. Nathan O. Hatch and Mark A. Noll (New York, Oxford University Press, 1982) 79–100, 101–20, and 121–38 respectively.

26. Noll, *Between Faith and Criticism*, 181–85.

27. *Hermeneutics, Authority and Canon*, ed. D. A. Carson and J. Woodbridge (Grand Rapids: Zondervan, 1986); and *Scripture and Truth*, ed. D. A. Carson and J. Woodbridge (Grand Rapids: Zondervan, 1983).

the perception persisted that evangelical attitudes toward the Bible reflected sometimes misguided if not naive ideas about truth, the human mind, and scholarly investigation. As Mark Noll concluded in the afterword to the second edition of *Between Faith and Criticism*, evangelical biblical scholarship, despite increasing sophistication, continued to be discounted in the academic establishment in part because among evangelicals "the influence of early modern science . . . remains strong, while in the university world modern and post-modern science . . . prevail."[28] The final verdict on Lindsell's accusation was decidedly ambiguous. On the one hand, the debate did prove his contention that inerrancy was a watershed in the sense that the controversy revealed great theological diversity among born-again Protestants, so much so that one could well conclude the movement was hollow at its theological core. On the other hand, the inerrancy debate was decidedly inconclusive because it raised more questions about historical origins of the doctrine than it answered.

MISSING IN ACTION: THE CHURCH

In the course of his history of Fuller Seminary, George M. Marsden observed that the controversy over inerrancy revealed a fundamental institutional weakness of American evangelicalism. Instead of appealing to recognized religious authorities, born-again Protestants invariably chose the court of popular opinion. "Whereas evangelicals appeal to the 'Bible alone' for authority," Marsden wrote, "they lack adequate mechanisms for settling differences on how the Bible is to be understood." As such, the inerrancy battle demonstrated the evangelical movement's lack of formal or ecclesiastical channels for determining the boundaries of evangelical identity. "Typically having weak views of the church or of central ecclesiastical authority, [evangelicals] cannot depend on synods or councils to adjudicate their disagreements."[29] What Marsden could have added was that the battle for the Bible pitted those who appealed to the evangelical people against those who were increasingly situated in the academy and looked to the authority of experts. While the International Council on Biblical Inerrancy sponsored conferences and produced literature designed to educate the masses, evangelicals who were uncom-

28. Noll, *Between Faith and Criticism*, 202.
29. Marsden, *Reforming Fundamentalism*, 291.

fortable with inerrancy learned some of that discomfort from advanced study. In either case, whether parachurch conferences and publications or academic articles and degrees, the authority of the church in its councils, synods, or denominational structures was a bystander.

For most evangelicals, the notion that the church has power is a surprise. So accustomed have American Protestants become to either parachurch organizations or to their own encounter with Jesus in their heart, that the idea that belonging to a church body is essential to true faith or that such a church body possesses some binding address upon her members through rightly appointed officers is foreign. In which case, church membership is little more than a preference, an option that comes with choosing the right Christian radio preacher from whom to learn, subscribing to the appropriate Christian magazines, and joining the best non-denominational support groups. Declarations of biblical teaching through creeds, confessions, and the decisions of deliberative assemblies are even farther removed from evangelical piety. Megachurches may have unknowingly attempted to address this problem by making church more accessible but have also provided an ecclesiastical structure with as much authoritative stature as Wal-Mart.

Protestantism was not always this way. The Westminster Standards, for instance, give an indication of that older Protestant outlook on the church in ways often missed even by the more conservative evangelicals. Chapter 31 of the Confession, for instance, declares that synods and councils "determine controversies of faith, and cases of conscience," "set down rules and directions for the better ordering of the public worship of God, and government of his church," and "receive complaints in cases of maladministration, and authoritatively to determine the same." The Westminster divines added what many conservative Protestants take for granted, namely, that these judgments and determinations are to "be received with reverence and submission . . . if consonant to the Word of God." Many Bible-only Protestants simply stop there, concluding that as long as the church does what the Bible says, then the church may have power because it is simply acting in accord with the one reliable authority, namely, Scripture. But the divines added a phrase that says believers are to submit to the rulings of synods and councils "not only for their agreement with the Word, but also for the power whereby they are made, as being an ordinance of God appointed thereunto in his Word." In other words, the church has power not simply to the degree that it is faithful to

Scripture but also as an authority to whom God has granted real power (in the same way that God ordained the state to administer justice). Of course, Protestants believe that churches err. But church errors do not strip them of their power any more than the errors of magistrates or parents might make the authority of the state or family illegitimate. How to handle the authoritative errors of God-ordained institutions is obviously a difficult question. But the right answer is not the prevailing one of acting as if the church has no authority.

The Westminster Standards also discuss church power at another place that the Reformed advocates of biblical inerrancy seldom notice—namely, in the chapter on Christian liberty (chapter 20). This is an odd section in which to find an assertion of church power since the point seems to be, as the second paragraph of chapter 20 states, "God alone is Lord of the conscience, and hath left it free from the doctrines and commandments of men, which are, in anything, contrary to his Word." Many evangelical Presbyterians interpret this chapter as yet another affirmation of *sola scriptura* at the expense of church authority, while also locating individual believers squarely under the Bible as their sole authority, not any church hierarchy. But, of course, the Westminster divines were not libertarians and were also very much concerned about social disorder. Consequently, they went on in the fourth paragraph to place substantial limits on Christian liberty. They wrote that Christian liberty can never be used to undermine any legitimate authority. The power they had in mind was not simply political, though with Parliament looking over their collective shoulder, they certainly had the civil magistrate in view. They also included the church in their idea of legitimate authority: "because the powers which God hath ordained, and the liberty which Christ hath purchased, are not intended by God to destroy, but mutually to uphold and preserve one another, they who, upon pretense of Christian liberty, shall oppose any lawful power, or the lawful exercise of it, *whether it be civil or ecclesiastical*, resist the ordinance of God" (emphasis added). Part of what was at stake, of course, was a political establishment that included the church. So to resist the church was to disregard the crown, which in England was still the supreme earthly authority over the church. Even so, when American Presbyterians revised the Westminster Standards to bring their teaching on the state into conformity with the realities of United States polity and ecclesiastical disestablishment they did not change this chapter. In which case, even in a voluntary church setting like the United States, chapter 20 cannot be used to deny either the power of the United States government or the authority of the church (whichever denomination it happens to be).

These sections of the Westminster Confession speak directly to the question of church power in ways that take Bible-only evangelicals by surprise. But they are not isolated assertions. They are bound up with other doctrines about the church that affirm the seriousness of her duties and church membership. In other words, the visible church is a divine ordinance not merely when assembled to deliberate its business, but also when gathered in local congregations for worship. After all, the means of grace, the word read and preached, baptism and the Lord's Supper are means of grace by which God communicates the benefits of redemption. The doctrine of the keys of the kingdom (Westminster Confession 30.2) is not simply a reference to church discipline, the third mark of the church, the one to follow word and sacrament. Actually, the rule of the church is implicated in the other marks since the church licenses and ordains those who may preach the word and administer the sacraments. For this reason, the task of church discipline is never simply a well-run, tightly organized church that excommunicates the unrepentant. Instead, it is bound up with the spiritual mission of the church, which the Confession describes in the following manner: "Unto this catholic visible church Christ hath given the ministry, oracles, and ordinances of God, for the gathering and perfecting of the saints, in this life, to the end of the world: and doth, by his own presence and Spirit, according to his promise, make them effectual thereunto" (25.3). This is no mere human institution that needs rules to be efficient, specific forms of motivation to inspire loyalty, and certain tasks to define institutional mission. Instead, the visible church is, at least according to some Protestants, "the kingdom of the Lord Jesus Christ, the house and family of God" (25.2). To raise the stakes and underscore that the church is an ordinance of God, the divines added that outside the church "there is no ordinary possibility of salvation" (25.2).

Although Protestants differ from Roman Catholics on important points of ecclesiology, the difference is not the way most American evangelicals imagine it. For instance, in their book *Is the Reformation Over?*, Mark Noll and Carolyn Nystrom conclude in standard low-church, Protestant fashion that the central difference separating evangelicals and Roman Catholics is "the nature of the church." "For Catholics," they write, "the visible, properly constituted, and hierarchally governed church is the principal God-ordained agent for the work of apostolic ministry." In contrast, for evangelicals "the church is the body of Christ made up of all those who have responded to the apostolic ministry . . ."[30] But if such older Protestant accounts of the church's ministry as the Westminster Standards are to be believed, then as defective as Protestant ecclesiology may be from Rome's perspective it is still closer to Roman Catholicism than to an evangelical faith that arrives at the Bible without going through the church.

In which case, the failure of evangelical Protestantism to take the church seriously is not simply the product of years of parachurch activity but also a misunderstanding of *sola scriptura*. Partly owing to the fallout from the battle with liberal Protestantism, conservatives have staked all of their fortunes on an inerrant Bible that will at least provide moral absolutes if not also point the way to Christ.[31] In the process, the church comes dangerously close to being merely a human institution that need not be believed or trusted any more than when it confirms what Bible readers already know. The dynamic of this relationship is a curious and very American one where church officers need to be subject to the voice of the people in the pew who refuse to use the pew Bible because they have brought their own. This democratic arrangement has no room for church members submitting to the teaching authority of the church. Ironically, then, the affirmation of the Bible's divine and authoritative nature nurtures distrust in the church's human officers only to give very human believers confidence in their own ability to read and interpret Scripture.

One way to illustrate the effects of Bible-onlyism on the authority of the church is to note evangelicalism's general disregard for systematic theology. To be sure, church creeds and confessions are by no means the same as systematic theology, even if both start from a similar task of striving to summarize the teaching of Scripture. Systematic theology is an academic discipline that, even when conducted by someone ordained to teach the word, is not authoritative in the way that a creed or

30. Mark Noll and Carolyn Nystrom, *Is the Reformation Over?: An Evangelical Assessment of Contemporary Catholicism* (Grand Rapids: Baker, 2005) 237.

31. For the effects of the fundamentalist controversy on evangelical ideas about the human character of the church versus the divine qualities of the Bible, see D. G. Hart, "The Irony of American Presbyterian Worship," in *Recovering Mother Kirk: The Case for Liturgy in the Reformed Tradition* (Grand Rapids: Baker, 2003) ch. 13.

confession adopted by the church is. And yet, the contemporary distrust of systematic theology is a function of the same kind of misunderstanding of *sola scriptura* that treats creeds and confessions as merely human products and that fails to see in the church any sort of legitimate authority beyond pious advice.

The most common way for conservative Protestants to display this distrust of theology is through biblicism. I ran across one example of such biblicism on a list-serve discussion group. Here the interlocutor felt compelled to settle a point of doctrinal debate by reference to Scripture alone, without ever referring to their Reformed confessional standards. At issue was the New Perspective on Paul and the propriety of using non-canonical material to understand the meaning of Scripture. One bright commentator made the sensible point that "the error of NPP scholars is not the fact that they study the literature of Second Temple Judaism and use it to shed light on the text, but the way in which they allow their reading of that literature to exercise a controlling authority in their exegesis." This interlocutor then anticipated the objection, "Isn't there a danger in allowing such non-canonical data to skew our exegesis?" In other words, "Shouldn't the canon alone shape our reading of any given passage?" To this he responded with an emphatic yes. But he did so with the following biblicistic qualification:

> there is a legitimate, secondary role for non-canonical data (particularly religious literature outside of Scripture) to help us interpret Scripture, even at a more substantive theological level. In general, I would argue that religious literature external to the canon of Scripture (whether Jewish or pagan) can be used in two main ways—to illuminate the continuities and discontinuities between Biblical revelation within the covenant community and the religious environment that exists outside of the covenant community.

Ironically, this same writer faults Reformed critics of the New Perspective for appealing mainly to history rather than employing sound exegesis. This is surprising since this particular exchange gave more weight to the non-canonical material of Second Temple Judaism than to the creed of the church in which this interlocutor was an officer.

Of course, simply appealing to the Westminster Confession does not settle what the apostle Paul meant in Romans 9. Neither is it entirely clear why N. T. Wright or E. P. Sanders, who have not subscribed to the Westminster Confession and have not agreed to work within the bounds of its interpretations, should receive as much attention from Presbyterians as the Westminster Standards. The reason for the popularity of the New Perspective on Paul is likely the influence of biblicism. Even though the New Perspective is at odds with the Reformed tradition at any number of points, it receives constant scrutiny and consideration because its advocates, like biblicists, go directly to the Bible without remembering they are part of a particular interpretive and ecclesial community (apart from, say, the Society of Biblical Literature, whose membership fees are high but whose penalties are slight). And the church has far more at stake in arriving at a right understanding of Paul than any scholarly guild.

Another form of biblicism—the high-brow variety—prevalent among conservative Protestants comes from John Frame, professor at Reformed Theological Seminary in Orlando. He has written self-consciously in defense of biblicism and has produced lengthy critiques of so-called "traditionalists," those whom Frame believes give more weight to history than to what the Bible alone teaches. In an essay on the Bible and theological method, Frame concluded that the Bible "must be primary in relation to history, sociology, or any other science. It is Scripture that supplies the norms of these sciences and governs their proper starting points, methods, and conclusions." Frame appealed to Cornelius Van Til's assertion—Scripture "speaks of everything"—to defend "something close" to biblicism. Frame admitted that Van Til did not think the Bible spoke directly of "football games, atoms, cosmology, philosophy." But, Frame added, "like the biblicist, Van Til believed that every human thought must be answerable to God's word in Scripture."[32] Frame's purpose was to counter those who appealed to Reformed confessions to settle theological debates. As he explains in another essay, "'Traditionalism' exists where *sola Scriptura* is violated, either by adding to or subtracting from God's Word." For Frame, Roman Catholicism has been guilty of this when relying upon the Magisterium just as liberal Protestantism departed from Scripture by relying upon autonomous reason. But the bigger issue for Frame is the resurgence of Reformed

---

32. John M. Frame, "In Defense of Something Close to Biblicism: Reflections on *Sola Scriptura* and History in Theological Method," *Westminster Theological Journal* 59 (1997) 274.

Protestants who appeal either to the Westminster Standards or the Three Forms of Unity, instead of the Bible.[33]

These examples of Presbyterian ideas about biblical authority, of course, give Roman Catholics considerable ammunition. The private reading of Scripture by individuals shorn of hermeneutical ties to the church is one of those emblems of nineteenth-century Protestantism that they used to show how Roman Catholics, by swearing fidelity to a foreign power, could not be truly patriotic.[34] Of late, this low-church version of Bible-onlyism has been harder to maintain with a straight face because of a hermeneutical environment much more self-conscious about the problems of individualistic interpretation and more engaged with the importance of interpretive communities. On the one hand, once Rome started to look less frightening and more thoughtful about sexual ethics and maybe even worship, the idea of church authority began to look better. On the other, Protestant liberalism early in the twentieth century with its maddening ambiguity, and postmodernism later with its critique of objectivity, taught some Protestants that the idea of the lone interpreter, sitting down with the Bible and getting it right while using the right manuscripts and correct grammatical tools, appeared to be considerably naive. The reasons had much to do with the acknowledgement of the situatedness of each and every reader. Because interpreters of the Bible—even ones with good intentions—bring a host of motives to the text, the idea of a neutral reading came to be regarded as hermeneutical folly.

But these hermeneutical developments rarely dent the authority of private readings of the Bible that still prevail among conservative Protestants, even among those Presbyterians who thought they had learned from Cornelius Van Til that presuppositions condition knowledge, including the kind derived from Scripture. A form of biblicism continues to manifest itself among conservative Protestants without a second thought. It has especially become evident in discussions about the authority of creeds or confessions for ministers or church members. These ecclesial statements are considered subordinate standards (which they are) and so much less authoritative than the Bible that they function

33. John M. Frame, "Traditionalism," online at http://www.frame-poythress.org/frame_articles/1999Traditionalism.htm.

34. The classic expression of such Bible-only anti-Catholicism was Lyman Beecher, *A Plea for the West* (1835; repr. Bedford, MA: Applewood, 2009).

like a reference work—something to pull off the shelf to inspect about a particular entry but of no binding authority on a person's conscience even when he has taken vows to propagate and defend its teaching.

Of course, the problem of looking at creeds and confessions this way, aside from their manifestation of legitimate church power and so functioning as an ordinance of God, is that those taking exception to creeds do so not simply on the authority of the Bible but on the authority of their own interpretation of the Bible. To say that a creed or confession or a church errs is of course a Protestant point of long standing. Not so clear however is who has the power to make that determination. So when an officer rises in presbytery or in an informal conversation at a tavern and says that a specific creedal conviction is not biblical, he has just established that his own creed is biblical. For both creeds and biblical objections to creeds are forms of interpretation to their core. As William G. T. Shedd, professor of theology at Union Theological Seminary (New York), observed during late-nineteenth-century debates about the revision of the Westminster Confession:

> Of course Scripture is the only infallible rule of faith. But this particular way of appealing to Scripture is specious and fallacious. In the first place, it assumes that Calvinism is not Scriptural, an assumption which the Presbyterian Church has never granted. . . . Secondly, this kind of appeal to Scripture is only an appeal to Scripture as the reviser understands it. "Scripture" properly means the interpretation of Scripture; that is, the contents of Scripture as reached by human investigation and exegesis. Creeds, like commentaries, are Scripture studied and explained, and not the mere abstract and unexplained book as it lies on the counter of the Bible House. The infallible Word of God is expounded by the fallible mind of man, and hence the variety of expositions embodied in the denominational creeds. But every interpreter claims to have understood the Scriptures correctly, and, consequently, claims that his creed is Scriptural, and if so, that it is the infallible truth of God. The Arminian appeals to the Articles of Wesley as the rule of faith, because he believes them to be the true explanation of the inspired Bible. . . . The Calvinist appeals to the creeds of Heidelberg, Dort, and Westminster as the rule of faith, because he regards them as the accurate exegesis of the revealed Word of God. By the "Bible" these parties, as well as all others who appeal to the Bible, mean their understanding of the Bible. There is no such thing as that abstract Scripture to which the revisionist of whom we are speaking appeals; that

is, Scripture apart from any and all interpretation of it. When, therefore, the advocate of revision demands that the Westminster Confession be "conformed to Scripture," he means conformation to Scripture as he and those like him read and explain it. It is impossible to make abstract Scripture the rule of faith for either an individual or a denomination. No Christian body has ever subscribed to the Bible merely as a printed book. A person who should write his name on the blank leaf of the Bible and say that his doctrinal belief was between the covers, would convey no definite information as to his creed.[35]

To pit the Bible against a church's confession of faith from one angle is akin to pitting the individual against the church since the individual and church are both appealing to the Bible for their theological convictions. To be sure, the question of whether individuals have as much power as the church is one that may well be revisiting. Are lone interpreters of the Bible ordinances of God in the same way that the church is? Massachusetts Bay Puritans surely didn't think so when they banished Anne Hutchison from their colony. When those lone interpreters are ordained do they have any more authority than the lone lay person? Again, if the case of Massachusetts Bay's disposal of Roger Williams is any indication, ordination would not seem to elevate individual interpretations above that of a synod, council, or general assembly.

To put the problem this way may strike evangelicals as odd, especially those who do live with creeds. Episcopalians put a fair amount of power in the hands of one man and they usually call him bishop. Baptists and Congregationalists on the other side are fairly squeamish about episcopacy but not so leery of the laity and so vest great authority in the democratic interpretive capacities of the local congregation. But Presbyterians and Reformed Christians are by nature conciliarists, that is, they believe committees are the height of decency and order. Church power, accordingly, is dispersed among elders, both lay and ministerial, who as a body make determinations that Episcopalians leave to a bishop and that Baptists grant to congregations. As unpleasant as committee meetings may be, there is great wisdom in denying power to one person and dispersing it among different branches of government or collective bodies. Divine-right monarchy may be in the distant past, but most civil societies in the modern era have come to

---

35. William Shedd, *Calvinism: Pure and Mixed* (1893: repr. Carlisle, PA: Banner of Truth, 1986) 146–47.

terms with the folly of giving executive power to one person exclusively (America's flirtation with imperial presidency notwithstanding).
And yet, when conservative Protestants, who love their country and
its system of government with a balance of powers, turn to their Bibles
they seem to forget their Republican and Democratic sensibilities and
regard their individual judgments as sovereign. Ironically, then, Bible-
onlyism has returned us to rule by the papacy, except that now rather
than having one Bishop of Rome, we have, if polls of the American
public are to be believed, close to a quarter of a billion American bish-
ops—that is, the percentage of the American population that affirms
the Bible is the word of God and infallible.

The way that Presbyterians and Reformed Protestants assert the
authority of synods and councils over individual readings of Scripture,
whether lay or ordained, is by adopting confessions and creeds whose
teaching sets the boundaries for fellowship, the terms for ordination,
and defines the corporate witness of the church. Part of what a candidate
for the ministry, for instance, must show is his knowledge of and agreement with his communion's confessional teaching. What is more, his
ability to remain a minister in good standing depends on not teaching
anything contrary to the church's creedal standards. And even though
he is not obligated when handling a particular passage to relate his three
points back to his denomination's doctrinal standards, he would be well
advised to if he is to fulfill the catechetical duty of the pastoral ministry. (Another way to do this, of course, is to reinstitute the catechetical
sermon, but that might require an afternoon or evening service, which
is a subject for another day.) The reason Presbyterians and Reformed
Christians have historically required assent to their confessions and
creeds is not simply for uniformity of clerical product, what some used
to call the corporate witness of the church. They have also done it because, as good Calvinists, they recognize that even Christians are prone
to error and are even more so when left to themselves and their own
intelligence and wisdom. Creedal subscription regulated by a church ju-
dicatory, then, is simply the tribute Presbyterianism pays to peer review.
If second opinions are good for medical treatment, and if journal editors regularly rely on panels of outside readers to evaluate manuscripts
submitted for publication, why not do the same with the interpretation
of the Bible? A theological second opinion may come in the form of
conforming one's interpretation of Scripture to the received teaching of

a particular communion. The challenge for contemporary Protestantism is to reconceive *sola scriptura* in a way that does justice to the Bible's teaching about the church.

DIVINE BOOK, HUMAN READERS

The challenge for conservative Protestants to recover an ecclesial and confessional outlook and identity to undergird a high view of Scripture is even greater than the twentieth-century conflict over inerrancy suggests. American evangelicals, as anti-traditional as they may be, are part of a Protestant habit reaching back to the beginning of the United States in which they have instinctively regarded the human as inherently defective and fallible in contrast to the reliability and error-free nature of the divine. One consequence of this binary outlook was to discount the human aspects of Scripture, explored in great detail by the biblical critics, and stress the Bible's divine origins. A related occurrence has been to neglect divinely ordained human institutions, such as the church, and assume that a human officer lacks real power because prone to error. Consequently, in addition to harboring a doctrine of Scripture that stumbles over the phenomena of the Bible, evangelicalism also trips over an authoritative church because it is populated by humans.

The best evidence of the historic evangelical ambivalence over church authority comes from Nathan O. Hatch's book *The Democratization of American Christianity*.[36] He argues that the political and cultural changes wrought by the American Revolution provided a setting that revealed the darker side of the Protestant soul once freed from the restraints of state-controlled churches and universities. In this new environment evangelicals inverted "the traditional modes of religious authority." Rather than "revering tradition, learning, solemnity, and decorum," as Calvinist clergy did, according to Hatch, "a diverse array of populist preachers exalted youth, free expression, and religious ecstasy." Evangelicals assumed that "divine insight was reserved for the poor and humble rather than the proud and learned."[37]

36. The following paragraphs are adapted from D. G. Hart, "Overcoming the Schizophrenic Character of Theological Education in the Evangelical Tradition," in *A Confessing Theology for Postmodern Times*, ed. Michael S. Horton (Wheaton, IL: Crossway, 2000) 114–16.

37. Nathan Hatch, *The Democratization of American Christianity* (New Haven, CT:

This inversion of traditional religious authority tapped three evangelical convictions, all of which have profoundly shaped the way born-again Protestants regard ministers and the churches in which they officiate. The first was an anti-creedal impulse that repudiated all theological formulations, whether historic or novel, as a device to keep the theologically illiterate in their place. Since Calvinism was the chief theological formulation in the United States, upstart evangelicals such as Baptists and Methodists took aim at Reformed orthodoxy's soteriology because it made God active and people passive. Still, evangelical hostility to Calvinism was rooted in a profound contempt for all traces of systematic thought, whether Arminian, Lutheran, or Socinian. As one Kentucky pastor who joined the Disciples put it, "we are not personally acquainted with the writings of John Calvin, nor are we certain how nearly we agree with his views of divine truth; neither do we care."[38]

Closely connected to anticreedalism was anticlericalism. Just as no theological opinion was better than any other, so the holder of that doctrinal conviction, whether living or dead, was no better than any other believer. Of course, most Americans have some sympathy with aspects of these low-church convictions since some Protestant clergy in the new nation were part of the political establishment and so were implicated in all of the inconsistencies and tensions that have bedeviled state churches since Constantine.[39] Still, once having conceded the political dimension of antebellum evangelical anticlericalism, its egalitarian presumptions remain. Both anticreedalism and anticlericalism manifested a proud and radical egalitarian streak that threatened any attempt to discriminate among social arrangements or cultural expressions. According to Daniel Parker, a Kentucky Baptist, "[T]he preaching manufactories of the east appear to be engaged in sending hirelings to the west, and should any of those *man-made, devil sent*, place-hunting gentry come into our country, and read in our places, we shall likely raise against *them* seven shepards [*sic*], and eight principle [*sic*] men."[40] Still, the point

---

Yale University Press, 1989), 35.

38. Robert Marshall and J. Thompson, quoted in Hatch, *Democratization*, 174.

39. For a perceptive critique of Constantinianism, see Stanley Hauerwas, *After Christendom?: How the Church Is to Behave If Freedom, Justice, and a Christian Nation Are Bad Ideas* (Nashville: Abingdon, 1991).

40. Quoted in Hauerwas, *After Christendom?*, 178.

stood: for evangelicals, creeds and clergy were bad because they came between God and man, thus smacking of Romanism.

The only men that evangelicals recognized as having some authority were the prophets and apostles who wrote the Bible. In other words, anticlericalism and anticreedalism were simply different ways of expressing the third prong of the evangelical attack upon religious authority, namely, *sola scriptura*. Yet the words of the men contained in Holy Writ were different because they were divinely inspired. Thus, the not-so-subtle evangelical political philosophy was that divine was good and human was bad. To put it another way, the only legitimate authority in this world was God's, a presumption that made rebellion against a king all right but posed a few dilemmas when the ox being gored was headship in the home. Not only did Bible-onlyism threaten all earthly authorities, but ironically it made the individual sovereign. Without the communion of the saints to guide, a fellowship that would typically extend to clergy of the present and worthies of the past, everyone could interpret the Bible for themselves. So deep was the conviction that men should not submit to any human authority that evangelicals read and distributed a book as old and complex as the Bible as if it were the news running off the penny press.[41]

The neo-evangelicals who created many of the institutions during the middle decades of the twentieth century and who appealed to biblical inerrancy as the hedge against infidelity were clearly fighting an uphill battle if they thought they could corral such egalitarian and individualist impulses into a coherent movement. They were clearly working with the best of evangelical materials handed down to them from the evangelical mainstream of the nineteenth century and the fundamentalist cause of the twentieth. To conclude that this effort was doomed to failure because these evangelicals lacked a good confession of faith and a proper view of the church is to imply that Protestants with creeds and church polities have been successful, an implication that twentieth-century denominational history would surely undercut.

Yet, a plausible conclusion, at least from the lights supplied by older Protestant voices, is that evangelicals made their work much harder because they neglected those divinely ordained institutions responsible for rightly dividing the word of God. Of course, given their history and their convictions, evangelicals need to be persuaded that churches, ministers,

41. See Hatch, *Democratization*, 174–79; Marsden, "Everyone."

and creeds are valuable let alone have any real authority. But if the in-errant Scriptures do actually teach about the nature of ordination, the power of the church, and the need for the peace, unity, and purity of Christ's body, then perhaps convincing evangelicals of the value of creeds and ecclesiology will not be so difficult. Either way, the doctrine of iner-rancy was incapable of supplying evangelicalism with peace, unity, and purity. The reason had a lot to do with an inability to establish firm lines of governance among evangelical leaders, institutions, and adherents. The divine word, in other words, never comes to sinners or believers apart from human hands, either those of the writers of Holy Writ them-selves or of the interpreters of Scripture. For this reason, a recovery of a Protestant ecclesiology that acknowledges divine authority delegated to human religious authorities could go a long way in harmonizing the tensions that have bedeviled evangelical Protestants and their exclusive attachment to the Bible.

2

The Subordination of Scripture to Human Reason at Old Princeton[1]

Paul Seely

THE BELIEF THAT GOD-BREATHED Scripture must be inerrant in all of its statements including those about science[2] is a reasonable and natural assumption. It seems quite unnatural to suppose that God would make a mistake. At the same time, this supposition is completely a priori. There is no biblical teaching that God would not speak to his children in terms of *their* scientific understanding rather than in terms of absolute truth. In fact, Jesus indicated that inspired Scripture could at times be accommodated to the merely cultural ideas that were dominant in the inspired writer's time—even when those ideas were sinful (Matt 19:7–9/Mark 10:2–9). Calvin accepted this teaching of Jesus and often employed it.[3] He spoke of accommodation to "notions which then prevailed,"[4] including accommodation to "error."[5]

1. "Old Princeton" refers to Princeton Theological Seminary between the time of its founding in 1812 and its reorganization in 1929.

2. By "science" and "scientific" I mean any belief about the natural world that is ultimately derived from empirical evidence and/or can be tested by empirical evidence. History is accordingly included.

3. David F. Wright, "Calvin's Pentateuchal Criticism: Equity, Hardness of Heart, and Divine Accommodation in the Mosaic Harmony Commentary," *Calvin Theological Journal* 21 (1986) 33–50; D. F. Wright, "Accommodation and Barbarity in John Calvin's OT Commentaries," in *Understanding Poets and Prophets*, ed. A. Graeme Auld (Sheffield: Sheffield Academic, 1993) 413–27.

4. John Calvin, *Commentaries IX: Jeremiah 1–19* (Grand Rapids: Baker, 1979) 7.

5. John Calvin, commentary on Psalm 58:4, cited in Davis Young, *John Calvin and*

At Old Princeton, however, the natural assumption of *absolute* inerrancy was an ultimate commitment to which, as we shall see, not only the biblical concept of accommodation was sacrificed but even the historical-grammatical meaning of Scripture. I fully agree with the Princetonian scholars of the nineteenth century that Scripture teaches that it is one hundred percent inspired, and this means it is authoritative for the purpose for which it was given, namely, instruction in matters of faith and morals.[6] The extension of this authority to the areas of history and science, however, goes beyond the divine purpose and beyond the teaching of Scripture. The concept of *absolute* inerrancy cannot be proven from Scripture either directly or indirectly.[7] Nor did the Princetonian scholars attempt to support this concept with more than a cursory appeal to any Scripture except 2 Tim 3:16 and 2 Pet 1:20, 21. Their concept of absolute inerrancy was so completely a priori that they repeatedly assumed that by proving *all* of Scripture was inspired, they had *automatically* proven *absolute* inerrancy.[8] This a priori assumption that inspiration guarantees *absolute* inerrancy is like the assumption that a 10,000-pound weight released from a high building on a windless day will strike the ground before a one-pound weight that is released at the same time. Both beliefs are a priori. Both beliefs rest ultimately upon pure human Reason. It was Reason, therefore, to which Scripture was being subordinated at Old Princeton.

the Natural World (New York: University Press of America, 2007) 186. The concept of accommodation that I am championing in this paper is not identical with Calvin's concept, but it is in agreement with his concept in principle and similarly in agreement with Jesus in principle and hence fully biblical.

6. 2 Tim 3:16. Although the historical and scientific notions of the times were assumed by Jesus, the prophets, and the apostles to be true, the purpose of their teaching was always spiritual; it was never to correct or even authenticate the scientific or historical notions of their times.

7. See my book *Inerrant Wisdom* (Portland, OR: Evangelical Reform, 1989) for the evidence that Scripture does not teach absolute inerrancy. Compare James D. G. Dunn, "The Authority of Scripture according to Scripture," *Churchman* 96 (1982) 104–22, 201–25.

8. This is done repeatedly in Benjamin B. Warfield's *Revelation and Inspiration* (Grand Rapids: Baker, 1981) and is the primary argument in Warfield and A. A. Hodge, *Inspiration*. The title of Warfield's book *Limited Inspiration* is most telling because the book is about limited inerrancy. In his *Systematic Theology* (1:163), Hodge argued Scripture must be historically and scientifically inerrant because what the biblical writers assert, God asserts.

Sadly, as we shall see, the leading lights at Old Princeton had clear opportunities to recognize that Scripture is accommodated to the science of its times, and they missed their opportunities. They repeatedly rejected the historical-grammatical meaning of Scripture in favor of interpretations that took the Bible out of context in order to sustain the natural assumption of human Reason that Scripture always agrees with scientific facts. They thus led evangelicalism down a path where today one can scarcely be "orthodox" unless willing to either take Scripture out of context in order to make it agree with modern science (concordism) or reject modern science (obscurantism) in favor of a private interpretation of the scientific data.

Let us look now more closely at how this all came to pass.

CHARLES HODGE

Charles Hodge held a high view of genuine science. While editor of the *Biblical Repertory and Princeton Review* (*BRPR*), he kept his readers informed about recent scientific developments. Some twenty percent of the book reviews in that journal concerned scientific books—not books about science and the Bible, but about science pure and simple.[9] He was so far from believing in a retracted or isolated fideism that he believed "this infallible Bible must be interpreted by science."[10] When criticized for publishing an article in *BRPR* that a critic thought gave too much credence to science compared to the Bible, Hodge responded with these telling statements:

> The proposition that the Bible must be interpreted by science is all but self-evident. Nature is as truly a revelation of God as is the Bible; and we only interpret the Word of God by the Word of God when we interpret the Bible by science. . . . There is a two-fold evil on this subject against which it would be well for Christians to guard. There are some good men who are much too ready to adopt the opinions and theories of scientific men, and to adopt forced and unnatural interpretations of the Bible, to bring it to accord with those opinions. There are others, who

9. Ronald Numbers, "Charles Hodge and the Beauties and Deformities of Science," in *Charles Hodge Revisited*, ed. J. W. Stewart and J. H. Moorhead (Grand Rapids: Eerdmans, 2002) 78.

10. Numbers, "Charles Hodge," 82.

not only refuse to admit the opinions of men, but science itself to have any voice in the interpretation of Scripture. Both of these errors should be avoided. Let Christians calmly wait until facts are indubitably established, so established that they command universal assent among competent men, and then they will find that the Bible accords with those facts. In the meantime, men must be allowed to ascertain and authenticate scientific facts in their own way, just as Galileo determined the true theory of the heavens. All opposition to this course must be not only ineffectual, but injurious to religion.[11]

Hodge rightly refused to suppress the facts of science and refused to "adopt forced and unnatural interpretations of the Bible, to bring it to accord with those opinions," that is, with the opinions of scientists that had not yet been proven. Hodge was "certain that there can be no conflict between the teachings of the Scriptures and the facts of science."[12] If he had restricted the "teachings of Scripture" to matters of faith and life, as the context of 2 Tim 3:16 implies, or if he had allowed for the principle of accommodation which Jesus accepted and Calvin frequently employed,[13] or if he had realized Scripture nowhere teaches the doctrine of *absolute* inerrancy[14] and we ought not to go beyond Scripture, he could have maintained a biblical approach to the relationship between modern science and the Bible. Unfortunately, the natural assumption to which he was committed had no place for any of these biblical options. Looking back at history, Hodge saw only two options: "scientific theories have either proved to be false or to harmonize with the Word of God properly interpreted."[15]

Hodge and the Proper Interpretation of Scripture

What did Hodge mean by "properly interpreted"? Judging by his earlier statement, he did not mean "forced and unnatural interpretations" made in order to bring the Bible "to accord with" science. In his *Systematic*

11. Charles Hodge, "Letter to the *New York Observer*, March 26, 1863," 98–99, cited in Mark Noll, "Science, Theology, and Society: From Cotton Mather to William Jennings Bryan," in *Evangelicals and Science in Historical Perspective*, ed. D. N. Livingstone, D. G. Hart, and M. Noll (New York: Oxford University Press, 1999) 109.

12. Hodge, *Systematic Theology*, 1:573.

13. Young, *John Calvin*, 157–234.

14. See note 7 above.

15. Hodge, *Systematic Theology*, 1:573.

Theology (1:187), he spelled out in a positive way the rules of proper biblical interpretation. His first rule was that "The words of Scripture are to be taken in their plain historical sense. That is, they must be taken in the sense attached to them in the age and by the people to whom they were addressed."[16] His second rule was that "Scripture must explain Scripture." His third and final rule was that "The Scriptures are to be interpreted under the guidance of the Holy Spirit." The first rule is the most critical because the second rule depends upon it, and the third rule will not violate it unless there is a *sensus plenior*. Modern conservative evangelicals have agreed with Hodge's rules, and their most basic rule is to follow the historical-grammatical interpretation of Scripture.[17] Conservative theologians at least from the Reformation on have realized from past church history that if the historical-grammatical interpretation of Scripture is set aside, the door is open to purely subjective interpretations, and such interpretations, used as they have been to support merely human traditions, undermine the authority of Scripture.

Nevertheless, in spite of his commitment to historical-grammatical interpretation, Hodge, as noted above, had a higher hermeneutical rule stemming from the natural assumption of human Reason: a true interpretation of the Bible must agree with scientific facts. As we shall see, Hodge was willing to set aside the historical-grammatical interpretation of Scripture if necessary (and thereby undermine the authority of Scripture) to maintain his assumption that the Bible would always agree with scientific facts.

One example of Hodge's ultimate commitment to human Reason is found in his statements about Scripture in relation to the findings of Copernicus. He tells us that because of the findings of Copernicus the church "has been forced . . . to alter her interpretation of the Bible to accommodate the discoveries of science. But this has been done without doing any violence to the Scriptures or in any degree impairing their authority."[18] Indeed, Hodge tells us that although the old views made it difficult to change interpretations, in time faith "grew strong enough to

16. Hodge, *Systematic Theology*, 1:187.

17. Compare *The Chicago Statement on Biblical Hermeneutics*, article 15. See Norman L. Geisler, *Explaining Hermeneutics: A Commentary on the Chicago Statement on Biblical Hermeneutics* (Oakland, CA: International Council on Biblical Inerrancy, 1983).

18. Hodge, *Systematic Theology*, 1:574.

take it all in and rejoice to find that the Bible, and the Bible alone of all ancient books, was in full accord with these stupendous revelations of science."

The "old views" said that the Scriptures taught that the sun was literally moving. As seen in the writings of Turretin, these views were based primarily on Josh 10:12, 13 and Eccl 1:5.[19] Hodge seems to have reinterpreted these passages as "phenomenal language," that is, referring just to appearances. But is this reinterpretation in accord with Hodge's first rule of interpretation? Is he taking the words of these passages "in the sense attached to them in the age and by the people to whom they were addressed"? What did the words about the sun "going down" mean in the age and to the people of Joshua's and Solomon's day? Hodge himself had answered this question in his essay "Inspiration." Speaking of the current opinions of the generation to which the biblical writers belonged, he said, "To them the heavens were solid, and the earth a plane; the sun moved from east to west over their heads."[20] Hodge is, of course, quite correct: given the age and the culture of the people to whom Josh 10:12, 13 and Eccl 1:5 were originally addressed, the words "go down" and "hasteth to its place where it ariseth" with reference to the sun were understood literally. Since both author and readers understood the sun to be literally moving, they would not agree that they were just using phenomenal language. But Hodge overrode his first rule of interpretation in order to sustain his a priori commitment to the idea that the Bible would always agree with the scientific facts. Human Reason's natural assumption that Scripture must be scientifically inerrant trumped the historical-grammatical interpretation of Scripture.

A second example of Hodge setting aside the historical-grammatical meaning of Scripture in order to maintain his commitment to Reason's natural assumption is found in his resolution of the conflict between Genesis 1 and geology. Geology was the science that pressed most strongly against the Bible in Hodge's day. Although Hodge was not willing to follow unproven theories, he was convinced that the Christian geologists who were leading scientists at the time must be taken seriously.

19. Josh 10:12, 13 read, "and the sun stayed in the midst of heaven, and hasted not to go down about a whole day," while Eccl 1:5 states, "The sun also ariseth, and the sun goeth down, and hasteth to its place where it ariseth."

20. Charles Hodge, "Inspiration," reprinted in *The Princeton Theology*, ed. Mark Noll (Grand Rapids: Baker, 1983) 137.

Since two of them in particular (Dana at Yale and Guyot at Princeton University) had interpreted the "days" of Gen 1 as long ages so that the Bible agreed with geology, Hodge accepted their day-age interpretation and said, "the friends of the Bible owe them [Dana and Guyot] a debt of gratitude for their able vindication of the sacred record."[21]

Hodge admitted that apart from a consideration of the scientific facts it would be most natural to understand the word "day" of Gen 1 "in its ordinary sense, but if that sense brings the Mosaic account into conflict with facts and another sense avoids such conflict, then it is obligatory on us to adopt that other." But if the interpretation of the word "day" in Gen 1 in its ordinary sense is "most natural," then interpreting it as a geological age is by definition "unnatural." The historical and biblical contexts of Gen 1 confirm that a day-age interpretation is unnatural.[22] The fact that no one until the rise of modern science interpreted the days of Gen 1 as long ages seals the case that such an interpretation is unnatural. Consequently, Hodge was accepting an approach to the Bible that he had earlier disavowed: a "forced and unnatural interpretation of the Bible, to bring it to accord with" the opinions of scientists—albeit these scientists had well-founded opinions.

Hodge's approach to the solidity of the firmament in Gen 1 reveals again his ultimate commitment to Reason's assumption that inspired Scripture must agree with the scientific facts. Interestingly, Hodge, like E. J. Young, accepted the grammatical meaning of the Hebrew word for "firmament" and hence did not deny that Gen 1 was speaking of a solid sky.[23] He also knew that the Israelites believed the sky was literally solid.[24] One would expect, therefore, that he would realize that the historical-grammatical meaning of the Hebrew word for "firmament" in Gen 1 is a literally solid sky. As Hodge said, "The words of Scripture [such as firmament] are to be taken in their plain historical sense. That

---

21. Hodge, *Systematic Theology*, 574.

22. Paul H. Seely, "The First Four Days of Genesis in Concordist Theory and in Biblical Context," *Perspectives on Science and Christian Faith* 49 (1997) 85–95. Available online at http://www.asa3.org/ASA/PSCF/1997/PSCF6-97Seely.html.

23. Hodge, *Systematic Theology*, 1:569–70. Hodge elsewhere writes, "When the Bible speaks of . . . the solid heavens . . ." Compare E. J. Young, *Studies in Genesis One* (Philadelphia: Presbyterian and Reformed, 1964) 90n94. Consulting *HAL*, one finds "the firm vault of heaven."

24. See *Inspiration*, cited above; and Hodge, *Systematic Theology*, 1:569.

is, they must be taken in the sense attached to them in the age and by the people to whom they were addressed."[25]

Indeed, one would expect not only that Hodge would follow his first rule of interpretation, but that he would also draw the rather obvious conclusion that the biblical statements about a solid sky were accommodations to the science of the times. But when asked why Scripture spoke of a solid sky, he kept his ultimate commitment to Reason's assumption in tact by lifting the biblical text out of its historical context. For support, he gives a quotation from Calvin's *Institutes* (1:14:3) in Latin, wherein Calvin said (translation mine), "Moses accommodating himself to the ignorance of the masses, mentions no other works of God in the account of creation except those which meet our eyes."[26] By citing Calvin's phrase "meet our eyes," Hodge exchanged the historical-grammatical meaning of a solid sky to mere phenomenal language.

Hodge thus missed another great opportunity to recognize that the Bible is accommodated to the scientific ideas of the times. He violated his own first rule of hermeneutics just as he did when he dealt with the sun's movement. He subordinated the historical-grammatical meaning of Scripture to the natural assumption of human Reason that inspired Scripture must be *absolutely* inerrant.

BENJAMIN B. WARFIELD

Benjamin Breckinridge Warfield, who taught systematic theology at Princeton from 1887 until 1921, apparently had no disagreements with Charles Hodge when it came to science and the Bible. He certainly upheld the idea that the Bible was inerrant in its scientific statements.[27] At the same time Warfield apparently had no problem accepting Genesis and the theory of evolution[28] and therein the long ages taught by geology. His praise of Sir John William Dawson's work shows that he ac-

---

25. Hodge, *Systematic Theology*, 1:187

26. Hodge, *Systematic Theology*, 1:569–70.

27. Archibald A. Hodge and Benjamin B. Warfield, *Inspiration* (1881, repr. Grand Rapids: Baker, 1979) 28.

28. See Mark Noll and David Livingstone, "Introduction: B. B. Warfield as a Conservative Evolutionist," in *Evolution, Scripture, and Science*, ed. Noll and Livingstone (Grand Rapids: Baker, 2000) 36–44.

cepted the day-age theory of Genesis just as Hodge did.[29] In so doing, his ultimate hermeneutic was not to understand "days" in Gen 1 "in the sense attached to them in the age and by the people to whom they were addressed." Rather, like Hodge he was subjecting the Bible to the findings of modern science on the basis of Reason's natural assumption that the Bible, being divinely inspired, would always be in agreement with the truths of science.

Similarly, because of the short time that humanity has existed on earth according to the Bible (from Adam to the present day, about six thousand years) and the long period of ten to twenty thousand years asked for by science in Warfield's day, Warfield said, "There was thus created the appearance of a conflict between the biblical statements and the findings of scientific investigators, and it became the duty of theologians to investigate the matter."[30] Warfield then proceeded to solve the conflict by noting that the biblical genealogies often have missing names, so the genealogies in Gen 5 and 11 could have missing names, and hence they could be stretched to the length of time demanded by science.

Although it is impossible to prove that the genealogies in Gen 5 and 11 do not have missing names, it is improbable that "in the age and by the people to whom they were addressed," *these* genealogies would have been thought of as having missing names. Unlike any other genealogies in the Bible or known in the ancient Near East, the genealogies in Gen 5 and 11 give the age of the father at the time of the birth of his son. This unique configuration makes it natural to understand these genealogies as providing an unbroken series of births from the time of Adam to that of Abraham. It is unnatural to interpret them any other way, and, as far as I have been able to determine, no one did so until the rise of modern geology. In fact, it is so natural to use these genealogies to calculate a continuous chronology that Jews from the beginning of intertestamental literature[31] until New Testament times[32] regularly did so.

29. See Warfield, "Review of Dawson, *Eden Lost and Won*," in *Evolution, Scripture, and Science*, ed. Noll and Livingstone, 175–76.

30. B. B. Warfield, "On the Antiquity and Unity of the Human Race," in *The Princeton Theology, 1812–1921: Scripture, Science, Theological Method from Archibald Alexander to Benjamin Breckinridge Warfield*, ed. Mark Noll (Grand Rapids: Baker, 1983) 290.

31. See Demetrius the Chronographer 2:18 in *The Old Testament Pseudepigrapha*, ed. James H. Charlesworth (Garden City, NY: Doubleday, 1985) 2:851–52; compare *2 Enoch* 72:6 and *The Assumption of Moses* 1:2, 3.

32. For example, Josephus, *Antiquities* 1.1.13: "The things narrated in the sacred

Christians continued this practice. Virtually *all* Christians from the beginning of Christianity until the rise of modern geology interpreted the genealogies in Gen 5 and 11 as indicating that the world is less than six thousand years old.[33] Even as sophisticated a thinker as Augustine interpreted these genealogies that way and employed the result to correct an opposing viewpoint. He wrote, "They . . . being deceived by a kind of false writing, that say: 'The world has continued many thousand years,' whereas the holy scripture gives us not yet six thousand years since man was made."[34]

In the sixteenth century, Calvin commented on Gen 5, "In this chapter Moses briefly recites the *length of time* which had intervened between the creation of the world and the deluge." He also said, "They will not refrain from guffaws when they are informed that but little more than five thousand years have passed since the creation of the universe."[35] Luther likewise wrote, "we know from Moses that about six thousand years ago the world was not yet in existence . . ."[36] Most Christians and commentaries in the nineteenth century were still holding that view.[37]

Given this centuries-long approach (third century BCE to the nineteenth century CE) of Jews and Christians, we must conclude that interpreting Gen 5 and 11 as giving a reliable chronology from Adam to Abraham is the most natural way to interpret these chapters.[38] Warfield's

---

scriptures . . . embrace the history of 5000 years . . ."

33. For the first and second century, see *Theophilus to Autolycus* 3:28, in *The Ante-Nicene Fathers* vol. 2, ed. A. Roberts and J. Donaldson (New York: Scribner's, 1899) 120; F. C. Haber, *The Age of the World: Moses to Darwin* (Baltimore: Johns Hopkins University Press, 1959) 246n25.

34. Augustine, *The City of God* (New York: E. P. Dutton, 1945) 12.10 (p. 317).

35. John Calvin, *Institutes of the Christian Religion*, 2:925 (emphasis mine).

36. *Luther's Commentary on Genesis* (Grand Rapids: Zondervan,1958) 1:3.

37. See, for example, John Gill, *Complete Body of Doctrinal and Practical Divinity*, vol. 1 (1839; repr. Grand Rapids: Baker, 1978) 370. Adam Clarke's commentary (1810–1825) also gives a chart showing Adam's death is in 930 Anno Mundi ("the year of the world").

38. Given the strong chronological interest in the chapters between Gen 5 and 11 (Gen 7:6, 11, 13; 8:4, 5, 13, 14; 9:28; 11:1) along with the unique configuration of these genealogies, it is natural indeed to use them to calculate the time from Adam to Abraham and then go on to calculate the age of the earth. It is an argument from silence that the author of Gen 5 and 11 did not add up the data to provide a chronology. He did not add up the data in the genealogy in Gen 11 to calculate the life span of each patriarch either, but his doing so in chapter 5 shows that he is leaving this calculation up to the reader.

approach is accordingly unnatural. It arose not from the biblical text, but from a strong desire to make the Bible agree with science. It was an interpretation born of the natural assumption of human Reason that inspired Scripture must always agree with scientific truth.

At the same time, Warfield defined biblical inerrancy as allowing for the possibility that an inspired writer could

> share the ordinary opinions of his day in certain matters lying outside the scope of his teachings, as, for example, with reference to the form of the earth, or its relation to the sun; and, it is not inconceivable that the form of his language when incidentally adverting to such matters, might occasionally play into the hands of such a presumption.[39]

This statement shows that Warfield knew as well as Hodge did that the Israelites believed the earth was literally flat, the sun literally moved, and, by implication from "the ordinary opinions of his day," that the sky was literally solid. And he allowed in the above quote that inspired Scripture might incidentally mention such things while at the same time not actually teach them. The only logical conclusion one could draw from these premises is that the mention of a flat earth, or a literally moving sun, or a solid sky in Scripture must be an accommodation. Only by means of an accommodation could such a cosmology be set forth in God-breathed Scripture without teaching it.

Yet the logical implication of Warfield's words apparently never fully dawned upon him. In his essay "Limited Inspiration," rather than admitting that science in Scripture may be accommodated and hence not necessarily inerrant, he said that if one accepted Henry P. Smith's view that Scripture was only infallible in matters of religion (faith and life), not in history or science, "the facts which he [a biblical writer] gives as natural facts may be of the order of the Oriental cosmogony, which stands the earth on the back of an elephant and the elephant on the back of a tortoise and the tortoise on nothing."[40] Warfield was thus insisting that inspiration guaranteed the truth of Scripture even in matters of science, and of cosmology in particular.

39. B. B. Warfield, "The Real Problem of Inspiration," in *The Inspiration and Authority of the Bible* (Philadelphia: Presbyterian and Reformed, 1948) 166–67.

40. Benjamin B. Warfield, *Limited Inspiration* (Philadelphia: Presbyterian and Reformed, 1962) 36.

Admittedly, Smith's assumption that inspiration guarantees inerrancy and hence the errant science in Scripture must not be inspired is just as faulty as Warfield's view. Inspiration is not limited. Regardless of Smith's failure to accept the full inspiration of Scripture, Warfield had the opportunity to explain the ancient Near Eastern cosmology that does appear in Scripture as an accommodation,[41] and failed to do so. It appears that in Warfield's/Smith's time, the word "inspiration" was regarded as synonymous with "revelation." If so, this would explain Smith's error and why Warfield was unable to see that Scripture was accommodated. Warfield's failure was nonetheless unfortunate. His failure perpetuated the assumption of human Reason that whatever God says must be *absolutely* true. And because Scripture accommodates the science of the times, that assumption has necessarily led to either twisting Scripture so that it agrees with modern science or to twisting science so that it agrees with Scripture. If Warfield had just been consistent with his own words and accepted biblical accommodation, evangelicals could have been spared more than a century of thinking that committed Christians must obscure either the Bible or science or both.

JOHN D. DAVIS

John D. Davis was the next significant name at "Old Princeton." William Henry Green had been professor of Old Testament before him, but Green's work primarily dealt with higher criticism and had little to say about science and the Bible. What makes John Davis particularly important is that he was the first OT scholar at Old Princeton to deal with the ancient Near Eastern literature recently discovered in Mesopotamia (1850–75), especially the creation and flood story parallels from Babylonia. In dealing with the Babylonian parallels, he extended the ra-

---

41. The Bible's ancient Near Eastern cosmology, with its solid sky and ocean above it, its flat earth floating on an ocean below, is ultimately no less unbelievable than the Eastern cosmology Warfield mentions as prohibited by inspiration. See Paul H. Seely, "The Firmament and the Water Above, Part I: The Meaning of raqia' in Genesis 1:6–8," *Westminster Theological Journal* 53 (1991) 227–40; "The Firmament and the Water Above, Part II: The Meaning of 'The Water above the Firmament' in Genesis 1:6–8," *WTJ* 54 (1992) 31–46; "The Geographical Meaning of 'Earth' and 'Seas' in Genesis 1:10," *WTJ* 59 (1997) 231–55; John H. Walton, *Ancient Near Eastern Thought and the Old Testament* (Grand Rapids: Baker, 2006) 165–78.

tionalizing concordism that his predecessors had used to sustain human Reason's assumption that inspired Scripture must be absolutely inerrant.

Genesis One

Davis began well in his discussion of Gen 1 and its parallels in the Babylonian creation account. He noted the great differences especially in theology between the biblical account of creation and the Babylonian account, and he forthrightly admitted the "kinship" between the two traditions. He explained the "kinship" as being partially due to the "ancient common habitat in Babylonia of the two peoples who transmitted these accounts."[42] That is, Abraham came from Babylonia.[43] The second reason he gives for saying there is "no reasonable doubt of a relationship between the two traditions" is because of "the community of conception, Hebrews and Babylonians uniting in describing the primitive condition of the universe as an abyss of waters shrouded in darkness and subsequently parted in twain in order to the formation of heaven and earth."

In addition, Davis saw that the idea of creation beginning with a watery abyss was not common just to Genesis and the Babylonian creation tradition, but was a widespread Mesopotamian concept that "permeates the native literature." He cited a Sumerian text to illustrate this fact.

Since Davis should have known from the science of his day (the nebular hypothesis) that the earth did not begin covered with an ocean but was rather too hot to have an ocean upon it (and especially an ocean that was divided into two parts with half placed above the sun, moon, and stars), one would think that Davis would have drawn the rather obvious conclusion that the biblical account is reflecting Mesopotamian beliefs about the natural world, beliefs Abraham probably brought into the biblical tradition. Scientifically informed contemporaries of Davis drew this logical conclusion.[44] One such writer said, "Upon the false

42. John D. Davis, *Genesis and Semitic Tradition* (1894; repr. Grand Rapids: Baker, 1980) 8.

43. Compare: "The tradition of the flood was current among the peoples from whom the Hebrews sprang. In the ancestral home of Abraham the flood was remembered as a great crisis in human history." See Davis, "Flood," *A Dictionary of the Bible*, ed. John Davis (Philadelphia: Westminster, 1898) 225.

44. Henry Morton, "The Cosmogony of Genesis and Its Reconcilers," *Bibliotheca Sacra* (April 1897) 267–68; and see Driver's list of scholars.

science of antiquity its author has grafted a true and dignified representation of the relation of the world to God."[45]

Similarly, a noted scientist at that time, Henry Morton, writing in the conservative journal *Bibliotheca Sacra* in 1897, demonstrated from the writings of experts in Hebrew that the meanings of the words in Gen 1 did not agree with the findings of modern science.[46] Since it was common knowledge in educated circles that Gen 1 did not agree with modern science and Davis could see that the "science" in Gen 1 was in agreement with ancient Near Eastern concepts, it seems like Davis should have realized that the "science" in the Bible was an accommodation. But Davis drew no such conclusion. In fact he seems to have thought that Gen 1 is an accurate scientific description that was given to mankind at an early age.

As for the "days" in Gen 1, Davis gives reasons why they are not to be taken as literal, 24-hour, sequential days. He suggests the Framework Hypothesis might be true. He suggests the days might be recounted not in the order in which things came into existence, but in their "period of prominence." He suggests the days might be figurative. He notes that the days do not have the definite article in the Hebrew text, so they could have big gaps between them; and, since the Babylonian account comes from the same original tradition as the biblical account and in the Babylonian account "the successive stages in the development of the ordered universe occupied long periods of untold duration," the "presumption becomes strong that the Hebrew writer likewise conceived of the creation period not as seven times 24 hours, but as vastly, indefinitely long."[47] Davis thus used the Babylonian creation epic to interpret the biblical account in a concordistic manner. In his *Dictionary of the Bible*, the facts of geology are merged with the biblical-Babylonian tradition, and the conclusion is drawn that "All facts at present available indicate that between the successive days long periods of time intervened."[48]

It is quite evident, of course, that it is the science of geology that was determining Davis's day-age interpretation. As mentioned earlier, no one before the rise of modern science interpreted the days of Gen

45. S. R. Driver, *The Book of Genesis*, 3rd ed. (New York: E. S. Gorham, 1905) 33. Driver footnotes a number of scholars who reached the same conclusion.

46. Morton, "The Cosmogony of Genesis."

47. Davis, *Genesis and Semitic Tradition*, 18.

48. Davis, "Creation," *Dictionary of the Bible*, 146.

1 as long ages. In fact, virtually all Christians believed the Bible taught that the earth was not more than six thousand years old.[49] Are we then to suppose that the simple Hebrews, who, as Hodge rightly said, believed the earth was flat, the sky was solid, and the sun was literally moving, nevertheless believed that the creation week was "vastly, indefinitely long"? I think not. Nor is Davis's reference to the long periods between the creation events in the Babylonian creation epic of any relevance, for they have to do with the creation of the gods, not of heaven and earth (which is mentioned later). The only basis for interpreting the days of Gen 1 as long ages is modern geology, and that basis violates Hodge's first and legitimate rule of hermeneutics.

In order to square science with the Bible's saying that vegetation appeared on day 3 before the sun on day 4, Davis pointed to how no one knows whether vegetation preceded the sun throwing off its planets or not. This is an odd claim since the vegetation mentioned on day 3 is clearly subsequent to the formation of the earth, which is, after all, one of the sun's planets. The article "Creation" in Davis's *Dictionary of the Bible* appeals to a form of the day-age theory, explaining, "plant life possibly did not respond to the divine decree until the sun appeared."

So Davis's approach to Gen 1 honestly acknowledged some of the parallels with the Babylonian creation epic. Yet he missed the fact of accommodation in the biblical text, and set forth instead a basket of varying concordist ideas, none of which are in agreement with the historical-grammatical meaning of Gen 1, and all of which were motivated by the strong desire to make Gen 1 agree with modern science. In the end Davis's interpretation of Gen 1 goes back to his ultimate commitment to the assumption of human Reason that inspired Scripture must agree with the facts of science.

The Flood

Regarding the Babylonian and biblical accounts of the flood, Davis pointed out a number of differences in addition to the theological differences, but he also saw the many similarities. He concluded that the Hebrew narrative, at least as a whole, was not derived directly from the

49. F. C. Haber, *The Age of the World: Moses to Darwin* (Baltimore: Johns Hopkins University Press, 1959) 246. Compare John Gill, *Complete Body of Doctrinal and Practical Divinity*, vol. 1 (repr., Grand Rapids: Baker, 1978) 370; and Adam Clarke's (1810–25) chart showing Adam's death is in 930 Anno Mundi (see notes 20–25 above).

cuneiform; but the accounts do have a common origin and describe the same flood. They are variant versions: "Two independently transmitted traditions of the same event."[50] Modern scholars agree with this assessment.[51]

But Davis also thought that "Confirmation of the historical character of the Semitic tradition is afforded by the existence of similar stories among other races."[52] Few, if any, modern scholars would agree with that assessment. Davis's contemporary S. R. Driver more realistically realized that "the principles of comparative mythology show that the traditions of a Flood current in different parts of the world do not necessarily perpetuate the memory of a single historical event."[53]

In order to establish the historicity of the biblical flood, Davis appealed to the then-noted geologist Eduard Suess as offering a credible geological explanation of the flood, which involved sea water rushing onto the land. Davis, accordingly, translated the Gilgamesh Epic, tablet 11, line 133, which refers to the end of the flood: "the sea withdrew to its bed." Driver, however, translated it: "the sea was calm." In our time, Speiser likewise translated it: "the sea grew quiet" (*ANET*). Dalley also translated it: "the sea became calm." It seems clear that Davis was reading Suess's theory into the cuneiform text in order to support the historicity of the flood.

Similarly, Davis was reading Suess's theory into the biblical account. When he dealt with the "fountains of the great deep" (Gen 7:11; 8:2), which are regularly understood in the OT to be fresh-water fountains[54] coming up from the ocean beneath the earth, Davis saw nothing of this ancient cosmology. Instead, he read Suess into the biblical text, saying, "the sea [which is not fresh water] disturbed perhaps by earthquakes,

---

50. Davis, *Genesis and Semitic Tradition*, 121.

51. Donald J. Wiseman, *Illustrations from Biblical Archaeology* (London: Tyndale, 1958) 8; John H. Walton, *Ancient Israelite Literature in Its Cultural Context* (Grand Rapids: Zondervan, 1989) 40; Alfred J. Hoerth, *Archaeology and the Old Testament* (Grand Rapids: Baker, 1998) 196; Alan R. Millard, "A New Babylonian 'Genesis' Story," *Tyndale Bulletin* 18 (1967) 17.

52. Davis, *Genesis and Semitic Tradition*, 122–23.

53. Driver, *Book of Genesis*, 99.

54. Gerhard F. Hasel, "The Fountains of the Great Deep," *Origins* 1 (1974) 67–72. Compare the "*great* waters" of the "*deep*" in Ezek 31:4, 5 (= the "great deep"), which made a cedar tree grow and hence must have been fresh waters.

rolled its waves upon the land."[55] As for the windows of heaven opening up to cause the flood (Gen 7:11), Davis recognized that this was not ordinary rain, yet he completely missed the fact that the text is referring to the ocean above the firmament pouring down. Most evangelical OT scholars today recognize that Gen 7:11 refers to a reversal of the second day of creation: the waters above the firmament came pouring down upon the earth; the waters beneath the earth came up. Waltke's comment is typical: "The earth is being returned to its precreation chaos by the release of the previously bounded waters above and by the upsurge of the subterranean waters (see 1:2, 6–9; 8:2)."[56]

Gen 7:11 (8:2) handed Davis a great opportunity to realize the biblical account was accommodated to ancient Near Eastern concepts, but he completely failed to see the ancient cosmology. No doubt Davis's assumption that Scripture must be scientifically inerrant played an important part in blinding him to the meaning of the biblical text. S. R. Driver, on the other hand, clearly saw the ancient cosmology in this verse.[57] Ironically, the "liberal," Driver, was interpreting the Bible in accord with Hodge's first rule of interpretation, while the "conservative," John Davis, was rewriting the Bible to make it agree with modern science!

Davis realized from geology that the flood was probably not global, so he attempted to explain the biblical text in ways that would negate its most natural and traditional interpretation. He said the phrase "all the high mountains under heaven" just means those "within man's changing horizon." He added that the language used cannot be interpreted beyond that which the people addressed would have understood, so the flood did not cover the whole earth, just the "earth" of Moses' day, which Davis described as being about a third the size of the United States.

Davis's view of the extent of the flood more or less agrees with the fact that the word "earth" is defined in the flood account as covering the greater ancient Near East.[58] But it overlooks two important facts: 1) the people addressed would have understood "all the high mountains under heaven" as including the Ararat mountains, and hence the flood was

---

55. Davis, *Genesis and Semitic Tradition*, 126.

56. Bruce Waltke, *Genesis* (Grand Rapids: Zondervan, 2001) 139. For similar statements by other evangelical Old Testament scholars, see Paul H. Seely, "Noah's Flood: Its Date, Extent, and Divine Accommodation," *WTJ* 66 (2004) 297–98.

57. Driver, *Book of Genesis*, 90.

58. Seely, "Noah's Flood," 303.

thousands of feet deep; and 2) if the flood covered "the earth of Moses' day" (one third the size of the United States) it would have covered the entire globe since water seeks its own level.

Davis was on the right track when he defined the extent of the flood as corresponding to the extent of the earth as understood in Moses's day. If he had been consistent he would have added that the sources of the flood's waters corresponded to the cosmology as understood in Moses's day. But such consistency would have revealed that the flood account does not correspond to modern science. Since Davis's ultimate commitment was to Reason's natural assumption that inspired Scripture must necessarily agree with the facts of modern science, he was unable to accept the full historical-grammatical meaning of the biblical account.

Thus we see at Old Princeton in the writings of Hodge, Warfield, and Davis an unwavering commitment to the natural assumption of human Reason that inspired Scripture must always agree with the scientific facts. Although this commitment was undoubtedly inspired in part by a desire to uphold the authority of Scripture, it was so strongly rooted in human Reason that the historical-grammatical meaning of Scripture (which is integral to its authority) was regularly subordinated to it. Thus Reason reigned at Old Princeton. Since the influence of Old Princeton on conservative evangelical thinking has been great, it laid the foundation for both the concordistic rationalizing that even today remains an integral part of most conservative evangelicalism and the scientific obscurantism that is integral to fundamentalism's "creation science."

Is there a better road for evangelicalism? Yes, and Scripture demands it. As children of light, Christians must refuse to obscure the Bible by forcing its words into agreement with modern science. Similarly, we must refuse to force the data of modern science into agreement with the Bible. In place of human Reason's natural assumption that Scripture must be *absolutely* inerrant, we ought to accept the teaching of our Lord that inspired Scripture is sometimes accommodated to ingrained cultural ideas of the times (Matt 19:7–9/Mark 10:2–9). Such accommodation has clearly occurred in Gen 1–11, and that accommodation absolves the Bible's references to ancient "science" from being errors (because they are not being taught). At the same time, it removes all pressure to obscure either the Scriptures or the facts of science. In this way, evangelicalism can thus affirm the inerrancy of Scripture as defined by Scripture, not by human Reason.

The Modernist-Fundamentalist Controversy, the Inerrancy of Scripture, and the Development of American Dispensationalism

Todd Mangum

THE CONTEXT IN WHICH THE DOCTRINE OF INERRANCY WAS DEVELOPED

THE ENLIGHTENMENT ERA EMPHASIZED individual discovery and encouraged an attitude of suspicion towards authority and tradition. By the late nineteenth century, this "enlightenment" had backfired on conservative Christian faith as church tradition and ecclesiastical authority came also within the crosshairs of its suspicion and critique. Biblical authority itself eventually came under suspicion.[1]

1. This is a sweeping summarization of six hundred years of Western intellectual history, of course, but there is wide agreement with the substance of this paragraph among historians, sociologists, and philosophers. See *The Cambridge History of Christianity*, vol. 7: *Enlightenment, Reawakening and Revolution: 1660–1815*, ed. Stewart J. Brown and Timothy Tackett (New York: Cambridge University Press, 2006); Margaret C. Jacob, *The Enlightenment: A Brief History with Documents* (New York: Bedford/St. Martin's, 2000); Jacques Barzun, *From Dawn to Decadence, 1500 to the Present: 500 Years of Western Cultural Life* (New York: HarperCollins, 2000); Nathan O. Hatch, *The Democratization of American Christianity* (New Haven, CT: Yale University Press, 1989); Nathan O. Hatch and Mark A. Noll, eds., *The Bible in America: Essays*

By the early twentieth century, disagreements over how to respond to critical theories of the Bible set off hostilities between people of faith within Christian churches and schools. Two opposing sides formed: "modernists" and "fundamentalists" (also called "liberals" and "conservatives," respectively). "Liberals" were those who suggested a strategy of candid concession to Enlightenment criticism, declaring that the ethical core of the Christian faith was what was most crucial to maintain. "Conservatives" objected that such concessions actually gave up the core of the Christian faith and insisted that Enlightenment critiques must simply be repelled.[2] Within this debate, conservatives developed the doctrine of inerrancy to guard the Bible against attack. They also used the doctrine as a diagnostic tool, to quickly discern whether an individual's doctrine of Scripture was "liberal." Fundamentalists thus used the doctrine as both a shield and a weapon.[3]

None of this says anything yet about the correctness or incorrectness of the doctrine. Understanding the context of formulation merely puts us in a better position to analyze its suppositions and intents, alerting us to what is central and what is peripheral to the doctrine's framing. Additional analysis is required to determine what is useful and correct, or what is unhelpful or inaccurate. By way of analogy, we

---

in *Cultural History* (New York: Oxford University Press, 1982); James Byrne, *Religion and the Enlightenment* (Louisville: Westminster John Knox, 1997); Kenneth L. Grasso, "Christianity, Enlightenment Liberalism, and the Quest for Freedom," *Modern Age* 4.4 (Fall, 2006) 10–14; Bruce K. Ward, *Redeeming the Enlightenment: Christianity and the Liberal Virtues* (Grand Rapids: Eerdmans, 2010); Michael Legaspi, *The Death of Scripture and the Rise of Biblical Studies* (New York: Oxford University Press, 2010).

2. See Stewart G. Cole, *The History of Fundamentalism* (New York: Richard R. Smith, 1931); Norman F. Furniss, *The Fundamentalist Controversy: 1918–1931* (New Haven, CT: Yale University Press, 1954); Bradley J. Longfield, *The Presbyterian Controversy: Fundamentalists, Modernists, and Moderates* (New York: Oxford University Press, 1991); Ernest R. Sandeen, *The Roots of Fundamentalism: British and American Millenarianism, 1800–1930* (Chicago: University of Chicago Press, 1970); Steve Bruce, *Fundamentalism* (Malden, MA: Blackwell, 2000); and George M. Marsden, *Fundamentalism and American Culture: The Shaping of Twentieth-Century Evangelicalism: 1870–1925* (New York: Oxford University Press, 1980). Compare Gary J. Dorrien, *The Making of American Liberal Theology: Imagining Progressive Religion 1805–1900* (Louisville: Westminster John Knox, 2001); idem, *The Making of American Liberal Theology: Idealism, Realism, and Modernity, 1900–1950* (Louisville: Westminster John Knox, 2003); and idem, *The Making of American Liberal Theology: Crisis, Irony, and Postmodernity, 1950–2005* (Louisville: Westminster John Knox, 2006).

3. Some details of these developments are provided below; see the section titled, "Inerrancy and the Fundamentalist-Modernist Controversy."

might ask whether the doctrine of inerrancy is more like the invention of the jeep or the splitting of the atom. (Both of these innovations contributed significantly to the Allied victory in World War II.) Granting that the original context for its formulation was unfortunate, was the result something praiseworthy, the hostilities merely bringing about a more rapid and clear advancement in understanding? Or was its very formulation unfortunate, its destructiveness highlighted in hindsight, its positive potential accessed only with extreme caution?

DISPENSATIONALISM AS A MICROCOSM OF CONSERVATIVE REACTION TO THE MODERNIST-FUNDAMENTALIST CONTROVERSY

Besides consideration of the role of inerrancy in the fundamentalist-modernist controversies generally, we wish to explore how the doctrine of inerrancy contributed to the rise of dispensational theology specifically. This gives us one window into the dynamics at work in the early development of American evangelicalism.

The fundamentalist coalition was a complex alliance of co-belligerents against modernism. New combinations of shared conviction were forming, as well as tenuous alliances that soon fell apart once the fight with liberalism was disengaged.[4] As fundamentalists separated from the main denominational bodies in pursuit of a more positive embodiment of their vision—all of them seeking a "pure, right" church as the reward for losses endured in the fundamentalist-modernist fights[5]—the

4. See Marsden, *Fundamentalism and American Culture*; idem, *Understanding Fundamentalism and Evangelicalism* (Grand Rapids: Eerdmans, 1991). See also Paul Kemeny, "Princeton and the Premillenialists: The Roots of the *marriage de convenance*," *American Presbyterians* 71.1 (1993) 17.

5. The language of separating to form a "true, pure" church was used most explicitly by the Presbyterian fundamentalists but is present in the language of fundamentalists within other denominations as well. For example, see Carl McIntire, "The True Presbyterian Church," *Christian Beacon* 1 (11 June 1936) 3–5; J. Gresham Machen, "The Changing Scene and the Unchanging Word: A True Presbyterian Church at Last," *Presbyterian Guardian* 2 (22 June 1936) 110; R. B. Kuiper, "Why Separation Was Necessary," *Presbyterian Guardian* 2 (12 September 1936) 225–27; Edwin H. Rian, *The Presbyterian Conflict* (Grand Rapids: Eerdmans, 1940) 234–35; George P. Hutchinson, *The History behind the Reformed Presbyterian Church Evangelical Synod* (Cherry Hill, NJ: Mack, 1974) 224; D. G. Hart and John Muether, *Fighting the Good Fight: A Brief History of the Orthodox Presbyterian Church* (Philadelphia: Committee on Christian

differences between them became more acute. The rise of dispensation-alism from this bubbling turmoil represents one manifestation of how conservative Christianity reconstituted itself through the aftershocks of the modernist-fundamentalist fallout. We are thereby alerted to issues and concerns with which evangelicals have been wrestling ever since.[6]

INERRANCY AND THE FUNDAMENTALIST-MODERNIST CONTROVERSY

It is hard to imagine now, but there was a time when American intel-lectuals in general assumed a view of Scripture that revered its divine authority—not just pastors, but university professors too. Ironically, the way was opened for the "liberalization" (and then secularization) of the academy by a pious but naive assumption: that open and honest exploration would lead inevitably to greater Christian ideals.[7] To this day, it is common to find people on either side of the conservative-liberal divide who look back on the evolution of American intellectual history from traditional Christian conservatism to progressive secular humanism with either bemusement or bereavement. One side views this history as a story of heroic pioneers gradually overcoming resistance to Enlightenment breakthroughs; the other side sees it as a tragic story of

---

Education and the Committee for the Historian of the Orthodox Presbyterian Church, 1995) 47; and George W. Dollar, *A History of Fundamentalism in America* (Greenville, SC: Bob Jones University Press, 1973). Compare also the writings of fundamentalist Baptists, William Bell Riley (founder and head of the World's Christian Fundamentals Association, organized in 1919) in his journal, *The Christian Fundamentalist*, and J. Frank Norris in his paper, *The Fundamentalist* (formerly, *The Searchlight*, and before that, *The Fence Rail*), throughout the early twentieth century.

6. I have chronicled in significant detail the rise of dispensationalism in the af-termath of the modernist-fundamentalist controversies in R. Todd Mangum, *The Dispensational-Covenantal Rift: The Fissuring of American Evangelical Theology from 1936 to 1944* (Waynesboro, GA: Paternoster, 2007).

7. George M. Marsden and Bradley J. Longfield, eds., *The Secularization of the Academy* (New York: Oxford University Press, 1992); also Marsden, *The Soul of the American University: From Protestant Establishment to Established Nonbelief* (New York: Oxford University Press, 1994). See also William F. Buckley Jr., *God and Man at Yale: The Superstitions of "Academic Freedom"* (New York: Regnery, 1951). Compare also Mark A. Noll, *Between Faith and Criticism: Evangelicals, Scholarship, and the Bible in America* (New York: HarperCollins, 1986); and idem, *The Scandal of the Evangelical Mind* (Grand Rapids: Eerdmans, 1994).

degeneration into apostasy by the very leaders entrusted with preserving the faith, save for a courageous remnant holding fast.

By the late nineteenth century, naiveté had given way to a battle mentality as conservative Bible-believers grew alarmed at theories they heard propagated by teachers even in their own denominational schools. These conservatives came to see themselves as fighting for orthodoxy. That barely describes their depth of feeling and strength of conviction, though. Reading their rhetoric even today is jolting.[8] And, of course, fundamentalist stridency was part of what their opponents found so off-putting.

The Briggs Heresy Trial: Catalyst for the Development of the Doctrine of Inerrancy

One of the first major flashpoints of the fundamentalist-modernist controversy was the "Charles A. Briggs Heresy Trial" in the early 1890s. Two renowned conservative stalwarts, both Princeton Seminary theologians, led the case against Briggs: Archibald A. Hodge (son of the legendary Charles Hodge) and Benjamin Breckinridge Warfield. Hodge and Warfield eventually succeeded in getting Briggs's appointment to a chaired professorship revoked by the Presbyterian General Assembly (1893), but this only led Briggs—and Union Seminary at which he taught—to withdraw from the Presbyterian Church USA denomination, thereby preserving Briggs at Union.

Central to Hodge's and Warfield's charge against Briggs was the claim that, by conceding to certain aspects of higher-critical theories, he had abandoned an orthodox view of scriptural inspiration as demanded by the Presbyterian Church's doctrinal standards. It was in framing this charge against Briggs that Hodge and Warfield first developed a full-fledged defense of biblical inerrancy.

---

8. The June 4, 1936, headline of *The Christian Beacon*, set in large, bold type, provides a clear example: "Jesus Christ Dethroned! Fundamentalists Ousted—Church to Split." While this headline may have been particularly sensationalistic, it is representative of the kind of fervor that characterized fundamentalist publications of the period, as even cursory perusal of fundamentalist magazines of the period—*The Christian Beacon*, *The Fundamentalist*, or *The Christian Fundamentalist*—quickly demonstrates.

The Development of the Doctrine of Inerrancy as a Reaction to Historical Criticism

The conflict between Hodge, Warfield, and Briggs did not start out at such a boiling point. In the early stages of the controversy, the inter-locutors all seemed to regard their discrepancy of view as a difference of scholarly opinion—vigorous, but academic. In 1880, Charles Briggs initiated the founding of a new journal, *The Presbyterian Review*, and invited A. A. Hodge to serve as coeditor with him. As a joint publication of Union Seminary in New York and Princeton Seminary in New Jersey (both Presbyterian Church USA schools at the time), the journal was to serve as a means of dialoguing, mediating differences, and sharpen-ing each other's perspective in a way that would foster harmony within the denomination.[9] Unfortunately, the result was just the opposite of its intention. The journal instead served to further polarize the two institu-tions and the ideas embraced by their leading thinkers.

One year after the founding of *The Presbyterian Review*, in 1881, Hodge and Warfield coauthored an article on "Inspiration." We are tipped off to this representing a very early stage in the development of the doctrine of inerrancy in part because the term "inerrancy" is never actually used in this article, but clumsy precursors are. For example, the word "errorless" occurs seven times within such awkward phrases as "absolutely errorless"[10] and "errorless infallibility."[11] The article sets forth what would become for a century thereafter the standard fundamental-ist-evangelical position on the inspiration (and inerrancy) of Scripture:

Statement of the Doctrine

> During the entire history of Christian theology the word Inspiration has been used to express either some or all of the ac-tivities of God, cooperating with its human authors in the genesis of Holy Scripture. We prefer to use it in the single sense of God's continued work of superintendence, by which, His providential, gracious, and supernatural contributions having been presup-posed, He presided over the sacred writers in their entire work of

9. Frank Luther Mott, *A History of American Magazines* (London: Oxford University Press, 1938), 74; M. James Sawyer, *The Survivor's Guide to Theology* (Grand Rapids: Zondervan, 2006), 182–84; Charles A. Briggs and Archibald A. Hodge, "The Idea and Aims of *The Presbyterian Review*," *The Presbyterian Review* 1.1 (January 1880) 3–7.

10. Archibald A. Hodge and Benjamin B. Warfield, "Inspiration," *The Presbyterian Review* 2.6 (April 1881) 237.

11. Hodge and Warfield, "Inspiration," 240.

> writing, with the design and effect of rendering that writing an errorless record of the matters He designed them to communicate, and hence constituting the entire volume in all its parts the Word of God to us.[12]

The tone of the entire article is one of seriousness and concern, its sense of distress signaling that the temperature in the debate is rising. The hostilities simmered barely beneath the surface in 1889, when Warfield replaced Hodge (who died in 1887) as coeditor, and, in that position, promptly refused to publish one of Briggs's articles.[13]

What brought the conflict to full boil in 1891 was Briggs's address on the "The Authority of Scripture" at his inauguration to the Edward Robinson Chair of Biblical Theology. The address went for two hours and seemed intended to lay down the gauntlet against views of biblical inspiration that would insist upon "inerrancy"—a term that Briggs *does* use, ironically (and lists as a modern-day *obstacle* to a proper understanding of biblical authority!).[14] In thinly veiled references to Hodge and Warfield, Briggs ridiculed their views as built on "pure, conjectural tradition! Nothing more!"[15] and as representing "a ghost of modern evangelicalism to frighten children."[16]

At this point, some of the personal and political dynamics are as relevant as the theological differences. Clearly, for Briggs, closed-minded conservatism had audaciously banned his views from the very journal he started, but, at his inauguration, he would settle the score. Warfield and his colleagues, who he knew would have to sit there and take it, might find his views out of bounds, but his own school's faculty supported him, and his own board of trustees had voted unanimously to confirm him in this honor. Furthermore, Charles Butler, chairman of the board and financier of the Edward Robinson Chair he was filling, had

---

12. Hodge and Warfield, "Inspiration," 232.

13. Mark Massa, *Charles Augustus Briggs and the Crisis of Historical Criticism* (Minneapolis: Fortress, 1990) 53–68. Lefferts A. Loetscher, *The Broadening Church: A Study of Theological Issues in the Presbyterian Church since 1869* (Philadelphia: University of Pennsylvania Press, 1954) 29–37; Harvey Hill, "History and Heresy: Religious Authority and the Trial of Charles Augustus Briggs," *U.S. Catholic Historian* 20.3 (Summer 2002) 1–21.

14. Charles Augustus Briggs, *The Authority of Scripture: An Inaugural Address* (New York: Scribner's, 1893).

15. Briggs, *Authority*, 33.

16. Briggs, *Authority*, 36.

encouraged him to choose the subject of biblical authority as the topic of his inaugural address.[17]

Warfield was indeed outraged, as could be expected. It was not just personal, though. Briggs was the first occupant of the newly established Edward Robinson Chair, but the *vacancy* on the faculty, which opened this position for Briggs, was brought about by the retirement of William G. T. Shedd, a stalwart conservative and high Calvinist who had taught theology at Union Seminary for the previous twenty-seven years. From a traditionalist Presbyterian perspective, Briggs's combative assault on the veracity of Scripture signaled the demise of a cherished theological heritage that Princeton and Union previously had shared as a Presbyterian core value since their founding.

The polarities of response to Briggs's inaugural address played out in several ecclesiastical tribunals thereafter. Warfield filed formal charges of heresy against Briggs. In a pattern that would become familiar over the next several decades, Briggs's own presbytery (the Presbytery of New York) refused to try him and then acquitted him when the General Assembly demanded that they investigate the charges—at which point the General Assembly itself took up the case. In June of 1893, the General Assembly overruled the verdict of the New York Presbytery and charged him with holding views contrary to the church's doctrinal standards; the General Assembly vetoed Briggs's appointment to the Robinson professorship and defrocked him. The faculty of Union Seminary, however, voted to withdraw the school from the Presbyterian Church USA denomination rather than abide by the General Assembly ruling; and the Episcopal Church USA reinstated Briggs's ordination and appointed him a priest in that denomination.[18]

The battle lines drawn in the Briggs case were essentially the same ones drawn in various contexts throughout the fundamentalist-modernist controversies over the next fifty years. The doctrine of inerrancy,

17. Briggs, *Authority*, 1–10. Compare the synopsis of Union Seminary's website: http://www.utsnyc.edu/Page.aspx? pid=807. The webmaster has titled this section, "Freedom to Learn, Freedom to Teach."

18. Numerous treatises chronicle the details of these events, including: J. R. Laidlaw, *The Trial of Dr. Briggs before the General Assembly: A Calm Review of the Case* (New York: A. D. F. Randolph, 1893); Carl E. Hatch, *The Charles A. Briggs Heresy Trial: Prologue to Twentieth-Century Liberal Protestantism* (New York: Exposition, 1969); Loetscher, *Broadening Church*, 30–55; and Ronald F. Satta, "The Case of Professor Charles A. Briggs: Inerrancy Affirmed," *Trinity Journal* 26 (Spring 2005) 69–90.

submitted in response to higher critical theories of the Bible, was a key plank and flashpoint all along the way. It was no coincidence that the first two volumes of *The Fundamentals*, published in 1909–10, were largely devoted to refuting the claims of higher criticism, seeking to expose its fallacies, and defending biblical inerrancy over against it.[19]

Inerrancy as the First "Fundamental" of the Faith

In 1910, the Presbyterian General Assembly set forth a Doctrinal Deliverance in which five doctrines were deemed "essential and necessary" for all ordination candidates to affirm. All five were aimed at some aspect of the historical-critical approach that Briggs had advocated. The first of these formed the main point: "It is an essential doctrine of the Word of God and our Standards, that the Holy Spirit did so inspire, guide and move the writers of the Holy Scriptures as to keep them from error."[20]

Although the 1910 Doctrinal Deliverance of the Presbyterian General Assembly represented the height of conservative power in the church at the time, the tide was now turning. The trial and defrocking made Briggs a martyr among those sympathetic to his views and to those sympathetic to him on a personal level. The loss of Union Theological Seminary, New York, was also a blow to the denomination. Twenty years of infighting proved wearying; eventually, the agitators— i.e., those perceived as persecuting others for their sincerely held views—fell out of favor.

Fundamentalism Falls Out of Favor in the Mainline Denominations

Already in the 1890s, prominent clergymen and leaders had voiced frustration with antagonists in the Presbyterian Church USA who seemed to value doctrinal agreement over peace and harmony. Henry van Dyke, a prominent Presbyterian minister and professor of English literature at Princeton, in 1893 composed "A Plea for Peace and Work," urging the General Assembly to accept the acquittal of Briggs by the

---

19. *The Fundamentals: A Testimony to the Truth*, ed. Amzi C. Dixon, Louis Meyer, and Reuben A. Torrey (Chicago: Testimony, 1910).

20. "Historic Documents of American Presbyterianism: The Doctrinal Deliverance of 1910," PCA Historical Center, Archives and Manuscript Repository for the Continuing Presbyterian Church, St. Louis.

New York Presbytery and end the hostilities.[21] It garnered 100 signatures from clerics and elders from all over the country within the Presbyterian Church USA. It proved to no avail in rescuing Briggs, but, at the very least, it indicates an undercurrent of pronounced frustration with the controversies.

In 1922, Harry Emerson Fosdick delivered his famous sermon, "Shall the Fundamentalists Win?" at the First Presbyterian Church of New York City.[22] This sermon portrayed the controversy within the churches as one provoked by backward, doctrinaire traditionalists inveighing against thoughtful scholarship and refusing to engage levelheadedly with the modern findings of history, science, and religion. In fact, Fosdick's framing of the conflict as a "modernist-fundamentalist controversy" has been with us ever since.

In 1923, J. Gresham Machen, professor of New Testament at Princeton, published his now-famous book *Christianity and Liberalism*, which claimed that the views of modernists like Briggs and Fosdick suggest not just a misguided form of Christianity but actually represent a different religion altogether.[23] That same year, Machen became the stated pulpit supply of First Presbyterian Church of Princeton, home church of Henry van Dyke, who had just returned from serving a ten-year stint as US Ambassador to the Netherlands. Even though van Dyke was a family friend of the Machens, he relinquished his (rented) pew in protest and publicly denounced Machen's "bitter, schismatic, and unscriptural preaching" in an op-ed piece that was carried by newspapers all over the country.[24]

In 1924, 1,274 clerics, ministers, and elders of the Presbyterian Church USA signed the Auburn Affirmation, which protested the 1910 Doctrinal Deliverance and, once again, framed the controversy as being between overly doctrinaire conservatives and level-minded peacemakers (some of whom shared the conservative views, the Affirmation

---

21. "They Plead For Peace; Presbyterians Who Are Tired of Controversy. Prominent Clergymen and Laymen—In This and Other Cities Join in Earnest Protest—Fearful that the Church's Influence May Be Lessened," *New York Times*, 18 February 1893, 8.

22. Harry Emerson Fosdick, "Shall the Fundamentalists Win?," *Christian Work* 102 (10 June 1922) 716–22.

23. J. Gresham Machen, *Christianity and Liberalism* (Grand Rapids: Eerdmans, 1923).

24. "Van Dyke's Pew," *TIME* 3.2 (14 January 1924) 18.

stated, but not the unchristian political tactics).[25] This Affirmation signaled the beginning of the end for conservative ecclesiastical power in the mainline denominations. From 1924 onward, the Presbyterian General Assembly consistently and systematically overturned previous rulings of the General Assembly that had favored the conservative cause; most significantly, the General Assembly repealed any requirement to subscribe to doctrines not explicit in the Westminster Confession itself. These notable reversals served to further energize both sides.

Fundamentalist Separation from the Mainline Bodies

In 1929, when the Presbyterian General Assembly took up investigation of the continuing controversy at Princeton, it found J. Gresham Machen and the conservative-fundamentalist faction at fault. Through the early 1930s, a series of trials took place in both the church and civil courts. Machen himself was defrocked in 1936. Progressives doubtless saw these events as an example of what goes around comes around, of conservatives simply reaping what they had sown in the late 1890s in their attacks on Briggs, which had led to his defrocking. Conservatives had drawn first blood.

Conservatives certainly understood that actions taken against them were done in part out of vengefulness, and they protested the severity of actions taken against them as inappropriate in both rationale and in proportion; they endured not just multiple instances of defrocking, but seizure of their church properties as well, with the pastors under discipline literally locked out of their churches. Conservatives came to

---

25. "AN AFFIRMATION: Designed to safeguard the unity and liberty of the Presbyterian Church in the United States of America," included as Appendix B in Charles E. Quirk, "The Auburn *Affirmation*: A Critical Narrative of the Document Designed to Safeguard the Unity and Liberty of the Presbyterian Church in the United States of America in 1924," (PhD diss., University of Iowa, 1967) 397–99, see also 116–35, 261–79, 498–516; Carl McIntire, "'Auburn Affirmation,'" *Christian Beacon* 1 (20 August 1936) 1–2, 7–8; Gordon H. Clark, "The Auburn Heresy," *Christian Beacon* 1 (20 August 1936) 3; idem, "The Auburn Heresy," *Southern Presbyterian Journal* 5 (15 July 1946) 7–9; Murray Forst Thompson, "The Auburn Betrayal: Parts I–V," *Presbyterian Guardian* 10 (10 November 1941) 113–14, 125–27; (25 November 1941) 133–34; (10 December 1941) 154–55; (25 December 1941) 165–67; and 11 (25 January 1942) 24–25; and L. Nelson Bell, "The Auburn Affirmation Is Actually Not an Affirmation of Faith But a . . . [sic] Dissent from Evangelical Truth," *Southern Presbyterian Journal* 10 (10 October 1951) 3–4.

regard their persecution as suffering for Jesus' sake, the price they had been called to pay to combat the growing apostasy within the church.[26]

Conservatives have never forgotten what happened to them in the early twentieth century; whole separatist denominations exist to this day as a result of these events. When conservatives tell what happened, it is a story of wolves coming into the church unawares in sheep's clothing, using sheep's language, and masquerading under sheep's pseudo-piety.[27] Therefore, of utmost importance to conservatives was the formulation of litmus tests and effective shibboleths by which subversive forces within the churches (and particularly within the churches' academic institutions) could be rooted out. The doctrine of inerrancy served effectively as just such a litmus test and shibboleth.

We have up to now reviewed the modernist-fundamentalist controversy almost entirely within the framework of the Presbyterian Church USA. This is mainly because the Presbyterians kept the best records of the period and also because the doctrinal framing of this controversy was formed within the Presbyterian stage of the conflict. We are now in position to pick up the dispensationalist aspect of the story.

Fundamentalism and Premillennialism

While Warfield and Hodge were taking on Briggs's higher critical views in the Northeast, James Hall Brookes was cheering them on from St. Louis and sounding his own alarms against modernist departures from the truth.[28] This is telling. The Briggs case seemed to crystallize issues and trends that were taking place (both openly and underground) across the country and across denominational lines. It galvanized forces on both sides—and that the "two sides" were forming across denomina-

26. See Rian, *Presbyterian Conflict*, 248–57; Robert K. Churchill, *Lest We Forget: A Personal Reflection on the Formation of the Orthodox Presbyterian Church* (Philadelphia: Committee for the Historian of the Orthodox Presbyterian Church, 1986); and Hutchinson, *The History behind the Reformed Presbyterian Church Evangelical Synod*. For the most detailed account of the history of this period, see articles from 1935–1938 in both the *Christian Beacon* and the *Presbyterian Guardian*, two publications from the conservative side of the argument, which chronicled these events in detail.

27. See, for example, Merrill T. MacPherson, "Why I Am Pastor of an Independent Church," *Christian Beacon* 2 (12 August 1937) 3–4, 7.

28. George M. Marsden, *Fundamentalism and American Culture: The Shaping of Twentieth-Century Evangelicalism, 1870–1925* (New York: Oxford University Press, 1980) 71.

tional lines is itself a significant historical and sociological phenomenon. Brookes was an important leader in the early premillenarian movement, which would eventually evolve into a movement called "dispensational-ism." (See the next section below.) But this and various other movements really were still evolving, which can be observed if one scrutinizes the situation carefully.

For instance, Charles R. Erdman was a leader, too, in the early premillenarian movement; in fact, he was the one to write the chapter on premillennialism in *The Fundamentals*, ironically enough.[29] Why ironic? Because Erdman was the very one who, as moderator of the 1925 Presbyterian Church USA General Assembly, opposed J. Gresham Machen's stance at Princeton and was instrumental in the restructuring of Princeton that led to Machen's departure. Clearly, the forces of po-larization were still emerging in the early 1920s, the sides forming and changing until well into the early 1930s.

This is where the early dispensationalist aspect of the story becomes interesting and relevant. The early premillenarians were reliable conser-vatives theologically, but they also tended to diminish denominational distinctives (sometimes in favor of the premillennial distinctive). While the *degree* of Erdman's magnanimity was unusual for premillennialists, in that he ended up extending toleration towards even those who did not affirm the "fundamentals,"[30] it was not unusual for premillennialists to extend toleration to fundamentalists of most any *denominational* variety in a way that other kinds of fundamentalists may not. Most premillen-nialists tended to regard the fundamentals as the *only* requirement for (interdenominational) cooperation and fellowship. In this, they were a distinctive *kind* of conservative, distinguishable from other kinds of conservatives; e.g., denominational conservatives (such as Landmark Baptists who would regard "believer's baptism" by immersion as cen-tral to the faith, or "truly Reformed" Presbyterians who would insist on

29. Charles R. Erdman, "The Coming of Christ," *The Fundamentals*, 11:98.

30. "Erdman responded to Machen's claims by standing on his platform of 'purity and peace and progress.' Erdman repeatedly defended his orthodoxy. 'I have always been a Fundamentalist in my beliefs,' he declared. 'I refuse to be labeled as a Modernist or as a liberal, but if any men of liberal theological views desire to vote for me this year it is, of course, their privilege to do so.' Erdman's protest failed to address Machen's con-cerns: Erdman's willingness to cooperate with liberals for the sake of evangelism–not his personal orthodoxy–was at the heart of Machen's opposition" (Longfield, *Presbyterian Controversy*, 149).

Calvinism as a standard for shared fellowship and cooperation).[31] This distinctive kind of conservatism is what evolved into dispensationalism.

We are now ready to examine the various elements of conservatism that blended in fundamentalist opposition to modernism to form the soil in which dispensationalism sprouted.

THE FUSION OF DARBYITE PLYMOUTH BRETHRENISM, SOUTHERN PRESBYTERIANISM, AND PREMILLENIALISM INTO A SINGLE MOVEMENT (CALLED "DISPENSATIONALISM")

In the late nineteenth century, Plymouth Brethrenism, Southern Presbyterianism, and premillennialism all shared two common characteristics: 1) they believed that the "true church" was a distinct entity to be sharply distinguished from and in opposition to the world; and 2) that the world would likely grow in its opposition to Christ and Christian values until Jesus returned. Of these three, Southern Presbyterianism was the most positive about the church's status and future (even about the possibility of reversing the tide of wickedness and rebellion in favor of the kingdom of God). Plymouth Brethrenism was the most pessimistic about both the world and the church (which the Brethren regarded as having largely falling away into apostasy, which they likewise believed would pave the way for the Antichrist).

These three movements—Plymouth Brethrenism, Southern Presbyterianism, and premillennialism—were distinguishable from one

31. See Rollin Thomas Chafer, "Eschatological Freedom," *Bibliotheca Sacra* 93 (July–September 1936) 387–88; Carl McIntire, "Premillennialism," *Christian Beacon* 1 (1 October 1936) 4. Compare the response of R. B. Kuiper, who rebuked McIntire for his commendation of "eschatological freedom"; it was such freedom, Kuiper claimed, that had (inadvertently) permitted the increase of "naturalistic postmillenarians" in the old denomination. See "Has the Presbyterian Guardian Attacked Premillennialism?: The Reply of Dr. Kuiper," *Presbyterian Guardian* 3 (14 November 1936) 54–55. Compare also Allan A. MacRae, "Dr. Allan A. MacRae Resigns Seminary: Founder of Westminster Seminary Opposes Its Present Stand," *Christian Beacon* 2 (29 April 1937) 1–2, 8. See also Leslie W. Sloat, "Should Conservatives Cooperate?" *Presbyterian Guardian* 19 (February 1950) 23; idem, "Calvinists Can and Do Cooperate!" *Presbyterian Guardian* 19 (March 1950) 43; and D. G. Hart and John Muether, *Fighting the Good Fight*, 38–39. For a fascinating survey of how this debate over grounds of cooperation—and separation—unfolded among Presbyterian fundamentalists after Machen, see John M. Frame, "Machen's Warrior Children," in *Alister E. McGrath and Evangelical Theology*, ed. Sung Wook Chung (Grand Rapids: Baker, 2003) 113–46.

another in the late nineteenth century. They were three streams that converged to form what would come to be known as "dispensationalism"
in the twentieth century. It is worth our while to devote some further
analysis to each.

Premillennialism is the oldest and broadest of the three, and is
more a description of ideas in the abstract, rather than a label of how
those ideas operate within a sociological movement, like the other two
terms. It is a term describing an eschatological model: an interpretive
scheme in which Christ's return is believed to initiate the "thousand-
year reign" of Revelation 20. Its views are clarified by juxtaposing it
with the other eschatological choices: postmillennialism suggests
that Christ's reign began with Christ's resurrection, such that his return to earth is the culmination—not the initiation—of his reigning.
Amillennialism suggests that trying to sort out the chronology at all is
wrongheaded; that what the Bible means to portray (including in the
Book of Revelation) is an ongoing battle between the kingdom of God
and the kingdom of this (evil) world, with victories and losses continuing for both sides until Christ's return.[32]

Premillennialists are fond of asserting that the earliest known
eschatology is premillennialist.[33] This may be true insofar as what was
expressly articulated; there are references among the early church fathers to Christ returning to rescue his people from calamity, and his
setting right the earthly affairs of human beings by replacing pagan
rulers with his own reign—these themes sound more premillennialist
in overall import than postmillennialist or amillennialist.[34] However,
even if premillennialism is granted bragging rights as the earliest known
eschatology for sake of argument, it is also true that nothing like the
full-blown dispensationalist variety of premillennialism existed before

32. For a helpful synopsis of each of these millennialist views, see Stanley J. Grenz,
The Millennial Maze: Sorting Out Evangelical Options (Downers Grove, IL: InterVarsity,
1992).

33. See, for example, George N. H. Peters, *The Theocratic Kingdom*, vol. 1 (New York:
Funk & Wagnalls, 1884) 480–500; Lewis Sperry Chafer, "A Survey of the History of
Chiliasm," in *Systematic Theology*, vol. 4 (Dallas: Dallas Seminary, 1948) 264–84; John
F. Walvoord, *The Millennial Kingdom: A Basic Text in Premillennial Theology* (Grand
Rapids: Zondervan, 1959) 19, 37–45, 113–23; J. Dwight Pentecost, *Things to Come: A
Study in Biblical Eschatology* (Grand Rapids: Zondervan, 1958) 16–25, 370–94.

34. Irenaeus, Justin Martyr, Papias, and Tertullian are among the most notable of
the early fathers to sound these themes and are cited most often by premillennialists as
proof of the claim that the early church embraced a premillennial eschatology.

the late nineteenth century.[35] (If the apostle Paul was assuming a dispensationalist template, as dispensationalists have often claimed, the early church failed to preserve that hermeneutical template.)

The hermeneutical approach of modern-day premillennialism seems actually to have gotten its start in the eschatology of Martin Luther. This is a startling suggestion, at first, given how vehemently opposed Luther was to the premillennialism of his day and given how vigilantly opposed Lutheranism historically has been to both premillennialism in general and the dispensational emphasis on ethnic Israel in particular.[36] All that acknowledged, it was Luther's identification of the pope as the Antichrist and his exposition of the visions of Revelation in support of this contention that gave Protestant apocalypticism its

35. For one thing, persecution of Christians by the Jews (and vice versa) created animosities that discouraged early church fathers from embracing any eschatology that envisioned a revival of blessing upon ethnic, national Israel. This aversion to Jewish Zionism among the church fathers was the main point that James Bear identified as distinguishing "historic premillennialism" from "dispensational premillennialism," a distinction made more famous a decade later by George Eldon Ladd. See James E. Bear, "Historic Premillennialism," *Union Seminary Review* 55 (May 1944) 193–222; idem, "The People of God," *Union Seminary Review* 52 (October 1940) 33–63; idem, "The People of God According to the Fathers of the Early Church," *Union Seminary Review* 52 (July 1941) 351–74; idem, "The People of God in the Light of the Teaching of the New Testament," *Union Seminary Review* 52 (January 1941) 128–58; and also George Eldon Ladd, *The Blessed Hope* (Grand Rapids: Eerdmans, 1956); idem, *Crucial Questions about the Kingdom of God* (Grand Rapids: Eerdmans, 1952); idem, *Jesus and the Kingdom* (Waco, TX: Word, 1964). In more recent years, "progressive dispensationalism" has arisen as an intra-dispensationalist movement that is seeking self-consciously to moderate some of traditional dispensationalism's idiosyncratic distinctives and peculiarities; many have observed that the movement has taken dispensationalism in a "Laddian" direction. See, for example, Charles C. Ryrie, "Progressive Dispensationalism," in *Dispensationalism* (Chicago: Moody, 1995), 161–82; Stephen J. Nichols, "The Dispensational View of the Davidic Kingdom: A Response to Progressive Dispensationalism," *The Master's Seminary Journal* 7.2 (Fall 1996) 213–39. Nevertheless, progressive dispensationalist Robert L. Saucy suggests that the emphasis on a revival of ethnic, national Israel remains a point that distinguishes dispensational theology from non-dispensational systems. See Saucy, "The Crucial Issue between Dispensational and Non-dispensational Systems," *Criswell Theological Review* 1 (Fall 1986) 149–65, a suggestion with which fellow progressive dispensationalist Darrell Bock concurs; see Bock, "Charting Dispensationalism," *Christianity Today*, 12 September 1994, 26–29; and "Why I Am a Dispensationalist with a Small 'd,'" *Journal of the Evangelical Theological Society* 41 (July 1998) 386–88.

36. Martin Luther, *Von den Jüden und iren Lügen* (1543); see also Heiko Oberman, "The Growth of Antisemitism," in *The Impact of the Reformation* (Grand Rapids: Eerdmans, 1994) 81–172.

start.[37] Twentieth-century dispensationalist apocalypticism may have become the most popular version of this approach, but, in historical hindsight, we can see it accurately as being merely the fruit of a tree that Luther planted.

The heart of Luther's approach to the Book of Revelation, which eventually gave root to premillennialist ideas, was the supposition that its visions intended to portray historical events that would take place long after the original readers of Revelation had passed off the scene.[38] While Luther's specific exegesis and calculation of the numbers of Revelation never caught on, his identification of the pope as the Antichrist and his assertion that Revelation's "whore of Babylon" was the

37. "While earlier in his career Luther viewed the Antichrist as a figure to come in the future, in 1520 Luther came to view the pope and the papacy as the Antichrist. Luther's view of the Antichrist and of the papacy shifted suddenly, dramatically, and permanently. Scholars have often noted that the events of 1518 and 1519—the growing indulgence controversy, his appearance at Augsburg, and his forthcoming papal ban—all played a role in changing Luther's view" (David M. Whitford, "The Papal Antichrist: Martin Luther and the Underappreciated Influence of Lorenzo Valla," *Renaissance Quarterly* 61.1 [Spring 2008] 26). Luther's apocalypticism has been a subject of renewed scholarly interest and exploration in recent years. Reformation scholars generally acknowledge that Luther's apocalyptic emphases became more pronounced as he got older and as opposition from the established (Catholic) church increased, but there is much discussion as to what the specific reasons were and what the impact of his apocalyptic speculations on his theology and thought was overall. For further analysis of these points, see Robert Kolb, *Martin Luther as Prophet, Teacher, Hero: Images of the Reformer, 1520–1620* (Grand Rapids: Baker, 1999) 17–28; Heiko A. Oberman, "Teufelsdreck: Eschatology and Scatology in the 'Old' Luther," in *The Impact of the Reformation* (Grand Rapids: Eerdmans, 1994) 51–68; idem, *Forerunners of the Reformation* (London: Lutterworth, 1967); idem, *Luther: Man between God and the Devil* (London: Fontana, 1993); Roland Bainton, *The Reformation of the Sixteenth Century* (Boston: Beacon, 1985) 44f; T. F. Torrance, "The Eschatology of Faith: Martin Luther," in *Luther: Theologian for Catholics and Protestant*, ed. George Yule (Edinburgh: T. & T. Clark, 1985) 145–213; Scott H. Hendrix, *Luther and the Papacy* (Philadelphia: Fortress, 1981). The 2001 *JETS* contains two excellent articles that summarize and analyze the salient points of this discussion: Michael Parsons, "The Apocalyptic Luther: His Noahic Self-Understanding," 44.4 (December 2001) 627–45; and Stephen J. Nichols, "Prophecy Makes Strange Bedfellows: On the History of Identifying the Antichrist" (March 2001) 75–85.

38. This was a hermeneutical approach proposed as early as the third century by such fathers as Hippoloytus (*Christ and the Antichrist*, in *Ante-Nicene Fathers*, vol. 5: *Fathers of the Third Century: Hippolytus, Cyprian, Caius, Novatian*, ed. Alexander Roberts, James Donaldson, and A. Cleveland Coxe [Grand Rapids: Eerdmans, 1956] 204–19); my thanks to patristics scholar David G. Dunbar for bringing this to my attention.

Roman Catholic Church did gain wide affirmation among Protestants.[39] Likewise, Luther's historicist scheme, by which the numbers and years of Revelation were recalculated as a cryptic riddle playing out in current-day events, fell out of favor in Lutheranism, but was picked up by other Protestant subgroups. The early-nineteenth-century Millerites (today's Seventh-Day Adventists) are the ones most famous for preserving this historicist approach to Revelation.[40]

Nineteenth-century apocalyptic fervor in turn created renewed interest in how the prophecies of the Bible—the visions of Revelation particularly—might be coming to fulfillment in contemporary events; this is what gave rise to premillennialist impulses. Especially as Christians came to take current events as indication of God's judgment on ungodliness and rebellion, an approach to the Bible became popular that suggested these things were predicted so that the faithful remnant would be encouraged to persevere until Christ comes back to rescue them. That really is the heart of premillennialism: the world gets worse and worse until Christ returns to forcefully and cataclysmically reverse their afflictions. His returning in glory brings the imposition of his own righteous reign on earth. Ergo, Christ's return is "pre-millennial"; he comes *before* the "thousand-year reign" of righteousness, peace, and glory with Satan bound, as referred to in Revelation 20.

Premillennialism tends to grow more popular when things are not going well in the world, especially if things are not going well for a subgroup of Christians whose members regard themselves as the faithful remnant of "true" Christians. The context was right for new waves of premillennialist fervor in Europe during the Napoleonic Wars and in the US in the twentieth century, with World War I followed in rapid succession by the Great Depression, World War II, the Cold War, and then the Middle East Gulf Wars.[41] All these twentieth-century events

39. See Whitford, "Papal Antichrist."

40. Leroy Edwin Froom, *The Prophetic Faith of Our Fathers: The Historical Development of Prophetic Interpretation*, vol. 2 (Hagerstown, MD: Review and Herald, 1950) 267–79.

41. Robert G. Clouse, Robert N. Hosack, and Richard V. Pierard, *The New Millennium Manual: A Once and Future Guide* (Grand Rapids: Baker, 1999). Hal Lindsey's *The Late Great Planet Earth* (Grand Rapids: Zondervan, 1970) was the first Christian prophecy manual to land a spot on the *New York Times* bestseller list. Other, similar dispensational premillennialist writings, speculating about how current events might serve as fulfillments of biblical prophecy, have since joined it in sales and popu-

help explain the popularity of premillennialism among American evangelicals. But, these events really just fanned the flame of premillennialist embers already flickering. The real impetus for premillennialism in the US is found in the nineteenth-century South—after the South lost a bloody Civil War, followed by the indignities of Reconstruction imposed on them.[42]

This is where the merger of Southern Presbyterianism and premillennialism becomes interesting and relevant. Southern Presbyterianism—a

larity. Most well known, of course, is the fictional *Left Behind* series by Tim LaHaye and Jerry Jenkins. The nonfiction book *Armaggedon, Oil, and the Middle East Crisis* (Grand Rapids: Zondervan) by John Walvoord was originally published in 1974 during the crisis of the Nixon-era Arab oil embargo, but the book has gone through multiple editions and republications as events in the Middle East have unfolded, and crises there have taken on different faces and phases—e.g., Gulf War I and Gulf War II each were accompanied with a fresh revision and republication of this book. These are but recent versions of a practice made popular by dispensationalists through writings, pamphlets, and prophecy conferences from the late nineteenth century to the present day. See, for example, James Hall Brookes, *Maranatha, or, The Lord Cometh*, 10th ed. (New York: Revell, 1889); idem, *Till He Come* (Chicago: Gospel Publishing, 1891); idem, *I Am Coming* (Glasgow: Pickering & Inglis, 1895); *Light on Prophecy: The Proceedings and Addresses of the Philadelphia Prophetic Conference, May 28–30, 1918* (New York: Christian Herald Bible House, 1918); Arno C. Gaebelein, *Studies in Prophecy* (New York: Our Hope, 1918); idem, *The Return of the Lord: What the New Testament Teaches about the Second Coming of Christ* (New York: Our Hope, 1925); idem, *World Prospects: How Is It All Going to End?* (New York: Our Hope, 1934)—these books by Gaebelein were all expansions of articles he initially had published in his magazine, *Our Hope* (originally, *The Hope of Israel Monthly*), which he founded with his friend and fellow German immigrant and fellow dispensational premillennialist Ernest F. Stroeter, in 1893, and which he published every month for over fifty years; C. I. Scofield, *The World's Approaching Crisis* (Philadelphia: Philadelphia School of the Bible, 1913); James Gray, *Prophecy and the Lord's Return* (New York: Revell, 1917); Harry A. Ironside, *Lectures on the Book of Revelation* (New York: Loizeaux, 1919); idem, *The Lamp of Prophecy* (Grand Rapids: Zondervan, 1940); idem, *Looking Back over a Century of Prophecy Fulfillment* (New York: Loizeaux, 1930); John Hagee, *From Daniel to Doomsday: The Countdown Has Begun* (Nashville: T. Nelson, 1999). For scholarly assessment of this prophetic/apocalyptic phenomenon as a notable distinctive of dispensational premillennialism, see Paul Boyer, *When Time Shall Be No More: Prophecy Belief in Modern American Culture* (Cambridge, MA: Harvard University Press, 1992); Timothy P. Weber, *Living in the Shadow of the Second Coming: American Premillennialism, 1875–1982* (Chicago: University of Chicago Press, 1997); and idem, *On the Road to Armageddon: How Evangelicals Became Israel's Best Friend* (Grand Rapids: Baker, 2005).

42. James H. Moorehead, "Between Progress and Apocalypse: A Reassessment of Millennialism in American Religious Thought: 1800–1880," *Journal of American Religion* 71 (December 1984) 524–42; idem, "The Erosion of Postmillennialism in American Religious Thought, 1865–1925," *Church History* 53 (March 1984) 61–77.

distinctive brand of Old School Presbyterianism—emphasized the idea of the "spiritual nature" of the church. This pious-sounding theological idea was submitted originally in defense of the South's "peculiar institution": slavery. At root, this Southern Presbyterian distinctive is a classic example of Southern gentility coupled with romantic, flowery rhetoric—unpleasant underpinnings disguised by euphemism. "The spiritual nature of the church" meant, in plain terms, that political and civil concerns—such as slavery!—were not matters the church should seek to address. The church might exhort its people to maintain properly submissive attitudes to authority or for those in authority to exercise their power in righteousness and love—all these attitudes of heart were "in bounds." But the social institutions of secular society itself were not to be a focus of the church's concern, because the church, in Southern Presbyterian framing, is a "spiritual institution."[43]

This idea of the spiritual nature of the church, when combined with premillennial eschatology, forms the basic core of dispensational theology. Yet rather than setting the church's spiritual nature solely over against the earthly nature of the political realm in contemporary society, dispensationalism came to set the spiritual nature of the New Testament church over against the earthly nature of Old Testament Israel (and also over against the earthly nature of the future kingdom of Israel).[44]

43. In the words of James Henley Thornwell: "[The Church] has no right to interfere directly with the civil relations of society. Whether Slavery be perpetuated or not, whether arrangements shall be made to change or abolish it, whether it conduces to the prosperity of the State or hinders the progress of a refined civilization,–these are questions not for the Church but the State, not for Ministers but for statesmen. Christian men may discuss them as citizens and patriots, but not as members of the Church of Jesus Christ" (*The Collected Writings of James Henley Thornwell*, vol. 4, ed. John B. Adger and John L. Girardeau [Richmond: Presbyterian Committee of Publication, 1873] 500–501). Compare Robert L. Dabney, "Lecture LXXIII: The Civil Magistrate," and "Lecture LXXIV: Religious Liberty," in the *Syllabus and Notes of the Course of Systematic and Polemic Theology Taught in Union Theological Seminary, Virginia* (Richmond: Presbyterian Committee of Publication, 1890) 862–87. For a helpful analysis of the formation and establishment of these viewpoints in the Presbyterian Church, USA, see Ernest Trice Thompson, *Presbyterians in the South*, vol. 1: *1607–1861* (Richmond: John Knox, 1963) 323–412, 510–71. See also J. Sprole Lyons, "The Problem of Relation of White and Colored Races," *Presbyterian Standard* 60 (8 October 1919) 4; L. Nelson Bell, "Race Relations—Whither?" *Southern Presbyterian Journal* 2 (March 1944) 4–5; William Childs Robinson, "Distinguishing Things that Differ," *Southern Presbyterian Journal* 5 (15 January 1947) 3–4; and J. E. Flow, "Is Segregation Un-Christian?" *Southern Presbyterian Journal* 10 (29 August 1951) 4–5.

44. See, for example, James Hall Brookes, *Israel and the Church* (Chicago: Bible

These core elements absorbed from premillennialism and Southern Presbyterianism were then given a distinctive twist—and intensified—by the third major factor in the development of early dispensationalism: Darbyite Plymouth Brethrenism. Much has been written about the contribution of John Nelson Darby to the early development of dispensationalism; a common mistake is to suggest that dispensationalism and Darbyism are simply synonymous; likewise, the direct connection between Darby and American dispensationalism is commonly exaggerated. These mistakes notwithstanding, the influence of Darby (and Plymouth Brethrenism generally) on the development of American dispensationalism was very significant—but not because the latter is simply a natural outgrowth of the former. Rather, dispensationalism was given a distinctive character by how Darby's ideas merged and synergized with the ideas of premillennialism and Southern Presbyterianism already on the rise among American Christian conservatives.[45]

Darbyite influence was what gave dispensationalism its characteristic suspicion of Christian apostasy in response to the modernist-fundamentalist controversies.[46] Already in the mid nineteenth century, Darby was thundering against the apostasy of the church in the modern age.[47] Whereas he (with Plymouth Brethrenism generally) advocated

Institute Colportage Ass'n, 1900) 12; and C. I. Scofield, *Scofield Reference Bible: 1917 Edition*, 1204n2. Lewis Sperry Chafer adopted Scofield's distinction between Israel and the church and greatly elaborated upon it. See Chafer, *Grace* (Wheaton, IL: Van Kampen, 1922) 238–39; idem, "Dispensationalism," *Bibliotheca Sacra* 93 (October–December 1936) 406, 448; and idem, *Systematic Theology* (Dallas: Dallas Seminary, 1947–48) 1:28–29, 4:3–426, 6:166–67, 7:211–12. Compare also Floyd Elmore, "A Critical Examination of the Doctrine of the Two Peoples of God in John Nelson Darby," ThD diss., Dallas Theological Seminary, 1990; and Carl E. Sanders II, *The Premillennial Faith of James Brookes: Reexamining the Roots of American Dispensationalism* (Lanham, MD: University Press of America, 2001) esp. ch. 2, "Spiritual Church/Heavenly Church."

45. Mark Sweetnam, "British and Irish Roots of the Scofield Reference Bible," and "The Impact of *The Scofield Reference Bible* on British Premillennialism," in R. Todd Mangum and Mark Sweetnam, *The Scofield Reference Bible: Its History and Impact on the Evangelical Church* (Colorado Springs: Paternoster, 2009) 54–72 and 135–68; also Mark Sweetnam and Crawford Gribben, "J. N. Darby and the Irish Origins of Dispensationalism," *JETS* 52.3 (September 2009) 569–77. See also Sanders, *Premillennial Faith.*

46. See Larry V. Crutchfield, *The Origins of Dispensationalism: The Darby Factor* (Lanham, MD: University Press of America, 1995).

47. See Joe L. Coker, "Exploring the Roots of the Dispensationalist/Princeton 'Alliance': Charles Hodge and John Nelson Darby on Eschatology and Interpretation of Scripture," *Fides et Historia* 30 (Winter–Spring 1998) 41–56.

separation from all denominations, few American advocates of his ideas followed him on that particular point. Instead, they seemed to believe that the denominations in general were not the problem; it was the modernist ideas that had infected the denominations that were the problem.

Thus, when the modernist-fundamentalist controversies broke out, the Southern Presbyterian premillennialists who had come under some Darbyite influence rallied to the fundamentalist alarms. These—James Hall Brookes, C. I. Scofield, Lewis Sperry Chafer, John Walvoord, J. Dwight Pentecost, S. Lewis Johnson—eventually became better known as representatives of "dispensationalism."

A CONCLUDING SUMMARY AND BEGINNING ANALYSIS OF DISPENSATIONALISM AND INERRANCY

We noted above that the type of premillennialism that would evolve into dispensationalism was a special brand of (fundamentalist) conservatism. I will conclude this chapter with a closing analysis of this point.

As the fundamentalist-modernist battles heated up in the early twentieth century, conservatives generally "found" one another across denominations; premillennialists, especially, found one another. Part of what drew them together, across denominational lines, was the annual prophecy conferences, which provided a vehicle for fellowship, spiritual renewal, and "retreat," as well as providing a forum to instill a deeper and wider commitment to premillennial eschatology. What perhaps should have been foreseen, but which instead seems to have taken the conservative alliance by surprise, was that premillennial eschatology and its distinctive hermeneutical commitments eventually became a source of tension between conservatives, rather than a source of harmony.

So long as modernism remained a common foe of them all, premillennialists and non-premillennialists were happy to remain in common cause against it, seemingly unaware of how great the differences between them potentially were. Once fundamentalists separated from the main denominational bodies and sought to establish a more positive vision for their future, however, the differences and tensions between them became acute. Conservatives all shared concern for what they perceived as the undermining of biblical authority by scholars employing historical-critical methods. However, premillennialists tended to have a distinctive set of responses to the problems raised by historical criticism. All conservatives rejected an approach to the Old Testament narratives that denied their historicity or their supernatural quality. All conservatives were wary of approaches to the Old Testament that relegated them to the realm of myth or fable, with the moral of the story left too much within the eye of the beholder. From there, though, premillennialist conservatives and non-premillennialist conservatives veered in very different directions.

Whereas non-premillennialist conservatives sought to demonstrate that the teaching of the various segments of the Bible could be harmonized, premillennialists commonly suggested that such harmonization was not possible, but neither was it intended—by the biblical writers or by God himself. Rather, the way to achieve an overall unity of biblical teaching, according to the premillennialist scheme, was to recognize the various divisions of biblical teaching, designed to remain disparate.[48]

In the early twentieth century, the patterns were still forming, and the "sides" were not yet clearly drawn. Nonetheless, this difference in response to historical critical challenges is significant. The strategy that dispensational premillennialists were suggesting was something like interpretive jujitsu, where the points of alleged contradictions in biblical teaching were conceded but absorbed into an overall interpretive approach that distinguished the Bible's contrasting segments, called "dispensations."[49]

Non-premillennialist conservatives were not impressed by this strategy, no matter how well-meaning or conservative its intent. Non-premillennialist conservatives were actually the ones who coined the (originally derogatory) term "dispensationalists"—a label meant to underscore for criticism the alleged excess of this approach in chopping up the Bible into "dispensations."[50]

---

48. See, for example, Clarence Larkin, *Rightly Dividing the Word of Truth* (Philadelphia: E. W. Moyer, 1920); C. I. Scofield, *Rightly Dividing the Word of Truth* (Oakland, CA: Western Book and Tract Co., 1921); Chafer, "Dispensationalism," 395–426; idem, "Are There Two Ways to Be Saved?," *Bibliotheca Sacra* 105 (January–March 1948) 1–2; Charles C. Ryrie, "The Necessity of Dispensationalism," *Bibliotheca Sacra* 114 (July–September 1957) 243–54; Nickolas Kurtaneck, "Excellencies of Dispensationalism," *Grace Journal* 3 (1962) 3–11.

49. Ibid.

50. Philip Mauro, *The Gospel of the Kingdom with an Examination of Modern Dispensationalism* (Boston: Hamilton Bros., 1928); B. W. Baker, "Is There Modernism

This is the backdrop to a fascinating story of how an intra-conservative division unfolded, which captured much of the attention of evangelical theologians throughout the twentieth century: the dispensational-covenantal rift (a story I have covered elsewhere).[51] The point made in this chapter is threefold: 1) the doctrine of inerrancy arose as a point of distinction in American evangelicalism when historical criticism arose as a point of controversy within the American denominations; 2) the doctrine of inerrancy was the "first fundamental," designed to alert fellow conservatives as to who was "safe" and who was apostate; and 3) the doctrine of inerrancy seems intended to provide a point of shared common ground among conservatives, but history has proven it insufficient to do so; in fact, it sometimes has been taken up in such a way as to exacerbate tensions between conservatives rather than uniting them.

Since the modernist-fundamentalist fights of the early twentieth century, evangelicals have clarified, qualified, and refined their understanding of what is "fundamental" to the faith regarding biblical inspiration and inerrancy in at least two significant, published forums: the Lausanne Covenant of 1974[52] and the Chicago Statement on Biblical Inerrancy of 1978.[53] The latter is far more detailed and also

in the Teachings of Dr C. I. Scofield?," *Presbyterian of the South* 109 (28 February 1934) 6–7; idem, "Is There Modernism in the Teachings of Dr. C.I. Scofield?: II," *Presbyterian of the South* 109 (7 March 1934) 7–8; Oswald T. Allis, "Modern Dispensationalism and the Doctrine of the Unity of the Scriptures," *Evangelical Quarterly* 8 (1936) 22–35; idem, "Modern Dispensationalism and the Law of God," *Evangelical Quarterly* 8 (1936) 272–89; John Murray, "The Reformed Faith and Modern Substitutes, Part VI: Modern Dispensationalism," *Presbyterian Guardian* 2 (18 May 1936) 77–79; idem, "The Reformed Faith and Modern Substitutes, Part VII—Modern Dispensationalism: The 'Kingdom of Heaven' and the 'Kingdom of God,'" *Presbyterian Guardian* 2 (17 August 1936) 210–12; idem, "The 'Kingdom of Heaven' and the 'Kingdom of God,'" *Presbyterian Guardian* 3 (9 January 1937) 139–41; also see Edwards E. Elliot, "Rightly Dividing St. Augustine," *Presbyterian Guardian* 11 (25 December 1942) 355–56.

51. R. Todd Mangum, *The Dispensational-Covenantal Rift: The Fissuring of Evangelical Theology from 1936 to 1944* (Colorado Springs: Paternoster, 2007).

52. F. F. Bruce, "The Lausanne Covenant 2: The Authority and Power of the Bible," *The Harvester* 55 (November 1976) 320–33. The full text, along with information on the history and background of the Lausanne Covenant, is online at http://www.lausanne. org/covenant.

53. *The Chicago Statement on Biblical Inerrancy* (Chicago: International Council on Biblical Inerrancy, 1978). The full text is accessible online at http://65.175.91.69/ Reformation_net/COR_Docs/01_Inerrancy_Christian_Worldview.pdf.

represents the more restricted framing of American evangelicalism; the former represents the broader framing and perspective of British (international?) evangelicalism. Together, they represent valuable contributions to understanding biblical inspiration and authority from an evangelical perspective.

Like most good doctrines, affirmation of inerrancy historically has helped to discover and clarify truths about God's character and work; in the case of the doctrine of inerrancy: how biblical authority works. This doctrine has helped foster a spirit of submissiveness to biblical teaching among evangelicals. By their very nature, doctrinal affirmations are tools by which insight into high and holy mysteries is accessed, obscurities clarified, and obstacles to understanding removed—like unto the value of a screwdriver in the physical world. When such a tool is taken up as a weapon, however, people get hurt.

As we go into the twenty-first century, with US culture threatening to become post-Christian like unto Western Europe, it is good for evangelicals to reconsider both the value and the damage that affirmation of biblical inerrancy has brought with it in our history. Affirmation of biblical inerrancy need not degenerate into a weapon by which the ideas (or character) of fellow believers are attacked. We have enough lessons from our history to do better than that; we just need the humility, competence, and courage to do so.

4

The Cost of Prestige

E. J. Carnell's Quest for Intellectual Orthodoxy

Seth Dowland

IN 1948, TWENTY-NINE-YEAR-OLD THEOLOGIAN Edward John Carnell won a $5,000 book prize, a spot on the faculty at Fuller Theological Seminary, and a ThD from Harvard. He added a PhD from Boston University the next year. This heady run presaged a decade in which Carnell would publish seven books and ascend, at the ripe age of thirty-five, to the presidency of Fuller. The seminary was just seven years old when, in 1954, it appointed Carnell as the school's second president. The youth of both the school and its new president suggested the vibrancy of "new evangelicalism," a movement of fundamentalists trying to shake the constricting aspects of the old faith without abandoning theological orthodoxy. Owing to his intellect, ambition, and productivity, Carnell stood alongside his colleague Carl F. H. Henry as a leading intellectual light of this "new evangelical" movement. The bully pulpit of Fuller's presidency provided Carnell an influential platform to articulate a theological program for evangelicalism. Yet Carnell's presidency was marked by conflict with colleagues and trustees, and he resigned after five controversial years in office. Fundamentalists accused him of heresy, and donors worried about Fuller's theological integrity.

Carnell served as an intellectual lightning rod in the storm raging throughout conservative American Protestantism in the mid twentieth century. "New evangelicals," eager to engage non-fundamentalists in discussion, rejected the fundamentalist premise of separation from both "worldly" influences and less dogmatic Christians. Fundamentalists saw evangelicals' eagerness to engage with doctrinal moderates as pandering and possibly heretical. Though both fundamentalists and "new evangelicals" claimed to uphold orthodox Christianity, their divergent impulses—separatism for fundamentalists, engagement for evangelicals—warred for supremacy among conservative Protestants in the middle of the twentieth century. Fundamentalists were convinced that evangelicals had abandoned orthodoxy in a quest for acceptance, while evangelicals thought fundamentalists had neglected a biblical mandate to engage the broader culture with the gospel. For instance, when evangelist Billy Graham accepted the sponsorship of the National Council of Churches for his 1957 New York City crusade, fundamentalists long suspicious of Graham marked him as an apostate. Fundamentalists viewed cooperation with the liberal NCC as an unpardonable sin. Graham, on the other hand, thought fidelity to the gospel demanded speaking to the widest possible audience—and the alliance with the NCC allowed that. Moreover, Graham even tried repeatedly to meet with theologian Reinhold Niebuhr, who dismissed the evangelist as a simpleton. While Graham handled Niebuhr's rejection with class, fundamentalists used the incident both to condemn Graham's "apostasy" and to note the futility of cooperation with liberals. To fundamentalists, the "new evangelicals" like Graham had abandoned orthodoxy.

Carnell, though not as popular or as influential as Graham, brought into sharp relief one of the most important sources of the tension between evangelicals and fundamentalists at mid century: the doctrine of scriptural inerrancy. Fundamentalists had broken with "modernists" in the early twentieth century in large part because modernists rejected a literal reading of the Bible. Major battles over the relationship of modern science to the biblical creation story resulted in a hardening of fundamentalists' commitment to the doctrine of scriptural inerrancy, which held that the Bible, in its original form, was free from any errors of fact and held no contradictions. Men like Wilbur Smith and Charles Woodbridge—faculty members at Fuller—came of age in a subculture where defending scriptural inerrancy was the *sine qua non* of conservative Protestantism. At the same time, liberal and Neo-orthodox theologians were hardening in their rejection of scriptural inerrancy. Carnell's push for "enlightened orthodoxy" had to navigate this impasse. As he tried to narrate the doctrine of scriptural inerrancy in terms that appealed to liberals, Carnell alienated his fundamentalist peers.

Carnell thereby reflected the evolving nature of conservative Protestantism during his lifetime. What seemed like a unified movement of conservative Protestants in the 1930s and 1940s became, by the 1950s, more clearly divided into camps of people committed to separatism (fundamentalists) and those committed to engagement with the larger culture (evangelicals). While this dichotomy overstates the differences between fundamentalists and evangelicals—there were, after all, plenty of fundamentalists eager to engage with the larger culture[1]—it helps explain why someone like Carnell would happily self-describe as a fundamentalist in 1948 only to disown that label in 1959.[2] The "new evangelicals" (henceforth simply referred to as evangelicals) aspired to greater cultural and intellectual relevance. As one of evangelicalism's brightest thinkers, Carnell realized that the moldy anti-intellectualism of conservative Protestantism had to go. "Fundamentalism" became for Carnell a scapegoat. By the late 1950s, he defined any intellectually embarrassing doctrines (like premillennialism) as fundamentalist. Scriptural inerrancy, however, was Carnell's bridge too far. He labeled traditional views of biblical inspiration (those forwarded by B. B. Warfield, Charles Hodge, and James Orr) as "fundamentalist" and therefore misguided. At the same time, Carnell insisted that he was defending scriptural inerrancy even as he admitted the possibility of factual mistakes or contradictions in biblical texts. Fundamentalists blasted him. Evangelicals found his work defending biblical inspiration weak. And liberals thought his position on Scripture laughably naive. For all of Carnell's creative theological work, he never produced a convincing defense of inerrancy. And his story ended in disappointment and tragedy: Carnell's scholarly output plummeted after five stressful years in the presidency, and he died of a drug overdose at the age of 47. This chapter explores both the personal and intellectual causes behind Carnell's rise and his demise. In his career we can see both the energy behind mid-century evangelicalism and the

---

1. Joel A. Carpenter, *Revive Us Again: The Reawakening of American Fundamentalism* (New York: Oxford University Press, 1997) 141–60, 187–210, 233–46.

2. See Edward John Carnell, "Post-Fundamentalist Faith," *The Christian Century*, 26 August 1959; Edward John Carnell, *The Case for Orthodox Theology* (Philadelphia: Westminster, 1959).

growing pains it faced as it sought to define new parameters for conservative Protestantism.

THE EDUCATION OF E. J. CARNELL

Born and reared in a fundamentalist household, Carnell spent his early years moving with his family to a series of Baptist churches in the upper Midwest. Biographer Rudolph Nelson noted that Carnell's father Herbert, a long-time Baptist minister, "was never part of the militantly separatist wing of fundamentalism."[3] Herbert Carnell brought one of his churches back into fellowship with the Wisconsin Baptist Convention—at a time when many fundamentalist churches broke away from denominational bodies—and served a brief stint as president of the Michigan Baptist Convention. Though Herbert Carnell never attained the level of education that his son did, his disposition toward church unity and his willingness to express reservations about fundamentalist strictures mirrored later attitudes of his son Edward.[4] E. J. Carnell's parents certainly taught their son proper fundamentalist decorum, but Carnell grew up with a more irenic view of the world than did many fundamentalists.

Carnell's undergraduate studies at Wheaton College stimulated a lifelong interest in philosophy and exposed him to "fundamentalism with a touch of class."[5] Like many of his fellow students, Carnell gravitated toward Professor Gordon Clark, in whose demanding philosophy courses Carnell excelled. Clark held significant sway over an "inner circle" of undergraduates, and he opened Carnell's eyes to the possibility of intellectually respectable Christianity. Clark displayed impatience with the anti-intellectual tendencies of many students and some of his colleagues at Wheaton. Students, for instance, remembered Clark stewing over lengthy chapel services that cut into class time. In his classes, Clark offered a rationalist apologetic for Christianity, which used logic

3. Rudolph Nelson, *The Making and Unmaking of an Evangelical Mind: The Case of Edward Carnell* (New York: Cambridge University Press, 1987) 23–24.

4. Nelson, *Making and Unmaking*, 23. Nelson noted several instances in Herbert's memoir where he criticized fellow fundamentalists, specifically Herbert's refusal to condemn moderate alcohol consumption and his condemnation of Moody Bible Institute's "hush-hush atmosphere" concerning sex and masturbation. (Herbert studied at Moody.)

5. Nelson, *Making and Unmaking*, 39.

and philosophy to prove the truths of the faith. Clark believed one could apprehend these truths through deduction and inference. Carnell would initially adopt and later discard Clark's rationalism. But in Clark, Carnell had discovered his strongest model for an intellectually engaged faith.[6]

Carnell subsequently went to Westminster Seminary in Philadelphia, where he developed a more mature understanding of theology. Founded when fundamentalist New Testament scholar J. Gresham Machen broke with Princeton Theological Seminary in 1929, Westminster represented an evangelical Calvinist theology that Carnell never fully appropriated. Yet he did excellent work at Westminster, earning two masters degrees. During his final year there, Carnell married Shirley Rowe, a Wisconsin schoolteacher who left her job to join Carnell in Philadelphia. The newlyweds' one-night honeymoon betrayed Carnell's obsession with his work. He surprised nobody when he announced his intention to enroll in Harvard's doctoral program.[7]

Carnell's graduate studies at Harvard demonstrated to him the intellectual torpor of recent fundamentalism and provoked in Carnell a profound desire to transform Christianity's intellectual landscape. Though fundamentalists had long since forsaken any hope of reclaiming Harvard for conservative Christianity, in 1944 Carnell joined a cadre of other bright fundamentalist scholars who tested their wits in Cambridge, Massachusetts. He struggled both financially and academically in his first year. Carnell told other students he had arrived at Harvard "with a sack full of arguments in defense of the faith, only to find to his dismay . . . that the sack was empty."[8] Nobody at Harvard read Gordon Clark or Cornelius Van Til (Carnell's teacher at Westminster). Harvard professors and students viewed fundamentalism as an intellectual backwater. This experience left Carnell frustrated with the intellectual trends of his natal faith—and determined to change them. Seeing the intellectual shallowness of twentieth-century fundamentalism challenged Carnell to develop an intellectually robust case for conservative Christianity. Carnell never significantly altered nor abandoned the ambitious goal

6. Nelson, *Making and Unmaking*, 36–39.

7. Nelson, *Making and Unmaking*, 42–53. Also see George M. Marsden, *Reforming Fundamentalism: Fuller Seminary and the New Evangelicalism* (Grand Rapids: Eerdmans, 1987), 31–44.

8. Nelson, *Making and Unmaking*, 60.

he set for himself at Harvard: restoring intellectual respectability and theological relevance to conservative Christian orthodoxy.[9]

Carnell did not dally in embarking upon his mission. He simultaneously wrote dissertations on Reinhold Niebuhr and Søren Kierkegaard, as well as a prize-winning book called *An Introduction to Christian Apologetics*. Carnell's theses on Niebuhr and Kierkegaard both developed clear expositions and well-conceived critiques of those men's theological systems, and both later went into publication. He earned doctorates from Boston University and Harvard in little over four years. But more than either degree, the Eerdmans book award proved critical to Carnell's early evangelical stardom. Eerdmans' $5,000 prize amounted to nearly a year's salary—a healthy prize in itself—but it also attracted the attention of Harold Ockenga and Charles Fuller, who would soon invite Carnell to join the Fuller faculty in Pasadena.[10]

Carnell's remarkable scholarly production suggested an unusually strong need to find intellectual defenses for his faith. Carl F. H. Henry, Carnell's colleague at Boston and Fuller, wrote, "Carnell was almost always serious and intellectually engaged; he wrestled speculative problems as personal inner tensions and pressed for precision."[11] Henry's recollection depicted a man who saw theological and intellectual inquiry as his reason for being. Carnell never enjoyed the ability to separate his academic work from his personal life. Theology and apologetics dominated his world.

9. For a good account of fundamentalists' (and especially Carnell's) experience at Harvard, see Rudolph Nelson, "Fundamentalism at Harvard: The Case of Edward John Carnell," in *Modern American Protestantism*: vol. 10: *Fundamentalism and Evangelicalism*, ed. Martin E. Marty (New York: K. G. Saur, 1993) 228–41.

10. Edward John Carnell, *An Introduction to Christian Apologetics: A Philosophic Defense of the Trinitarian-Theistic Faith* (Grand Rapids: Eerdmans, 1948); Carnell, *The Theology of Reinhold Niebuhr* (Grand Rapids: Eerdmans, 1951); Carnell, *The Burden of Søren Kierkegaard* (Grand Rapids: Eerdmans, 1965). For a fuller account of Carnell's apologetic system, see Gary Dorrien, *The Remaking of Evangelical Theology* (Louisville: Westminster John Knox, 1998) 61–68. While acknowledging the rational nature of *An Introduction to Christian Apologetics*, Dorrien perceptively uncovers in that text hints of Carnell's later disillusionment with rational apologetics.

11. Carl F. H. Henry, *Confessions of a Theologian: An Autobiography* (Waco, TX: Word, 1986) 121.

EXPANDING INFLUENCE AT FULLER

Carnell moved to California in 1948, hoping to carve out space for himself on a Fuller faculty already dominated by confident theologians. Fuller Seminary had opened its doors in 1947 with gaping holes to fill. Of the original four faculty members—Wilbur Smith, Everett F. Harrison, Carl F. H. Henry, and Harold Lindsell—only Lindsell taught church history, and Lindsell considered himself more a scholar of missions than a church historian. None of the four specialized in Old Testament. Henry and Smith had already established themselves with significant works in apologetics and theology. The theologian Carnell, then, seemed an odd hire for a young school with needs elsewhere. Moreover, except for Harrison, each of the four founding faculty members held aspirations to power. As historian George Marsden points out, Smith, Harrison, Henry, and Lindsell "were all in on the ground floor and each knew he could have a shaping role [at Fuller]." Carnell brought ambition and theological interests into a group already overflowing with generous helpings of both.[12]

Yet early in his career, Carnell seemed destined for success as he quickly earned a reputation as a master teacher and scholar. Alumni from Fuller's 1950–1952 graduating classes overwhelmingly chose Carnell as the seminary's most influential professor.[13] He published with remarkable frequency. Carnell followed up his 1948 apologetics text with the publication of *Television: Servant or Master?* in 1950. Two more academically rigorous books followed in successive years: the publication of his Harvard dissertation on Niebuhr in 1951, and another work on apologetics, 1952's *A Philosophy of the Christian Religion*. Meanwhile, *An Introduction to Christian Apologetics* went through its fourth edition. Carnell's reputation as an evangelical theologian soared.[14]

12. Marsden, *Reforming Fundamentalism*, 24–30.

13. Marsden, *Reforming Fundamentalism*, 301. Marsden's appendix, compiled from surveys of Fuller alumni, shows that Carnell maintained this distinction for the graduating classes of 1957–1959 and 1965–1967, though his popularity dimmed slightly over time. In the survey of 1950–1952 alumni, Wilbur Smith, Everett Harrison, Carl Henry, and William La Sor followed Carnell, in that order.

14. Edward John Carnell, *Television: Servant or Master?* (Grand Rapids: Eerdmans, 1950); Carnell, *Theology of Reinhold Niebuhr*; Carnell, *A Philosophy of the Christian Religion* (Grand Rapids: Eerdmans, 1952). For a discussion of Carnell's early career at Fuller, see Nelson, *Making and Unmaking*, 73–86.

As his reputation grew, Carnell angled to gain more power in the seminary. Like other faculty members, Carnell had grown anxious about the geographical remove of Harold Ockenga, Fuller's founding president. Though he seemed an obvious choice for the presidency of Fuller at the time of the seminary's founding in 1947, Ockenga did not wish to leave his influential pulpit at Park Street Church in Boston. Charles Fuller thus agreed to allow Ockenga to become president *in absentia*, with the stipulation that Ockenga would eventually move to Pasadena. Yet entreaties from his congregation repeatedly convinced Ockenga to stay in Boston. By 1954, the seminary possessed a full faculty and its own buildings, and faculty members had tired of Ockenga's indecision. Ockenga himself attended the 1954 board meeting intending to make a final decision about whether to move to Pasadena or to relinquish the presidency. At that board meeting, Ockenga met secretly with Carnell and offered him the presidency if Ockenga decided against moving to California. In the end—and despite Ockenga's stated decision to move to Pasadena announced at the board meeting—that is exactly what happened. Ockenga wired Charles Fuller in September 1954 to say he would not be moving west after all. Other faculty members, unaware of Carnell's arrangement with Ockenga, assumed that Charles Fuller would convene a search for a new president. Instead, they found out within a week that the matter had been decided. Carnell assumed the presidency of Fuller at age thirty-five.[15]

Carnell's decision not to disclose his arrangement with Ockenga to his colleagues, alongside his correspondence with Ockenga, suggested a growing rift between the young theologian and the rest of the faculty. During the summer of 1954, the faculty—already worried that Ockenga would back out of his commitment to move to Pasadena—convened a discussion to discuss what to do in the event Ockenga reneged on his promise. Carnell did not share details of his agreement with Ockenga made at the May board meeting. After the faculty meeting, Carnell wrote Ockenga with details of the discussion and complained, "they" [the faculty] wanted "an evangelical Dale Carnegie to be a front and public relations man . . . one who could soak the rich." This image hardly matched Carnell's presidential ideal. Moreover, Carnell's use of "they" to refer to the Fuller faculty evinced a divide between himself and his colleagues. He believed the faculty entertained false notions of their own

15. Marsden, *Reforming Fundamentalism*, 138–43.

academic success and wrote to Ockenga, "I refuse to be party to their fantastic schemes."[16] Carnell's extensive correspondence with Ockenga revealed a man convinced of his intellectual gifts and worried about his relationship with colleagues.[17]

And he was right to worry: Carnell's faculty colleagues took the news of his ascension as a bit of a shock. Only thirty-five years of age and lacking administrative abilities or experience, Carnell seemed an odd selection. Dean Harold Lindsell appeared distraught about the choice of Carnell. Professor Wilbur Smith threatened resignation.[18] A few weeks prior to the announcement, Ockenga and Charles Fuller had invited Carl Henry to comment on the possibility of Carnell's presidency. Henry balked. He told Ockenga and Fuller that by promoting Carnell, "Fuller would lose an astute scholar and writer and a popular teacher to administrative work in which he had no experience whatsoever."[19] Henry's concerns proved prescient, as Carnell struggled throughout his tenure with administrative duties and a nagging desire to return to full-time scholarship. Yet Ockenga and Fuller had already decided to promote Carnell when they talked with Henry. Perhaps they sought from him confirmation of their wisdom in choosing Carnell. Instead, Henry's comments hinted at the deep ambivalence among Fuller's faculty about Carnell's presidency.

Yet most of Carnell's first year as president went well. Since his ascension to the presidency occurred so close to the arrival of students, Carnell began the 1954–55 school year teaching a full load of courses. After turning his classes over mid-year to new professor Paul Jewett, Carnell spent two successful weeks in March on a cross-country fundraising trip. The seminary added faculty members in pastoral care

16. Nelson, *Making and Unmaking*, 89.

17. Two studies of Carnell make particularly good use of his correspondence with Ockenga: Marsden, *Reforming Fundamentalism*; Charles Allan Poole, "Splintered Light: E. J. Carnell and the New Evangelicalism," (ThM thesis, Duke University, 2003).

18. Marsden, *Reforming Fundamentalism*, 143; Nelson, *Making and Unmaking*, 90. Carnell reported to Ockenga about his meeting with Lindsell, whom he said was "deeply crushed" by the choice of Carnell. Carnell suggested Lindsell should be promoted to vice president, a position that was never created. Smith retracted his threat of resignation within a week, but upon his resignation in 1963, he traced his disillusionment with Fuller to the beginning of Carnell's presidency. See Marsden, *Reforming Fundamentalism*, 221–23.

19. Henry, *Confessions of a Theologian*, 139–40.

and developed plans to add a position in evangelism. Morale improved noticeably among both faculty members and students. In many of his letters, Carnell seemed energized about the work of building Fuller Seminary. The future looked bright.[20]

The forecast dimmed significantly after Carnell's inauguration ceremony, which took place on May 17, 1955, at Pasadena's Lake Avenue Congregational Church. With much of the evangelical intellectual world literally at his feet, Carnell ascended the podium to deliver "The Glory of a Theological Seminary." He divided the address into the three sections. In the first, Carnell promised to uphold the seminary's "theological distinctives" with "conviction and firmness," a promise that echoed fundamentalism's concern for doctrinal purity. The second and third sections of the address, however, ruffled fundamentalist feathers. Carnell argued for full engagement with "all the relevant evidences—damaging as well as supporting" and for "an attitude of tolerance and forgiveness towards individuals whose doctrinal convictions are at variance with those that inhere in the institution itself." He privileged love over truth and implicitly accused fundamentalists of "arrogance." He cautioned against thinking that "sheer possession of truth is an index to the virtue of the person," and instead encouraged charity and tolerance.[21] Though all of the Fuller professors accepted Carnell's refusal to thunder declarations of damnation at liberals, they still expected Carnell to stand firm for the faith. Carnell's declaration that Fuller's "glory" rested in "an attitude of tolerance and forgiveness toward individuals whose doctrinal convictions are at variance with those that inhere in the institution"[22] infuriated some of his colleagues. Conservative faculty member Wilbur Smith led a group of four faculty members who cornered Carnell in his office the next day, repudiating his speech and forcing Carnell to withhold it from publication. Shaken by the incident, Carnell said he developed "a lump in my stomach that didn't leave the entire time I was president."[23]

20. Marsden, *Reforming Fundamentalism*, 143–47; Nelson, *Making and Unmaking*, 90–95.

21. Edward John Carnell, "The Glory of a Theological Seminary," (Pasadena, CA: Fuller Theological Seminary Alumni Association, 1967 [delivered 1955]) 12–13.

22. Carnell, "Glory of a Theological Seminary," 12.

23. Nelson, *Making and Unmaking*, 96. An excellent account of the speech and its immediate aftermath is Marsden, *Reforming Fundamentalism*, 147–52. Fuller's alumni association eventually published the speech two years after Carnell's death (see note 21).

Carnell's inaugural address came at a moment when his own thinking was evolving. In 1955, Carnell had already published four books and won considerable praise from both students and colleagues. Few of them, however, understood that Carnell was moving away from Gordon Clark's rationalism and toward a more existentialist apologetic. Clark had taught Carnell how to build a rigorously logical defense of the faith, beginning with the (impossible-to-prove) assumption of a Triune God who had revealed truth in Scripture. From that assumption, however, Clark believed it possible to defend Christianity rationally. Carnell's popular first book, *An Introduction to Christian Apologetics* (1948), promoted a similar view, and it went through four printings in as many years. By 1952, however, Carnell had become convinced that apologetics demanded an engagement with "the whole man." As he put it, "Man is not simply *nous* . . . he happens to be a complexity of intellect, emotions, and will—plus a lot more. Whole truth must satisfy the whole man."[24] As such, a rigorously logical approach to apologetics seemed increasingly unsatisfactory to Carnell. Moreover, Scripture itself did not present a coherent philosophical system of faith. So, beginning with the 1952 publication of *A Philosophy of the Christian Religion*, Carnell endeavored to develop a defense of the faith that moved away from rationalism.[25]

This intellectual shift signaled Carnell's dissatisfaction with the approach favored by the vast majority of conservative Protestant thinkers at mid century, and it worried his colleagues. When they launched Fuller Seminary, founders Charles Fuller and Harold Ockenga had explicitly stated their intentions to establish a first-rate postgraduate evangelical seminary. That meant different things to different people. Older conservatives like Fuller, Wilbur Smith, and Charles Woodbridge understood the need for strong academics, but preserving their charges from doctrinal error remained paramount. More progressive figures like Henry and Ockenga gently nudged the seminary toward a post-fundamentalist faith, unsure of what that required and still cautious to maintain certain biblical and theological boundaries. Carnell, though still committed to the doctrine of inerrancy and to what he referred to as "orthodox Christianity," stood on the far end of the intellectual spectrum at the seminary. He was attempting a daunting intellectual feat at a moment

24. Carnell, *Philosophy of Christian Religion*, 38.

25. Dorrien, *Remaking of Evangelical Theology*, 71–75. See also Poole, "Splintered Light," 22–37.

when the seminary was still trying to find its footing. The stresses of administration and intellectual challenges eventually forced Carnell out of the presidency and into a period marked by a decline in productivity and poor reception of Carnell's work.

AN INTELLECTUALLY HONEST DEFENSE OF "HISTORIC CHRISTIANITY"

After the inauguration debacle, Carnell understood the precariousness of his situation. But he also felt emboldened to cast a vision for evangelicalism. The presidency of Fuller was a powerful bully pulpit, and Carnell determined to use it to deploy an intellectually robust defense of "historic Christianity."[26] Carnell had launched this mission while studying under Gordon Clark and continued pursuing it under Cornelius Van Til, a theologian at Westminster. Those men had taught Carnell that the battlefield of the mind was crucially important to the survival of Christianity, and they encouraged Carnell to make a robust intellectual defense of his faith. But in time Carnell distanced himself from both the rationalism of Clark and the presuppositional theology of Van Til. When Carnell had studied at Harvard, he discovered that nobody there read any fundamentalists after J. Gresham Machen, who wrote in the early twentieth century. Liberal and Neo-orthodox theologians viewed fundamentalism as naive. Carnell, then, decided that he needed to make a radical break with the intellectual trends of fundamentalism—including those he learned at Wheaton and Westminster. As he wrote to Carl Henry, "I want to command the attention of [Paul] Tillich and [John] Bennett; then I shall be in a better place to be of service to the evangelicals. We need prestige desperately."[27]

In his first year as president, Carnell eliminated the premillennialist clause from Fuller's statement of faith. Over the past fifty years, premillennialism (the belief that Christ's return would occur before the thousand-year reign of Christ prophesied in the Book of Revelation) had

26. Carnell did not particularly like the word "evangelical," feeling it caused misunderstanding and confusion. As president, he once attempted to eliminate use of the word at Fuller, encouraging faculty and students to refer to the seminary as the "Home of Historic Christianity." That phrase never caught on. See Marsden, *Reforming Fundamentalism*, 173.

27. Henry, *Confessions of a Theologian*, 137.

become a standard article of faith for fundamentalists. Carnell viewed strict premillennialism with disdain. He complained to Ockenga privately that because of the seminary's premillennialist restriction, "neither Calvin, Warfield, Hodge, nor Machen could teach at Fuller."[28] Along with progressive faculty members Paul Jewett, George Ladd, Clarence Roddy, and—most important—Charles Fuller's son Dan, Carnell convinced Charles Fuller to assent to a statement releasing the seminary from the premillennialist clause upon the elder Fuller's death.[29]

Carnell also began writing for a wider audience. His 1956 *Christian Century* article "A Proposal to Reinhold Niebuhr" typified Carnell's strategy. Reasoning that he needed to distance himself from intellectually deficient conservative dogmas, Carnell criticized the "easy perfectionism" that permeated Billy Graham's revival sermons. Though he meant to support Graham's efforts with the article, Carnell often sounded patronizing toward the evangelist. After arguing that Graham's doctrine of grace is "biblically inaccurate," Carnell conceded, "I find it easy to be patient with Billy Graham." He then went on to denounce Reinhold Niebuhr's "patronizing" treatment of conservatives without any apparent sense of irony. He proposed that Niebuhr view Graham and his upcoming New York crusade with a bit more charity. But Carnell's equivocal statements about Graham's theology suggested his dissatisfaction with the evangelist. Moreover, he concluded with the admission, "each of us cultivates some heresy or other"—hardly the robust defense Graham might have hoped for.[30]

At the same time, Carnell was working overtime to complete his third book of apologetics, *Christian Commitment*, which was published by Macmillan (a respected trade press) in 1957. Before the publication of *Christian Commitment*, Carnell exuded optimism. He predicted to faculty and students that *Commitment* would transform the field of apologetics.[31] *Commitment* continued Carnell's journey towards a more existential apologetic. In the first few pages he wrote, "I am lifting the veil from *my* experiences in order that others might be guided into a

28. Letter from Carnell to Ockenga, dated 14 October 1955, quoted in Marsden, *Reforming Fundamentalism*, 150.

29. Dorrien, *Remaking of Evangelical Theology*, 77–78.

30. Edward John Carnell, "A Proposal to Reinhold Niebuhr," *The Christian Century*, 17 October 1956, 1197–99.

31. Nelson, *Making and Unmaking*, 103.

more accurate understanding of their own." He thought his effort "to unbosom the self" would prove painful but rewarding.[32] This autobiographical opening confirmed Carnell's dissatisfaction with his earlier apologetic works, focused as they were on rational approaches to defending the faith. In *Commitment*, Carnell argued for a "third way of knowing." The first two ways of knowing—knowledge by acquaintance (or experience) and knowledge by inference—could not, according to Carnell, apprehend the fullness of truth. Instead, one had to "place himself in the center of those obligations which form the moral and spiritual environment of his life." Only then could one grasp "truth as personal rectitude." As such, Carnell's apologetic work depended not on propositional arguments but on an unmasking of how his *commitment* to "powers greater than himself" shaped and transformed his understanding of truth.[33]

Commitment, however, confused readers and fell well short of Carnell's hopes for success. Reviewers panned the book. Neo-orthodox theologian William Hordern, writing for *The Christian Century*, blasted Carnell's "amazing lack of understanding" of modern theological concepts and wrote, "The most serious weakness of the book . . . lies at the very heart of its argument." Hordern thought Carnell made God's judgments dependent on human decisions. Though Hordern applauded Carnell's willingness to "repent of the sins of fundamentalism," he concluded with a penetrating query: "Could it be that the errors of earlier modernism, such as overconfidence in man's goodness and rationality and an uncritical view of the immanence of God, are going to be brought back by the new fundamentalists?" Hordern's review undercut the central thesis of *Commitment* and left readers with the impression that Carnell had neglected his historical and theological homework.[34]

More devastating, Carnell's former mentor Gordon Clark gave *Commitment* a scathing evaluation in *Christianity Today*. In the review, Clark said *Commitment* opened the door to universalism, disparaged foreign missions, and undercut God's omnipotence. Quite simply, Carnell's argument in *Commitment* "is standard procedure of those who

32. Edward John Carnell, *Christian Commitment: An Apologetic* (New York: Macmillan, 1957) 3.

33. Carnell, *Christian Commitment*, 22, 16.

34. William Hordern, "Uncritical Conservative?," *The Christian Century*, 4 September 1957, 1039–40.

wish to oppose the theology Dr. Carnell stands for." Clark felt personally insulted by Carnell's insistence that the "third way of knowing"
required constant introspection if a Christian desires righteousness. "I
am not flattered when it is said that my lack of insight," wrote Clark,
"is the result of my insincerity."[35] Clark recognized *Commitment* for
what it was: a book-length rejection of the rationalism he had taught
Carnell at Wheaton. Clark's review wounded Carnell deeply and likely
torpedoed any hope the book had at popular success among conservative Protestants. Macmillan grew impatient with the book's slow sales
and sold the outstanding copies of *Commitment* as remainders. Carnell
managed to joke about the book's failure on occasion—once quipping to
a class that Macmillan had just called with the exciting news of the sale
of one copy—but friends reported that Carnell took the book's failure
hard. Biographer Rudolph Nelson called the dismissal of *Commitment*
"the greatest disappointment of [Carnell's] professional life."[36]

SCRIPTURAL INERRANCY AND CARNELL'S BREAK WITH FUNDAMENTALISM

In arguing for a "third way of knowing," Carnell implicitly departed from
fundamentalists' commitment to scriptural inerrancy. Carnell himself
wrote comparatively little about scriptural inerrancy, preferring to deal
with philosophical questions like those raised in *Commitment*. But his
later work revealed both an experiential epistemology and an overriding
concern for Christian fellowship—factors that made holding the line on
scriptural inspiration increasingly difficult. If, as *Commitment* argued,
the fullness of truth came through autobiographical introspection,
propositional truths gleaned through Scripture were not true simply
because they appeared in the Bible. Rather, their truth rested upon their
correspondence both with the theology forwarded by Jesus and Paul and
with their ability to push believers into closer relationship with God.[37]
Moreover, fundamentalists' insistence on maintaining separation from

35. Gordon H. Clark, "Book Review: Christian Commitment," *Christianity Today*,
2 September 1957, 36–38.

36. Nelson, *Making and Unmaking*, 103.

37. Edward John Carnell, *The Case for Orthodox Theology* (Philadelphia:
Westminster, 1959) 92–111.

believers who did not share their view of scriptural inspiration struck
Carnell as narrow-minded and even unchristian. Carnell increasingly
worried that fundamentalists had sacrificed love on the altar of truth and,
in so doing, lost both. In a 1958 article for *The Handbook of Christian
Theology*, he described fundamentalism as a "religious mentality" that
"forgets that orthodox truth without orthodox love profits nothing."[38] By
focusing his later apologetic work on experiential aspects of faith and on
establishing connections with theological liberals, Carnell paved the way
for many subsequent evangelical theologians. He also offered a biting
critique of fundamentalists and a pale defense of scriptural inerrancy.

Carnell's most notable salvo against fundamentalists also contained
his lengthiest discussion of biblical inspiration. In 1959, Carnell published *The Case for Orthodox Theology*, one of a series of three volumes
commissioned by Westminster Press about competing theological
positions.[39] Carnell spent most of the book distancing historic orthodoxy from fundamentalism, which Carnell defined as "orthodoxy gone
cultic."[40] In a twenty-page chapter titled "Difficulties," Carnell wrestled
with the problem of scriptural inspiration. While claiming to defend
inerrancy, Carnell faulted the two main traditions defending the divine
inspiration of Scripture: the Princeton theology found in the works of
Charles Hodge and B. B. Warfield, and the British tradition articulated
by James Orr. The Princeton theologians—who held considerably more
influence in American fundamentalism—focused on the "plenary inspiration" of Scripture, or the notion that Scripture is true because God
says it is true. According to Warfield, the Bible made countless assertions
of its divine inspiration. As a result, all of Scripture—every word—was
"God-breathed" and therefore true. Orr, on the other hand, argued that
scriptural truth derived from its ability to push people towards Christ.
"The proof of the inspiration of the Bible," he wrote, "is to be found in
the life-giving effects which that message has produced, wherever its
word of truth has gone."[41] Both approaches to the Bible were flawed, in

38. Edward John Carnell, "Fundamentalism," in *A Handbook of Christian Theology*, ed. Marvin Halverson (New York: Meridian, 1957) 142–43.

39. The other two books were L. Harold DeWolf, *The Case for Theology in Liberal Perspective* (Philadelphia: Westminster, 1959); William Hordern, *The Case for a New Reformation Theology* (Philadelphia: Westminster, 1959).

40. Carnell, *Case for Orthodox Theology*, 113.

41. Carnell, *Case for Orthodox Theology*, 100.

Carnell's reading. Hodge and Warfield too easily dismissed "inductive difficulties"—those moments where Scripture contradicted modern science or itself. On the other hand, Orr made a "perilous admission" of historical errors in the Bible.[42]

Carnell articulated a problematic solution to this dilemma. He argued first that the doctrine of inspiration rested on the testimony of Christ and the apostles—a relatively uncontroversial claim among fundamentalists. But Carnell went on to argue that the divine inspiration of Scripture ensured only that biblical writers gave "infallible accounts" of the materials presented them. This meant, for instance, that the biblical histories contained in the book of Chronicles might contain mistakes if the writer of Chronicles possessed mistake-ridden genealogies. The Holy Spirit, according to Carnell, may or may not have inspired biblical scribes to correct the errors in manuscripts they copied. If scholars proved the history and genealogy in the book of Chronicles incorrect, Carnell claimed, "the doctrine of Biblical inerrancy would *not* be destroyed." Locating the error exclusively in the lists copied by the author of Chronicles preserved the possibility of a mistake-free transcription, argued Carnell, and thus sustained the doctrine of biblical inerrancy.[43]

This dubious defense of inerrancy led many conservative Protestants to reject or ignore *The Case for Orthodox Theology*. After all, what self-respecting inerrantist wanted a Bible full of perfectly copied mistakes? *Christianity Today*'s review of the book claimed that Carnell did not give "proof or vindication of the authority of the written Word." Reviewer Philip E. Hughes pointed out the lack of constructive arguments for conservative Christianity. Frankly, wrote Hughes, "this is a disappointing book."[44] Carnell had a chance to defend evangelicalism against its theological foes, but he torpedoed his project with an overly caustic attack on fundamentalists and an unconvincing attempt to defend inerrancy.

Carnell, however, continued to distance himself from fundamentalists. In a 1959 article for *The Christian Century* titled "Post-Fundamentalist Faith," Carnell wrote, "It was by a discovery of

42. Carnell, *Case for Orthodox Theology*, 111.

43. Carnell, *Case for Orthodox Theology*, 111. Compare Robert M. Price, "Neo-Evangelicals and Scripture: A Forgotten Period of Ferment," *Christian Scholar's Review* 15 (1986) 315–30.

44. Philip E. Hughes, "Defending the Faith," *Christianity Today*, 4 January 1960, 42–43.

[fundamentalists'] pompous theological error that I awoke from dog-matic slumber." By "pompous theological error," Carnell referred to fun-damentalists' convictions that all other Christians were apostates and that they alone possessed truth.[45] One year later, Carnell offered *Century* readers an autobiographical account of why he now seemed so intent on attacking fundamentalism. In 1949 Carnell had used the Revised Standard Version of the Bible in one of his books. Several fundamental-ists charged him with "outright heresy" for using a translation other than the King James Version. After initially deciding to "ride out the storm," Carnell later decided he had to fight back. Fundamentalists had made it impossible for Carnell to defend a "sane Protestant orthodoxy" be-cause they (and he, for a time) had forgotten that "Jesus names *love*, not possession of doctrine, as the sign of a true disciple." Carnell castigated fundamentalists as defenders of "cultic orthodoxy" and suggested that any conservative Protestant with half a brain fell into his camp.[46] Note both the rhetoric and the venue in which Carnell attacked fundamen-talists. By airing his concerns in the self-proclaimed organ of mainline Protestantism, *The Christian Century*, and by casually dismissing fun-damentalists as "cultic" and attitudinally disposed toward separation, Carnell made enemies quickly.

Carnell attacked fundamentalists with passion because he came to see them as the central impediment to his theological project. Fundamentalists' insistence on the preeminence of truth accorded with Carnell's determination to provide a robust intellectual defense of Christianity, but fundamentalists' most important truths held none of the intellectual respectability Carnell craved. Like other "new evan-gelicals," Carnell wanted non-fundamentalists to understand orthodox Christianity as intellectually robust. He knew that a defense of plenary inspiration would never convince liberal and Neo-orthodox theologians. And he also wrestled internally with the defenses of inerrancy provided by fundamentalists. Faced with scientific and historical evidence that seemed to contradict scriptural teaching, Carnell—like many evangeli-cals before him and since—found it increasingly difficult to maintain a

45. Carnell, "Post-Fundamentalist Faith," 971.

46. Edward John Carnell, "Orthodoxy: Cultic vs. Classical," *The Christian Century*, 30 March 1960, 378, 377. Carnell argued for evangelicals' right to sit at the table of dis-cussion with liberals, evincing some degree of dissatisfaction with the progress he had made. Carnell never managed to achieve the prominence among liberals he thought he deserved.

belief in inerrancy. Though he felt it essential to hold the line, the solution for scriptural inspiration he proposed in *The Case for Orthodox Theology* was weak. And yet, Carnell's overall theological project presaged many themes of late-twentieth-century evangelicalism, including a desire to find "points of contact" between the gospel and culture and to develop a theology that took human experience seriously. As his biographer Allan Poole noted, "one of the mysteries surrounding Carnell is his rapid disappearance from the scene of later twentieth century theology."[47]

Carnell's "disappearance" stemmed both from his inability to deal with scriptural inerrancy and from the personal and scholarly troubles of his final years. Carnell's shift to a more experiential apologetic in the late 1950s rendered rational and presuppositional defenses of Christianity untenable. As a result, though Carnell never explicitly repudiated the doctrine of inerrancy, he found it both hard to defend and restrictive in his mission to speak to the broader culture. Fundamentalists had used the gospel as an "ideological weapon," insisting on a defense of inerrancy that appeared increasingly absurd to non-fundamentalists.[48] As a result, Carnell focused his later books on love and Christian fellowship. He could not abide fundamentalists' tendency to elevate a particular view of scriptural inspiration as *the* mark of a true disciple. And fundamentalists noted this. For instance, John R. Rice used his widely circulated periodical *The Sword of the Lord* to denounce *The Case for Orthodox Theology*. If Fuller Seminary did not repudiate Carnell, wrote Rice, "I do not believe that out-and-out Bible believers can safely send students to Fuller Seminary or send any money to support the seminary." Rice's shot found its mark, and Charles Fuller and Harold Lindsell scrambled to assure supporters that the seminary and Dr. Carnell maintained the necessary doctrinal standards. Even so, Carnell's actions took their toll on Fuller Seminary.[49]

Furthermore, the intellectual and financial battles fought during Carnell's presidency pushed him to the brink of collapse. Carnell resigned the presidency in 1959 after five stressful years in office. He immediately took a sabbatical for rest and writing, but it proved insufficient to heal

47. Poole, "Splintered Light," 36. Compare John G. Stackhouse Jr., "Pioneer: The Reputation of Edward John Carnell in American Theology" (MA Thesis, Wheaton College, 1982).

48. Carnell, *Case for Orthodox Theology*, 128.

49. Marsden, *Reforming Fundamentalism*, 188–92, quote on 191.

his damaged psyche. Historian George Marsden perceptively captured Carnell's dilemma: "At age forty, with spectacular successes behind him, he felt not only a sense of nowhere else to go, but even a failure at what he had already done."[50] Carnell fell into serious depression and required hospitalization in the summer of 1961. Subsequent shock therapy and prescription drugs restored some of Carnell's health, and he taught at Fuller for six more years.

Yet the drastic reduction in Carnell's scholarly output in the 1960s suggested the negative effects of his battle with fundamentalists. Carnell's inability to maintain intellectual vibrancy deprived him of his life's passion. Carnell died of a mild drug overdose in an Oakland, California, hotel room in April 1967. The coroner declared the death "undetermined whether ACCIDENTAL or SUICIDAL." His former pastor told biographer Rudolph Nelson, "Carnell's death was certainly unfortunate, but it was not as shocking as it might have been. He was dying inside."[51]

Laboring under the heavy load of a self-imposed burden to transform Christianity, Carnell never shook off the failure, disappointment, and disinheritance that resulted from the publications he produced while president of Fuller Seminary: *Christian Commitment* and *The Case for Orthodox Theology*. While the books argued themes that would later come to define evangelicalism, they also reflected confusion about Carnell's intellectual inheritance and an unrealized goal to make conservative Protestantism relevant to the larger intellectual world. Although Carnell forwarded a creative theological program that inspired a generation of students and won accolades from his colleagues, this fell far short of his ambitions. Intellectual elites brushed him aside as casually as the fundamentalists he had worked so hard to distance himself from. He found himself isolated even among the new evangelical movement he had helped to shape and faded quickly from evangelical memory. His inspiring vision for an intellectually robust evangelicalism foundered as he wrestled with inerrancy. Fundamentalists charged him with heresy even as liberals labeled him naive. Carnell was, in a sense, stuck between two intellectual worlds: unable to make peace with the dogmas of his youth and equally unable to leave them behind.

50. Marsden, *Reforming Fundamentalism*, 191–93.

51. Nelson, *Making and Unmaking*, 120, 215; see 106–21 for a fuller account of Carnell's final years.

5

"Inerrancy, a Paradigm in Crisis"

Carlos R. Bovell

IN THIS CHAPTER, I provide a synopsis of how some contemporary inerrantists are constructively critiquing inerrancy and comment on some of the effects this is having on conservative evangelicalism. To help establish an ideational context for the overview, I reappropriate Thomas Kuhn's account of scientific revolutions as a description of contemporary evangelical discussions regarding the nature and authority of Scripture. In section 1, I refer to relevant primary and secondary philosophical literature to provide a cursory account of Kuhn's philosophy of science.[1] In section 2, I posit that inerrancy is the dominant paradigm for conservative evangelical considerations regarding Scripture. In section 3, I suggest that the state of contemporary evangelical discussions on Scripture seems to approximate the pattern of crisis described by Kuhn. In section 4, I offer examples of inerrantist scholars trying to deal with anomalies that those involved in evangelical biblical studies are presently confronting. In the fifth and last section, I integrate Kuhn's notion of "crisis" and "extraordinary science" into the evangelical inerrantist context. My aim is to help readers better appreciate the epistemological and sociological impasse separating contemporary evangelical disputants who are writing on the inerrancy of Scripture today.

---

1. See Thomas Kuhn, *The Structure of Scientific Revolution*, 3rd ed. (Chicago: University of Chicago Press, 1996).

KUHN'S PHILOSOPHY OF SCIENCE

For the sake of space, I will only mention those features of Kuhn's philosophy of science that are directly germane to the aims of the present chapter, namely Kuhn's observations regarding the relationship between "paradigms," "anomalies," and "crises." I shall begin with a quote from Kuhn's *The Structure of Scientific Revolutions*:

> Let us then assume that crises are a necessary precondition for the emergence of novel theories and ask next how scientists respond to their existence. Part of the answer, as obvious as it is important, can be discovered by noting first what scientists never do when confronted by even severe and prolonged anomalies. Though they may begin to lose faith and then to consider alternatives, they do not renounce the paradigm that has led them into crisis. They do not, that is, treat anomalies as counterinstances, though in the vocabulary of philosophy of science that is what they are . . .[2]

Hanson's inquiry into the foundations of classical particle physics provides a helpful illustration of what Kuhn is talking about here. The following reflection concerns the first of Newton's three laws of motion:

> The law encapsulates and extrapolates much information about events, yet it seems beyond disconfirmation: it could not but be true. "But surely, after having been kicked across the smoothest ice a rock could stop abruptly. It could return to where it was kicked, or even describe circles. This could happen without ground glass, magnets, or anything else. Is this not possible?" Here some will reply "Yes," and others "No." As before this is not an experimental issue; *it concerns the organization of concepts.* . . . When others would regard anomalous events as falsifying the law, [the person saying "No"] would say, "That only shows the presence of some hidden mechanism. Or else what we took for a rock is not a rock at all." The law is less vulnerable to experience for him than for others. . . . Whatever proves a body's motion not to be rectilinear also proves that it is acted on by forces.[3]

---

2. Kuhn, *Structure*, 77.

3. Norwood R. Hanson, *Patterns of Discovery: An Inquiry into the Conceptual Foundations of Science* (New York: Cambridge University Press, 1961) 96; emphasis mine. Newton's first law: a body at rest remains at rest and a body in motion continues to move at a constant velocity unless acted upon by an external force.

When scientists are practicing what Kuhn calls "normal science," anomalies are accounted for in a manner consistent with the dominant paradigm.[4] Yet there almost always lurks a group of practitioners who encounter the very same anomalies and for various reasons decide that the dominant paradigm is in crisis.

Alasdair MacIntyre proffers the following criterion for telling whether a tradition has entered into crisis: "One of the signs that a tradition is in crisis is that its accustomed ways for relating *seems* and *is* beginning to break down. Thus the pressures of skepticism become more urgent and attempts to do the impossible, to refute skepticism once and for all, become projects of central importance to the culture and not mere private academic enterprises."[5] Kuhn's own interpretation of the relation between anomalies and crises reads:

> The reasons for doubt sketched above were purely factual; they were, that is, themselves counterinstances to a prevalent episte-mological theory. As such, if my present point is correct, they can at best help to create a crisis or, more accurately, to reinforce one that is already very much in existence. By themselves [anomalies] cannot and will not falsify that philosophical theory, for its defenders will do what we have already seen scientists doing when confronted by anomaly. They will devise numerous articulations and *ad hoc* modifications of their theory in order to eliminate any apparent conflict. . . . If, therefore, these epistemological counterinstances are to constitute more than a minor irritant, *that will be because they help to permit the emergence of a new and different analysis of science within which they are no longer a source of trouble.*[6]

4. With uncanny prescience, Ludwig Fleck wrote of these very same dynamics some twenty-five years earlier: "In more modern, more remote, and still complicated fields, in which it is important first of all to learn to observe and ask questions properly, this situation does not obtain—and perhaps never does, originally, in any field—until tradition, education, and familiarity have produced *a readiness for stylized (that is, directed and restricted) perception and action*; until an answer becomes largely pre-formed in the question, and a decision is confined merely to 'yes' or 'no,' or perhaps to a numerical determination; until methods and apparatus automatically carry out the greatest part of our mental work for us" (Fleck, *Genesis and Development of a Scientific Fact*, trans. F. Bradley [Chicago: University of Chicago Press, 1979] 84; emphasis original).

5. Alistair MacIntyre, "Epistemological Crises, Dramatic Narrative, and the Philosophy of Science," *The Monist* 60 (1977) 459.

6. Kuhn, *Structure*, 78; emphasis mine.

In short, Kuhn's philosophy of science proposes that scientists typically conduct their experiments and other investigations under the auspices of a consensual paradigm, and when scientists do this, they are practicing "normal science." During times of crises, however, anomalies—counterinstances that rascally present themselves to every scientific paradigm, whether dominant or not—help magnify a sense of uncertainty regarding the exemplar and motivate at least some specialists in the field to conduct their activities in a more or less troubled state of paradigmatic agnosticism. A scientist who practices science under such "frontier" conditions is said to be practicing "extraordinary science."

INERRANCY AS A DOMINANT PARADIGM

In this section, I shall survey a handful of evangelical and Reformed writings to illustrate how inerrancy is conceived as the dominant paradigm by quoting from standard texts in systematics.

Millard Erickson explains in his *Christian Theology* that "[t]he inerrancy of Scripture is the doctrine that the Bible is fully truthful in all of its teachings."[7] Inerrancy is presented as a result of the manner in which the Bible has been inspired. Regarding inspiration, he has the following to say:

> Inspiration is herein conceived of as applying to both the writer and the writing. In the primary sense, it is the writer who is the object of inspiration. As the writer pens Scripture, however, the quality of inspiredness is communicated to the writing as well. It is inspired in a derived sense. . . . We have observed that inspiration presupposes an extended period of God's working with the writer. This not only involves the preparation of the writer, but also the preparation of the material for this use.[8]

Erickson candidly admits that the experience of actually reading the Bible can sometimes give the impression that the doctrine of the inerrancy of Scripture is incompatible with the data of Scripture, yet his counsel on the matter is patently conservative and evangelical:

> We must, then, continue to work at the task of resolving whatever tensions there are in our understanding of the Bible. . . . Rather

7. Millard Erickson, *Christian Theology*, 2nd ed. (Grand Rapids: Baker, 1998) 247.

8. Erickson, *Christian Theology*, 244–45.

than giving fanciful explanations, it is better to leave difficulties unresolved in the confidence, based on the doctrine of Scripture, that they will be removed to the extent that additional data become available.[9]

Lewis and Demarest in their systematic effort, *Integrative Theology*, speak about inerrancy of the Old Testament in the following terms:

> Summing up, the data show that the Old Testament is more than a human witness to revelation. . . . The teachings of these faithfully copied books were endorsed by the Lord Jesus Christ as conveying objectively valid (inerrant) truth factually and ethically, and so authoritative and necessary to healthy Christian beliefs and experience in the world.[10]

Their conclusions regarding the New Testament read along similar lines:

> Summing up the data on the New Testament, the Lord Jesus Christ, the supreme revelation of God, prepared the disciples for additional revelation after his departure and delegated authority to his authentic apostles to write, as well as speak, revealed truth foundational for the building of the church in every century and culture. . . . What the New Testament teaches, God teaches. What it affirms is objectively valid truth: logically, factually, and ethically (inerrant), and so it is authoritative for Christians in the development of healthy, coherent convictions by which to live in the church and the world (infallible).[11]

Wayne Grudem in his *Systematic Theology* comes to the following conclusions regarding both testaments:

> With evidence such as this we are now in a position to define biblical inerrancy: *The inerrancy of Scripture means that Scripture in the original manuscripts does not affirm anything that is contrary to fact.* . . . The definition in simple terms just means that *the Bible always tells the truth*, and that it always tells the truth *concerning everything it talks about.*[12]

---

9. Erickson, *Christian Theology*, 263.

10. Gordon R. Lewis and Bruce A. Demarest, *Integrative Theology*, vol. 1 (Grand Rapids: Zondervan, 1987) 148.

11. Lewis and Demarest, *Integrative Theology*, 154.

12. Wayne Grudem, *Systematic Theology* (Grand Rapids: Zondervan, 1994) 90–91; emphasis original.

In conservative Reformed circles, Boice describes the same biblio-logical viewpoint: "Inerrancy means that when all the facts are known, the Scriptures in their original autographs and properly interpreted will be shown to be wholly true in everything they teach, whether that teaching has to do with doctrine, history, science, geography, geology, or other disciplines or knowledge."[13] Robert Reymond is representative of both Reformed and evangelical theologians in his estimation of iner-rancy as the default Christian position:

> The church worldwide has properly seen that the rational char-acter of the one living and true God would of necessity have to be reflected in any propositional self-revelation which he deter-mined to give to human beings, and accordingly has confessed the entire truthfulness (inerrancy) and noncontradictory char-acter of the Word of God.[14]

Finally, the *Evangelical Dictionary of Theology* has this to say about inerrancy:

> Inerrancy is the view that when all the facts become known, they will demonstrate that the Bible in its original autographs and cor-rectly interpreted is entirely true and never false in all it affirms, whether that relates to doctrine or ethics or to the social, physi-cal, or life sciences.[15]

It should be obvious to those who live and move and have their being in conservative evangelicalism that inerrancy is the dominant paradigm, not only for reflecting upon and thinking about the Bible, but for reflecting on and thinking about every aspect of Christian living, and that at an existentially fundamental level. Inerrancy is the functional equivalence of Newton's first law of motion in the example given above: if some kind of doubt should ever surface regarding the inerrancy of Scripture it is because some external force is affecting one's reading of Scripture. The problem cannot lie with Scripture; it must lie with our-selves, whether it is because we do not yet possess all the evidence or that our sin is somehow getting in the way of us seeing things aright.

13. Paul Enns, *The Moody Handbook of Theology* (Chicago: Moody, 1989) 167, cit-ing J. M. Boice, *Does Inerrancy Matter?*

14. *A New Systematic Theology of the Christian Faith* (Nashville: T. Nelson, 1998) 110.

15. P. Feinberg, "Bible, Inerrancy and Infallibility of," in *Evangelical Dictionary of Theology*, ed. W. A. Elwell (Grand Rapids: Baker, 1984) 142.

INERRANCY A PARADIGM IN CRISIS

An evangelical doctrinal trend is underway that has yet to plateau. According to the US Religious Landscape Survey conducted by the Pew Forum on Religion and Public Life, only 16 percent of Protestants were raised outside of Protestantism. Yet 29 percent of evangelicals have moved from one evangelical tradition to another, and of the number of persons who claim they are unaffiliated with any religion, 44 percent claim to be former Protestants.[16] In a 2003 *Scientific American* article, Rodger Doyle reports the results of a Gallup "General Social Survey" to the effect that the percent of American adults believing in the doctrine of inerrancy has fallen from almost 40 percent in 1975 to about 25 percent by the turn of the millennium.[17] For evidence of this trend, one need look no further than to past presidents of the Evangelical Theological Society.

For starters, in 2003 Norman Geisler resigned his membership from the society upon hearing ETS's judgment regarding the open theism debate. On his website, Geisler gives an account of his decision:

> First and foremost among my reasons for resigning is that ETS has lost its doctrinal integrity. For decades it has had a single Doctrinal Basis: "The Bible alone, and the Bible in its entirety, is the Word of God written and is therefore inerrant in the autographs." With the official decision to retain in membership persons who clearly deny what the ETS framers meant by this statement, ETS has lost its doctrinal integrity . . .
>
> Further, the society has knowingly adopted a revisionist hermeneutic that undermines all for which it stands. For the report of the Executive Committee, confirmed by the membership vote, knowingly allows in its membership persons who do not hold the same view on inerrancy as that of the framers of the doctrinal statement. This they have knowingly done since 1976 when the Executive Committee confessed that "Some of the members of the Society have expressed the feeling that a measure of *intellectual dishonesty prevails among members who do not take the signing of the doctrinal statement seriously.* Other members of the

16. The survey was published February 25, 2008. Available online at http://religions.pewforum.org.

17. Rodger Doyle, "Sizing Up Evangelicals: Fundamentalism Persists but Shows Signs of Moderation," *Scientific American* 288.3 (2003) 37. Not all evangelicals will find the poll's definition of inerrancy useful.

Society have come to the realization that they are not in agreement with the creedal statement and have voluntarily withdrawn. That is, *in good conscience* they could not sign the statement."[18]

Geisler is decrying a fundamental shift within the ETS regarding the meaning of inerrancy, a shift that is, according to Geisler, at considerable variance with the intentions of the framers of the society's doctrinal statement.

Another past president who bears mention is Francis Beckwith. Beckwith resigned his ETS membership in 2007 upon converting to Roman Catholicism. He explained online that: "Although I firmly believe that I can sign the ETS doctrinal statement in good conscience, my high-profile presence in ETS will likely result in the sort of public conflict that occurred during the debate over the openness view of God and the attempt on the part of some members to oust believers in that view."[19] The ETS executive committee, however, did not agree:

> The work of the Evangelical Theological Society as a scholarly forum proceeds on the basis that "the Bible alone and the Bible in its entirety, is the Word of God written and is therefore inerrant in the autographs."... Confessional Catholicism, as defined by the Roman Catholic Church's declarations from the Council of Trent to Vatican II, sets forth a more expansive view of verbal, infallible revelation. Specifically, it posits a larger canon of Scripture than that recognized by evangelical Protestants, including in its canon several writings from the Apocrypha. It also extends the quality of infallibility to certain expressions of church dogma issued by the Magisterium . . . as well as certain pronouncements of the pope . . .

> We recognize the right of Roman Catholic theologians to do their theological work on the basis of all the authorities they consider to be revelatory and infallible, even as we wholeheartedly affirm the distinctive contribution and convictional necessity of the work of the Evangelical Theological Society on the basis of the "Bible alone and the Bible in its entirety" as "the Word of God written and . . . inerrant."[20]

18. Source: http://www.normangeisler.net/etsresign.htm. Geisler is citing the 1976 Minutes, italics his.

19. Source: http://rightreason.ektopos.com/archives/2007/05/my_resignation.html.

20. Source: http://www.etsjets.org/?q=announcements/frank_beckwith_re-signs. Cited: March 2, 2008. Beckwith responds in *Return to Rome: Confessions of an Evangelical Catholic.* (Grand Rapids: Brazos, 2009), 121-26.

Although inerrantist Dan Wallace, for example, does not see anything in the ETS doctrinal statement that should prevent Beckwith from continuing as an ETS member,[21] Beckwith's conversion to Catholicism from the vantage of the ETS executive committee necessitates a concomitant change in his doctrine of inerrancy.

The two cases of former ETS presidents Geisler and Beckwith show, at the very least, that there are some fundamental disagreements over what inerrancy means and what exactly one might expect the dogma to entail. This snapshot of the inerrantist landscape illustrates how evangelical scholars are creating a social need for engagement with anomalies *"to permit the emergence of a new and different analysis of inerrancy within which they might no longer be a source of trouble."*[22]

EXAMPLES OF PRACTITIONERS DEALING WITH ANOMALIES

In this section, I present for consideration a sampling of evangelical scholars engaging inerrancy's anomalies. The examples are representative of the anomalies contributing to paradigmatic crisis.

Some writers find an anomaly in the incongruity that appears between the treatment of Scripture in much of the primary literature one finds when studying historical theology and the standard account of inerrancy one finds in contemporary evangelical inerrantist literature. For example, Thomas Buchan concludes that

> we ought not be surprised if we fail to find inerrancy as it has been articulated in twentieth-century evangelicalism in the theology of the patristic, medieval or Reformation periods. Accordingly, it may be that the goal of determining a "central Christian tradition" of biblical authority is not ultimately feasible. . . . It is possible that inerrancy might be better conceived, defended and employed as an interpretive strategy, a theological hermeneutic that called for the suspension of disbelief in favor of faith in what Scripture reveals and that was developed as a strategy of resistance to the pressures of the historical-critical method, rather than as a polemic in the service of ecclesial or doctrinal purity

21. Source: http://blog.christianitytoday.com/ctliveblog/archives/2007/05/ets_on_beckwith.html.

22. Paraphrase of the Kuhn quote cited above, notably replacing the word "science" with "inerrancy."

or as an apologetic argument for supposed generically verifiable epistemological soundness of the sacred text.[23]

Others see anomalies in the issues that the Dead Sea Scrolls raise for the traditional way of framing the doctrine of inerrancy in terms of invoking an inerrant set of autographs. For example, J. Daniel Hays counsels that

> it is important to move off the fence and to make a decision concerning Jeremiah based on the best data available. . . . I think that the evangelical doctrines of inerrancy, inspiration and original autographs do not necessarily preclude inspired literary development, and I suspect that we will struggle with the implications of this in the years to come. . . . In Jeremiah, the LXX reflects a text that is closer to the original than the MT does. Let's use it that way.[24]

Others find anomalies in the textual practices evident in the work of ancient scribes. For example, John Brogan makes the following plea to his fellow evangelicals:

> Our doctrine of Scripture must allow for the editorial development of certain biblical texts, affirming that the writing was "God's Word" at every stage of the process. It must acknowledge that the scribes who copied the texts had other interests and motives in addition to copying the text. It must affirm that the people of God have never had access to the "inerrant autograph," but that they have always had access to the authoritative Word of God. . . . God's Word has come to God's people sometimes through quite exact copies of the text and sometimes through inferior copies that contained unintentional and intentional errors; sometimes through complete copies that contained all sixty-six books and sometimes through only portions of the Bible or even copies that contained additional, non-canonical writings; sometimes

23. T. Buchan, "Inerrancy as Inheritance? Competing Genealogies of Biblical Authority," in *Evangelicals and Scripture: Tradition, Authority and Hermeneutics*, ed. V. Bacote, L. C. Miguélez, and D L. Okholm (Downers Grove, IL: InterVarsity, 2004) 54.

24. J. Daniel Hays, "Jeremiah, the Septuagint, the Dead Sea Scrolls and Inerrancy: Just What Exactly Do We Mean by the 'Original Autographs?,'" in *Evangelicals and Scripture*, 149. In his contribution to the present collection (ch. 6), Hays mentions this anomaly and observes that evangelical Old Testament scholars are still holding to inerrancy. He concedes, however, that an "older, simplistic" inerrantist approach is now no longer possible. Compare his remarks on "fine-tuning" inerrancy.

through very literal translations of the original languages and sometimes through translations of translations of translations.[25]

Others are troubled by anomalies that stem from considerations of the formation of the biblical canon. For example, Craig Allert charges that

> a high view of Scripture should be just as concerned with how the New Testament came to exist in the form we have it as with what it says. What the Bible says is certainly important, but a knowledge of what the Bible says is intimately related to where the Bible grew—in the church—and how it grew. . . . Any examination of the history of the formation of the New Testament canon cannot miss the vital role played by its leaders.[26]

Others see anomalies in the ways that Scripture so closely resembles extrabiblical materials. For example, Ben Witherington III explains:

> Perhaps the most difficult concept to get across to modern readers of Paul's letters and the other NT documents that appear to be letters is that they are oral documents. . . . In other words, they are geared for oral performance and meant to create an aural effect. And because they are basically speeches or sermons rather than pure texts, most of them follow the rules for ancient speeches, namely the rules for rhetoric. . . . But alas, conservative Christians today are far more likely to treat Paul's letters as compendiums of theological nuggets, propositional truths, and ethical rules and regulations than they are to see this material as part of an ongoing dialogue, a conversation in context, that is being played out by the rules of rhetoric. These documents should be heard and appreciated like fine sermons or powerful discourses, not read as if they were texts written by Miss Manners.[27]

Some writers consider the lack of theological unity they encounter in Scripture as an anomaly for inerrancy. For example, Kent Sparks has been particularly bothered by the phenomenon of theological diversity in the Bible. He responds by proposing: "God could make our

25. John J. Brogan, "Can I Have Your Autograph?: Uses and Abuses of Textual Criticism in Formulating an Evangelical Doctrine of Scripture," in *Evangelicals and Scripture*, 109–10.

26. Craig D. Allert, *A High View of Scripture?: The Authority of the Bible and the Formation of the New Testament Canon* (Grand Rapids: Baker, 2007) 173.

27. Ben Witherington III, *The Living Word of God: Rethinking the Theology of the Bible* (Waco, TX: Baylor University Press, 2007) 65.

behaviors perfect when we become Christians, but he evidently does not. Similarly, the theological and ideological diversity of Scripture suggests that God did not rid his text of fallible human elements."[28] The anomaly of theological diversity exacerbates Sparks' sense of paradigmatic crisis and helps motivate his search for an alternative to the standard accounts of inerrancy.[29]

Sparks has also just published a monograph that takes evangelicals to task for the way they tend to treat the arguments of critical scholars. He recounts how there were times when he himself had become convinced of some critical position, not from his encounter with the historical critics, *but by his reading of evangelical engagements with historical criticism.* One aspect of the problem is that "[i]f the practitioners of biblical criticism are right on even a modest portion of their claims, then God's written Word certainly reflects far more humanity than traditional evangelicals might expect." Another aspect is that "[i]t seems clear to me that, for the most part, evangelical efforts to challenge the standard results of biblical criticism not only fail but often fail badly. . . . Fideism, specious arguments, misconstruing evidence, strained harmonizations, leaving out evidence, special pleading, and various kinds of obscurantism are par for the course in this conservative apologetic."[30] To paraphrase, Sparks has found that the critics are right, evangelical denials notwithstanding; inerrantist doctrines of Scripture must duly account for these and other scholarly developments.

Although there are other examples that come to mind, I conclude the present adumbration with the case of an evangelical's reflection on self-critical postmodern analysis. Clark Pinnock writes:

> My journey toward renewal in the evangelical understanding of biblical authority led me from a "philosophical biblicism" to a "simple biblicism." The postmodern-like shift had begun with an earlier preoccupation with verifiable revelational data that could speak with rational certainty to the world. I championed the assumption of divinely given propositional truths that could save

28. Kent Sparks, "The Sun Also Rises: Accommodation in Inscripturation and Interpretation," in *Evangelicals and Scripture*, 130.

29. In his contribution to the present volume (ch. 7), Richard Schultz argues that the anomaly of theological diversity, though a real part of divine accommodation, is "not a threat" to inerrancy.

30. Kenton Sparks, *God's Word in Human Words: An Evangelical Appropriation of Critical Biblical Scholarship* (Grand Rapids: Baker, 2008) 132, 169.

humankind from relativism. The journey later moved me to a focus that I always had in an incipient way, but one that became dominant for me and now lacked that foundationalist overlay.[31]

The examples adduced suffice to illustrate the point. A number of evangelicals have been spurred on by anomalies to sustain a paradigmatic crisis regarding the inerrancy of Scripture. Such inerrantist specialists are self-consciously conducting research in their respective disciplines in ways that *permit the emergence of a new and different analysis of inerrancy within which the anomalies might no longer be a source of trouble.*

EXTRAORDINARY SCIENCE

When an evangelical carries on his or her work in a context of paradigmatic crisis, that work can take on a special character with regard to its allegiance to the dominant paradigm. In the case of evangelicals reflecting upon the doctrine of inerrancy, it is ironic that it is precisely their single-minded faith commitment to Scripture that makes the crisis and all subsequent phases of extraordinary science so acute in the first place.[32] In Kuhn's words:

> When . . . an anomaly comes to seem more than just another puzzle of normal science, the transition to crisis and to extraordinary science has begun. The anomaly itself now comes to be more generally recognized as such by the profession. More and more attention is devoted to it by more and more of the field's most eminent men. If it still continues to resist, as it usually does not, many of them may come to view its resolution as *the* subject

31. Clark H. Pinnock, *The Scripture Principle: Reclaiming the Full Authority of the Bible*, 2nd ed. (Grand Rapids: Baker, 2006) 257.

32. Not only that, but there is an incredibly powerful social taboo against performing extraordinary science for the paradigm of inerrancy. In fact, this taboo is so strong within conservative evangelicalism that practitioners engaging in extraordinary science often go to great lengths to make it look to the establishment as if they are still carrying out normal science. Hagner traces the most recent wave of this trend to the publication of Harold Lindsell's *The Battle for the Bible*. See D. Hagner, "The Battle for Inerrancy: An Errant Trend among the Inerrancists," *The Reformed Journal* (April 1984) 19–22. For a psychological account of the construction of fundamentalist identity, see Wayne C. Booth, "The Rhetoric of Fundamentalist Conversion Narratives," in *Fundamentalisms Comprehended*, ed. M. Marty and R. S. Appleby (Chicago: University of Chicago Press, 1995) 367–98.

matter of their discipline. For them the field will no longer look quite the same as it had earlier.[33]

Presently, for a new generation of evangelical scholars, the anomalies appear to them to be "resisting," i.e., refusing to conform to the dominant paradigm of inerrancy, thus making it possible for these evangelicals to not conduct their scholarship under the strictures of normal science. For Kuhn, not to engage in normal science means not to engage the "puzzles" that accepted theories of a normal science regularly supply to the specialist; these puzzles are what suggest a gamut of possible research topics for students and scholars to undertake. This helps explain why some postconservatives write as if they have reached the end of their hermeneutical ropes.[34] The business of evangelicalism has always been, at least in my mind, to find out what God wants his people to do and believe, to know only insofar as these things are revealed in Scripture, and to act upon it, i.e., upon whatever it is that is learned from sustained engagement with Scripture (be it through homilies, liturgy, personal study, etc.).

Normal science in this context would involve a prolonged engagement with Scripture toward the end just described (or some end comparable to it), but *extraordinary* science would involve attempts to carry on the usual scholarly activities with little to no regard for finding out what it is that God is saying to his people. The inquiries are of a different order. Instead, the problems that singularly arise from the presence of persistent anomalies preoccupy researchers to such an extent that they begin to see the research they do in a totally different light. Kuhn (and others) shows how this can happen in science. D. A. Anapolitanos describes how it happens in mathematics.[35] The purpose

33. Kuhn, *Structure*, 82–83; emphasis original.

34. I have come across critical remarks regarding the seemingly thoroughgoing skepticism that sets in at this phase, particularly how long it takes to come out of it, but I wonder whether such remarks fully appreciate how deeply upsetting the crisis can be. After all, MacIntyre observes, "My ability to understand what you are doing and my ability to act intelligently (both to myself and to others) are one and the same ability" (MacIntyre, "Crises, Narrative and Science," 453–54). For the critical remarks, compare Kevin Vanhoozer, "Lost in Interpretation?: Truth, Scripture, and Hermeneutics," *Journal of the Evangelical Theological Society* 48 (2005) 92; and James K. A. Smith, "Questions about the Perception of 'Christian Truth': On the Affective Effects of Sin," *New Blackfriars* 88 (2007) 586n4.

35. D. A. Anaplitanos, "Proofs and Refutations: A Reassessment," in *Imre Lakatos and Theories of Scientific Change*, ed. K. Gavroglu, Y. Goudaroulis, and P. Nicolacopoulos

of the present chapter is to impress upon readers that the same can happen in theology and is happening now in evangelicalism with regard to inerrancy as a paradigm.

CONCLUSION

I find Kuhn's own account of extraordinary science to be remarkably apropos for contemporary discussions involving inerrancy—so much so that I want to conclude by paraphrasing him to the following effect:

> Because they can ordinarily take the doctrine of inerrancy for granted, exploiting rather than criticizing it, evangelical scholars are freed to explore Scripture to an esoteric depth and detail otherwise unimaginable. Because that exploration will ultimately isolate severe trouble spots, they can be confident that the pursuit of normal science will inform them when and where they can most usefully become Popperian critics. . . . It is the strategy appropriate to those occasions when something goes wrong with normal science, when the doctrine of inerrancy encounters crisis.[36]

It seems to me that this is precisely the phase in which conservative evangelicalism presently finds itself with regard to one of its most elemental doctrines.[37] Conservative evangelical professors and students are presently engaging in both normal theologizing and extraordinary theologizing about inerrancy within the same seminaries, within the same universities,

(Dordrecht: Kluwer, 1989) 338: "These periods are marked, among other things, by the transformation of loose and potentially fruitful philosophical (especially metaphysical) ideas into focused ideas which allow one to see an area no longer through a glass darkly, but with completely new eyes. The overall mathematical activity taking place during and immediately after a foundational crisis (activity which is mainly spurred by such a crisis) is usually centered around the construction of a new conceptual framework with which one hopes to remedy or avoid the problems which caused the crisis."

36. Thomas Kuhn, "Reflections on My Critics," in *Criticism and the Growth of Knowledge*, ed. I. Lakatos and A. Musgrave (New York: Cambridge University Press, 1970) 247.

37. Some regard the fact that inerrancy has been officially established as the most fundamental doctrine for conservative evangelical poses a major problem for conservative evangelicalism. See, for example, D. G. Hart, *Deconstructing Evangelicalism: Conservative Protestantism in the Age of Billy Graham* (Grand Rapids: Baker, 2004) 131–51; and C. Bovell, *Inerrancy and the Spiritual Formation of Younger Evangelicals* (Eugene, OR: Wipf and Stock, 2007) 149–54.

and within the same learned societies, amounting to an excruciating tension.[38] Interestingly enough, Kuhn suggests that this "unbearable" tension might be one of the prime requisites for the very best sort of scientific research.[39] Unfortunately, however, in some conservative schools the tension has proven so intolerable that a palpable acrimony has overtaken both faculty and students. Nevertheless, a preliminary application of Kuhn's account of the structure of scientific revolutions to the context of evangelical inerrancy debates can provide a helpful vantage point from which to interpret some of the intramural dynamics brought about by renewed rounds of controversy surrounding the doctrine. It is hoped that the foregoing appropriation of Kuhn's philosophy of science might help affected younger evangelicals gain proper perspective on recent bibliological developments that appear to some to be upsetting evangelical Christian orthodoxy at its very core.

38. Compare Norris Cameron Grubbs and Curtis Scott Drum, "What Does Theology Have to Do with the Bible?: The Doctrine of Inspiration as an Illustration of Discipline Specialization Run Amok," paper presented at the national meeting of the Evangelical Theological Society, San Diego, California, November 2007.

39. See Kuhn, "The Essential Tension: Tradition and Innovation in Scientific Research," in *The Essential Tension: Selected Studies in Scientific Tradition and Change* (Chicago: University of Chicago Press, 1977) 225–39.

BIBLICAL PERSPECTIVES

6

Inerrancy and Evangelical Old Testament Scholarship

Challenges and the Way Forward

J. Daniel Hays

INTRODUCTION

THIS CHAPTER ATTEMPTS TO discuss the contemporary intersection of evangelical Old Testament scholarship and the doctrine of inerrancy. There are numerous current issues within the field of Old Testament studies that have implications for one's view of Scripture. Several of the more significant issues include: 1) literary development, text criticism and the "original autographs"; 2) the nature of history and history writing in the Old Testament; 3) the relationship between the Old Testament and the literature of the ancient Near East; and 4) the nature of evangelical Old Testament hermeneutics, especially in regard to "propositional truth" approaches.[1] This chapter will attempt to explore

1. Obviously this is an abbreviated list. The issue of theological diversity in the Old Testament—another very important issue—will be discussed in the next chapter by Richard Schultz; thus it is not included here. One might add "the use of the Old Testament in the New Testament" to this list, but this issue is largely a New Testament issue, dealt with primarily by New Testament scholars (Walt Kaiser and Peter Enns are noted exceptions), and it is also largely a hermeneutical issue. Thus it will not be discussed here in any detail. Very briefly, at the heart of this issue is the extent to

these issues, particularly in regard to how these issues are impacting the understanding of inerrancy by evangelical Old Testament scholars. This chapter is not attempting to suggest solutions or final answers to these very complex issues, but rather to identify the direction that evangelical Old Testament scholarship is heading and to probe into some of the implications this movement has for the evangelical doctrine of Scripture.

CATEGORIES AND DEFINITIONS

Although defining the entire spectrum of evangelicalism can be challenging (especially around the edges), this chapter will understand "mainstream evangelicalism" according to the characteristics delineated by Alister McGrath:

> 1) A focus, both devotional and theological, on the person of Jesus Christ, especially his death on the cross; 2) The identification of Scripture as the ultimate authority in matters of spirituality, doctrine and ethics; 3) An emphasis upon conversion or a "new birth" as a life-changing religious experience; and 4) A concern for sharing the faith, especially through evangelism.[2]

Within mainstream evangelicalism, large numbers of believers use the term "inerrancy" to describe their belief that the Bible is true

---

which New Testament writers appear to employ the interpretive methods of Second Temple Judaism in their understanding of the Old Testament and the question of *sensus plenior*. There is no "evangelical consensus" on this issue. For example, note the three different evangelical views described by Walter Kaiser, Darrell Bock, and Peter Enns in *Three Views on the New Testament Use of the Old Testament* (Grand Rapids: Zondervan, 2007). See also Richard N. Longenecker, *Biblical Exegesis in the Apostolic Period*, 2nd ed. (Grand Rapids: Baker, 1999); G. K. Beale, ed., *The Right Doctrine from the Wrong Texts? Essays on the Use of the Old Testament in the New* (Grand Rapids: Baker, 1994); and Peter Enns, *Inspiration and Incarnation: Evangelicals and the Problem of the Old Testament* (Grand Rapids: Baker, 2005) 113–65. Although a lively debate over this issue continues, it should be noted that a large number of the evangelical scholars writing in this area hold to inerrancy and show no signs that the issue will lead them away from this doctrine. Note the large number of contributors to the recent volume *Commentary on the New Testament Use of the Old Testament* (Baker, 2007) who are members of the ETS (i.e., professing inerrancy): Craig Blomberg, David Pao, Eckhard J. Schnabel, Andreas J. Köstenberger, Mark A. Seifrid, Roy E. Ciampa, Moisés Silva, Frank S. Thielman, G. K. Beale, Jeffrey A. D. Weima, Philip H. Towner, George H. Guthrie, and D. A. Carson.

2. Alister E. McGrath, *A Passion for Truth: The Intellectual Coherence of Evangelicalism* (Downers Grove, IL: InterVarsity, 1996).

and historically accurate. The most widespread accepted technical definition of inerrancy within evangelicalism is the Chicago Statement on Biblical Inerrancy, produced in 1978 by the International Council on Biblical Inerrancy. Unless otherwise qualified in the context, this chapter will assume the understanding of the term inerrancy as expressed in that document.

Although a large percentage of evangelicalism uses the term inerrancy to describe their belief in the truthfulness and historicity of the Bible, this chapter recognizes that not all evangelicals do. Many evangelicals, especially those in a European context, prefer the term "infallibility."[3] Nonetheless, a large percentage of evangelicals, including a large number of evangelical Old Testament scholars, adhere to the doctrine of inerrancy. These scholars are most easily (but not exhaustively) identified by their membership in the Evangelical Theological Society (ETS), which requires its members to subscribe to the society's doctrinal basis, which includes the following statement: "The Bible, and the Bible in its entirety, is the Word of God written and is therefore inerrant in the autographs."[4]

BRIEF HISTORY AND AN OVERVIEW OF THE FOUNDATIONAL ISSUE

During the twentieth century, Western (i.e., European-American) conservative Protestant Christianity split into two loosely defined and overlapping camps: fundamentalism and evangelicalism.[5] The issues are

3. A. T. B. McGowan, *The Divine Authenticity of Scripture: Retrieving an Evangelical Heritage* (Downers Grove, IL: InterVarsity, 2007).

4. Old Testament scholars mentioned in this chapter who are members of ETS include Tremper Longman, Daniel Block, J. Daniel Hays, Michael Grisanti, John Walton, Gordon Johnston, Todd Beale, Bruce Waltke, Ronald Youngblood, Herbert Wolf, Peter Enns, John Oswalt, Jeffrey Niehaus, Walt Kaiser, and G. K. Beale, who is technically a New Testament scholar, but who does frequently engage with Old Testament issues.

5. Obviously, there are aspects of American evangelicalism that predate the gundamentalist movement and that can be traced back to the early history of the United States. For a history of evangelicalism, see the five-volume series entitled *A History of Evangelicalism: People, Movements and Ideas in the English-Speaking World* (Downers Grove, IL: InterVarsity). This series includes Mark Noll, *The Rise of Evangelicalism* (2003); John R. Wolffe, *The Expansion of Evangelicalism* (2007); David W. Bebbington, *The Dominance of Evangelicalism* (2005); Geoff Treloar, *The Disruption of Evangelicalism* (projected); and Brian Stanley, *The Global Diffusion of Evangelicalism* (projected). For

complex, but one of the critical factors dividing evangelicalism from fundamentalism was how they viewed and employed critical scholarship. Fundamentalism, growing out of the conservative-modernist controversies and believing that the veracity of the Bible itself was at stake, tended to have defensive, anti-intellectual characteristics, and thus was generally hostile toward critical scholarship. Mainstream evangelicalism, while agreeing with the fundamentalist on many aspects of the faith, nonetheless aspired for a higher level of intellectual inquiry and scholarship. Thus they endeavored to eclectically engage with critical scholarship. Nonetheless, a high view of Scripture and its truthfulness, characteristic of fundamentalism, was likewise carried over into evangelicalism. In the United States the term most commonly used for this high view of Scripture was "inerrancy."[6]

Mainstream evangelicalism has attempted to combine faith in the basic "fundamentals" of orthodox Christianity with intellectual, well-educated scholarly inquiry. The emphasis on scholarship within evangelicalism (especially within the fields of New Testament, Old Testament, and theology) is something that appears to have picked up steam in the latter years of the twentieth century and into the twenty-first. This is an ongoing process and something of a balancing act. Integrating faith with critically oriented academic scholarship will always have its tensions. Indeed, New Testament scholar I. Howard Marshall comments:

> Here two things are happening. The first is that, after a lengthy period of comparative (but never total) neglect of scholarship, many, but not all, evangelicals have returned to a recognition of the need for a believing criticism which employs all possible means that can shed light on the text. The second is that, we have identified the ways in which various new approaches and tools have been recognized to be both legitimate and essential in understanding the text more adequately. A continuing task must be

---

a standard discussion on the relationship between fundamentalism and evangelicalism, see George Marsden, *Understanding Fundamentalism and Evangelicalism* (Grand Rapids: Eerdmans, 1991); and *Reforming Fundamentalism: Fuller Seminary and the New Evangelicalism* (Grand Rapids: Eerdmans, 1995).

6. Mark Noll, *Between Faith and Criticism: Evangelicals, Scholarship and the Bible in America*, 2nd ed. (Vancouver: Regent College, 2004). For more discussion, see Kenneth Collins, *The Evangelical Moment: The Promise of an American Religion* (Grand Rapids: Baker, 2005) 41–47; and A. T. B. McGowan, *Divine Authenticity of Scripture*, 84–122.

the evaluation of such approaches to ensure that we do not lapse unawares into unbelieving criticism.[7]

Evangelical Old Testament scholarship has continued to develop and mature. Driven primarily by the desire to improve their understanding and interpretation of the biblical text, significant numbers of evangelical Old Testament scholars have acquired top academic degrees and have set about engaging with the methodologies and the conclusions of historical-critical study. Yet generally they have carried out this engagement from within the faith presuppositions of evangelicalism.[8]

7. I. Howard Marshall, "Evangelicals and Biblical Interpretation," in *The Futures of Evangelicalism: Issues and Proposals*, ed. Craig Bartholomew, Robin Parry, and Andrew West (Grand Rapids: Kregel, 2003) 120. Of course differences will emerge over what constitutes "believing criticism" and what constitutes "unbelieving criticism." Kenton Sparks, for example, in his recent book *God's Word in Human Words: An Evangelical Appropriation of Critical Biblical Scholarship* (Grand Rapids: Baker, 2008), proposes that evangelicals embrace practically *all* of the conclusions of critical scholarship, including a denial of the historicity of most of the Old Testament. The things in the Bible that should be believed, Sparks adds, are only those events that are affirmed by the early church creeds. Since he advocates belief in the basics of the faith as expressed in the creeds, Sparks calls his approach "believing criticism." Yet Sparks appears to have moved well beyond any traditional evangelical approach to Scripture and to faith, scoffing at both inerrancy and infallibility. His approach calls for the denial of most of the Old Testament, including the exodus event (p. 319). For many scholars within evangelicalism, Sparks has moved well outside of the movement, precisely into what could be called "unbelieving criticism."

8. Sparks, *God's Word*, seems oblivious to this development. In fact, throughout his book he argues that those non-evangelical critical scholars developing the conclusions of historical criticism are really smart people ("experts") and should be listened to (58, 70, 146). Sparks then declares that evangelical scholars, on the other hand, are "poorly trained in the critical issues of biblical scholarship" (168). He goes on to explain that "conservative evangelicals have always had difficulty securing advanced university degrees in biblical studies, particularly in the Old Testament." This is a rather curious and ill-informed statement, especially in light of the education of those particular evangelical Old Testament scholars that Sparks critiques harshly throughout that particular chapter: Tremper Longman (PhD, Yale), Raymond Dillard (PhD, Dropsie University), Richard Schultz (PhD, Yale), V. Phillips Long (PhD, Cambridge), Ian Provan (PhD, Cambridge), and James Hoffmeier (PhD, University of Toronto). Are these the ones that are "poorly trained in the critical issues of biblical scholarship" and who have "had difficulty securing advanced university degrees in biblical studies"? Ironically, G. K. Beale comes at this issue from the other end of the spectrum, pointing to this phenomenon (evangelicals receiving OT PhDs at top-ranked "critical" institutions) as leading to an "erosion" of the evangelical doctrine of inerrancy. Beale writes: "A second factor leading to reassessment of the traditional evangelical view of the Bible's inspiration is that over the last twenty-five years there have been an increasing number of conservative students graduating with doctorates in biblical studies and theology from non-evangelical

One of the issues to be explored in this chapter is the extent to which this increase in scholarly intensity and engagement with critical schools of thought has impacted the doctrine of inerrancy as articulated by mainstream evangelical Old Testament scholarship, and in what manner these scholars are reformulating this doctrine.

LITERARY DEVELOPMENT, TEXT CRITICISM AND THE "ORIGINAL AUTOGRAPHS"

Central to the evangelical understanding of inerrancy is the concept that the Scriptures are inerrant in the original autographs. That is, when each particular book of the Bible was written, that first document was inerrant. Inerrancy does not cover the transmission (later copying) of the text or the translation of the text, steps where errors can (and obviously do) find their way into the text.[9] This process is fairly straightforward

institutions. A significant percentage of these graduates have assimilated to one degree or another non-evangelical perspectives, especially with regard to higher-critical views of the authorship, dating, and historical claims of the Bible, which have contributed to their discomfort with the traditional evangelical perspective of the Bible. On the other hand, these same scholars, while significantly qualifying their former view of inerrancy, have not left their basic position about the truth of the gospel and the Bible's basic authority. Thus they continue to want to consider themselves 'evangelical' but at the same time reformers of an antiquated evangelicalism, represented, for example, by the Chicago Statement on Inerrancy" (Beale, *The Erosion of Inerrancy in Evangelicalism: Responding to New Challenges to Biblical Authority* [Wheaton, IL: Crossway, 2008] 20–21).

9. Most evangelical scholars, both in Old Testament studies and in New Testament studies, are simply not troubled by textual variants and the necessity of carrying out textual criticism to determine what was probably the original text (or very close to it). For them it is the concept of the "original autograph" that drives them to practice text criticism; that is, they believe that the closer they can get to the original the more accurate their text is. Lee Martin McDonald, who argues against both inerrancy and infallibility, seems to miss this close connection between the need for text criticism and the belief in inerrancy. Curiously, he argues that the reality of textual variants should convince evangelical scholars to abandon inerrancy. Apparently misunderstanding (or ignoring) the close involvement of many evangelical and inerrantist Old Testament and New Testament scholars in textual criticism, McDonald writes, "Christian scholars who advocate an inerrant biblical text regularly make use of the eclectic Greek or Hebrew texts of the Bible [*sic*, Hebrew texts like BHS or BHK are not eclectic], and ignore the fact that we do not have the original texts and that all translations are based on the only ancient texts that we do have, namely those with many copyists' errors in them. . . . If inerrancy does not extend to the full phase of the history of the transmission and preservation of the Scriptures as well, then the infallibility of the former, the inerrant

if we envision someone like the Apostle Paul sitting down to write (or dictate to a scribe) one of his epistles. When Paul finishes this text (complete with his own editing interaction with the scribe), it is inerrant. So for the New Testament the "original autograph" component of inerrancy is relatively straightforward.

In the Old Testament, however, the concept of "original autograph" is not as clear. Many evangelical Old Testament scholars are underscoring the fact that the issue of original composition and the "original autographs" is much more complicated than is often acknowledged in discussions on inerrancy. In addressing this issue, Michael Grisanti writes, "I seek to show that some commonly used definitions of key terms, especially 'autographa' and 'canonicity,' are defined primarily from a NT perspective and do not give sufficient attention to some of the realities of the OT text."[10] Likewise, Daniel Block states, "The notion of 'autographs,' an expression that theologians apply to 'the first or original copies of the biblical documents,' is not as tidy as many claim."[11]

Non-evangelical critical scholarship throughout the twentieth century argued consistently that many of the Old Testament books reflect numerous stages of literary development and editorial activity rather than an "all at once" composition by one original author. While not accepting the extent of this literary development or many of the implications arising from this development for dating the written materials, nonetheless, in recent years evangelical scholars have recognized that the books of the Old Testament do not specifically claim an "all at once"

---

original manuscripts, seems irrelevant" (McDonald, *Forgotten Scriptures: The Selection and Rejection of Early Religious Writings* [Louisville: Westminster John Knox, 2009] 203, 221). At many evangelical institutions where inerrancy is affirmed (e.g., Dallas Theological Seminary, Wheaton College, Westminster Theological Seminary), the rigorous study of text criticism is a standard part of the curriculum. To evangelical scholars in this context, McDonald's argument seems rather odd.

10. Michael A. Grisanti, "Inspiration, Inerrancy, and the OT Canon: The Place of Textual Updating in an Inerrant View of Scripture," *Journal of the Evangelical Theological Society* 44 (2001) 577.

11. Daniel I. Block, "Recovering the Voice of Moses: the Genesis of Deuteronomy," *JETS* 44 (2001) 405. See also J. Daniel Hays, "Jeremiah, the Septuagint, the Dead Sea Scrolls, and Inerrancy: Just What Exactly Do We Mean by the 'Original Autographs'?" in *Evangelicals and Scripture: Tradition, Authority, and Hermeneutics*, ed. V. Bacote, L. Miguélez, and D. Okholm (Downers Grove, IL: InterVarsity, 2004) 133, who writes, ". . . the systematic theologians who write on inerrancy and inspiration seem almost oblivious to the particularites of the Old Testament textual problem."

composition by one specific author. Thus, some of them are suggesting that literary development (at least to some limited degree) and editorial activity does not necessarily conflict with inspiration and inerrancy. This is true particularly in the Old Testament prophetic books. Mark Boda, for example, writes, "It is consistent with an evangelical view of Scripture that close associates of the prophets took the words revealed to the prophets by God and shaped them into a powerful message for later generations to read and profit from."[12] The book of Jeremiah in particular poses a special challenge because the Septuagint version of Jeremiah reflects an edition of the text that is around 2,700 words shorter than the edition reflected in the Masoretic Text. Evangelical scholars recognize that this "two-edition" situation probably reflects some significant literary development. Thus Tremper Longman writes:

> While the shorter text could conceivably represent an abridgement of the longer text, it is more likely that the longer version represents the later stage. As remarked above, the end of Jeremiah indicates that there were multiple editions of the book during the lifetime of the prophet and we have speculated that there may well have been post-Jeremiah editions as well.[13]

Thus the situation in Jeremiah poses an interesting problem for evangelical scholars. Is literary development included under the concept of inerrancy? And if so, in the book of Jeremiah, when does literary development (inspired and inerrant) stop and textual transmission (with human copyist errors) begin? There are at least three plausible possibilities.[14] There

---

12. Mark Boda, *Haggai, Zechariah*, NIV Application Commentary (Grand Rapids: Zondervan, 2004) 37. Likewise, see the discussion of literary development in the OT Prophets by J. Daniel Hays, *The Message of the Prophets: A Survey of the Prophetic and Apocalyptic Books of the Old Testament* (Grand Rapids: Zondervan, 2010) 27–30.

13. Tremper Longman III, *Jeremiah, Lamentations*, New International Biblical Commentary (Peabody, MA: Hendrickson, 2008) 9.

14. The three basic possibilities are: 1) the shorter version (as represented in the Septuagint and perhaps one of the Dead Sea Scrolls) was the original inerrant text and the longer version (as in the Masoretic Text) reflects "uninspired" textual transmission scribal additions; 2) the shorter version reflects an early stage in the inspired literary development process and thus all of the expansions and additions found in the longer Masoretic Text are inspired and therefore inerrant (perhaps the majority view among evangelical scholars); and 3) the two versions were produced separately (one in Egypt and one in Babylonia) and both of them were inspired and inerrant. For a more detailed discussion of this problem, see Hays, "Jeremiah, the Septuagint," 133–49.

is no consensus view among evangelical Old Testament scholars on this issue and the problem is still currently being debated.[15]

Furthermore, the concept of literary development and the challenge of relating it to the original autographs are not limited to the Old Testament Prophets. For example, although maintaining Moses as the primary author, Daniel I. Block nonetheless underscores the evidence for some literary development/editorial activity within the book of Deuteronomy. Block then raises the question: When did the inspiration and inerrancy phase of the development stop and the uninspired and errant phase of textual transmission begin? He writes:

> Is the task of textual criticism to establish the text as it stood at the time the canon was closed, or as it stood when the book of Deuteronomy as a unitary literary work was composed and accepted as normative for Israel's faith, cult, and conduct? On the other hand, even if autographs are defined as "the first or original copies of the Biblical documents," what do we mean by "Biblical documents"? Does the expression refer to the individual speeches of Moses transcribed on separate parchment scrolls by Moses' own hand and recognized immediately to be canonical? Or the collection of the three speeches on one scroll? Or the edited version of the book of Deuteronomy, complete with its narratorial stitching? Or the grammatically updated version of the book? Or the Pentateuch as we have it, with Deuteronomy as the last book?[16]

It should be noted that these evangelical scholars working with literary development in the Old Testament are not abandoning inerrancy. But neither are they falling back on older, simplistic understandings of inerrancy that often ignore the Old Testament data. Rather, they are exhorting their evangelical colleagues to rethink how the concepts of inspiration, inerrancy, and original autograph apply in those situations where literary/editorial development occurred. Thus within the field of evangelical Old Testament scholarship there is an ongoing dialogue emerging over how inspiration and inerrancy relates to literary development and

15. Several papers have been presented in recent years at the national ETS conferences attempting to engage with this issue, but coming to varying conclusions. See, for example, Steven Anderson, "The Formation of the Book of Jeremiah: An Argument for One Edition," (2009); Todd S. Beall, "4QJer and the Text of Jeremiah," (2007); and J. Daniel Hays, "Jeremiah, the Septuagint, the Dead Sea Scrolls, and Inerrancy: Just What Exactly Do We Mean by the 'Original Autographs'?" (2000).

16. Block, "Recovering the Voice of Moses," 406.

editorial activity. Michael Grisanti has recently proposed that inspiration and inerrancy be extended to cover editorial activity that occurred after the initial primary text was written and up until the final canonical form was established.[17] Likewise, in the article mentioned above regarding Deuteronomy, Daniel Block states: "In view of these considerations, we affirm that the process of inspiration encompasses Yahweh's original guidance of the thoughts of Moses, Moses' oral communication of the message to the people, Moses' transcription of the message to text, and finally the collation and editing of those texts."[18] No clear final consensus has emerged yet, and indeed, scholars will probably debate this issue more specifically on a book-by-book basis. While this phenomenon is not leading evangelical Old Testament scholars away from inerrancy, it is leading them to refine the traditional, overly simplistic understanding of "original autographs."

THE NATURE OF HISTORY AND HISTORY WRITING IN THE OLD TESTAMENT

Since the Enlightenment many critical scholars in the Western world have attempted to study the Old Testament with a "scientific" approach, primarily using the tools of modern "social science" historiography. This approach involved removing any presuppositions by which the Bible is viewed as revelation from God and, as a corollary, any presuppositions about the inherent truthfulness of the text. Thus many non-evangelical critical scholars will not accept biblical events as historical unless the events are corroborated by other historical evidence (archaeological, non-Israelite literature, etc.). This approach has led many of these critical scholars to express skepticism about the historicity of the Old Testament. For these scholars, very few of the events described

---

17. Grisanti, "Inspiration, Inerrancy," 577–98. For support, Grisanti cites several scholars who make statements affirming some manner of inspired editorial activity, including Bruce K. Waltke, "Historical Grammatical Problems," in *Hermeneutics, Inerrancy, and the Bible*, ed. Earl Radmacher and Robert Preus (Grand Rapids: Zondervan, 1984) 78; Ronald Youngblood, *The Book of Genesis: An Introductory Commentary*, 2nd ed. (Grand Rapids: Baker, 1991) 241; Herbert Wolf, *An Introduction to the Old Testament Pentateuch* (Chicago: Moody, 1991) 60; and Duane Garrett, *Rethinking Genesis: The Sources and Authorship of the First Book of the Pentateuch* (Grand Rapids: Baker, 1991) 85–86.

18. Block, "Recovering the Voice of Moses," 405.

in the Bible that occurred prior to the ninth century BCE are historical (the life of Abraham, the life of Moses, the exodus, the conquest
of the promised land, the Davidic kingdom, etc). Likewise, as these
scholars apply their historical-critical approach to the Bible they often
note inconsistencies and discrepancies that they perceive in the text.
As evangelical Old Testament scholars engage with this scholarship,
how are they responding and what impact does this response have on
their doctrine of inerrancy?

Kenton L. Sparks (who rejects both inerrancy and infallibility), in
*God's Word in Human Words: An Evangelical Appropriation of Critical
Biblical Scholarship*, exhorts evangelical Old Testament scholars to
abandon their presuppositions (and extensive arguments) regarding the
veracity of the Old Testament and to embrace all of the conclusions of
mainstream critical scholarship (i.e., deny the historicity of Abraham,
the exodus, etc.).[19] Sparks's proposal is quite radical and not likely to be
well received by the majority of evangelical scholars. Although the term
"evangelical" can be a slippery term and can mean different things to
different people, to most "ETS-style" evangelical scholars, Sparks's proposal appears to be well outside of evangelicalism. While evangelicalism
certainly reflects a spectrum of views on many issues of biblical scholarship, many evangelical Old Testament scholars would consider Sparks's
proposal as off the spectrum. Thus his proposal is probably not an option that mainstream evangelical Old Testament scholarship is likely to
consider seriously.

In *Inspiration and Incarnation: Evangelicals and the Problem of the
Old Testament*, Peter Enns offers another approach to handling some of
the tensions he sees regarding historicity in the Old Testament. Enns describes his approach as "incarnational" and views some of the tensions
as indications of God's accommodation to human limitations. Unlike
Sparks's proposal, Enns's approach appears to be within the evangelical
umbrella, albeit perhaps left of center. Enns continues to advocate the inerrancy of Scripture, but he argues that the concept of inerrancy must be

---

19. Sparks argues that the "essential" events in the Bible are true (i.e., the resurrection of Jesus), and that one should rely on the early church creeds to determine which
events in the Bible should be accepted by faith. For Sparks, the exodus (and most of the
rest of the OT) does not rank as one of the "essential" events. It is unlikely that Sparks
will convince many within the field of evangelical Old Testament studies to drop the
historicity of the exodus. See Sparks, *God's Word*, 281–85, 319–22.

driven by and refined by what is actually in the text itself and not rigidly regulated by past evangelical traditions on how to understand it.[20]

At the heart of the "historicity" issue is the nature of history writing in the Old Testament. Should the history recorded in the Old Testament be evaluated as accurate or inaccurate history based on modern perceptions of history writing? Or should the conventions of history writing in the Old Testament be evaluated on its own terms? Evangelical Old Testament scholarship has, by and large, opted for the second option, and something near to a consensus is emerging, represented by works such as *A Biblical History of Israel* by Iain Provan, V. Philips Long, and Tremper Longman; *The Art of Biblical History* by V. Philips Long; *Exploring the Old Testament: A Guide to the Historical Books* by Philip E. Satterthwaite and J. Gordon McConville; and "An Evangelical Approach to Old Testament Narrative Criticism" by J. Daniel Hays.[21] All of these scholars stress that the Old Testament historical books must be viewed as "theological narrative." Provan, Long, and Longman use the term "narrative historiography" to describe the genre.[22] They write: "The key point is that *biblical accounts must be appreciated first as narratives before they can be used as historical sources . . .*"[23] Drawing on the work of Jewish scholar Meir Sternberg, Hays argues that the authors of the Old Testament histories balanced three primary concerns: aesthetics (the artistic way the story was crafted), theology (the point of the story intended by the divine author), and historicity (they proclaimed

20. In response to a review article for the sake of clarification, Enns writes: "Inerrancy, in other words, must be understood in ways that are respectful and conversant with the parameters set by Scripture's own witness understood in its varying historical contexts. Otherwise, we run the risk of basing our doctrine of inerrancy on a foundation outside of Scripture, and then expecting Scripture to behave in ways that we presume it should (in this case, comporting with familiar notions of rationality), rather than trying to define such categories as best we can from within Scripture" (Enns, "Response to G. K. Beale's Review Article of *Inspiration and Incarnation*," *JETS* 49 [2006] 321).

21. Iain Provan, V. Philips Long, and Tremper Longman, *A Biblical History of Israel* (Louisville: Westminster John Knox, 2003) 75–97; V. Philips Long, *The Art of Biblical History* (Grand Rapids: Zondervan, 1994); Philip E. Satterthwaite and J. Gordon McConville, *Exploring the Old Testament: A Guide to the Historical Books* (Downers Grove, IL: InterVarsity, 2007) 9–25; and J. Daniel Hays, "An Evangelical Approach to Old Testament Narrative Criticism," *Bibliotheca Sacra* 166 (2009) 3–18.

22. Provan, Long, Longman, *Biblical History*, 88–96.

23. Provan, Long, Longman, *Biblical History*, 93.

these events as true occurrences).[24] It is the recognition of the artistic elements (aesthetics) in the Old Testament historical narratives that is relatively new and is leading to a slight revision in how evangelical Old Testament scholars view the problems of Old Testament history. With this approach, for example, many supposed "discrepancies" between 1–2 Kings and 1–2 Chronicles are explained by the different narrative and theological purposes of the two histories,[25] and when analyzed properly within the conventions of the genre being used, these supposed "discrepancies" do not constitute "errors."

THE RELATIONSHIP BETWEEN THE OLD TESTAMENT AND THE LITERATURE OF THE ANCIENT NEAR EAST

Over the past 150 years a tremendous wealth of literature from ancient Egypt and Mesopotamia has been discovered, translated, and studied, some of it predating the Old Testament. Throughout this period Old Testament scholars have been in constant discussion and debate over the relationship between this ancient literature and the Old Testament.[26] Over the last thirty to forty years evangelical Old Testament scholars have become more and more involved in using comparative studies of this literature to shed light on biblical texts. Jeffrey Niehaus writes, "No study of biblical material can now be complete without some understanding of its ancient background. Comparative studies have become virtually mandatory for a proper understanding of the Old Testament."[27] Also, in recent years there has been a strong concerted effort by evangelical scholars and evangelical publishers to make the results of these

24. Meir Sternberg, *The Poetics of Biblical Narrative: Ideological Literature and the Drama of Reading* (Bloomington: Indiana University Press, 1985) 41–48; Hays, "Narrative Criticism," 7–17.

25. Provan, Long, Longman, *Biblical History*, 93–96.

26. See brief discussions of this engagement from an evangelical perspective in John H. Walton, *Ancient Near Eastern Thought and the Old Testament* (Grand Rapids: Baker, 2006) 15–18, 29–40; Jeffrey J. Niehaus, *Ancient Near Eastern Themes in Biblical Theology* (Grand Rapids: Kregel, 2008) 13–33; and John N. Oswalt, *The Bible among the Myths: Unique Revelation or Just Ancient Literature?* (Grand Rapids: Zondervan, 2009) 11–31.

27. Niehaus, *Ancient Near Eastern Themes*, 13–14.

comparative studies accessible to audiences at the pastoral—and even popular—level.[28]

One of the most basic issues emerging from the comparative study of the Old Testament and the literature of the ancient Near East regards the many parallels and similarities between the culture, stories, cultic practices, and religious thinking of the ancient Israelites and that of their neighbors throughout the ancient Near East. Many critical scholars outside of evangelicalism have stressed the similarities and argued that Israelite religion has nothing particularly unique about it. They conclude that the ideas and religious faith reflected in the Old Testament merely evolved out of the religious milieu of the region. Thus they would not see any type of "divine revelation" in the religion of the Old Testament.[29] Evangelical Old Testament scholars reject this notion. They agree that ancient Israel shared a common cultural heritage with many of her neighbors. They acknowledge that obviously many cultural, including some religious, similarities exist. Likewise they agree that acknowledging these similarities and studying them are critical to understanding the biblical text. On the other hand, many evangelical scholars argue, the differences between the religion of Israel (as described in the Old Testament) and that of her neighbors are huge and highly significant, testifying to the divine revelation.[30]

---

28. For example, in addition to the works mentioned above by Niehaus, Walton, and Oswalt, see John H. Walton, Victor H. Matthews, and Mark W. Chavalas, *The IVP Bible Background Commentary: Old Testament* (Downers Grove, IL: InterVarsity, 2000); Daniel I. Block, *The Gods of the Nations: Studies in Ancient Near Eastern National Theology*, 2nd ed. (Grand Rapids: Baker, 2000); John H. Walton, *Ancient Israelite Literature in Its Cultural Context: A Survey of Parallels between Biblical and Ancient Near Eastern Texts* (Grand Rapids: Zondervan, 1989); *Genesis*, NIV Application Commentary (Grand Rapids: Zondervan, 2001); and *The Lost World of Genesis One: Ancient Cosmology and the Origins Debate* (Downers Grove, IL: InterVarsity, 2009); Tremper Longman III, *How To Read Genesis* (Downers Grove, IL: InterVarsity, 2005); John H. Walton, ed., *Zondervan Illustrated Bible Backgrounds Commentary*, 5 vols. (Grand Rapids: Zondervan, 2009); and Walter C. Kaiser and Duane Garrett, *Archaeological Study Bible: An Illustrated Walk through Biblical History and Culture.* (Grand Rapids: Zondervan, 2006).

29. For a recent example, see Mark Smith, *The Origins of Biblical Monotheism: Israel's Polytheistic Background and the Ugaritic Texts* (New York: Oxford University Press, 2001).

30. Block, *Gods of the Nations*, 149–53; Oswalt, *Bible among the Myths*, 185–94; Walton, *Ancient Near Eastern Thought*, 331–34; and Beale, *Erosion of Inerrancy*, 215–18.

More relevant to the issue of inerrancy is the question of how much God "accommodated" the commonly held ancient Near Eastern understanding of the world and religion into his revelation to the Israelites. Enns, for example, argues that God *intentionally* accommodated his message to the ancient Israelites by speaking in terms (and in "realities") that they could comprehend, rather than in terms and realities that modern era people expect. Enns does not see this as an "error" or "mistake" but an intentional decision by God: "This is surely what it means for God to reveal himself to people—he accommodates, condescends, meets them where they are."[31]

This issue is particularly pertinent to how one approaches Genesis 1, and it is at this point that contemporary evangelical Old Testament scholars (many of whom are inerrantists) are plowing some new ground and will probably change the way evangelicals understand Genesis 1. Enns, as mentioned above, proposes that God intentionally accommodated his revelation in Genesis 1 to the cosmological understanding that Israel had at that time period. Other scholars compare Genesis 1 with non-Israelite creation accounts in the ancient Near East and from that context they underscore the polemical nature of the biblical account. Gordon Johnston, for example, suggests that Genesis 1 is a polemic specifically against Egyptian creation myths:

> Genesis 1 appears to be a literary polemic designed to refute ancient Near Eastern creation mythology in general and ancient Egyptian creation mythology in particular. Although several elements in this passage surely reflect a general Semitic background, the majority of parallel elements are cast against the Egyptian mythologies. This suggests that Genesis 1 was originally composed, not as a scientific treatise, but as a theological polemic against the ancient Egyptian models of creation which competed against Yahwism for the loyalty of the ancient Israelites.[32]

In his recent book *The Lost World of Genesis One*, John H. Walton acknowledges the concept of divine accommodation in Genesis 1

---

31. Enns, *Inspiration and Incarnation*, 56.

32. Gordon H. Johnston, "Genesis 1 and Ancient Egyptian Creation Myths," *Bibliotheca Sacra* 165 (2008) 194. Johnston presented much of this material to the ETS at the national meeting in 2006 in a paper entitled, "Genesis 1—2:3 in the Light of Ancient Egyptian Creation Myths: Context and Contextualization of Ancient Israelite Cosmogony."

(similar to Enns's proposition),[33] but he argues that Genesis 1 is describing the creation of the *function* of the cosmos and not the *material* nature (as most modern readers assume). Walton proposes that Genesis 1 is not describing the creation of the material matter of the universe, but rather describing the inauguration of the cosmos as the functioning temple in which God resides and rules. Walton notes that this understanding helps to defuse some of the tension between those who have an inerrant view of Genesis 1 and those who embrace the theory of evolution, for he argues that his view does not contradict the modern theory of evolution, and yet it also reflects the intended meaning of the biblical author. Walton sees this view as consistent with inerrancy.[34] G. K. Beale, a strong defender of inerrancy, espouses a similar view and argues that viewing the world as the "cosmic temple" of God is a consistent and important feature of biblical theology, occurring throughout the Old Testament and climaxing in the New Testament book of Revelation.[35] Similar to Walton, Beale maintains that such a view does not contradict inerrancy but rather serves to answer many of the alleged problems.[36]

THE NATURE OF EVANGELICAL OLD TESTAMENT HERMENEUTICS, ESPECIALLY IN REGARD TO "PROPOSITIONAL TRUTH" APPROACHES

One of the commonalities running throughout evangelical Old Testament scholarship is the commitment to sound exegesis and a her-

33. Walton, *Lost World*, 16, writes, "So what are the cultural ideas behind Genesis 1? Our first proposition is that Genesis 1 is ancient cosmology. That is, it does not attempt to describe cosmology in modern terms or address modern questions. The Israelites received no revelation to update or modify their 'scientific' understanding of the cosmos. They did not know that stars were suns; they did not know that the earth was spherical and moving through space; they did not know that the sun was much further away than the moon, or even further than the birds flying in the air. They believed that the sky was material (not vaporous), solid enough to support the residence of deity as well as to hold back waters. In these ways, and many others, they thought about the cosmos in much that same way that anyone in the ancient world thought, and not at all like anyone thinks today. And God did not think it important to revise their thinking."

34. Walton, *Lost World*, 162–73.

35. G. K. Beale, *The Temple and the Church's Mission: A Biblical Theology of the Dwelling Place of God*, ed. D. A. Carson New Studies in Biblical Theology 17 (Downers Grove, IL: InterVarsity, 2004).

36. Beale, *Erosion of Inerrancy*, 213–18.

meneutic that builds upon solid exegesis. By their nature and training, evangelical Old Testament scholars tend to be "biblical theologians" rather than "systematic theologians." Thus they tend to always start with text and then move from their exegesis to doctrine. They generally react negatively toward methods that seem to start with doctrine and then move into texts to see how such texts support that doctrine (popularly called prooftexting).

Likewise, mainstream evangelical Old Testament scholars regularly stress that the text must speak for itself, even regarding the issue of inerrancy. Block states this clearly:

> When we interpret the Scriptures as they are intended to be understood, we will find them to be completely reliable preservers of truth. But this high view of the Scriptures means that we must let them say what they want to say. . . . Whether we are considering the oral event or the written record, we must abandon tight mechanical theories about the process of inspiration.[37]

Likewise, Grisanti writes, "Theological definitions should draw on biblical evidence rather than stifle it."[38] Thus many evangelical Old Testament scholars would object to methods that force Scripture into modern genre categories and then incorporate this mistaken genre classification into the doctrine of inerrancy. For example, in some areas of evangelicalism, the belief in inerrancy is wedded to the concept that "the Bible expresses God's truth in propositional statements" (Article 6 of The Chicago Statement on Biblical Hermeneutics).[39] In general, evangelical Old Testament scholars who hold to inerrancy reject this connection, recognizing that God's truth in the Old Testament is expressed through many different genres and not always through propositional statements.[40]

---

37. Block, "Recovering the Voice of Moses," 403–4.

38. Grisanti, "Inspiration, Inerrancy," 595.

39. Earl D. Radmacher and Robert D. Prues, ed., *Hermeneutics, Inerrancy, and the Bible: Papers from ICBI Summit II* (Grand Rapids: Zondervan, 1984) 882–87.

40. Many theologians also note that the Bible speaks in numerous ways other than just propositional truth statements. David S. Dockery and David P. Nelson, for example, write: "Nevertheless, the term *inerrancy* may not go far enough. The Bible, like other forms of human communication, is certainly more that true assertions. Communication involves emotions, aesthetic and affective abilities, and the will, in addition to propositional statements. Certainly praise is more than a proposition" (Dockery and Nelson, "Special Revelation," in *A Theology for the Church*, ed. Daniel L. Akin [Nashville: Broadman & Holman, 2007] 160).

•

Many evangelical Old Testament scholars who embrace inerrancy and the Chicago Statement on Biblical *Inerrancy* would nonetheless agree with much of Iain Provan's incisive critique of The Chicago Statement on Biblical *Hermeneutics*, particularly in regard to its view of the truth of the Bible as completely composed of "propositional truth statements."[41]

Likewise, most evangelical Old Testament scholars would reject the idea that inerrancy implies certain *necessary* interpretive conclusions in certain texts. For example, as discussed above, many evangelical Old Testament scholars would reject the idea that if one believes in inerrancy then he/she *must* believe that Genesis 1 describes a literal account of a seven-day creation of the physical world. In contrast, most contemporary evangelical Old Testament scholars would assert that inerrancy leads one to search for the interpretive meaning that the text claims for itself and not one imposed upon it.

This disagreement over the implications of inerrancy surfaced as an important side issue during the "Openness Controversy" within the Evangelical Theological Society as played out at their national conventions during 2002–2004. Some systematic theologians argued that one could not believe in inerrancy and still maintain that God changes his mind (as inferred in several Old Testament texts). According to this line of thinking, if one believed that God did indeed change his mind, he/she would be violating the doctrinal statement of the ETS regarding inerrancy. Numerous Old Testament scholars in ETS, however, although they did not embrace or defend Openness, nonetheless rejected the idea that inerrancy demanded a certain interpretive conclusion from the Old Testament texts that seemed to describe God as "changing his mind," especially since this interpretive conclusion appeared to be devoid of serious exegesis.[42] So while mainstream ETS-style evangelical Old Testament scholarship remains firmly committed to the doctrine of inerrancy, they are also firmly committed to the theological method that starts with

41. Iain Provan, "'How Can I Understand, Unless Someone Explains It to Me?' (Acts 8:30–31): Evangelicals and Biblical Hermeneutics," *BBR* 17 (2007) 1–36. Note also the caution expressed by Old Testament scholar Robert L. Cate, "The Importance and Problem of Distinguishing between Biblical Authority and Biblical Interpretation," in *The Proceedings of the Conference on Biblical Inerrancy, 1987* (Nashville: Broadman, 1987) 373–409.

42. For example, see the reaction by J. Daniel Hays, "Does Systematics Drive Old Testament Exegesis, or Can God Still Change His Mind?: Questions Regarding Interpretive Method," presented at the 2002 ETS national meeting.

serious exegesis and then moves to doctrine. Thus when some within systematics "over-defines" inerrancy, linking this doctrine to certain presupposed "propositional truth" conclusions that appear to contradict solid evangelical Old Testament exegesis, many Old Testament scholars balk at the definition.

Evangelical Old Testament scholars do believe that the Old Testament contains "propositional truth." Yet they would be quick to point out that such propositional truth statements in the Old Testament might well be six chapters long and embedded in the subtle nuances of a complex narrative. To interpret this propositional truth correctly requires some serious and sound Old Testament exegesis.

IS THERE A MOVEMENT AMONG EVANGELICAL OLD TESTAMENT SCHOLARS TO ABANDON INERRANCY OR TO CHANGE TERMS?

In recent years some scholars and writers have called for an abandonment of the term "inerrancy."[43] Some have predicted that the younger generation of evangelicals will abandon inerrancy in large numbers (or are already in the process of doing so).[44] Kenneth Collins writes:

> Though the authority of the Bible was expressed by means of a doctrine of biblical inerrancy for most of the twentieth century, principally by those evangelicals whose stories lie in historic

43. McGowan urges evangelicals to replace the term "inerrancy" with "infallibility." See McGowan, *Divine Authenticity.* McDonald rejects both inerrancy and infallibility, but he is particularly critical of those who advocate inerrancy. He writes: "In an age when Christians are taught to read critically in university training, they will invariably bring a number of critical questions to Bible studies in their churches and will not be convinced by flimsy arguments about inerrancy that ignore the data of Scripture itself" (McDonald, *Forgotten Scriptures,* 201–21, 204). Sparks consistently throughout his book *God's Word* ridicules evangelical scholars who hold to inerrancy, stating that any truly good scholar would reject the doctrine.

44. Carlos R. Bovell writes: "Nevertheless, many young evangelicals have helplessly watched their views shift from the evangelical inerrantist position to a more nebulous, I-know-that-it-has-*some*-kind-of-authority position that becomes less and less defined and more and more obscure over time." Bovell, however, seems to be as much bothered by the pedagogical methods that some use to teach inerrancy as he is by the doctrine. He does react against the doctrine, even denying it, but one wonders if he is reacting to one particular expression of the doctrine (particularly in some areas of systematics) rather than the doctrine of inerrancy as espoused by mainstream evangelical Old Testament scholarship. See Bovell, *Inerrancy and the Spiritual Formation of Younger Evangelicals* (Eugene, OR: Wipf and Stock, 2007) 151.

fundamentalism, it is unlikely that the majority of twenty-first-century evangelicals will continue in this vein. . . . Evangelical thinking about the authority of Scripture in general and inerrancy in particular is already undergoing significant and most likely lasting change. To illustrate, according to Douglas Jacobsen, a "growing number of evangelicals have rejected the traditional inerrantist position." And James Davison Hunter, ever careful in his scholarship, cites the hard data that substantiates all such assertions: "Nearly 40 percent of all evangelical theologians have abandoned the belief in the inerrancy of Scripture."[45]

Is this true? First of all note that the two sources Collins cites above (Jacobsen and Hunter) were published in 1987, over twenty years ago! These predictions did not seem to come about, either at the popular level or in the evangelical academy. Citing Barna Research, *Christianity Today* recently quipped that 56 percent of *Americans* think the Bible has no errors.[46] Likewise, there is no indication that the evangelical academy is abandoning the doctrine of inerrancy. Membership in the Evangelical Theological Society, where affirmation of belief in inerrancy is a membership requirement, has continued to grow, and total membership currently stands at over 4,500. University and seminary textbooks that affirm inerrancy continue to lead evangelical textbook sales, indicating that the vast majority of evangelical institutions of higher education are continuing to teach inerrancy (or at least are continuing to maintain the doctrine as a viable option).[47] Likewise, within the field of evangelical Old Testament scholarship, there does not appear to be any large-scale drift away from inerrancy as a foundational belief and as defined by the Chicago Statement on Biblical Inerrancy.[48]

45. Kenneth J. Collins, *The Evangelical Moment: The Promise of an American Religion* (Grand Rapids: Baker, 2005) 45. Collins cites Douglas Jacobsen, "The Rise of Evangelical Hermeneutical Pluralism," *Christian Scholar's Review* 16 (1987) 328; and James Davison Hunter, *Evangelicalism: The Coming Generation* (Chicago: University of Chicago Press, 1987) 31.

46. *Christianity Today*, December 2009, 14.

47. For example, in theology note the popularity of Wayne Grudem's *Systematic Theology* (Grand Rapids: Zondervan, 1995), and in hermeneutics note J. Scott Duvall and J. Daniel Hays, *Grasping God's Word*, 2nd ed. (Grand Rapids: Zondervan, 2005).

48. G. K. Beale argues that there is a new movement of sorts represented by Peter Enns's *Inspiration and Incarnation* that is really seeking to substitute the doctrine of infallibility in place of inerrancy. Beale, however, does not provide any firm evidence for a "movement." Evangelical Old Testament scholarship within ETS tends to be somewhat irenic on this issue. Thus the lack of hostility or negativity among evangelical Old

Several writers who have challenged the continuing usage of "inerrancy" as the primary term for the authority of the Scriptures have argued that the lengthy definition required for inerrancy and the need for numerous qualifications for the term render the term ineffective for the church. McGowan writes, ". . . surely there must be a better word we could use?" He then cites I. H. Marshall, who states, "It [inerrancy] needs so much qualification, even by its defenders, that it is in danger of dying the death of a thousand qualifications."[49]

Yet it is precisely because the term "inerrancy" is so firmly embedded within the language of the American evangelical church that many evangelical Old Testament scholars opt for retaining it. One of the defining features of evangelical scholarship in general is that most evangelical scholars see themselves as servants of the church and not independent academicians. That is, they do not see themselves as sitting up in an ivory tower, disconnected to the church, discussing theoretically or esoterically which term might best be used to express the church's belief in the truthfulness of the Bible. Inerrancy is the term that is used by many, many evangelical churches. For the most part, evangelical Old Testament scholars see their responsibility as helping the church to understand the doctrine of Scripture by using the terminology that is currently in use. If these scholars suddenly told the church that they have decided to shift terms (say, from inerrancy to infallibility), many church members would interpret that as indicating that these scholars no longer believe that the Bible is true, thus creating a huge and harmful uproar in the church.[50] The observation that the doctrine of inerrancy takes a lot of effort to define properly (the Chicago Statement is indeed numerous pages in length) simply reflects the reality that the process and product of inspiration is complex and complicated. The Bible is a very complex book produced in a very complicated manner. Most scholars would

---

Testament scholars towards Enns's proposal should not be interpreted as a sign that they are embracing his position. See Beale, *Erosion of Inerrancy*, 220–21.

49. See McGowan, *Divine Authenticity of Scripture*, 106; I. Howard Marshall, *Biblical Inspiration* (London: Hodder & Stoughton, 1982) 72–73. This is also an issue raised by Bovell, *Inerrancy*, 151.

50. McGowan's proposal that evangelicalism use the term "infallibility" instead of "inerrancy" is much more plausible in Britain, where the evangelical church is much more comfortable with the term "infallible," than it is in America, where many churches normally use the term "inerrancy."

agree that in regard to theological definitions, accuracy is more important than simplicity.

So among mainstream evangelical Old Testament scholars there is no significant movement to abandon inerrancy or to substitute the term infallibility. On the other hand, there is an ongoing discussion about how best to fine-tune the definition of inerrancy.

SUMMARY AND CONCLUSIONS

Several conclusions can be drawn from the discussions above.

1. There is no widespread movement away from inerrancy among evangelical Old Testament scholars.

2. On the other hand, many evangelical Old Testament scholars are suggesting that certain "fine-tunings" or clarifications in the doctrine of inerrancy are needed in order to match the claims coming from the text itself. Thus, for example, the concept of inerrancy and original autographs must be defined in such a way that it includes some literary development in the formation of the Old Testament books. Likewise when discussing what constitutes "fact" and "error" in the Old Testament historical books and other narrative texts, the genre and conventions of ancient historiography, including such issues as aesthetics, must be taken into account. This issue becomes particularly acute in Genesis 1, where many evangelical Old Testament scholars are proposing understandings of the nature of the text that are quite different than that derived from a simple reading of the text as if it were a modern day account of how God literally created the world. In addition, but related to this, evangelical Old Testament scholars reject the connection between inerrancy and predisposed hermeneutical conclusions that ignore standard evangelical exegetical processes, as well as the notion that the Bible is to be understood and interpreted as if it were a collection of one-sentence propositional truth statements only.

3. There does not seem to be any widespread call among mainstream evangelical Old Testament scholars for abandoning the Chicago Statement on Biblical Inerrancy. Most evangelical Old Testament scholars within the ETS appear to maintain that the Chicago State-

ment is nuanced enough and contains enough genre-specific qualification that they are still comfortable with it.[51]

4. Evangelical Old Testament scholars will continue to engage vigor-
ously with critical scholarship while attempting to retain evangelical faith presuppositions. They will continue to seek to raise
the bar for evangelical Old Testament scholarship and they will
continue to send sharp students to top-tier graduate schools to
receive top PhDs.

5. The focus of evangelical Old Testament scholarship will continue
to be on exegesis and biblical theology. They will not center their
efforts on defending doctrines such as inerrancy, although it will
continue to be an important foundational doctrine for them.

6. While staying within the Chicago Statement on Biblical Inerrancy
umbrella, mainstream evangelical Old Testament scholarship,
however, is applying inerrancy in ways that are different than the
traditional evangelical understanding of a generation ago, especially that expressed within the discipline of systematic theology.
Thus they are widening the definition of inerrancy.

In a sense one could place the varying understandings of inerrancy
within evangelicalism on a spectrum. On the right can be placed the
views represented by very conservative evangelical theologians such as
Geisler and Nix, while on the left one should probably place the proposal
of Peter Enns.[52] The left end of the spectrum of inerrancy probably overlaps to some degree with the right (i.e., the more conservative) end of the
spectrum for the doctrine of infallibility.[53]

Yet most of inerrantist evangelical Old Testament scholarship, as
represented by the members of the ETS, is probably in the middle. They

51. Of the scholars discussed in this paper, several go out of their way to underscore
that their views are within the scope of the Chicago Statement on Biblical Inerrancy.
For example, see Block, "Recovering the Voice of Moses," 408; and the opening paragraph in Grisanti, "Inspiration, Inerrancy," 577. Likewise note the affirmation of the
Chicago Statement on Biblical Inerrancy in Duvall and Hays, *Grasping God's Word*, 412.

52. Norman Geisler and William Nix, *General Introduction to the Bible* (Chicago:
Moody, 1985); Enns, *Inspiration and Incarnation*.

53. McGowan's definition of infallibility reflects a very high view of Scripture and
its historicity, and probably overlaps with what some scholars are calling inerrancy.
Although Peter Enns continues to affirm inerrancy, Beale, *Erosion of Inerrancy*, 220,
argues that Enns's view is really that of infallibility.

are sympathetic to Enns's argument, while not embracing his conclusions. On the other hand, they are leery and skeptical of the hermeneutical fusion of inerrancy with certain dogmatic presupposed conclusions about the meaning of specific texts as practiced by some evangelical systematic theologians.

7

Theological Diversity in the Old Testament as Burden or Divine Gift?

Problems and Perspectives in the Current Debate[1]

Richard Schultz

"It is possible to view canonical diversity not as a *problem* to be solved but as a *blessing* to be received with thanks. It is precisely its diversity—call it plentitude, an embarrassment of riches, a Pentecostal plurality—that enables Scripture to speak on so many levels to so many different kinds of situations."[2]

TWO CONTRASTING POSITIONS

IF YOU CONSULT ANY lengthy treatment of biblical theology or of the nature of Scripture, sooner or later you will come upon a discussion of unity and diversity. This is hardly surprising. Taking up the task of doing biblical theology is premised upon the assumption that a sufficient amount of unity can be found in the biblical canon to make such

1. Parts of this chapter were originally delivered at the 2006 and 2007 annual meetings of the Evangelical Theological Society.

2. Kevin J. Vanhoozer, *The Drama of Doctrine: A Canonical Linguistic Approach to Christian Theology* (Louisville: Westminster John Knox, 2005) 275; emphasis mine.

a task feasible. Similarly, the conviction that the Bible is in some sense the word of God naturally brings with it the expectation that such divine oversight should result in a demonstrable degree of theological unity, despite the involvement of diverse human authorial agents.

Unfortunately, too often the debate has been conducted in terms of unity *versus* diversity, rather than unity *amidst* or *despite* diversity. The rhetoric employed sometimes gives the impression that diversity is *perversity* or that unity requires *uniformity*. Conservative biblical scholars have understandably been vocal advocates of unity. Daniel Fuller's monograph *The Unity of the Bible* is typical of this approach. Fuller clearly states his goal in the opening sentence of his first chapter, entitled "Evidence for the Bible's Unity": "to discover and express the basic theme that gives coherence to the Bible's teachings."[3] For Fuller, unity and inerrancy are closely related,[4] although he understands "unity" quite broadly in terms of the overall subject or message of Scripture rather than its specific content. After the initial two chapters, he assumes unity for the rest of the book. In his recent monograph, *Recovering the Unity of the Bible*, Walter Kaiser Jr. takes an analogous approach, although he offers a more comprehensive apologetic.[5]

As we shall see in the course of this chapter, however, the subject of the unity of the Bible has been of interest to a wide range of biblical scholars and theologians, for many of them unrelated to issues of divine inspiration and inerrancy. For example, David Noel Freedman seeks to demonstrate the unity of the Bible in terms of "the organization, arrangement, and amalgamation of the different individual literary entities into the whole that we call the Hebrew Bible."[6] Here one can note as well that the secondary literature on this subject reflects a wide range of understandings regarding unity.

Although there has been a considerable number of scholars during the past half-century who were intent on demonstrating or defending the unity of the Bible, the majority have preferred to discuss the relationship

3. Daniel P. Fuller, *The Unity of the Bible: Unfolding God's Plan for Humanity* (Grand Rapids: Zondervan, 1992) 21.

4. Fuller, *Unity of the Bible*, see xviii.

5. Walter C. Kaiser Jr., *Recovering the Unity of the Bible: One Continuous Story, Plan, and Purpose* (Grand Rapids: Zondervan, 2009). Fifteen of his sixteen chapters contain the word "unity."

6. David N. Freedman, *The Unity of the Bible* (Ann Arbor: University of Michigan Press, 1991) vi.

between unity and diversity by acknowledging the presence of both and seeking to affirm the one without downplaying or denying the other. In either case, some degree of unity has normally been assumed. In recent decades, however, the pendulum has swung toward emphasizing diversity. Several significant publications have made the case that the extent of theological diversity in the Bible compels us to rethink how we do biblical theology—and how we construe the nature of Scripture. These publications will be the point of departure for the present chapter. Since the authors in view are all Old Testament specialists, we will focus our discussion on the Old and only occasionally refer to parallel concerns in the New.

Recent Contributions to the Debate: Non-Evangelical and Progressive Evangelical

In his *magnum opus*, Walter Brueggemann discerns both testimony and countertestimony in the Old Testament, which together serve to deconstruct the biblical theologian's efforts to formulate universalizing, generalizing, or totalizing statements. Since "the texts themselves witness to a plurality of testimonies concerning God and Israel's life with God . . . Old Testament theology must live with that pluralistic practice of dispute and compromise, so that the texts cannot be arranged in any single or unilateral pattern."[7] By focusing on "disputatious testimony that refuses closure,"[8] Brueggemann responds to and indirectly affirms the contemporary view that Old Testament theology as traditionally practiced is impossible, noting that "any notion of Old Testament Theology is thought, by definition, to be reductionist, thus riding roughshod over the rich diversity of the text."[9]

Erhard Gerstenberger states the situation more bluntly: "we should first of all recognize the enormous theological diversity of this marvelous collection of testimonies to our God-talk instead of leveling out these invaluable distinctions."[10] Furthermore, we "can no longer afford

---

7. Walter Brueggemann, *Theology of the Old Testament: Testimony, Dispute, Advocacy* (Minneapolis: Fortress, 1997) 710.

8. Brueggemann, *Theology of the OT*, 717.

9. Brueggemann, *Theology of the OT*, 716.

10. Erhard S. Gerstenberger, "Contextual Theologies in the Old Testament?," in *"A Wise and Discerning Mind": Essays in Honor of Burke O. Long*, ed. Saul M. Olyan et al., Brown Judaic Studies 325 (Providence, RI: Brown Judaic Studies, 2000) 131–32.

'eternal' truisms . . . because all alleged absolute truths have proven to be contextually conditioned and far from eternal."[11] As a result, the Old Testament "has no unitary theology, nor can it," but such plurality (and even religious syncretism) should be viewed as "as an extraordinary stroke of good fortune," freeing us from the task of "finding and formulating the 'right' faith in God."[12]

Brueggemann and Gerstenberger are prominent representatives of recent scholarly efforts, reflecting the influence of postmodern epistemologies, to move beyond the dominant modernist, historical-critical assertion of the utter theological diversity to be found in the Old Testament. Rather than lamenting such pluralism within biblical texts, they exploit it and call upon the community of faith to celebrate it. In the process, however, the church's ability to (pro-)claim any authoritative word of God is inevitably lost; Gerstenberger accordingly entitles his synthetic work "theologies in" rather than "theology of" the Old Testament. A divine word is replaced by contextually generated and, therefore, contingent human words.

The progressive evangelical camp provides somewhat different responses to the issue of diversity. In his 2005 book, *Inspiration and Incarnation*, Peter Enns proposes a modified "incarnational" analogy as the best model for understanding the inspiration process with respect to the Old Testament Scriptures. In his opinion, many traditional evangelical conceptions of Scripture emphasize its divine Author at the expense of its human authors, often leading conservative scholars to decide in advance what their Bible *can* or *cannot* say. Thus they sometimes ignore or distort textual features in order to defend the Bible's uniqueness, theological unity, and respect for authorial intention in its intertextual citations.

In his three major chapters, Enns argues against such an approach, citing various parallels between ancient Near Eastern and Old Testament texts and concepts (chapter 2), examples of theological diversity both within and between the major sections of the Old Testament canon (chapter 3), and appropriations of Old Testament texts by "inspired" New Testament authors whose interpretive methods would puzzle a present-day hermeneutics professor (chapter 4). Such textual evidence

---

11. Gerstenberger, "Contextual Theologies," 133.

12. Erhard S. Gerstenberger, *Theologies in the Old Testament*, trans. John Bowden (Minneapolis: Fortress, 2002) 1–2.

compels us, according to Enns, to freely acknowledge the degree of "divine accommodation" involved when the infinite God communicates with finite human beings. As a result, the Old Testament Scriptures are less unique and less unified, and perhaps even less coherent, than many conservative evangelicals assume a divinely inspired Bible should be.

Enns begins chapter 3 by discussing "The Problem of Theological Diversity in the Old Testament," contrasting Jewish approaches to "biblical tensions and ambiguities" with modern evangelical approaches. According to him, the former (which he clearly prefers) emphasize creative conversations, while the latter exhibit emotional stress and often strained solutions. By the term "diversity," Enns is referring to the types of phenomena that can lead critical scholars to conclude that "the Old Testament is full of contradictions and, hence, a quaint record of conflicting human opinions."[13] His examples include diversity in the Wisdom literature, Chronicles, and the Law, and with regard to the presentation of God (e.g., as One or one among many, as changing his mind or unchanging).

Enns rejects what he considers to be the shared assumption of critical and evangelical scholars—that "God's word and diversity at the level of factual and theological message are incompatible," leading the former to deny the divine origin of Scripture and the latter to deny (i.e., explain away) the existence of such diversity.[14] Enns's stated goal is to challenge the approaches and conclusions of both groups of scholars, but it is clear that his primary concern is ending what amounts to "intellectual dishonesty" on the part of conservative evangelicals by convincing them that the diversity within the Old Testament is substantial and undeniable but by no means incompatible with divine authorship. Instead of laboring to achieve forced harmonizations of biblical content, they should give more consideration to the question, "Why does God's word look the way it does?"[15]—what Enns refers to as the "messiness of the Old Testament," which is necessary in order for God to reveal himself in "the rough-and-tumble drama of human history."[16]

---

13. Peter Enns, *Inspiration and Incarnation: Evangelicals and the Problem of the Old Testament* (Grand Rapids: Baker, 2005) 73.

14. Enns, *Inspiration and Incarnation*, 73.

15. Enns, *Inspiration and Incarnation*, 107.

16. Enns, *Inspiration and Incarnation*, 110.

Although Kenton Sparks repeats approvingly a number of Enns's points in his 2008 monograph, *God's Word in Human Words: An Evangelical Appropriation of Critical Biblical Scholarship*, his primary focus is on the "assured results" of historical-critical scholarship, which he asserts that all scholars—evangelicals included—must affirm. These include numerous examples of contradictory factual and theological claims in the Old Testament: the conditional or unconditional nature of the Davidic covenant, legal diversity within the Pentateuch, and the differences between the primary history of the monarchy in Samuel-Kings and the Chronicles account.[17] He deems scholarly efforts to harmonize differences as "speculative" and even "misleading and illegitimate."[18]

Sparks, like Enns, speaks frequently of "divine accommodation" as a foundational explanation for the phenomena of Scripture. The "contradictions" in Chronicles are not really contradictions at all since "it was never the Chronicler's purpose to present history as it actually transpired," offering rather "a kind of realized eschatology." It therefore uses "so-called fictions" to express "profound theological truths." Since Chronicles makes no pretense of giving an accurate history, it is innocent of the charge of containing "errors."[19] Rather than seeking to demonstrate how divergent theological perspectives are compatible, we should ponder how the Bible speaks "as the authoritative voice of God if it includes the diverse and sometimes contradictory perspectives of its human authors."[20] That entails acknowledging, however, that, "[a]t face value, Scripture does not seem to furnish us with one divine theology; it gives us numerous theologies."[21]

What Is at Stake?

As this concluding quotation from Sparks indicates, the issue we are discussing is not simply academic—something that scholars with time on their hands enjoying debating. Rather, at stake is the question of whether the theological diversity in Scripture is so extensive and fundamental that

17. Kenton L. Sparks, *God's Word in Human Words: An Evangelical Appropriation of Critical Biblical Scholarship* (Grand Rapids: Baker, 2008). Compare Sparks's ch. 3 and Enns's ch. 3.

18. Sparks, *God's Word*, 159–64.

19. Sparks, *God's Word*, 221–22.

20. Sparks, *God's Word*, 227.

21. Sparks, *God's Word*, 121; emphasis original.

we should abandon the task of doing synthetic biblical theology. Since biblical theology, in turn, provides the building blocks for constructive systematic theology, the legitimacy of this enterprise may be questioned as well. And since there is an integral relationship between biblical theology and biblical ethics, affirming "numerous theologies" in the Bible (rather than a unified, normative theology of the Bible) leads naturally to highlighting conflicting ethical stances advocated in the Bible, some of them apparently sub-Christian. This can lead then to questioning the usefulness of the Bible (and certainly the Old Testament) in doing Christian ethics. Furthermore, both Enns and Sparks insist that honestly acknowledging the theological (and other types of) diversity in the Old Testament must lead us to modify our doctrine of Scripture—for Sparks, this involves a radical redefinition of "inerrancy" to express God's inerrant utilization of fully errant human writings.

Thus, there are (at least) two contrasting and broadly expressed assessments of theological diversity within the Old Testament (and New Testament) that one can find in the scholarly literature. One approach downplays or denies diversity and highlights unity, sometimes as a result of a prior commitment to the divine origin of Scripture. The other downplays or denies unity and highlights diversity, usually as a necessary result of the human origin of Scripture. The goal of this chapter is to explore options for fully embracing the diversity of Scripture as posing no real threat to a high view of Scripture or to the identification of significant aspects of unity that go beyond the bland assertion that its unity is to be found in Christ.[22] Furthermore, we will seek to demonstrate that such diversity, in reflecting the diverse authors and situations that produced these texts, promotes the application of the Scriptures to a diversity of contemporary circumstances.

DEFINITIONS AND CATEGORIES

First we must clarify what we mean by the terms "unity" and "diversity," for these are certainly used in very diverse ways!

---

22. Enns, *Inspiration and Incarnation*, 110. He praises this as "more subtle" and "deeper."

Diversity or Contradiction?

One of the common views is that "diversity" is basically synonymous with (or a euphemistic substitute for) "discrepancy" or "contradiction." Gerhard von Rad concludes on the basis of his tradition-historical analyses that "the Old Testament contains not merely one, but quite a number of theologies which are widely divergent both in structure and method of argument,"[23] claiming that "[e]xamples of extreme contradictions in the formation of the tradition can be multiplied at will."[24] If this involves historical traditions about Israel's past—and one possesses reliable criteria for determining the accuracy of such traditions—such contradictions could involve error.

With regard to theological statements, Enns is careful to point out that "diversity in no way implies chaos or error."[25] When responding, however, to those who would claim "that diversity (in law) implies inconsistency, which naturally raises the issue of error,"[26] he simply shifts the question to what such diversity tells us about the nature of Scripture and the nature of God. Sparks, though denying that divine "'accommodation' is merely a cipher for 'error,'"[27] nevertheless asserts that "the literary, historical, ethical, and theological diversity in Scripture that scholars have documented a thousand times over" clearly demonstrates that the biblical authors were subject "to their own finite and fallen interpretive horizons."[28] This certainly sounds like an indirect assertion of error.

In the most comprehensive study of this issue to date, John Goldingay helpfully distinguishes four degrees of "contradiction" that theological diversity in the Old Testament may present: (1) formal (relating to the words, e.g., the use of Hebrew *nikham* in 1 Sam 15:11, 29, 35 to both state and deny that God changes his mind), (2) contextual (relating to the circumstances, e.g., Zion theology in Isaiah and Jeremiah), (3) substantial (relating to the viewpoint, e.g., the perspectives of Job *versus* Proverbs regarding the utility of wisdom), and (4) fundamental

---

23. Gerhard von Rad, *Old Testament Theology*, trans. D.M.G. Stalker, 2 vols. (New York: Harper & Row, 1965) 2:414.

24. von Rad, *OT Theology*, 2:120.

25. Enns, *Inspiration and Incarnation*, 80.

26. Enns, *Inspiration and Incarnation*, 85.

27. Sparks, *God's Word*, 244.

28. Sparks, *God's Word*, 244.

(relating to ethical or religious outlook, e.g., Yahweh *versus* Baal).[29] The final category presents the strongest threat to the integrity of the biblical faith. The remaining three degrees may involve *complementary* rather than *contradictory* perspectives, that is, to conceive of a relationship differently does not necessarily entail polarity or inconsistency.

Unity or Harmonization?

One of the difficulties in dealing with this subject is that authors use the term "unity" in a variety of ways. The predominant use seems to be modeled by von Rad, who speaks repeatedly of the unity of the Old Testament in terms of "an all-embracing basic concept."[30] Similarly, as already noted, Enns find the unity of the Old Testament in Christ, a perspective that some interpreters would view as an imposition from the New Testament. As will be discussed further below, the idea of unity is often associated with the search for a theological center. Gerstenberger uses the term more narrowly to denote "a normative unity" in the sense of "one absolute affirmation."[31]

Several scholars have characterized the unity of the Bible in figurative terms. For example, according to D. A. Carson, "the Bible is like a jigsaw puzzle that provides five thousand pieces along with the assurance that these pieces all belong to the same puzzle, even though ninety-five thousand pieces are missing," rejecting the naive view that the Bible is like a 5,000-piece puzzle, of which all pieces are provided.[32] Donald Guthrie contrasts his understanding of unity with "[m]any modern approaches . . . where several jigsaws are mixed up together and the various pieces refuse to fit because they do not belong."[33]

Robert Wilson conceives of unity more in terms of overall coherence and consistency in thematic development, which he sometimes

---

29. John Goldingay, *Theological Diversity and the Authority of the Old Testament* (Grand Rapids: Eerdmans, 1987), 15–25.

30. von Rad, *OT Theology*, 2:415, although he dismisses this idea as "illusory" and "violently exploded" by the historical study of the OT, 2:414–15.

31. Gerstenberger, "Contextual Theologies," 131–32.

32. D. A. Carson, "Unity and Diversity in the New Testament: The Possibility of Systematic Theology," in *Scripture and Truth*, ed. D. A. Carson and John D. Woodbridge (Grand Rapids: Zondervan, 1983) 81–82.

33. Donald Guthrie, *New Testament Theology* (Downers Grove, IL: InterVarsity, 1981) 50–51.

finds lacking in 1–2 Kings.[34] This raises the issue of harmonization, both for conservative scholars and for those polemicizing against them. Harmonization involves offering an explanation for how two apparently contradictory factual or conceptual statements can be understood as not ultimately incompatible.[35]

For many scholars, such harmonizing efforts are anathema. According to William Johnstone, "The worst thing that one can do with a biblical text is—understandable though it may be and motivated with the highest of purpose—to propose a harmonizing reading. For in so doing, one may be destroying the very point that the respective writer is trying to make."[36] His point is well taken—if harmonizing two statements *replaces* interpreting a specific statement in its present literary context. For many conservative scholars, however, harmonization is instead a reflex action to defend the integrity of Scripture against the claims of historical-critical scholars that it is filled with contradictions (i.e., errors), and thus it is a theological-apologetic rather than a hermeneutical move.[37] Guthrie defends "the proper place" of harmonization: "it is as illogical to suppose that no attempt should be made to reconcile evidence, as it would be in a court of law to suppose that the only function in examining evidence was negative (to discover discrepancies) and never positive (to propose a valid reconstruction to account for apparently contrary evidence)."[38]

We will return later to the issue of "legitimate" harmonization. At this point, we will conclude with three methodological affirmations. First of all, the basic claim that some type of theological unity can be identified in the Old Testament (or Bible) is not necessarily dependent

34. Robert R. Wilson, "Unity and Diversity in the Book of Kings," in *"A Wise and Discerning Mind": Essays in Honor of Burke O. Long*, ed. Saul M. Olyan et al., Brown Judaic Studies 325 (Providence, RI: Brown Judaic Studies, 2000) 295.

35. Two of the most helpful discussions of harmonization are by Craig L. Blomberg, "The Legitimacy and Limits of Harmonization," in *Hermeneutics, Authority, and Canon*, ed. D. A. Carson and John Woodbridge (Grand Rapids: Zondervan, 1986) 135–74; and Raymond B. Dillard, "Harmonization: A Help and a Hindrance," in *Inerrancy and Hermeneutic: A Tradition, A Challenge, A Debate*, ed. Harvey M. Conn (Grand Rapids: Baker, 1988) 151–64.

36. William Johnstone, *1 and 2 Chronicles*, vol. 1: *1 Chronicles 1–2 Chronicles 9: Israel's Place among the Nations*, JSOTS 253 (Sheffield: Sheffield Academic, 1997) 22.

37. See Gleason L. Archer, *Encyclopedia of Bible Difficulties* (Grand Rapids: Zondervan, 1982) 30–31.

38. Guthrie, *NT Theology*, 56–57.

on harmonizing efforts. Secondly, since the default stance of most modern scholars is to emphasize diversity at the expense of—or to the exclusion of—unity, scholars who prefer to emphasize unity—or both—will need to employ harmonization to some degree in order to make their case. This is not to legitimate any and every harmonistic effort, no matter how forced. Thirdly, the constructive task of synthesizing biblical or systematic theology requires some type of harmonization of divergent theological statements. In this chapter, we will understand unity in terms of the basic, but complex, coherence of major theological themes within the Old Testament, which, despite diversity in presentation and emphasis, can be viewed as complementary rather than contradictory.

Categorizing Diversity

Before discussing unity and diversity in greater detail, it is helpful to categorize the various *types* of diversity that can be identified within the Old Testament. Scholars most frequently cite *historical* diversity, ranging from differences in the spelling of proper names and the numbers of individuals involved in specific events to differences in the indicated causation and outcomes of those events. A related category is *material* diversity, such as is reflected in parallel legal prescriptions, which often differ in remarkable ways. A third category is *ideological* diversity, such as differing attitudes toward the monarchy, a particular priestly line, or worship sites outside Jerusalem. This category may overlap somewhat with the fourth category, *theological* diversity, which involves divergent ways of construing God's relationship with his people Israel or with the nations (or individuals within either group).

Furthermore, one can distinguish various *forms* of theological diversity. Goldingay, for example, notes three major categories of diversity: (1) in the meaning of concepts (e.g., seeing God, God and the gods), themes (e.g., righteousness), and institutions (e.g., monarchy); (2) in the messages of individual Old Testament books (e.g., Kings *vs.* Chronicles, Proverbs *vs.* Ecclesiastes, Jeremiah *vs.* Ezekiel) and traditions (wisdom *vs.* historical books); and (3) in the significance found in particular events and motifs (e.g., creation, exodus, wilderness wanderings).[39]

Gordon McConville is dissatisfied with these categories because they blur the more important distinction between "simple disagreement

---

39. Goldingay, *Theological Diversity*, 2–12.

between biblical authors over given issues" and inherent "polarity."[40] McConville gives primary emphasis to such "polarities," for example, between law and grace, God known and unknown, ritual and spontaneous religion, individual and community, and faith and doubt/skepticism. He denies that these are best viewed in terms of "conflict and polemic," preferring to speak of "imbalance" and "counterbalance." Frequently, such polarities are analyzed as resulting from redactional reworking by editors in fundamental disagreement with prior authors and editors. Instead, one should acknowledge that one element often implies the other, giving expression to the complexity of theological assertions.[41] The other type of diversity that he identifies derives from the fact that the Old Testament story "develops and moves through many phases," resulting in diverse presentations of the relationship between creation and redemption, politics and religion, and election and universalism in the course of the Old Testament canon.[42]

THE NATURE AND LIMITS OF THEOLOGICAL UNITY IN THE OT

"That the biblical canon contains diversity is obvious to most readers; that it is nevertheless a unity is the conviction of those for whom it functions as Holy Scripture."[43]

Perspectives from the History of Interpretation

The unity and diversity in the Bible is a longstanding issue. According to James Kugel, ancient interpreters "assumed that the Bible contained no contradictions or mistakes. It is perfectly harmonious, despite its being an anthology"; in short, it is "an utterly consistent, seamless, perfect book."[44] Efforts to harmonize texts began already within the Bible itself. In 1 Chr 20:5, for example, the author is apparently seeking to reconcile

40. J. Gordon McConville, "Using Scripture for Theology: Unity and Diversity in Old Testament Theology," *Scottish Bulletin of Evangelical Theology* 5 (1987) 46.

41. McConville, "Using Scripture," 46–49.

42. McConville, "Using Scripture," 49–51.

43. John Barton, "Unity and Diversity in the Biblical Canon," in *Die Einheit der Schrift und die Vielfalt des Kanons* (*The Unity of Scripture and the Diversity of the Canon*), ed. John Barton and Michael Wolter, BZNW 118 (Berlin: de Gruyter, 2003) 11.

44. James L. Kugel, *How to Read the Bible: A Guide to Scripture, Then and Now* (New York: Free Press, 2007) 15.

discrepant accounts in 1 Sam 17:50 and 2 Sam 21:19 concerning who slew Goliath. John Barton clarifies that, in rabbinic Judaism, scriptural consistency was essential primarily in legal (*halakhic*) rather than historical matters, citing a Talmudic story of Hananiah son of Hezekiah who discovered a contradiction between Ezekiel and the Torah: "What did he do? Three hundred barrels of oil were taken up to him and he sat in an upper chamber and reconciled them."[45] But the first-century Jewish historian Josephus also asserted that the Jews "have not an innumerable multitude of books among [them], disagreeing from and contradicting one another [as the Greeks have]."[46]

Patristic and medieval theologians simply assumed the unity of Scripture, derived from its divine authorship, although various means were employed to preserve its "unity" in the face of obvious inconsistencies. These included discerning additional "levels of meaning" when two texts could not be reconciled on the literal level.[47] The rise of historical-critical approaches to the Bible ended this consensus. By 1875, Bernhard Duhm could confidently assert that the lack of "chronological and formal unity in the Old Testament goes without saying," making "the title 'theology of the Old Testament' indefensible" due to the lack of the requisite unity. "Unity" could be preserved only by resorting to verbal inspiration or allegorical or typological interpretation.[48] Accordingly, ever since the Enlightenment period, the unity of the Bible has been a disputed claim, something to be defended rather than assumed.

Unity in a Divinely Inspired Book: A Reasonable Expectation?

In making the case for theological unity in the Old Testament, it must be conceded from the beginning that an irrefutable argument cannot be constructed from the text alone, especially when so much rests on the interpretation of individual texts (see our discussion of Ecclesiastes

---

45. *B. Shabbat* 13b, cited by Barton, "Unity and Diversity," 11.

46. Josephus, *C. Ap.* 1.8, cited by Kaiser, *Recovering the Unity*, 13.

47. L. Schwienhorst-Schönberger, "Einheit und Vielheit: Gibt es seine sinvolle Suche nach der Mitte des Alten Testaments?," in *Wieviel Systematik erlaubt die Schrift? Auf der Suche nach einer gesamtbiblischen Theologie*, ed. Frank-Lothar Hossfeld, Quaestiones Disputate 185 (Freiburg: Herder, 2001) 48–49. See Kaiser, *Recovering the Unity*, 13–17, for a brief overview.

48. Bernhard Duhm, *Die Theologie der Propheten als Grundlage für die innere Entwicklungsgeschichte der israelitischen Religion* (Bonn: A. Marcus, 1875) 25–27, my translation and summary.

below), so that theological considerations are also necessary. James Barr
sets forth two approaches to understanding the relation between the
Bible as a whole and its component parts:

> it is possible to hold that the "unity" of the Bible is not a principle
> of authority or a principle of interpretation, but rather something
> to be *sought*; not a starting-point but a goal of the process of
> study, interpretation and theological thinking. If in fact the Bible
> in some sense comes from the one God, whether as inspired by
> him or given by him as authority, it would seem to follow that the
> end-product of its effect would have some sort of unity and not
> be absolutely self-contradictory.[49]

John Davis assumes unity in "a starting point" argument: "If the assertions of 2 Timothy 3:16 and 2 Peter 1:21 are true, then it is proper to
assume the essential unity of the Bible on *a priori* grounds."[50] He con-
structs the following syllogism: "Major premise: All that God creates is
in perfect unity with Himself and other elements of his creation; Minor
premise: God created the Old and New Testaments; Conclusion: The
Old and New Testaments are a perfect unity."[51] How simple he makes
it sound: "a perfect unity"! The sixteenth-century Lutheran theologian
Martin Chemnitz spoke rather of "a very concordant dissonance" in the
four canonical Gospels,[52] while contemporary evangelical theologian
Kevin Vanhoozer speaks of "Spirit-enabled polyphonic unity."[53]

The extensive theological diversity within the Old Testament raises
the question of whether Davis's argument is convincing. In fact, both
Enns and Sparks suggest that such "perfect unity" is a fundamentalist
fantasy. In their view, divine accommodation has produced (Enns) or
adopted (Sparks) such diverse texts that any claim of theological unity

49. James Barr, *The Bible in the Modern World* (New York: Harper & Row, 1973) 99.

50. John J. Davis, "Unity of the Bible," in *Hermeneutics, Inerrancy, and the Bible*, ed.
Earl D. Radmacher and Robert D. Preus (Grand Rapids: Zondervan, 1984) 644–45.
Harold H. Rowley, *The Unity of the Bible* (London: Carey Kingsgate, 1953) 8, states the
position more cautiously: "If God was revealing Himself, then there should be some
unity about the revelation, since it was the same Being Who was being revealed."

51. Davis, "Unity of the Bible," 645.

52. Cited in Timothy Ward, "The Diversity and Sufficiency of Scripture," in *The
Trustworthiness of God: Perspectives on the Nature of Scripture*, ed. Paul Helm and Carl
R. Trueman (Grand Rapids: Eerdmans, 2002) 192.

53. Vanhoozer, *Drama of Doctrine*, 276; also John Goldingay, *Models for Scripture*
(Grand Rapids: Eerdmans, 1994) 336, a symphonic metaphor.

is at best a heavy-handed imposition (i.e., an unwarranted harmonization), and at worst an intentional ignoring of the actual phenomena of
Scripture. In reading their work, however, one gets the impression that
they not only emphasize theological diversity, but, by labeling any effort
at harmonization illegitimate, are intent on preserving theological diversity. In fact, they even tend to glorify it because it more clearly demonstrates the nature and degree of divine accommodation that they assert.

It is in principle reasonable to assume, however, that if Scripture
faithfully records divine "speech acts" that are to serve as his self-com-
munication and instruction to humanity, the resultant writings should
be internally consistent and free of fundamental contradiction. And if,
as the Scriptures attest, that same God is actively involved in directing
the history of his people toward his goals for creation, a fundamental
unity of purpose should also be apparent, as expressed in his covenantal
commitments.[54] To be sure, most biblical scholars today no longer grant
these premises. For them, any striking unity within the Old Testament
must be the result of extensive editorial intervention in the final form
and ordering of the biblical books.

Contemporary Approaches to Unity

One approach to unity is what Barton calls "the search for a higher
unity," which involves subordinating obvious diversity. This can involve
claiming that "the Scripture writers really were communicating an essentially unified vision of the truth, even though they differed on points of
detail."[55] In Barton's view, most modern biblical theologians are engaged
in this quest, claiming that the inherent unity of the biblical witnesses
is "being *discovered*, not *imposed*." He also includes Brevard Childs's canonical approach under this rubric, although it makes no such empirical
claim: "What Childs suggests is that Christians *ought* to read the Bible as
a unified text because of what they believe about its status as Scripture
for the community."[56]

For Schwienhorst-Schönberger, the normative function of canon
means that the canonical text is ultimately to be understood as *one* text.
Thus individual biblical texts are to be read only in connection with the

54. See Roger T. Beckwith, "The Unity and Diversity of God's Covenants," *Tyndale
Bulletin* 38 (1987) 93–118.

55. Barton, "Unity and Diversity," 19.

56. Barton, "Unity and Diversity," 21.

macrotext of which they are a part, as evidenced by their extensive intertextual connections.[57] Wolter takes it a step further: what distinguishes
canon is "the desire for unity," so that, following Umberto Eco, the intentions of both the individual authors and readers are subordinated to the
intention of the (canonical) work as a whole.[58]

If unity is to be grounded both in the divine origin of Scripture and
in its canonical status, then some of the common approaches to unity
must be downplayed as too narrow in focus and potentially counterpro-
ductive. First of all, the "search for a center," prompted by the work of
Walter Eichrodt and so prominent in previous decades, must be viewed
primarily as an assertion of theological unity. But the identification of
such a central, unifying theme ultimately excludes more than it includes
and hardly demonstrates the unity of the whole. More promising in this
regard are the various "polarities" within the Old Testament mentioned
above, since they allow one to explore the potential complementarity
(i.e., coherence) of seeming opposites, holding them together and "seeking to clarify their interrelation rather than abandoning one member of
each pair."[59] The discussion of the relationship between the testaments
in terms of Christology, salvation history, typology, promise and fulfillment, continuity and discontinuity, or covenant[60] is similarly narrow in
focus (e.g., ignoring non-messianic or non-eschatological prophecy).
Not only is it irrelevant to the issue of the nature of theological unity
within the Old Testament, but it also does not address the type of diversity that authors like Gerstenberger and Enns highlight.

Instead, unity is to be sought in the unified "storyline" of the Old
Testament and the frequent allusions to it in the Psalms and prophetic
books, in its shared traditions (e.g., Exodus, Zion, God as rock or cloud-
rider), which are creatively employed by various authors, and in its rich
tapestry of intertextual (verbal) connections. Furthermore, unity is to be
affirmed through what Goldingay terms the "unifying or constructive

57. Schwienhorst-Schönberger, "Einheit und Vielheit," 67; also Michael Wolter, "Die Vielfalt der Schrift und die Einheit des Kanons," in Barton and Wolter, eds., *Unity of Scripture*, 65.

58. Wolter, "Vielfalt der Schrift," 66–67 (German: "der Wille zur Einheit").

59. John Goldingay, "Diversity and Unity in Old Testament Theology," *Vetus Testamentum* 34 (1984) 168.

60. See David L. Baker, *Two Testaments, One Bible: The Theological Relationship between the Old and New Testaments*, 3rd ed. (Downers Grove, IL: InterVarsity, 2010) 271–76.

approach." He explains his architectural metaphor: "The building must be appropriate to the materials themselves, and . . . the builder must work on the assumption that even where the stone may seem to have come from several different quarries, it all can be shaped into a satisfying whole." Shifting then to a mathematical analogy, Goldingay describes the Old Testament theologian's task as seeking the highest common factor in various expressions of Old Testament faith rather than the lowest common factor.[61] What we have in mind here—and will seek to illustrate in the case studies below—is that focusing exclusively on diversity can be as tendentious as focusing exclusively on unity. What one needs to do is to seek aspects of unity within diverse treatments of a given theological theme, while also exploring ways in which such statements can be fairly understood as complementary rather than contradictory.[62] And if this involves some degree of "harmonization," that is also warranted, as long as the dictum is not unity at any cost!

THE SOURCES AND SIGNIFICANCE OF THEOLOGICAL DIVERSITY

Unlike unity, there is no need to defend the presence of theological diversity in the Old Testament! The question is rather "how much 'dissonance' Scripture in fact possesses" and "how much 'dissonance' can be tolerated in a supposedly 'concordant' scriptural canon before we must give up and judge it 'discordant.'"[63]

Sources of Diversity

Any discussion of theological diversity must begin by identifying its various sources or "reasons." Goldingay offers the most extensive list: different historical settings, audiences, authors, literary forms, subjects, tradition circles, and rhetorical purposes (e.g., polemic).[64] It may be helpful to illustrate how these may result in theological diver-

61. Goldingay, *Theological Diversity*, 184.

62. For an earlier helpful effort to find unity in diversity, see Harold H. Rowley, "The Unity of the Old Testament," *Bulletin of the John Reynolds University Library* 29 (1946) 326–58; see also Rowley, *Unity of the Bible*, 1–29. Rowley describes this as "a dynamic unity," an ongoing development due to divine revelation (8).

63. Ward, "Diversity and Sufficiency," 193.

64. Goldingay, *Theological Diversity*, 12–15.

sity using examples from the Old Testament Prophets. Isaiah (Isa 7) and Jeremiah (Jer 7) employ the so-called Zion tradition differently because they are addressing different military crises (Assyrian *versus* Babylonian siege). The different attitudes of their audiences led to contrasting emphases, Isaiah rebuking the lack of trust in God's elective commitments and Jeremiah rebuking false reliance. Micah uses rural images more often than Isaiah, who is located in Jerusalem. Ezekiel develops the vine image more fully in a prose text (Ezek 14) than Isaiah does in a poetic "song" (Isa 5). Isaiah uses creation terminology in Isa 40:12, 22 in the context of an encouragement to trust God's promise of restoration, while Amos uses it in 2:13 to warn Israel of the certainty of the coming judgment. Jeremiah and Ezekiel, coming from priestly circles, conceive of the future in different terms (new covenant/new temple) than does Daniel, the statesman (kingdom of God). For Hosea, the Hebrew word *ba'al* becomes taboo because of its associations with Baal worship (2:16–17), while for Isaiah it expresses Israel's permanent "marriage" to the LORD (54:5).

Problematic Approaches to Diversity

There are clearly a number of problematic approaches to such diversity. We have already noted the common rejection of harmonization, or "reconciliation," as Barton calls it.[65] To be sure, some harmonizing attempts are justly infamous, such as Harold Lindsell's "solution" that Peter denied Jesus not *three* but *five* times,[66] and deserve E. J. Young's rebuke: "to employ strained and forced methods of harmonization is not intellectually honest."[67] But Young also protests one page earlier: "To force passages of Scripture to contradict one another when they can and do harmonize is to engage in an unwarranted type of exegesis."[68] Barton calls another improper approach "deletion and alteration,"[69] which includes the practice of distinguishing a "canon within a canon," and claims that "almost all Christians informally espouse such an approach."[70] Goldingay labels

---

65. Barton, "Unity and Diversity," 18.

66. Harold Lindsell, *The Battle for the Bible* (Grand Rapids: Zondervan, 1976) 176.

67. Edward J. Young, *Thy Word Is Truth: Some Thoughts on the Biblical Doctrine of Inspiration* (Grand Rapids: Eerdmans, 1957) 124.

68. Young, *Thy Word is Truth*, 123.

69. Barton, "Unity and Diversity," 13.

70. Barton, "Unity and Diversity," 16.

this an "evaluative or critical approach" (chapter 4), in which one's criterion for preferring one theological viewpoint over another may be the text's moral concern, developmental level, Mosaic or prophetic spirit, relationship to New Testament concerns, or one's own values. An emphasis on progressive revelation can also be problematic, since it can tend to denigrate earlier revelation, assume that God of necessity builds on the foundation of simpler truths, and dismiss unpalatable claims as stemming from a "pre-" period. While it is certainly inappropriate to dismiss the diversity in the Old Testament as merely superficial and inconsequential, it is equally inappropriate to openly acknowledge it without diligently seeking to relate diverse viewpoints to one another, instead "treating it as a bran-tub in which we rummage until we find something that gives us the pretext for accepting what we wanted to believe anyway."[71]

Proper Approaches to Diversity

So how should we properly approach theological diversity? First of all, we must recognize that diversity is an unavoidable feature of a divine-human book developed in the course of human history—but it is not therefore a necessary evil. Unless we insist on a dictation model of inspiration, we affirm that God uses diverse human agents not despite—but precisely because of—their diverse backgrounds and personalities. Although Sparks (or his publisher) appears to give priority to the human words of Scripture by printing "*HUMAN WORDS*" in an obviously larger font than "*GOD'S WORD*" on the book cover, traditional Christian theology has always given priority to the latter. What theological diversity in the Old Testament therefore indicates is quite simply that "diversity was the mode of biblical revelation," so we should "avoid . . . flattening out the inspired differences."[72]

Furthermore, as McConville points out, the fact that the Old Testament is "the deposit of people's actual experience of God in many situations over many centuries" fosters diversity, as does "the forward movement, or historical character," of Old Testament revelation.[73] Vang

71. Goldingay, "Diversity and Unity," 160.

72. David Wenham, "Appendix: Unity and Diversity in the New Testament," in *A Theology of the New Testament*, by George Eldon Ladd, 2nd ed. (Grand Rapids: Eerdmans, 1993) 715.

73. McConville, "Using Scripture," 55, 54.

notes another neglected "human" source of theological diversity—the presence of sin in the lives of God's people, which forces God to communicate to them both in terms of their *ideal* and their *actual* situations.[74] Paul Hanson similarly characterizes theological diversity as reflecting "God's living relationship with a people."[75] Accordingly, there is no basis for an evangelical scholar to seek to deny or downplay diversity.

Secondly, however, one needs to acknowledge that this diversity can present a theological problem. But what is the exact nature of that problem? Some scholars, such as Achtemeier and Sparks, cite examples of theological "discrepancies" alongside historical "discrepancies" as corroborating evidence of the humanness (i.e., errancy) of Scripture.[76] But it is considerably more difficult to demonstrate that theological viewpoints are mutually exclusive than with the details of parallel historical narratives. The former only become a problem when one feels compelled to take an evaluative or critical approach, choosing between the options—or rejecting them both.

Vanhoozer asserts, however, that "strictly speaking, the diverse canonical parts neither contradict nor cohere with one another, for both these notions presuppose either the presence or absence of conceptual consistency."[77] For example, there is no easy way to "cut the Gordian knot" and resolve the alleged tension between nationalism and universalism within the book of Isaiah, since not only do both emphases run parallel throughout the book but also no two expressions of either emphasis are identical. Furthermore, each occurrence of this theme has a unique contextual function.[78] Similarly, it is problematic to claim "theological diversity" simply by citing texts that indicate that God both *does* and *does not* repent (as in 1 Sam 15:11, 29, 35).[79] Not only is the Hebrew

74. Carsten Vang, "'Der HERR ist einer!' Von der Einheit und der Verschiedenheit in der Theologie des Alten Testaments," *European Journal of Theology* 4 (1995) 149.

75. Paul D. Hanson, *The Diversity of Scripture: A Theological Interpretation*, OBT (Philadelphia: Fortress, 1982) 3.

76. Paul J. Achtemeier, *Inspiration and Authority: Nature and Function of Christian Scripture* (Peabody, MA: Hendrickson, 1999) 53–54; Sparks, *God's Word*, 119–21.

77. Vanhoozer, *Drama of Doctrine*, 275.

78. See Richard L. Schultz, "Nationalism and Universalism in Isaiah," in *Interpreting Isaiah: Issues and Approaches*, ed. H. G. M. Williamson and D. L. Firth (Downers Grove, IL: InterVarsity, 2009) 122–44.

79. See the discussion by Enns, *Inspiration and Incarnation*, 103–7; also Sparks, *God's Word*, 231.

verb that is used here (*nikham*) notoriously difficult to translate, but it is also used differently in different syntactical expressions to express either God's emotional or volitional responses to human actions.[80]

Finally, one may even embrace diversity while still seeking to delimit it by clarifying the nature and extent of diversity presented by specific texts. Barton states the matter quite frankly: "To commend such a book honestly as a vehicle for the Word of God must somehow involve seeing this diversity not merely as no worse than neutral, but rather as in some respects a positive advantage."[81] Hanson effectively summarizes this positive attitude: "How much richer and more profound is our knowledge of God because of the diversity of expression."[82] Much of the diversity in the Old Testament, however, is simply a reflection of the fact that "truth is complex and many-sided"; that is, it is less a matter of conceptual conflict and more a matter of "the thrashing out of issues inherent in theologizing."[83] Therefore, seeking to demonstrate the context-specific functions and complementary nature of theologically divergent expressions is not an inappropriate apologetical ploy but a hermeneutical mandate.

CASE STUDIES IN APPROACHES TO THEOLOGICAL DIVERSITY

As we have seen, theological diversity within the Old Testament can take various forms and have various causes. Some of these issues are unique to (or posed more sharply by) a particular type of literature. In the next section of the chapter, we will discuss some of these, noting how Enns and Sparks have highlighted diversity in each corpus, as well as suggesting how one might view this diversity differently while also highlighting legitimate aspects of unity.

---

80. See Paul D. House, "God's Character and the Wholeness of Scripture," *Scottish Bulletin of Evangelical Theology* 23 (2005) 8–11.

81. Barton, "Unity and Diversity," 26.

82. Hanson, *Diversity of Scripture*, 3.

83. J. Gordon McConville, "Diversity and Obscurity in Old Testament Books: A Hermeneutical Exercise Based on Some Later Old Testament Books," *Anvil* 3 (1986) 36.

Historiography: Samuel/Kings versus Chronicles

Although the historical books of the Old Testament are clearly those in which scholars have identified the most *factual* discrepancies,[84] one can also note divergent theological themes within and between individual historical books. Robert Wilson, in his helpful discussion of unity and diversity within 1–2 Kings, detects "complex" thematic consistency in the work's account of the fall of the Northern Kingdom; however, he sees "multiple and contradictory explanations for the fall of Jerusalem and the exile."[85] Although concluding that "none of the major themes . . . seem to run consistently through the entire book,"[86] he acknowledges that the repentance theme—pertaining to both individuals and the nation as a whole—does serve to unite the history, even if derived from various redactional layers.

The relationship between Samuel-Kings and Chronicles, which in some respects is more problematic than that between the Synoptic Gospels, receives considerably more discussion. Enns summarizes the matter: Chronicles is "an *alternate* history of Israel . . . told from *a different perspective for different reasons*."[87] No one would dispute his claim that Chronicles is written from a later perspective than Samuel-Kings and that it is seeking to answer contemporary questions in light of previous history. As soon as one acknowledges that Old Testament historiography is not simply concerned with preserving a record of the past but also interpreting the past in order to address contemporary issues and questions, one understands how such concerns may have guided the selection, ordering, and presentation of material to give Chronicles a very different "feel" from Samuel-Kings, especially if the former was drawing on additional sources. Enns cites four aspects of Chronicles' theological diversity: diminishing David's sins, emphasizing the people's unity, focusing on the temple and Solomon's role in building it, and its theology of "immediate retribution."[88]

---

84. This is the major focus of Archer's *Encyclopedia of Bible Difficulties.*

85. Wilson, "Unity and Diversity," 306.

86. Wilson, "Unity and Diversity," 308. For a more positive assessment of the theological unity of 1–2 Kgs, see Iain W. Provan, *1 and 2 Kings*, NIBC (Peabody, MA: Hendrickson, 1995) 10–15.

87. Enns, *Inspiration and Incarnation*, 63; emphasis original.

88. Enns, *Inspiration and Incarnation*, 84.

Since biblical historiography is not "objective," according to Enns, but instead "attempts to communicate the significance of historical events . . . according to the historian's purpose," one should reject the common evangelical practice of seeking to harmonize them.[89] The biggest problem is that harmonization shifts the focus from viewing Chronicles as a message to be heeded to a problem to be solved. It appears, however, that Enns has replaced one problem-oriented focus with another, for he concludes his discussion of theological diversity in Chronicles: "However much we might struggle with this [diversity], it is important to understand that God himself is pleased to allow this tension to stand."[90]

But theological differences do not necessarily produce tension. Let us briefly examine Enns's treatment of some of these differences. First of all, Chronicles does not mention David's sins with Bathsheba and Uriah, but it does recount at length David's sin in conducting a military census (1 Chr 21). Contra Enns, however, this does not, in itself, turn David into a "glorified" or "messianic" figure,[91] especially if one understands that Chronicles is not intended to replace, contradict, or correct Samuel-Kings.[92] Furthermore, the silence of Chronicles regarding the "power struggles" described in 1–2 Kings does not necessarily offer a revisionist view of the David era as "an ideal age" of unity, which the post-exilic community now seeks to "relive" without the benefit of a Davidic king![93] The book's emphasis is more on the *one* people of God rather than on interpersonal unity.[94]

Enns sees additional evidence of the Chronicler's "messianic" interest in the divergence in Nathan's announcement of the "Davidic covenant" between 2 Sam 7:16 ("*Your* house and *your* kingdom will endure forever before me; *your* throne will be established forever.") and 1 Chr

89. Enns, *Inspiration and Incarnation*, 66.

90. Enns, *Inspiration and Incarnation*, 85.

91. Enns, *Inspiration and Incarnation*, 84; according to Sparks, *God's Word*, 103, both David and Solomon are presented as "entirely blameless and blessed by God."

92. The highly abbreviated accounts of Saul's reign in 1 Chr 10:13–14 and of the Babylonian envoys' visit with Hezekiah in 2 Chr 32:31 make it clear that a knowledge of the Samuel-Kings history is presupposed by the author of Chronicles and presumably also on the part of his readers.

93. Enns, *Inspiration and Incarnation*, 84.

94. Thus "Israel," used nine times 1 Chr 21, refers to the entire nation, rather than merely to the Northern Kingdom as it does in 1–2 Kings.

17:14 ("I will set him over *my* house and *my* kingdom forever; *his* throne will be established forever.") as indicative of how "the author shapes the events to suit his theological purpose,"[95] the latter account reflecting a post-exilic focus on God rather than on the Davidic line.

Rather than trying to harmonize these verses by arguing that perhaps Nathan delivered promises to David on two *different* occasions, says Enns, we should admit that we do not and cannot know what Nathan actually said. Such an admission is both honest and acceptable. The Chicago Statement on Biblical Inerrancy, article 13, denies that "the topical arrangements of material, variant selections of material in parallel accounts, or the use of free citations" negates inerrancy.[96] Nevertheless, it is problematic to contrast the emphases of 2 Sam 7 and 1 Chr 17 since *both* texts highlight God's involvement in upholding Nathan's promise as well as the enduring nature of the Davidic line. The claim that the Davidic monarchy also involves *God's* house and kingdom is hardly foreign to Samuel since it clearly states elsewhere that God remains Israel's true monarch, even after the monarchy has been divinely instituted (see 1 Sam 8:7; 12:12–13, 24). Assuming that 2 Sam 7 is earlier, Chronicles has likely been modified to reflect the significance of the Davidic covenant for that book's thematic emphasis on the kingdom of God.[97]

Secondly, Martin Selman considers the term "immediate retribution" too narrow and even inaccurate, for Judah and its leaders frequently experience mercy rather than deserved punishment and their hope is grounded in God's covenantal commitments, not in reward.[98] This too is not necessarily in tension with Kings' explanation of the nation's exile. Chronicles' author/editor has a greater interest in the immediate results of an individual ruler's obedience or disobedience—both for the ruler and for the nation (e.g., Joash in 2 Chr 24:1–16 and 17–27), while Kings is more interested in their cumulative effects leading to ultimate judgment. When the book of Chronicles offers an explanation for Judah's ex-

95. Enns, *Inspiration and Incarnation*, 64.

96. "The Chicago Statement on Biblical Inerrancy," in *Inerrancy*, ed. Norman Geisler (Grand Rapids: Zondervan, 1980) 496.

97. See Martin J. Selman, "The Kingdom of God in the Old Testament," *Tyndale Bulletin* 40 (1989) 163–71.

98. Martin J. Selman, *1 Chronicles*, TOTC (Downers Grove, IL: InterVarsity, 1994) 59–65.

ile in 2 Chr 36:14–16, it is quite similar to that in 2 Kgs 24 in describing the ongoing disobedience and apostasy of the people and their rejection of the prophetic message.

Sparks addresses comparable issues concerning Samuel-Kings and Chronicles but expresses the problem more strongly, speaking of the Chronicler's "ideological biases . . . which tend to slant" accounts or even "inspire the author to invent stories that suit his purpose."[99] In the case of contradictory accounts, one must conclude that "both cannot be historical" and that the end product is "well shy of a perfectly accurate account of Israel's past."[100] Thus the author of Chronicles, according to Sparks, simply "transformed" good King Asa into a wicked king (prompted by 1 Kgs 15:16–24) and wicked Manasseh into a good king (prompted by his unusually long reign) so that they conformed to his theological principle of "immediate retribution."[101]

Although admitting that both biblical accounts might be "partially correct,"[102] Sparks dismisses as "speculative" Brian Kelly's conclusion that 2 Chr 33 is "not an overpainting of Kings, and certainly not a whitewashing of Manasseh's reputation, but rather a second painting, a different perspective drawn from the materials available to the author."[103] But is not Sparks's approach equally or even more speculative in concluding that (1) one (or both) of the accounts is not historically correct; (2) these divergent accounts cannot be reconciled; (3) theology not only repeatedly trumps history in the Old Testament, but authors also willingly sacrifice historical accuracy in order to make theological points; (4) the Chronicler did not have access to any sources unavailable to the author of Kings; and (5) the authors of the two accounts had insufficient warrant for using Manasseh to illustrate two contrasting theological points—as the culmination of a long-term legacy of disobedience and apostasy by Davidic kings and as a representative Israelite repenting and being restored after being exiled for disobedience? The political pundits

---

99. Sparks, *God's Word*, 101.

100. Sparks, *God's Word*, 102.

101. Sparks, *God's Word*, 103–4.

102. Sparks, *God's Word*, 164.

103. Sparks, *God's Word*, 159–64; Brian E. Kelly, "Manasseh in the Books of Kings and Chronicles," in *Windows into Old Testament History: Evidence, Argument, and the Crisis of "Biblical Israel"*, ed. V. Philips Long et al. (Grand Rapids: Eerdmans, 2002) 145.

of today could easily draw opposite lessons from the personal lives and policies of the two most recent United States presidents![104]

Wisdom: Proverbs versus Ecclesiastes-Job[105]

Another much discussed example of theological diversity in the Old Testament is the claimed contrast or contradiction between the perspective on wisdom in Proverbs and that emphasized in Ecclesiastes and Job. Enns begins his discussion of theological diversity in the wisdom corpus with the frequently cited contrasting admonitions in Prov 26:4–5: "Do not answer a fool according to his folly, . . . Answer a fool according to his folly." This hardly constitutes theological or otherwise problematic diversity, but rather a call to evaluate each situation wisely before taking the appropriate action, by anticipating the recipient's likely reaction. These are also not isolated proverbs but are better understood as part of a structured coherent unit (26:1–12) that offers guidelines for how to deal appropriately with fools.

Next, Enns highlights the widely divergent statements about wealth that can be found throughout the book of Proverbs. In a fuller study of this topic, R. N. Whybray notes that even each subcollection within the book offers its own distinctive slant on this topic, likely reflecting the values and concerns of the particular socioeconomic group that produced it.[106] Here again, Enns treats individual proverbs in isolation from their contexts, contrasting proverbs such as 10:15 ("The wealth of the rich is their fortified city, but poverty is the ruin of the poor.") and 18:11 ("The wealth of the rich is their fortified city; they imagine it an unscalable wall.") rather than reading and qualifying each by the proverbs with which they are paired and juxtaposed (i.e., 10:15–16 and 18:10–11).

---

104. To take another example, one must at least acknowledge that some of the differences between the accounts of David's census in 2 Sam 24 and 1 Chr 21 stem from the respective authors' distinctive uses of this narrative. Whereas 2 Sam 24 serves as a contrast to 2 Sam 21:1–14, emphasizing one more time how David, unlike Saul, restored the nation to divine favor, 1 Chr 21 serves to describe how David identifies the appropriate site for the future temple, the preparations for which will then occupy him during his final years.

105. For a more detailed discussion of theological unity and diversity related to this OT genre, see Richard L. Schultz, "Unity or Diversity in Wisdom Theology?: A Canonical and Covenantal Perspective," *Tyndale Bulletin* 48 (1997) 271–306.

106. R. N. Whybray, *Wealth and Poverty in the Book of Proverbs*, JSOTS 99 (Sheffield: JSOT, 1990).

Although affirming that all biblical proverbs are wise and correct, he not only warns against universalizing the claims of any one proverb but also eschews any effort to "collate the diversity of Proverbs so that it yields a unified teaching on wealth," since this "renders unimportant the diversity that God himself has put there."[107]

But is there no way to synthesize these proverbial "slices of reality," as Ted Hildebrandt calls them,[108] into a complex but coherent perspective on wealth without "steamrolling" its diversity? Wealth, according to the book of Proverbs, can be understood (1) as a divine gift or reward (which brings with it a stewardship of benevolence), (2) as the outcome of wise planning and diligent efforts, or (3) as the spoils of violent or scheming exploitation, with only God and the wealthy person knowing which of these applies in a given case. As such, wealth may provide temporary ease and enjoyment but should never be relied on, since it may result in new problems or quickly disappear. Nearly every verse in Proverbs associated with wealth could find the "slice of reality" that it expresses both properly affirmed and qualified in this summary. It does not seem to me that such a synthesis is an affront to the God who was willing to "accommodate himself" by speaking to humanity through what Enns calls "a loose collection of diverse theological points of view."[109]

With regard to Ecclesiastes and Job, Enns points to the conceptual and theological diversity both *within* these respective books and *between* them and other Old Testament books (and Proverbs in particular). Enns labels these "internal tensions" within Ecclesiastes, such as 7:3 and 8:15, as "contradictions"[110]—whereas 7:3 commends sorrow, 8:15 praises enjoyment. Enns can view these verses as conflicting with one another only by ignoring the reasons underlying these evaluative statements. Could it not be that the purpose of including—or even juxtaposing—such apparently disjunctive proverbs is primarily rhetorical, seeking to lead the reader to a more nuanced view of reality? Enns's alternative explanation—that Ecclesiastes contains contradictions to mirror his fundamental view of life as "unpredictable, uncontrollable,

---

107. Enns, *Inspiration and Incarnation*, 76.

108. Ted A. Hildebrandt, "Proverbs," in *Cracking Old Testament Codes: A Guide to Interpreting the Literary Genres of the Old Testament*, ed. D. Brent Sandy and Ronald L. Giese Jr. (Nashville: Broadman & Holman, 1995) 42.

109. Enns, *Inspiration and Incarnation*, 109.

110. Enns, *Inspiration and Incarnation*, 77.

and contradictory"[111]—involves a too one-sidedly negative assessment of the book's theology.

In his analysis, Proverbs and Ecclesiastes differ fundamentally in that the former "hammers home . . . that 'wisdom works' and does not fail," while Qoheleth is resigned "to the notion that wisdom, although good *to a point*, ultimately won't bring home the goods."[112] One can agree with this assessment only in terms of their distinct *emphases* but not in terms of their *diverse claims*, for in the assessment of Thomas Krüger, "What the book of Qoheleth says about the possibilities and limits of human wisdom corresponds basically to the view of wisdom in the older parts of the book of Proverbs (Proverbs 10ff.): wisdom can lead to a happy and fulfilled life, but it cannot reliably guarantee such a life."[113] Proverbs may emphasize the benefits of acquiring wisdom and of living wisely in reverence before God, but it also acknowledges that the world of the wise and the righteous is populated by fools, as well as the wicked, lazy, mockers, gossips, adulteresses, and perverse, whose values and lifestyles are on a collision course with theirs. (Consider 17:12: "Better to meet a bear robbed of her cubs than a fool in his folly.") The God-fearing wise and righteous individual may still feel the pain of divine discipline (3:11–12), be impoverished (15:16; 16:8), have enemies (16:7), be condemned even though innocent (17:15; 18:5), experience the grief of having a foolish child (17:21, 25), fall seven times, though able to rise again (24:16), and need to wait for divine deliverance (20:22). Furthermore, wisdom can only succeed if aligned with God's purposes (21:30), and it is not human skill but rather "the blessing of the LORD that makes rich" (10:22; cf. 27:1).

Furthermore, Enns's contrast between Ecclesiastes and Proverbs is only valid if one also agrees with his interpretive assertions regarding the message of Qoheleth: that his viewpoint "borders on heresy," that the proper translation of *hebel hebalim* is "utterly meaningless" (rather than "ephemeral" or "utterly transient"), and that Qoheleth has "no notion of the afterlife," which reduces and relativizes all of wisdom's benefits.[114] This is an interesting point, since the high valuation of wisdom in the

111. Enns, *Inspiration and Incarnation*, 78.

112. Enns, *Inspiration and Incarnation*, 78–79; emphasis his.

113. Thomas Krüger, *Qoheleth: A Commentary*, trans. O. C. Dean Jr.. Hermeneia (Minneapolis: Augsburg Fortress, 2004) 22.

114. Enns, *Inspiration and Incarnation*, 79.

book of Proverbs does not appear to hinge on its "eternal" benefit, even though some scholars see evidence of a hope in the afterlife reflected in a few individual proverbs (e.g., 12:28; 15:24; 23:18; 24:14). More importantly, one can question whether Enns's interpretation does justice to the diverse statements in Ecclesiastes. Despite observing that prolific sinners can still live a long life, Qoheleth maintains his core theological conviction that those who fear God will *ultimately* be better off than the godless (8:12–13). Moreover, the book does affirm the existence of an eternal dimension (3:11) and a future (and perhaps final) judgment (3:17; 8:12–13; 11:9; 12:14), possibly also hinting at an ultimate reunion with God (3:21; 12:7).

If one takes the full range of Qoheleth's beliefs and claims into consideration, as summarized by Whybray,[115] and compares them with other Old Testament books, one must acknowledge that they are "fundamentally Hebraic." In sum, in light of the book of Proverbs' technique of exploring various facets of the same topic and Qoheleth's frequent juxtaposition of contrasting or even seemingly contradictory statements, one could suggest that their respective authors-editors utilize diversity of *content* for rhetorical ends without granting Enns's conclusion that these books are presenting divergent *theologies*.

Finally, with respect to Job, Enns claims that the book fundamentally questions "the relationship between deeds and their consequences." In his interpretation, Job's friends are simply affirming the retribution principle, as set forth in Deuteronomy (5:32–33) and Proverbs (3:1–2) so that "anyone well versed in Old Testament teaching would likely have drawn the same conclusion"[116] as Job's three companions did after observing his suffering. Following Enns's logic and given the late date that most scholars suggest for Job, however, Job's friends could also have taken into consideration David's relentless pursuit by Saul, Joseph's troubles at the hand of his siblings and Potiphar's wife, and Daniel's night in the lion's den, and consequently should have hesitated before drawing such a facile conclusion.

John Walton offers a different perspective on Job's friends, suggesting that, in urging Job "to appease God through a procedure of blanket confession," they were more in line with "a revered ANE wisdom

---

115. R. N. Whybray, *Ecclesiastes*, NCB (Grand Rapids: Eerdmans, 1989) 28.

116. Enns, *Inspiration and Incarnation*, 81.

tradition" than with Deuteronomic theology.[117] The book's final outcome, however, does uphold the deed-consequence nexus. The issue at stake is one of timing (i.e., God is just, but one might have to *wait* to experience justice) or of a too rigid application of a general principle, a perspective that all three wisdom books share. In sum, Enns is justified in pointing out diverse emphases and content both within and between the individual Old Testament wisdom books, but he has not demonstrated the degree of theological diversity that warrants his conclusion that "divine accommodation" has resulted in theologically "messy" Scriptures, which reflect "the rough and tumble drama of human history."[118]

Appropriate Strategies for Dealing with Diversity

According to Enns, Scripture is intentionally made or left "messy." Theologian William Placher suggests that the very messiness of the biblical texts (i.e., "diversity") is an embodiment of the God they try to bring to speech: "The narratives of this God who eschews brute force were not edited with the brute force necessary to impose a single, clear framework."[119] In our home "messy" is not tolerated for long, except in my younger son's room. Enns's primary admonition to evangelical theologians, however, is: "Stop messing with the messiness of Scripture!" Since, in his view, Scripture's intentional messiness offers unmistakable evidence of divine accommodation, any theological attempt to clean it up involves, at best, an imposition of order and, at worst, a distortion of Scripture.

What we have been suggesting in this chapter, rather, is that theological diversity is not to be feared as a threat to a conservative doctrine of Scripture. On the one hand, the amount or degree of diversity to be found in the Old Testament is often exaggerated. On the other hand, the identification of theological diversity can be taken as a call to examine why a particular emphasis is more appropriate in a particular historical, literary, and theological context—for example extolling the uniqueness of God ("I am the LORD, and there is no other; apart from me there is no God," Isa 45:5) rather than extolling his superior status ("For the

---

117. John H. Walton, *Ancient Near Eastern Thought and the Old Testament: Introducing the Conceptual World of the Hebrew Bible* (Grand Rapids: Baker, 2006) 308.

118. Enns, *Inspiration and Incarnation*, 109–10.

119. William C. Placher, *Narratives of a Vulnerable God: Christ, Theology, and Scripture* (Louisville: Westminster John Knox, 1994) 88.

LORD is the great God, the great King above all gods," Psa 95:3), and then considering how these two claims relate to one another within the Old Testament's diverse portrayals of God.[120] Such an approach can enrich one's exegesis theologically, rather than sidetracking the person into apologetic pursuits.

As Vanhoozer suggests, "the way forward is to acknowledge a unity in diversity," while bearing in mind that a "canonically circumscribed plurality admits of several voices and viewpoints, but not just any."[121] In doing so, one may indeed recognize the effect of divine accommodation on the production of Scripture, but not one that inherently negates unity and causes theological tension. Instead, such "inspired" diversity adds richness and texture to the divine communication and enables us more easily to apply it to the diversity of our life situations.

---

120. See the discussion by Daniel I. Block, "Other Religions in Old Testament Theology," in *Biblical Faith and Other Religions: An Evangelical Assessment*, ed. David W. Baker (Grand Rapids: Kregel, 2004) 56–60.

121. Vanhoozer, *Drama of Doctrine*, 275.

8

"But Jesus Believed that David Wrote the Psalms . . ."

Stephen Dawes

THE BOOK OF PSALMS

Psalms and Isaiah are the Old Testament books most extensively quoted in the New Testament, constituting rich sources of its imagery and theology.[1] From its use in monastic services, via Matins and Evensong in the *Book of Common Prayer* and the inclusion of Scottish paraphrases in many hymn books, Psalms has historically played an important role in the worship and spirituality of English Christianity. The same could be said, almost certainly, for its contribution to Christian worship and spirituality in every time and place. Anecdotal evidence suggests that in England at least, use of the Psalms in worship might be decreasing with

---

1. S. Moyise and M. J. J. Menken, ed., *The Psalms in the New Testament* (New York: T. & T. Clark, 2004) 2. Versions referenced below include: Douay-Rheims: Douay-Rheims translation of the Vulgate, Challenor revision; GNB: Good News Bible, 2nd ed., 1994; KJV: King James Version or Authorized Version, 1611; NEB: New English Bible, 1970; NETS: New English Translation of the Septuagint, 2007; NIV: New International Version, 1978; NJB: New Jerusalem Bible, 1985; NJPS: New Jewish Publication Society, *Tanakh*, 1999; NRSV: New Revised Standard Version, 1991; REB: Revised English Bible, 1989; RSV: Revised Standard Version, 1952; RV: Revised Version, 1898; Septuagint: *New English Translation of the Septuagint*, Oxford University Press, 2007, or http://ccat. sas.upenn.edu/nets; Targum: http://www.targum.info (Newsletter for Targumic and Cognate Studies); Vulgate: http://www.latinvulgate.com.

the demise of Morning and Evening Prayer in the Church of England, with the arrival of newer styles of worship generally, and with "worship songs" increasingly displacing traditional hymnody: but be that as it may, it remains true that for many Christians the Psalms are not simply "ancient hymns" but a great "resource of Christian prayer and praise."[2] There is, therefore, potential for varieties of unease and tension at the points where traditional understandings of the Psalms meet "academic" viewpoints. There is also, of course, potential for discovery, enlightenment, and further reflection.

CONSENSUS AND DISSENT

The psalm titles have traditionally sat on the periphery of Psalms studies; commentaries usually devote few pages to them and they normally receive little classroom time. Devotionally they feature minimally too, and versions of psalms for liturgical use almost always omit them, as did NEB (though its successor, REB, restores them). Part of this lack of interest is no doubt simply due to the fact that most titles add nothing to the appreciation of the individual psalms themselves, just as while some singers of hymns might note their author's name, few will be interested in the name of the tunes, their metres, or which guitar chords they use. Part is also, no doubt, due to their obscurity, which is at times impossible to penetrate. As long ago as 1919 the writer of the commentary on Psalms in the original *Peake's Commentary* called the psalm titles a "barren subject," devoting only half a column of his fifteen-column introduction to it,[3] and while there is evidence of some change since then (the new *Dictionary of the Old Testament: Wisdom, Poetry and Writings* gives them a substantial fifteen-column entry), Rodd's treatment in the *Oxford Bible Commentary* of 2001, which opens with a comment on their importance, only gives them two columns.[4] There is, however, one title point that invariably does create discussion and which most commentaries feel the need to address. It is the phrase *lᵉdawid*, traditionally translated as "of David," and the issue it raises is that of the Davidic

2. J. H. Eaton, *Psalms for Life*, (London: SPCK, 2006) ix.

3. W. E. Addis, "The Psalms," in *A Commentary on the Bible*, ed. A. S. Peake (London: T. Nelson, 1919) 373.

4. C. S. Rodd, "Psalms," in *The Oxford Bible Commentary*, ed. J. Barton and J. Muddimann (New York: Oxford University Press, 2001) 358.

authorship of the seventy-three psalms that carry this heading in the Hebrew Bible.

> The Davidic authorship enshrined in Jewish and Christian tradition has no credible historical grounding.[5]

> The so-called superscriptions or titles to individual psalms cause a disproportionate measure of difficulty to a translator, modern and ancient alike. . . . All in all . . . there is a variety of words/phrases that may be labelled "expressions of general reference." That is to say, they indicate without much specificity . . . that *x* has something to do with *y*. . . . One of these "expressions of general reference" is *tō dauid* (*tō asaph*, et al.). Since the Greek translator clearly did not assign authorship per se to such Psalms, I have opted for the reasonably neutral phrase, "Pertaining to Dauid" (et al.), since it allows for a range of perceived connections with the person(s) in question.[6]

These two statements, selected almost at random, one from a well-reviewed commentary by the doyen of literary critics who have written about the Bible, and the other from the general editor of a new translation of the Septuagint, illustrate the uncontroversial and long-accepted view of the "Davidic authorship" of the Psalms in what might be called, albeit controversially, the "mainstream" of Hebrew Bible/Old Testament scholarship. They may or may not also hint that this view might be problematic to some members of the faith communities who read the Psalms.

> The phrase 'of David' indicates that this song (*i.e.,* Psalm 3) either was written for David, in honor of David, or was placed in a collection to commemorate that great king.[7]

> Even greater caution is necessary in understanding psalm headings which seem to name authors . . . It seems probable, therefore, that while a number of psalms were written by David (e.g., Ps 3), some of his poems may have been edited for later congregational use; yet others not necessarily written by David have come down to us as items in a collection bearing his name . . . the great un-

---

5. R. Alter, *The Book of Psalms: A Translation with Commentary* (New York: Norton, 2007) xv.

6. A. Pietersma, *New English Translation of the Septuagint* (New York: Oxford University Press, 2007) 545.

7. J. F. D. Creach, *Psalms* (Louisville: Geneva Press, 1998) 6.

certainty surrounding all these psalm headings applies also to the ten which recall incidents in the life of David.[8]

These two statements from Christian scholars, "conservative" ones at that, written for a Christian public and also chosen almost at random, are slightly more cautiously expressed but clearly emerge from that same position. Lest this be thought a bold thing to write in such a commentary for such a constituency, and something of only relatively recent doing, here is the oldest instance of this kind of thing known to me in a Bible commentary intended for church use:

> After all that has been done to assign each Psalm to its author, there are few of which we can say positively, "These were made by David."

This comes from the introduction to the Psalms in volume 4 of the *Bible Commentary* by the English Methodist Adam Clarke, published in 1821. The commentary as a whole appeared in eight volumes between 1810 and 1826 and went through numerous reprints through the nineteenth century in British Methodism.

Needless to say there are contemporary scholars with impeccable academic credentials who hold a different view. In two important contemporary dictionary entries, Waltke[9] presents a passionate argument in support of the Davidic authorship of the psalms that bear his name, and Dale Brueggemann[10] offers a careful and nuanced argument for the same position, though Tucker,[11] in a shorter contribution in the same dictionary, does not appear to be taking the same line. The case for Davidic authorship is very clearly stated by Bullock[12] in his student introduction. The explicitly evangelical introduction to the Old Testament by Dillard and Longman must be noted here too, though its conclusion that "while

---

8. R. E. O. White, *A Christian Handbook to the Psalms* (Grand Rapids: Eerdmans, 1984) 26f.

9. B. K. Waltke, "Psalms: Theology of," in *New International Dictionary of Old Testament Theology and Exegesis*, ed. W. A. VanGemeren (Carlisle: Paternoster, 1996) 4:1101–3.

10. D. A. Brueggemann, "Psalms 4: Titles," in *Dictionary of the Old Testament: Wisdom, Poetry, and Writings*, ed. T. Longman and P. Enns (Downers Grove, IL: InterVarsity, 2008) 619.

11. W. D. Tucker, "Psalms 1: Book of," in *Dictionary of Old Testament*, 578–79.

12. C. H. Bullock, *Encountering the Book of Psalms* (Grand Rapids: Baker, 2001) 23–26.

the titles are not canonical, they may be reliable" raises more issues than it resolves.[13]

Gerald Sheppard offers an important corrective here when he argues that both so-called liberal and literalist preoccupations with questions of authorship are inadequate.[14] He sees the Davidic element in the psalm titles as an important editorial device in the canonical process in which psalms are transformed from what they were in their original settings, wherever and whatever they were, to what they are in the canon of Scripture, in which they are to be read alongside the equally canonical stories about David. So for him, as in his treatment of Ps 51 which he offers as an example, the links with the David story in 2 Sam 11–12 as indicated in the psalm heading, "when the prophet Nathan came to him, after he had gone in to Bathsheba," adds depth, richness, and insight to the reading of the psalm as Scripture in which "the ordinary words of women and men become God's word to me."[15] Thus, he argues, these editorial points are neither to be dismissed, as in much "liberal" interpretation, nor misunderstood, as in much "literalist" interpretation, but seen as examples of "inner-biblical" interpretation, which contributes significantly to richer readings of the Psalms as Scripture. Important though this way of reading the Psalms, and the Old Testament more generally, is and is becoming, for the purpose of this chapter it must simply be observed that it too is based on the premise that David wrote few, if any, of the psalms that bear his name.[16]

l^edawid

l^edawid

One hundred of the psalms contain a name in their headings: David (73), Asaph (12), Korah (11), Jeduthun (3), Solomon (2), and once each for Ethan, Heman and Moses (yes, that does add up to more than one hundred, four titles contain more than one name). We will pause at two of these names before considering David.

---

13. R. B. Dillard and T. Longman, *An Introduction to the Old Testament* (Leicester: Apollos, 1995) 216; compare Tucker, "Psalms 1," 579.

14. G. T. Sheppard, *The Future of the Bible: Beyond Liberalism and Literalism* (Toronto: United Church Pub., 1990) 74–98.

15. Sheppard, *Future of the Bible*, 89–95.

16. Sheppard, *Future of the Bible*, 80–81.

Psalm 90 is entitled "A Prayer of Moses, the man of God" (NRSV, etc). REB goes a slightly different way with "A prayer: ascribed to Moses, the man of God." Immediately we see one of the insoluble translation issues to which Pietersma alludes. Are "a prayer" and *lᵉmošeh* a single phrase, as NRSV reads them, or are they two separate expressions as REB reads them? Each is possible. As to the Mosaic authorship of this psalm, Anderson speaks for the mainstream of biblical scholarship when he writes:

> The Psalm is attributed to Moses, and as such it is unique in the Psalter. Few . . . would accept the Mosaic authorship of this lament; most scholars agree that the composition is of a post-Exilic date, late rather than early. The ascription of the Psalm to Moses may be (at least partly) an appreciation of the poem by later generations.[17]

Tate, in his commentary in the *Word Biblical Commentary* series from a more conservative position, says much the same:

> Though the context(s) of the psalm's composition and use cannot be absolutely fixed, the ascription of the psalm to Moses in the title is undoubtedly the result of later (probably post-exilic) scribal exegesis . . .[18]

Pss 72 and 127 are headed *lišᵉlomoh*, which is rendered "of Solomon" (NRSV, NIV, NJB, NIV, NJPS, NKJV, RSV, RV) or, rather differently, "for Solomon" (Alter, KJV, REB) and unambiguously, "by Solomon" (GNB).

In his excellent and widely-used introductory handbook on the Psalms, Lucas gives an excellent summary of the usual and important explanation that the Hebrew preposition used here (*l-*): ". . . may indicate authorship ('by'), ownership ('belonging to'), the person for whom it was written ('for')"; and adds that in Ugaritic ". . . the preposition *l-* seems to indicate the person who is the main character of a poem ('about')."[19]

And so to David. Seventy-three psalms are headed *lᵉdawid* (Pss 3–9, 11–32, 34–41, 51–65, 68–70, 86, 101, 103, 108–10, 122, 124, 131,

17. A. A. Anderson, *The Book of Psalms*, New Century Bible (London: Oliphants, 1971) 649.

18. M. E. Tate, *Psalms 51–100*, Word Biblical Commentary (Dallas: Word, 1990) 438, where he goes on to offer a possible explanation of what that unknown scribe or scribes was trying to do and why.

19. E. Lucas, *Exploring the Old Testament*, vol. 3: *The Psalms and Wisdom Literature* (London: SPCK, 2003) 19f.

138–145). Of these, thirteen contain a note in their titles of the event or incident "when" David uttered the psalm (Pss 3, 18, 34, 51, 52, 54, 56, 57, 59, 60, 63, 142) or, in the other case, the person about whom he did (Ps 7). Consistent with their translation of the references to Solomon, NRSV, NIV, NJB, NJPS, RSV, and RV translate the term as "of David" while REB has "for David." Alter, however, opts for the neutral "a David psalm," as does Peterson in *The Message*. KJV changes tack and joins the "of David" camp. GNB uses its own title for each psalm, but consistently in its footnotes gives, "A psalm by David."

The same construction is found in the superscription to the Song of Songs, which GNB translates, "The most beautiful of songs, by Solomon." There, however, it adds the footnote: "By Solomon; *or* dedicated to Solomon, *or* about Solomon." No such qualifying note appears about *lᵉdawid* in psalms, and that silence is a perfect illustration of the nervousness of the editors around this issue. Any indication of the academic consensus that *lᵉdawid* is not about authorship but about a psalm's dedication, or its belonging to "the royal collection" or the like, is absent from GNB and from most other translations.

THE "DAVIDIZATION" OF PSALMS

The Targum on Psalms has one less David psalm than the Hebrew Bible, omitting any David reference from the heading of Ps 131. It also adds "situations" to its titles of Pss 9 and 58. Among interesting details are the note that Ps 60 is a "copy made by David," that Ps 143 is "for David," that Ps 44 is "For David, composed by the Sons of Korah," but especially that its standard "of David" becomes "composed by David" for Pss 52–55 and 69 (with that as an editorial addition in italics also in Pss 70, 101, 103, 138–40, 142, and 144). It clearly understands that the Aramaic *l-* in these psalm headings can mean "composed by" ("by Solomon" [Ps 72], "by Asaph" [Pss 50, 73, etc.], and "by the sons of Korah" [Pss 42, 44, etc.]), but Braude chooses to render it like that regarding David only in these few instances.

When we turn to the Septuagint we find an interesting development. The number of *tō dauid* psalms increases by thirteen (using the Hebrew Bible numberings, these are Pss 33, 43, 71, 91, 93–99, 104, 133). Two of these, Ps 96 ("When the house was being rebuilt after the captivity") and

Ps 97 ("When his land is being brought to order"), have a "when" in their headings, but it is clear that these "whens" are much more akin to the situational title in Ps 30 than to those in the thirteen headings that refer to an event in David's life. Then an extra, unnumbered psalm is found at the end, which is not part of the collection, and is usually called Ps 151 for identification purposes. This is headed, "This psalm was written in his own hand by David, though outside the number, when he fought Goliad in single combat." It is written in the first-person singular and is autobiographical in a way none of the canonical David psalms are. Brenton's classic translation of the Septuagint renders this *tō dauid* as "of David," which is not the most obvious translation of the Greek, while NETS opts for the "reasonably neutral" and more open "pertaining to David," as we saw in the quote from Pietersma.

One hundred twenty-six of the Hebrew Bible's one hundred fifty psalms are found in longer or shorter fragments in the manuscripts from Qumran. Among those with headings or titles that have been preserved, Pss 33, 91, 99, 104, and 133 are attributed to David, as they are in the Septuagint. In addition, Pss 33 and 123 can be added to the David list. At least fifteen other psalms have been found at Qumran, one of which (the otherwise unknown "Third Exorcism Psalm," 11QPsAp[a]) is also attributed to David. Qumran psalms 151A (11QPs[a]: 151A) and 151B (11QPs[a]: 151B) are expansions of the supernumerary psalm at the end of the Septuagint. The first recounts that David was a shepherd and summarizes the eventful visit of Samuel (1 Sam 16); the second is fragmentary but is clearly recounting David's victory over Goliath (1 Sam 17).

11QPs[a], the Great Psalms Scroll, is the largest of the forty psalm scrolls from Qumran, and it ends with a selection of material clearly designed to assert its Davidic authorship. There is a fragment called "David's Last Words" (compare 2 Sam 23:1–7) and then this otherwise unknown note called "David's Compositions":

> And David, son of Jesse, was wise and a light like the light of the sun, and a scribe, and discerning and perfect in all his ways before God and men. And the Lord gave him a discerning and enlightened spirit. And he wrote 3600 psalms; and songs to sing before the altar over the whole-burnt perpetual offering for every day, for all the days of the year: 364; and for the Sabbath offerings, 52 songs; and for the offering of the New Moons and for all the days of the festivals, and for the Day of Atonement: 30 songs. And all the songs that he uttered were 446, and songs for making

music over the possessed, 4. And the total was 4050. All these he uttered through prophecy which had been given him from before the Most High.

Psalms 140 and 134 follow this (why is unclear) before Pss151A and 151B end the scroll.[20]

Pietersma's comment on the disproportionate amount of trouble caused to translators by these superscriptions can also be seen in a brief look at the Vulgate, which adds two psalms to the growing David list (Pss 67 and 71 in the Hebrew numberings), subtracts three (Pss 122, 124 and 145) and includes three new "situations" (Pss 27, 96 and 143). Three titles are worth noting here for the prepositions they use: "For Iduthun himself, a canticle of David" (Ps 39), "A psalm of David, the canticle of Jeremias and Ezechiel to the people of the captivity, when they began to go out" (Ps 65), and "A psalm for David, of the sons of Jonadab and the former captives" (Ps 71). In total in Douay-Rheims the prepositions used are: "to David" (4), "of David" (14), and "for David" (60), with three of the first set being "to David himself" and nineteen of the third being "for David himself." This is far more complex than the standard "of David" of the majority of English versions and Brenton's Septuagint.

Our final example of the growing list of David psalms, and of how he could write psalms about later events (i.e., "through prophecy," as in the compositional note from Qumran) is the Midrash on Psalms (*Midrash Tehillim*), containing material from the third to thirteenth centuries CE.[21] Here it is said that David "gave five Books of Psalms to Israel" (on Ps 1.2) and that he was the author of 148 "psalms of praise" (on Ps 104.2), including the keynote Ps 1. A lovely example of the complexities involved in all this is in the discussion of Ps 91, untitled in the Hebrew Bible and the Old Testament, but authored by David in the Septuagint, the Vulgate, and in a reconstructed text at Qumran (where it is the Fourth Exorcism Psalm, 11QPsApᵃ). In the Midrash, however, we find, "It is argued that Solomon composed this Psalm. It was composed, however, by none other than Moses," an assertion repeated in other comments later on the same verse.[22] David is also cited as author

---

20. M. Abegg Jr., P. Flint, and E. Ulrich, *The Dead Sea Scrolls Bible* (New York: HarperCollins, 1999) 583f.

21. W. G. Braude, *The Midrash on Psalms*, 2 vols. (New Haven, CT: Yale University Press, 1959) 1:xxxi.

22. On Ps 91:1, see Braude, *Midrash*, 100f.

in fifteen of the otherwise unattributed psalms, twelve of which are new to our growing David list (Pss 1, 2, 102, 105–7, 111, 114, 116, 119, 137, 149). No such credit is given to him, however, for the "royal psalms" in the 90s. The Midrash adds no new "situations" in the titles of its David psalms, but its reflections on at least six of them assume such a situation (Pss 17, 53, 55, 58, 122, and 144).

DAVID, "THE SWEETE SINGER OF ISRAEL"

Whether or not *l^edawid* is an indication of authorship in the Hebrew Bible, it is clear that the Davidic authorship of many, if not most, of the psalms in the canonical book of Psalms is assumed and promoted by the developing tradition. The beginnings of that tradition are quite minimalistic, lying in the story of David's soothing lyre-playing for King Saul in 1 Sam 16:14–23, a possible allusion to which is found in Amos 6:5. The tradition grows in the Chronicler's presentation of King David's wide-ranging involvement with liturgical music. With all Israel he "dances before God . . . with song, lyres, harps, tambourines, cymbals and trumpets" when he begins the process of bringing the ark up to Jerusalem (1 Chr 13:8). He organizes the music when the process is resumed (1 Chr 15:16–24) and leads the worship (vv. 25–28). He then "appointed the singing of praises to the Lord by Asaph and his kindred" (1 Chr 16:7) with Heman and Jeduthun involved too (1 Chr 16:41f). Whether he sings the psalm or commissions it is unsaid, but the Festive Psalm in 1 Chr 16:8–36 is a pastiche of parts of three canonical psalms, none of which is headed as Davidic (Pss 105:1–15, 96, and 106:1, 47–48). Towards the end of his life he makes the necessary arrangements for his son Solomon to build the temple he had been unable to build himself, and the arrangements includes musicians (1 Chr 23:5) and the special commissioning of the sons of Asaph and of Heman and Jeduthun to "prophesy with lyres, harps and cymbals" (1 Chr 25:1). At the end of all of this he "blessed the LORD in the presence of all the assembly" (1 Chr 29:10). Solomon might build the temple, but this leaves us in little doubt about whose temple it was intended to be—David's. As we have seen, the tradition of David the psalmist reaches its height in Judaism in that composition note from Qumran. This tradition clearly understands the David in question to be the historic king, successor to Saul and father of

Solomon, the "sweete singer of Israel" (2 Sam 23:1, Geneva Bible, 1560) and "father of liturgical psalmody" (Ecclus. 47:8–10), and it is this position that became firmly established in the tradition of both Judaism and Christianity, indeed the Talmud attributes all of the Psalms to David (Baba Bathra 14b, 15a; Pesahim 117a)!

In his recent, large, three-volume commentary, Goldingay adds another point, that the word "David" is in fact capable of other references than that to the historical shepherd-turned-king. It can refer to any of the kings of David's line, and after the demise of that royal line it can refer to the future king, the Anointed One, the Messiah who is to come, at least in the hopes of some,[23] or, as we might say, to "David, the Once and Future King."

THE TREASURY OF DAVID

In evangelical Christianity the image of David the psalmist is perhaps seen nowhere more clearly than in the title of C. H. Spurgeon's *The Treasury of David* and in the treatment of him as such throughout that classic. The same point is emphatically made in this historically important text:[24]

> The author of this book. It is, no doubt, derived originally from the blessed Spirit. They are spiritual songs, words which the Holy Ghost taught. The penman of most of them was David the son of Jesse, who is therefore called the 'sweet psalmist of Israel' (2 Sam 23:1). Some that have not his name in their titles yet are expressly ascribed to him elsewhere, as Ps 2:1–12 (Acts 4:25) and Ps 96:1–13 and Ps 105:1–45 (1 Chr 16:1–43). One psalm is expressly said to be the prayer of Moses (Ps 90:1–17); and that some of the psalms were penned by Asaph is intimated (2 Chr 29:30), where they are said to praise the Lord in the words of David and Asaph, who is there called a seer or prophet. Some of the psalms seem to have been penned long after, as Ps 137:1–9, at the time of the captivity in Babylon; but the far greater part of them were certainly penned by David himself, whose genius lay towards poetry and music, and who was raised up, qualified, and

23. Goldingay, *Psalms* (Grand Rapids: Baker Academic, 2006) 1:27

24. Section 2 of the introduction to Psalms in Matthew Henry's *Complete Commentary on the Whole Bible*, 1706.

animated, for the establishing of the ordinance of singing psalms
in the church of God.

This understanding and the use made of it in "devotional" readings of
the Psalms in church and synagogue continues in widespread use to this
day, and if evidence is needed then almost any contemporary devotional
commentary on Ps 23 will supply it, as will listening to sermons on
psalms or on David, to say nothing of googling either topic and seeing
what your trawl reveals on the Web.

CONTROVERSY

Thus far we have noted, and considered the evidence for, the strong academic majority view that *lĕdāwīd* is not to be understood as a statement
about authorship and that it is probably best taken to denote dedication
or ownership—"for David" or "belonging to David"—"David" being
understood to mean the old royal house of Judah. My own practice,
considering all of this, is to translate the term as "belonging to the royal
collection" or "dedicated to the king." And it is at this point that two
worlds collide. Here the long devotional tradition of David the psalmist
among traditional Bible-reading Christians meets an academic commonplace. Alert to this clash of cultures, Seybold concludes his discussion of authorship in the psalm titles in his widely used introduction to
the Psalms like this:

> Only with the personalisation of the originally anonymous Holy
> Scriptures and the distribution of the text-complexes under the
> names of great authors, Moses, David, Solomon, and the proph-
> ets, Ezra, etc., did the Psalms too come to be given an "author,"
> a simplification which may have had dogmatic advantages, but
> which in the long run has been at the cost of historical plausibil-
> ity and has led to ideological entrenchment.[25]

There is, however, something more.

---

25. K. Seybold, *Introducing the Psalms* (Edinburgh: T. & T. Clark, 1990) 38.

BUT JESUS SAID

Most discussions of the authorship of psalms do not go here, for good reason, as we shall see. In the classroom, however, there is usually someone who will quote Mark 12:36–37 or its parallels in which Jesus affirms that David wrote Ps 110. It is often the same person who in previous classes has quoted Matt 12:39–41 to demonstrate that Jesus believed the Jonah story to be history rather than parable, and Matt 24:37–39 to show that Jesus also believed in a real flood at the time of Noah. For such an interpreter, if Jesus said that David wrote those psalms then David must have written them. It is possible to respond to this point in a number of ways. One is to point out, with tongue in cheek, that Jesus admits that there are some things he does not know (Mark 13:32 and parallels). Another might be to refer to the ongoing "Jesus of history/Christ of faith" debate, if one can remember the latest of its twists and turns, and to point out that it is the "remembered Jesus" whose "voice" we hear in the Gospels, mediated through the interpreters Matthew, Mark, and Luke—though that approach (which needs serious attention in the appropriate New Testament class) usually gets the discussion into still deeper water. Much the best approach here is to draw on the resources of classical post-Chalcedonian Christology and remind the class that the orthodox position on this one is to acknowledge that if Christ was "fully human" then he did not know the geography of China or the formulae of nuclear physics. In the same way he would have believed that David wrote the psalms in question because that was what was thought at the time. One can even add the scriptural note that it was of such things that he "emptied himself" (Phil 2:7). Objecting students may not be convinced by any of this, but at least at this point the biblical lecturer can refer them to the theology tutors for a lesson in orthodox Christology.

As the discussion in class proceeds, however, some students might mention the views of Luke and Paul on this topic. For Luke they may cite Acts 1:16–20, which refers to the Holy Spirit speaking through David in Pss 69 and 109, Acts 2:25 about David writing Ps 16, and Acts 4:25 about him writing Ps 2 (which has no Davidic title in the Hebrew Bible, and is the second half of Ps 1 in the Septuagint, which has no Davidic heading either). For Paul, reference might be made to Rom 4:6 citing David as author of Ps 32, and Rom 11:9 about Ps 69. And finally, someone might add that Heb 4:7 follows the Septuagint and cites David as the author of Ps 95, which is unattributed in the Hebrew Bible. By which point, the discussion is not so much about the authorship of the Psalms as about the inspiration and authority of the Bible.

TIME TO GET PERSONAL, CONTEXTUAL, AND REFLECTIVE

It will be clear by now, I think, that I regard myself as both a fully paid-up, though minor, member of "the mainstream academic Old Testament community" and as a loyal and faithful "mainstream" Christian of the English Methodist variety; and that I see no conflict between these two aspects of my being and doing. No doubt some readers will regard my use of "mainstream" here, albeit in inverted commas, as begging too many questions, as tendentious or provocative, or all of the above. It is, however, the only label in both areas that I am prepared to use, in a world where labels are increasingly divisive rather than informative. It will also be clear in the reflections that follow that I am writing from the British church and university scene, which is in many ways quite different from the American one, if I can actually use the singular in either case.

Hearing the Davidic authorship of seventy-three psalms questioned in a class, seminar, or house group is obviously not as high on the trauma scale as first encountering questions around the resurrection of Jesus or the historicity of Abraham or the exodus, but for some students the challenge is real. Give in on this one, they say, and you are already beginning the slide down the slippery slope that ends in dismissing the Bible and everything it has to say. I have taken part in that sort of discussion throughout my ministry, in Methodist and other churches since I was ordained in 1971, and in academia. For the past twenty years I have worked with students training for ministry in the Anglican, Methodist, and United Reformed churches, together with public students working for theology qualifications, first in the University of Birmingham and then for longer in the University of Exeter. At the same time I have run programs—very similar in content to those that I have taught in these contexts—for the same three denominations in this part of the southwest of England, and published primarily for the same constituencies. What follows are my reflections on teaching the Bible with full academic rigor to adult Christians from a variety of church backgrounds, traditions, and faith perspectives.

In my classes and among my readership there have always been students who have been surprised to learn of commonplace academic issues about the Bible, including minor ones like psalm titles. Some of them are disturbed by what they encounter, others are relieved. There have also been students, thankfully, who are not surprised at all, because they come from that minority of churches where congregations are aware of these things and for whom there is no gap between the "devotional" and the "academic" reading of Scripture, between the worlds of the church and the academy, or between their minister's study and pulpit.[26]

The starting point of all my teaching is that the Bible as it is has to be taken seriously. My students, for example, get used to being told to read what a passage says, and not what they think it says, remember that it says, or have been told that it says, because for me close attention to the text as it stands is crucial. Hence the need to pay careful attention to how the Hebrew phrase *lĕdāwīd* is and should be translated. They also learn that saying "the Bible says . . ." is not enough, for first they have to say which Bible they are talking about because there is more than one canon. Hence the need to draw attention to the differences in psalm titles between the Septuagint and the Hebrew Bible, and to the fact that the NIV is not the same Bible as the NJB. Likewise they learn that, in that deceptively simple saying, there is a speaker who is controlling what is to be read from the Bible because he or she is the one who opens it, selects a passage, and gives it voice. Hence the need to know where different commentators and Bible versions are coming from, as well as recognize their own presuppositions and assumptions as readers—presuppositions and assumptions that their teacher needs to acknowledge too.

The other piece of essential early learning for my students is to recognise that genre is the key to all reading, reading the Bible included, and that if one gets the genre wrong then all kinds of strange things can happen. Thus for my students there is an early and rigorous encounter with the realities of text, canon, reader, and genre because these are, for me, the essentials of beginning to take the Bible seriously. My conviction is that we cannot understand what our Bible or Bibles say or mean until

---

26. This "gap" was the subject of a series of articles in the *Expository Times* in 2000 under the heading "In Honesty of Preaching," a lovely phrase from a modern hymn by Fred Pratt Green. My contribution was headed "Mind the Gap," *Expository Times* 11 (June 2000) 293–96.

we have looked at them as they are and recognised how they came to us; and the fact that I have written most of that sentence with "Bibles" in the plural is part of the learning curve. It follows that, for me, doctrines of the authority and inspiration of the Bible must begin from the Bible as it is, rather than be imposed upon it as the starting point for reading the Bible. And at this point my observation is that problems are often created for students because their churches have given them false expectations about the Bible that are exposed when the Bible is read seriously in the classroom. So for me, the problem is not with the academy teaching things that belittle the Bible (though I know that sometimes it does, which simply means that we must give the dogmas of the academy every bit as much critical scrutiny as we give the dogmas of the churches), but with some of the churches saying things about the Bible to which it cannot live up. Here the two classic examples of this are "inerrancy" for "evangelical" and "fundamentalist" Christians, and the Gospel procession for "catholic" ones. If you attend church week by week where you stand while the Gospel book is carried in procession, censed, kissed, and blessed before it is read only by a priest who introduces and concludes the reading with powerfully solemn words praising Christ for it, then you are almost inevitably going to be uneasy in a classroom discussing "the Synoptic problem." The "inerrancy" question, given the interests of this book, requires a couple of paragraphs of its own.

There is no doubt that the authority of the Bible has been and still is one of the most divisive issues among Christians, and we almost inevitably end up at this point even in classes discussing such a small matter as psalm titles. This is the fundamental issue threatening to split the Church of England and the Anglican Communion worldwide as I write this chapter. This is why labels like "evangelical," "fundamentalist," and "liberal" so often become battle banners. There is equally no doubt that big things are at stake here and that Christian students from all positions are right to get agitated about it. Discussion is, therefore, to be welcomed and encouraged. Strange as it may seem to readers in the USA, however, it is a fact that in all the serious and often heated discussions in university classes, church contexts, emails, and letters in which I have been involved over the years around the words "Bible," "authority," and "inspiration," the word "inerrancy" has almost never featured. Similarly, as an interested observer of the evangelical scene in the UK, I think it is fair to say that that word does not have a high profile in contemporary British evangelical discourse either. British evangelicals have much more to say about how the Bible's teaching is to be applied in today's church and world than they have about the doctrine of the inerrancy of Scripture.

I am not qualified to discuss why inerrancy does not appear to be an issue in the UK in the way that it clearly is in the USA, but I think there are a number of points worth noting. One is simply that the word "inerrant" does not feature in British "evangelical" self-description. The current Evangelical Alliance basis of faith, for example, works with a high definition of Scripture's authority, but the word "inerrant" does not feature in it, as it did not feature in the previous version of it. Another is that the "first wave" of fundamentalism in the early twentieth century, in which "inerrant" was such a key term, simply never caught on in the UK, or rather, the arguments against it won the day.[27] Here the obituary of A. S. Peake in *The Times* of 20 August 1929 has become famous:

> Perhaps it was Dr Peake's greatest service, not merely to his own communion but to the whole religious life of England, that he helped to save us from a fundamentalist controversy such as that which has devastated large sections of the Church in America. He knew the facts which modern study of the Bible has brought to light. He knew them, and he was frank and fearless in telling them, but he was also a simple and consistent believer in Jesus, and he let that be seen too, and therefore men who could not always follow him were ready to trust him, and let him go his own way. If the Free Churches of England have been able without disaster to navigate the broken waters of the last thirty years, it is largely to the wisdom and patience of trusty and trusted pilots like Arthur Samuel Peake that they owe it.

Similarly C. H. Dodd, writing in the *Dictionary of National Biography, 1922–30*, summarizes Peake's life and work so: "his work did much to save the Free Churches of Great Britain from the baneful effects of 'Fundamentalist' controversies."

Peake left another legacy too: the relationship between church and university exemplified by his life and his *Commentary* of 1919 has

---

27. The literature is enormous, but see the chapters in James Barr, *Fundamentalism*, 2nd ed. (London: SCM, 1981); idem, *Escaping from Fundamentalism* (London: SCM, 1984); Kathleen C. Boone, *The Bible Tells Them So: The Discourse of Protestant Fundamentalism* (London: SCM, 1990); Peter Herriot, *Religious Fundamentalism: Global, Local and Personal* (London: Routledge, 2009); and Christopher H. Partridge, ed., *Fundamentalisms* (Carlisle: Paternoster, 2001).

continued to be normative in the UK until very recently. This can be seen not only in "liberal" scholars like C. H. Dodd but also in the life and work of such great British evangelical scholars as F. F. Bruce, C. K. Barrett, and I. H. Marshall. The UK is currently experiencing the "new wave" of fundamentalism and what effect that will have remains to be seen, but so far the number of "ideological fundamentalists" in the British scene remains small. There are, needless to say, a larger number of "folk fundamentalists" in the British church, by which I mean those who are oblivious to academic questions about the Bible. My experience with such people is that, in the main, they respond positively, and often with relief, when they are introduced to these questions. Their move from Ricoeur's famous "first naiveté" to his second might not be painless, but few seem to regret the transition once it has been made.

Perhaps my final point on inerrancy might entail two questions. Is one possible reason for the British lack of interest in inerrancy the observation that the Bible as it is demonstrates that the doctrine does not fit the facts? Is another reason the recognition that the idea of inerrancy has no biblical warrant, in that it arises from an interpretation of a single word in 2 Tim 3:16—which the word itself does not need and does not justify? Whatever the reasons, the doctrine of the inerrancy of Scripture rarely comes up as the presenting issue when students in my classes in church or university are exposed to academic questions about the Bible.

CONCLUSION

The Davidic authorship of seventy-three psalms, or lack of it, is a small matter. We have noted the translation issue around the key Hebrew preposition. We have observed the fluidity of the growing tradition in the earliest versions, and its end point in the different canons of Scripture that emerge from them. We have seen the implication of this detail for doctrines of the authority and inspiration of the Bible. It seems to me that the phrase "honesty of preaching," from the modern hymn by Fred Pratt Green quoted in footnote 26, is too important to be confined to sermons. It should be the tenor of all teaching, and as such involve us in facing up squarely to the Bible as it is, and working outwards and onwards from there. The Bible itself, I am convinced, has nothing to fear from the honesty of "mainstream" academic rigor; neither, I am equally convinced, does the student, providing that academic rigor is accompanied by pastoral concern, which I take to be essential and a feature of all good teaching. It is true that some students and some congregations find the outworking of all this challenging, but since when has "challenge" been a dirty word in Christian discipleship? If someone is challenged because they can no longer "believe in the Bible" or "believe in the church" (to use two phrases that feature in these debates from time to time), is that not in fact a gospel challenge to them to put their faith "in" the only proper place in which Christian faith is to be put, namely, Christ?

What matters about the book of Psalms and the psalms it contains, of course, is not who wrote them, when, or where or why; nor the current big questions in Psalms study around the shape of the book or how it has been read and used down the centuries. Such technical and historical matters have a place, but it is a secondary one. What matters is what the Psalms say about God, faith, and life; how God engages with us as we sing them, pray them or meditate upon them; and how they enable us to bring the deepest emotions of praise or lament to God in worship and prayer. Beginning its life as a temple worship book, and morphing through *Torah* study book for godly living into a people's prayer book, the Psalms remains what it always was: "Words to God and Words from God," to use the title of a recent book.[28] Any teaching on the Psalms, or on Scripture more generally, that leaves students unable to read, sing, and pray them is simply bad Bible teaching, wherever it comes from. Good Bible teaching, on the other hand, enables faith to read, sing, and pray with heart and mind, even when they know that a "David psalm" almost certainly does not mean that he penned it.

---

28. H. N. Wallace, *Words to God, Word from God* (Aldershot: Ashgate, 2005).

9

Some Thoughts on Theological Exegesis of the Old Testament

Toward a Viable Model of Biblical Coherence and Relevance[1]

Peter Enns

INTRODUCTION

A RECENT MOVEMENT IN BIBLICAL interpretation is referred to as theological exegesis, and is represented by such well-known biblical scholars as Christopher Seitz, Francis Watson, and Joel Green.[2] The driving motivation behind this movement is an attempt to reclaim biblical interpretation as a decidedly theological exercise, which is something with which I am in enthusiastic agreement. My comments here will be

---

1. This chapter originally appeared in *Reformation and Revival Journal* 14 (2005) 81–204 and is included here by permission.

2. A recent summary of theological exegesis may be found in S. A. Cummings, "The Theological Exegesis of Scripture: Recent Contributions by Stephen E. Fowl, Christopher R. Seitz and Francis Watson," *Currents in Biblical Research* 2 (2004) 179–96. Joel B. Green and Max Turner have edited a volume focusing on NT studies that also contains valuable bibliographical information: *Between Two Horizons: Spanning New Testament Studies and Systematic Theology* (Grand Rapids: Eerdmans, 2003). Eerdmans is also planning to publish a commentary series (Two Horizons) that focuses on theological exegesis of the Bible.

restricted to the Old Testament, and I would like to begin by offering a working definition of theological exegesis that I trust will be allowed for the sake of discussion. Theological exegesis of the Old Testament is a distinctively Christian reading that seeks *coherence* and *relevance*: *coherence*, meaning it seeks to understand the parts in relation to the whole; *relevance*, meaning it seeks to focus on the theological significance of such exegesis for the church. Defined in this way, theological exegesis may be seen as a corrective to other approaches to Old Testament interpretation where it seems coherence and relevance are either ignored or even vilified, namely much of the history of higher-critical, post-Enlightenment exegesis.

Theological exegesis defined in this way is something with which I have an immediate affinity. This is because I am an evangelical/Reformed reader of Scripture. I read conscious of how the whole fits together (coherence), and seeking to understand where and how the ancient and modern horizons meet (relevance). I would go so far as to say that it is a basic Christian instinct to do so—bordering, perhaps, on common sense, although that may be overstating a bit. Yet it seems valid to observe that theological exegesis represents somewhat of an attempt at a recovery of the church's hermeneutical instincts *vis-à-vis* modern developments.

The purpose of this essay is to flesh out this rough definition of theological exegesis by observing how traditional models of coherence and relevance were challenged in early historical-critical scholarship on the Old Testament and in the fundamentalist response to that challenge. Specifically, the perspective I will take is to observe how historical criticism and fundamentalism collided precisely because they offered *alternate and competing models of coherence and relevance*. Although these early battles are technically over, trajectories were set during this time that are still felt by evangelicals today. I also am a firm believer that a strong grasp of our past is important for any forward progress we might wish to make. I will conclude with some very brief thoughts on how our own canon provides guidance for how the church today can read the Old Testament with coherence and relevance.

HISTORICAL-CRITICAL EXEGESIS OF THE OLD TESTAMENT: AN ALTERNATE MODEL OF COHERENCE AND RELEVANCE

I think it is important to state at the outset that the past 300 years of Old Testament interpretation have not been all bad. Among the benefits have been not only advances in our understanding of the nature of the biblical text, so-called lower criticism, but in our understanding of the Bible itself. I am thinking here mainly of the increased historical consciousness that largely defines modern scholarship, i.e., the issue of "Bible in context." It is the "quest for the historical . . ." Jesus, Abraham, Moses, or David that has helped us see something of the real-life, flesh-and-blood, incarnational dimension of Scripture—however erroneous some of the earlier quests may have been.

We need only think of how our understanding of the Bible and its world has been affected by such things as the discovery of ancient Near Eastern creation accounts, law codes, wisdom texts, various inscriptions—not to mention the Dead Sea Scrolls and, in their wake, the accompanying increased attention given to Second Temple Judaism in general. The effects of these and other discoveries from 1850 to 1950 have been felt by all serious students of the Bible, and no one would dare argue that these discoveries have been of little consequence, or that they have not affected—in many cases deepened—our interpretation of portions of Scripture.[3] This is why theological exegesis, if it is to be successful, cannot stand at a safe distance from modern scholarship. Instead, it must be truly progressive, meaning it must be a project undertaken *in light of* and *in conversation with* the Bible in the modern world, while at the same time having a chastening and even correcting role over against modernist hegemony and overconfidence in its own conclusions. This is what I, at least, perceive to be one of the potential strengths of theological exegesis, that it be neither *fearful* of nor in *bondage* to modern interpretation of the Bible.

The well-rehearsed rise and development of higher-critical Old Testament scholarship does not need to be repeated here, but at least one aspect is relevant. Its inception was driven in part by a desire to liberate the study of the Bible from the control of both Roman Catholic and post-Reformation dogmatics. These dogmatic systems were, to say the least, highly successful in their respective interpretive communities.

---

3. One need only turn to the *NIV Study Bible's* notes for Genesis to make the point.

They claimed an ancient pedigree and enjoyed official authority. And they employed Scripture in ways that were deemed highly coherent and relevant. They were coherent in that they were *systematic*; they were relevant in that they were to be *believed* by all the faithful. Spinoza's (1632–1677) goal was to undermine such dogmatic systems, at least in part because of how he felt dogma was used to maintain political control over the people. Spinoza sought to deconstruct dogma (and therefore, as he saw it, political oppression) by reading Scripture afresh—by wresting it from the control of the clergy and putting it into the hands of the common man, guided only by the light of reason, not ecclesiastical authority. And, thus, in the minds of some, modern biblical criticism was born, or at least conceived. Some of what Spinoza set in motion was picked up by subsequent biblical scholars.

The beginnings of modern Old Testament scholarship specifically are very clear. *The* question around which modern Old Testament scholarship was born and, in my opinion, from which subsequent scholarship proceeded, was, "Who wrote the Pentateuch?" More specifically, "Who wrote Genesis?"—since this is the portion of the Pentateuch to which neither Moses nor any other biblical author would have been an eyewitness. Specifically, two issues came to be the focus of attention beginning in the late seventeenth century. The first and most fundamental focus concerned the literary diversity of the Pentateuch, exemplified by use of the various Hebrew names for God, namely Elohim and Yahweh (translated "God" and "Lord," respectively, in English Bibles). These early investigations were the impetus for what eventually developed into the well-known Documentary Hypothesis (the four sources of the Pentateuch known as JEDP). The second focus was the "post-Mosaica" of the Pentateuch, those portions that seemed, on chronological and others grounds, to have originated later than the time of Moses.[4] Both of these foci were central to source criticism, the first Old Testament higher-critical methodology.

Then, in the nineteenth century, a third focus came into view, instigated by the explosion of extrabiblical data mentioned above. Now the question became, "What is the relationship between Genesis and the worldviews of Israel's ancient Near Eastern neighbors?" The field of "comparative religions" was born, which has dominated Old Testament

---

4. Some commonly cited examples include Deut 1:1; 34:5–8; Num 12:8; Gen 12:6; 36:31.

scholarship in general since then. Indeed, it is the foundation of every Hebrew Bible doctoral program I know of and to which evangelical professors are keen to send their best students. Although not always intended in this way, all three of these developments (literary diversity, post-Mosaica, ancient Near Eastern parallels) threatened—or were at least perceived to threaten—traditional, dogmatic notions of the Old Testament's coherence and relevance.

Whatever one might think about the strengths and weaknesses of source criticism, we must remember that source critics were not the first to address some of these Bible difficulties. Jewish and Christian interpreters had taken note, for example, of post-mosaic elements for quite some time. For example, both Jerome and the twelfth-century rabbi Abraham ibn Ezra seemed concerned about the implications for mosaic authorship of certain passages.[5] What was introduced in *modern* scholarship, however, was the *radical redefinition of Israelite origins* in light of these kinds of data. The theory of sources to explain the use of divine names, along with the post-Mosaica, eventually led to a consensus, a "critical orthodoxy": Moses not only did not write the Pentateuch as we know it, but what had been the very core of the Mosaic contribution—the Sinaitic law—was considered fundamentally postexilic, a thousand years removed from the traditional date for Moses. The Pentateuch was not simply divided into sources. The placing of the law in the postexilic period formed the basis for *an entire reconstruction of Israel's history.*

Now, there have been many nuances and developments in source criticism, and it is perhaps not necessary to mention that, like any academic field, scholars who self-consciously espouse source critical methodology have disagreed among themselves on many issues. Indeed, some literary trends in contemporary Old Testament scholarship question openly the validity of a source-critical analysis, and I am in agreement with such trends. But despite recent developments, the abiding effect of these early trajectories has been considerable: source criticism effectively challenged the traditional understanding of the coherence of the Pentateuch. The reason for this is that heretofore the traditional model of

5. Concerning Jerome's comments on Deut 34, see John N. Hritzu, trans., *Saint Jerome: Dogmatic and Polemical Works*, ed. R. J. Deferrari, vol. 53 of *The Fathers of the Church: A New Translation* (Washington, DC: The Catholic University of America Press, 1965) 19. Concerning Abraham ibn Ezra's comment on Gen 12:6, see *Ibn Ezra's on the Pentateuch: Genesis (Bereshit)*, trans. H. N. Strickman and A. R. Silver (New York: Menorah, 1988) 151.

coherence of the Pentateuch was *tied inextricably and fundamentally to a Mosaic core*. Once that Mosaic core was challenged—once the law was deemed a postexilic development, not a pre-monarchic foundation—to mix well-known metaphors—the dominoes began to unravel down the slippery slope. The Pentateuch came to be understood as a tendential, ideological, political, postexilic, priestly, and power-mongering pasting together of disparate sources, which not only cannot speak today, but ought not to, at least not until its parts can be properly reassembled (the task of source criticism). In other words, not only were older notions of *coherence* challenged, but the *relevance* of the Pentateuch—based as it was on the older model of coherence—was dismissed as untenable and even naive.

In my opinion, what inspired the well-documented visceral reactions from traditional Christian *and* Jewish thinkers alike was precisely this loss of a traditional model of coherence and relevance. People of faith can stomach Moses using older sources to write Genesis, as early source critics such as Simon, Semler, and Astruc argued.[6] E. J. Young allowed for such a view as well.[7] They can even stomach a post-Mosaic final formation of the Pentateuch; Jerome, mentioned earlier, alluded to the possibility of Ezra's role as editor, which is a commonly held position today. But people of faith cannot stomach a Pentateuch that, as it stands, is actually a hindrance to true knowledge of Israelite history and religion. Here the title to Wellhausen's 1883 source-critical masterpiece speaks volumes: ***Prolegomena** to the **History** of Israel*. One must *first* do a source-critical analysis—hence, *prolegomena*—*before* one can describe Israel's *history*, and therefore its faith. The simple folk religion reflected in the earliest sources (J and E) such as we see in the patriarchal narratives, with altars being built under every tree, is the oldest and therefore purest expression of Israelite religion. The Law—represented in both D and P—is the latest development by over-zealous, legalistic priests who want worship centralized and legislated. To say the least, things were turned topsy-turvy.

6. A very helpful source of information concerning these early source critics can be found in Edward McQuenn Gray, *Old Testament Criticism: Its Rise and Progress* (New York: Harper, 1923). Gray cites extensively from the works of these three scholars and a number of others.

7. E. J. Young, *An Introduction to the Old Testament* (Grand Rapids: Eerdmans, 1964), 153.

But what has proved to be an even greater challenge to conventional notions of the Pentateuch were the various ancient Near Eastern texts and archaeological discoveries mentioned earlier. Source criticism is based entirely on creative ways of handling internal data, and so was susceptible to focused critique. Ancient Near Eastern literature, however, introduced an external framework against which portions of the Old Testament now demanded to be understood. In other words, this was concrete data that had to be dealt with. The earliest and most celebrated example is the *Enuma Elish*, the Babylonian creation story discovered in the mid nineteenth century that bore noticeable similarities to Genesis 1.[8]

Scholarship eventually moved away from the pan-Babylonianism that characterized the early enthusiasm for these texts. It is now considered injudicious to view Genesis as any way dependent specifically on this Babylonian account, and the creation stories from other ancient cultures, namely Egyptian, must also be brought into the picture.[9] Nevertheless, the similarities between Genesis and *Enuma Elish* remain very real and so require some sort of explanation. And in my view, not nearly enough evangelical work has been done in helping us work though the implications of such ancient Near Eastern texts. The importance of such a conversation is highlighted when we consider other well-known examples: the parallels to the flood story (e.g., Atrahasis and Gilgamesh epics); the Code of Hammurabi and its relationship to biblical law; the Sargon birth story and Moses' birth in Exodus 2; Egyptian wisdom and portions of Proverbs.

Locating the Old Testament in its ancient Near Eastern environment has proved challenging for evangelicals, but not all the news has presented problems. Many discoveries have supported notions of basic historicity of Old Testament narratives.[10] And we must always remember that all data are to be interpreted, which introduces the issue of one's

8. This text was discovered and gradually translated beginning in 1848. For some comments on the impact of this and other discoveries on our understanding of the Old Testament, see Peter Enns, *Inspiration and Incarnation: Evangelicals and the Problem of the Old Testament* (Grand Rapids: Baker, 2005) 23–29, 48–56.

9. See John D. Currid, *Ancient Egypt and the Old Testament* (Grand Rapids: Baker, 1997).

10. On this see, for example, Kenneth Kitchen, *On the Reliability of the Old Testament* (Grand Rapids: Eerdmans, 2003); Iain Provan, V. Phillips Long, and Tremper Longman, *A Biblical History of Israel* (Louisville: Westminster John Knox, 2003)—hereafter *BHI*.

presuppositions. Hence, academic debates continue about how best to understand the impact of some of these discoveries. The "assured results of criticism" have not always proved so certain. But when the dust settles from detailed points of debate, the fact remains that the history of Old Testament historical criticism in general has posed real challenges for traditional understandings of coherence and relevance. These challenges have not gone away and so have provided part of the motivation for such things as theological exegesis.

It has happened more than once that when an evangelical student of Scripture opens the *Hebrew* Pentateuch (not a translation) and reads it knowledgeable of and in conversation with the internal and external data brought to bear through the modern study of the Old Testament, they come away saying, "I see the point." They may not have abandoned the faith, but they have certainly been affected by their studies. To make this observation is not a crass concession to liberalism, but a recognition of how our understanding of Scripture has been affected by its modern study and how that can be challenging for evangelicals. The question we must ask is not how best to resist the modern study of the Bible, but how best to proceed forward in light of it.

It is true to a certain point to say that modern scholarship on the Pentateuch has *disrupted* previous models of coherence and relevance. But we are mistaken if we think of this as merely a negative (i.e., "critical") exercise—simply an "attack" on the Bible. There is more to it. We must ask ourselves a question that I feel is too little asked in evangelical circles: Why did such a supposedly purely *disruptive, negative* approach become so widely accepted? Why was there a "critical orthodoxy" to begin with? There are *many* possible, valid, and complex dimensions to answering these kinds of questions, but surely there is much more to it than they were all rebels against God, looking for ways to undermine Scripture. That may very well be true in some instances (in fact I think it is), but that hardly explains this phenomenon as a whole.

Rather, higher criticism caught on because it was found to be *persuasive*—not simply because it *destroyed* coherence and relevance, as if all modern scholars were looking for ways to rid themselves of traditional belief. It was persuasive because it offered *an alternate means of achieving coherence and relevance*—one that spoke to many modern readers. The lasting impact of modern criticism on the Pentateuch—the reason why it was *persuasive* to so many, the reason why after 300 years

or so, although regularly adjusted and revised, it continues to set parameters in the academic study of Scripture, even now to a certain extent
for evangelicals—is not because it *rejected* coherence—*but because it
achieved far too much of it*. It did not simply tear the Bible apart, but it
put it back together again in ways that gained, perhaps not universal, but
broad scholarly consensus.

I do not want to be misunderstood. In being descriptive of modern
biblical scholarship I do not mean to imply that every modern development is ultimately correct. Moreover, I do not intend to suggest that the
rise of modern criticism is anything other than a complex matrix of all
sorts of underlying and competing issues, not to mention the never-to-
be-neglected spiritual dimension. My only point is that modern biblical
scholarship should rightly be understood as *an alternate model of coherence and relevance,* and one that has achieved significant success, and
therefore cannot be taken lightly.

It should be noted that the *type* of *coherence* offered by source criticism could only be achieved by moving *beyond* the surface, so-called
plain reading of the text toward a radical rereading of the text in light
of contemporary worldviews and expectations. But perhaps we should
not fault source criticism too much for this. For what is true of modern
criticism is generally true of *any* reading of the Old Testament—ancient
or modern—that seeks to be coherent and relevant. Let me put it this
way. Modern criticism is *more* than a *denial* of inerrancy or inspiration,
as is sometimes asserted. And neither is it the crowning achievement of
human thought, the climax of the human intellectual drama, as is sometimes asserted on the other side. Rather, as I have heard Jon Levenson
say, modern criticism is modern midrash. Midrash is the ancient hermeneutical exercise of reading older texts in ways that speak to current situations—whether it be ancient Greco-Roman politics, the sectarianism of
Qumran, medieval rabbinic concerns, etc. What is assumed in midrash
is that the texts *ought* to address the current situation—no matter how
much effort and ingenuity it takes to do so.

It may sound odd to describe modern scholarship as midrash, but I
suggest the description is helpful nonetheless. Both ancient midrash and
modern criticism have to "do something" to the text in order to *bring it
into* the contemporary context. Both assert, "Our real focus of attention
is what is *beneath*, what is *hidden* to the naked eye, what can be surfaced
only through 'proper' interpretive techniques." Both ask the question,

whether implicitly or explicitly, "In light of who we are *now*, in light of what we now understand *our world* to be, what do these *ancient* texts mean?" As bold and simplistic as it might sound, I have just described in principle not only Wellhausen, but the Qumran community—and in fact *any* interpretive paradigm.

As for the question of *relevance*, modern criticism may not be focused on personal, moral appropriation (although liberalism did attempt to address this issue through the social gospel movement). As I see it, the relevance achieved through modern criticism is largely a matter of intellectual compatibility rather than personal moral behavior. The Bible's relevance in modern criticism is seen in how the recently reconstructed coherence now makes the Bible compatible with the modern worldview—this is a Bible "we can live with." Again, and to tip my hand a bit, I have just described in principle the concern of *any* interpretive paradigm: How can we understand the *old* text in a *new* way, in a way that makes *sense to us* in light of the world *in which we live? How is our Scripture relevant?* This question is as old as the recorded history of interpretation of the Old Testament and can be seen in the pages of the Old Testament itself (see below).

The current theological exegetical project, therefore, must be seen for what it is, not *new* in the sense that it is introducing or even recapturing coherence and relevance over against the purely deconstructive influence of modern approaches. Rather, like all exegetical paradigms, it too is offering an *alternate, rival* way of reading Scripture. *Its* success will be determined by how persuasive *it* is, which is to say, by how it offers a scheme that is deemed *more* coherent and *more* relevant than that which it seeks to replace. The question before us is what such a persuasive model of coherence and relevance can look like. The total package of the modernist paradigm, despite true advances, is ultimately not going to be acceptable for evangelicals. But did the original fundamentalist response address the matter persuasively?

FUNDAMENTALIST REACTION: MAINTAINING AN OLDER MODEL OF COHERENCE AND RELEVANCE

I want to be clear that I am using the term "fundamentalism" in a neutral, historically descriptive manner, not pejoratively. So, historically understood, fundamentalism was born out of the controversies instigated by higher criticism. I would describe it as essentially a reaction to modern scholarship insofar as it seemed driven by an urgency to *resist* higher criticism and to *maintain* precritical models of coherence and relevance. On one level, the urgency is understandable in that higher criticism was seen as a threat to such notions as inspiration, inerrancy, and infallibility.

And in this regard there are certain aspects of the fundamentalist reaction to higher criticism that are worthy of serious consideration, even if they have not always swayed the general academic population. I am thinking here primarily of the detailed and foundational arguments of nineteenth-century, Princeton Old Testament professors Joseph Addison Alexander and William Henry Green,[11] and many others who have owed a debt to them. In fact, much of the history of Old Testament study at nineteenth-century Princeton was largely defined by a reaction to source criticism. Entire careers of brilliant men were dedicated to countering the influence of Wellhausen, and so a number of valid and important counterarguments were leveled. At the very least, these early conservative critics were very adept at pointing out how some of the Pentateuchal data had been exaggerated or made to serve possible but not necessary conclusions. And so attention was drawn to the bias of some higher critics where the theory began to drive the analysis of the data. Some conservatives were particularly effective in pointing out the highly subjective degree to which sources were precisely delineated and, more importantly, dated.

It is one thing, for example, to notice the differences between Gen 1 and 2, or the repetition in the flood story, and to theorize some notion of sources, and to do so in a way that is still largely compatible with traditional views (as Jean Astruc did in the eighteenth century—Moses had access to two memoirs, one of that used Yahweh and the other Elohim, which Moses combined to write Genesis). But when one takes a theory that was designed to address these types of phenomena and applies that theory to texts that don't seem problematic, e.g., the highly coherent Joseph story, then exegetical problems are caused rather than solved.

---

11 A very helpful summary of the teachings of these and other Princeton Old testament professors may be found in Marion Ann Taylor, *The Old Testament in the Old Princeton School (1812–1929)* (San Francisco: Mellen Research University Press, 1992).

Fundamentalists were quick to point out the inconsistencies, exaggerations, and blind spots in modern pentateuchal scholarship.

But why really expend all that energy? It strikes me that the threat to fundamentalism was not simply in having a competing model of coherence running around. Rather it was in how the alternate model of *coherence* affected the notion of Scripture's *relevance* for the church. Again, higher criticism was persuasive to many, so persuasive that it led brilliant men to lay down their entire careers in service to its defeat. The higher-critical model did not just say, "Watch how clever we can be in constructing a new model of Scripture's coherence—watch us play the game 'divide the Pentateuch into sources.'" It said, "*Now* at last we know what the Pentateuch is *really* like, and it's not at all what you had thought. Now everything is up for grabs, and we're going to have to rethink some things."

In other words, higher criticism was perceived as threatening to take the Bible *away* from Christians. In fact, it was, and still is, often put more strongly: It threatened to destroy *the gospel itself.* Dots were quickly connected, and the dominoes unraveling down the slippery slope centered around the doctrine of Scripture. "If the critics are right here in Genesis, at the very beginning of the Bible, then we can no longer trust Scripture as God's plain word *anywhere.* And then we are only a stone's throw from a denial of the virgin birth, the atonement, resurrection—*salvation itself*—the personal application of Scripture's story, *the* issue where the coherence of Scripture touches down in the very practical question of its *eternal relevance.*"[12]

I agree with the heart motivation to defend the gospel, to keep the Bible in the hands of Christians, so to speak, so they can read it and believe it with confidence as God's word. My comments here are actually directed to help that happen more and more. This is why I am concerned that an *inadequate* defense of the gospel, one that is more reaction than engagement, may have, for some, the exact opposite effect. Again, without wishing to minimize the legitimate observations of fundamentalism, there are elements of the fundamentalist critique that have made the

---

12. Parenthetically, the parallels between this issue and the current, visceral debates over the New Perspective are telling. Once again, things can be tolerated such as a Second Temple background to the New Testament. But if one is perceived as attacking salvation—in this case, justification by faith—the gloves come off very quickly. The perceived threat of the NP is not in how Second Temple Judaism might generally affect our broad picture of the New Testament, but in how it is perceived to affect its *relevance.*

argument as a whole less effective than it might have been. This, it seems to me, is because the arguments seemed geared to maintaining at all costs an older model of coherence and relevance, rather than offering some sort of synthesis, even of a very modified sort, between traditional views and newer data. In other words, what I wish had happened in the nineteenth century was an articulation of a high view of Scripture that was deliberately in dialog with the impact of things like ancient Near Eastern data or post-Mosaica. But rather than offering a *persuasive alternative* to the modern paradigm, it focused mainly on the salvaging of an older one. And the reason for this, to me, is very important to understand. It is because *the survival of the **gospel itself** was seen to be dependent upon the success of the older model.*

This is illustrated in the famous diatribe of W. H. Green against the Anglican bishop—and missionary—Colenso.[13] Colenso was thoroughly convinced of source-critical arguments, but he was not an ivory tower academic. He took his message to the mission field. On one level the sense of urgency one can see in Green's writings is understandable, but this urgency was often expressed by simply making counterassertions and even *ad hominem* remarks. Such a critique could only go so far. Green could show how a source-critical methodology as a whole, when applied consistently, could become increasingly haphazard, chaotic, and subjective. He could thus deride source criticism as a whole, by poking holes in biased arguments here and there. But the biblical and extrabiblical data that raised the questions in the first place still needed to be addressed, and this is where the fundamentalist critique could come up short at points.

For one thing—and I very much wish to be corrected on this if I am in error—I have found no sustained discussion concerning the impact of extrabiblical texts in the writings of the nineteenth-century Princeton Old Testament scholars. I may recall an occasional reference, but no attempt to work through the implications of even such a widely discussed text as *Enuma Elish*. The focus, rather, as I mentioned earlier, was on source criticism. I am not entirely sure why this is the case, unless source criticism was simply seen as more of a threat because of its placement of the law in the postexilic period (as mentioned above).

---

13. See Peter Enns, "William Henry Green and the Authorship of the Pentateuch: Some Historical Considerations," *Journal of the Evangelical Theological Society* 45 (2002) 385–403.

But thinking beyond nineteenth-century Princeton specifically, we can see certain rhetorical strategies surfacing here and there in the fundamentalist response. For example, I still often see appeals to what I like to call the "it's possible" argument, or similarly the "be patient" argument. So, for example, the well-known reference to Moses' humility in Num 12:3 ("Now Moses was a very humble man, more humble than anyone else on the face of the earth" TNIV) is reconciled to Mosaic authorship by saying, "*It's possible* for Moses to have written that if he were in fact the most humble man on the face of the earth." Apparently that is a sufficient defense to maintain the traditional model. A similar explanation is typically offered with respect to the record of Moses' death in Deut 34:5–6 ("And Moses the servant of the Lord died there in Moab, as the Lord had said . . . to this day no one knows where his grave is," TNIV): "We're not sure how to reconcile this with Mosaic authorship. *It's possible* it's prophetic. In any event, we are sure that *patient exegesis* will provide the answer." If one's aim is to persuade—which is what I think was needed—rather than maintain, the "it's possible" argument can come across as obscurantist, and the "be patient" argument can seem more like stalling for time—or perhaps worse, "Don't bother me with details." There is also an awkward tension in the fundamentalist argument. The higher-critical model was taken to task for handling data inconsistently and obscuring legitimate tensions in the model, but apparently the tensions within the fundamentalist model could be sufficiently addressed simply by showing that it remained possible, provided that one exercise patience.

Now that cuts both ways. At points both the higher critics and the fundamentalists could be considered guilty of the *same* fallacy: assuming the ultimate validity in their own model, and, hence, maximizing "friendly" data, while minimizing those that are less compliant. One could call this last polemical strategy the principle of "selective engagement." For example, tensions, repetitions, and post-Mosaic elements in the Pentateuch *can* lend themselves to a source-critical framework, but that is not necessarily so. And for evangelicals, for example, the Tel Dan and Siloam Tunnel inscriptions can be appealed to in order to lend nice support to the historicity of the monarchy (namely the historical David and Hezekiah's tunnel project, respectively). Likewise evidence of Semitic presence in second-millennium Egypt meshes with the patriarchal and exodus narratives. But the Babylonian creation and flood stories, just to name the two most prominent examples, are likewise ancient Near Eastern data, but one is struck by how little these parallels have been addressed, not only in nineteenth-century Princeton, but by evangelical scholarship in general—at least in anything other than a defensive posture.

Both sides of the debate can be faulted, but their mistakes need not be repeated. My very practical concern is how the "it's possible," "be patient," and "selective engagement" arguments have had some deleterious effects for evangelicals. First, we probably all know evangelicals over the years who have left the faith because they have been *persuaded* by critical advances—and not just in seminary or graduate schools, but in high school and college "Bible as literature" classes; by watching PBS or the History Channel; by flipping through *Time* or *Newsweek*; or by reading popular novels. I would suggest that at least one reason for this is that these individuals have not had at their disposal a workable, alternate theological model for incorporating the data of modern scholarship. The issue is not that "they denied the Bible" and that's that, but *why*. The path from conservatism to liberalism is well worn—and often with great pain—but far, far less frequently has the journey been taken in reverse, and this should tell us something.

Now, that journey need not take place, in any case. The scholarly work regularly produced by faculty at recognized evangelical colleges and seminaries shows a degree of comfort and familiarity with studying the Old Testament in its ancient Near Eastern environment, and even arriving at conclusions—although perhaps somewhat modified—that at one point would have been deemed wholly unacceptable to fundamentalism. But a very important scholarly and spiritual question for me is whether evangelicals today can move beyond a piecemeal and uneasy relationship with modern scholarship and offer theological paradigms that interact seriously with relevant data, but without getting caught up in the entire worldview package offered by modernity—which at times has certainly been characterized by such things as autonomy, rebellion, arrogance; sin. Perhaps a chastened modernity, and one that reflects the concerns of theological exegesis, can offer the option that many are looking for today.

A second negative effect of the fundamentalist response is that simple resistance encouraged hostility to modern scholarship *in general*, i.e., the notion that acceptance of *any* higher-critical insights is "caving into liberalism." It seems to me that contemporary evangelical biblical scholarship has more or less moved beyond that. Third, it has encouraged a bifurcation of scholarship and faith among evangelicals. What many of us here have observed among critical-scholars—a public life of scholarship that rarely if ever intersects with their private life of faith—this strikes me as not unattested among evangelicals. There are very gifted evangelical scholars who are experts in various fields whose work, if time were taken to connect the dots, would have some impact on how they view their Bible. But too often, in my view, their two worlds of scholarly work and doctrinal formulations are kept separate.

It seems to me that we evangelicals are at a bit of an impasse. Is there room for growth, where we—*together, without suspicion*—can hammer out a viable theological model of coherence and relevance, *helping each other* to be cognizant of both promises and pitfalls—where our exegesis is able to make *proper* use of the state of modern scholarship (again, without accepting every conclusion or assumption)—and to bring that exegesis to bear on the church, the lives of God's people, in a way that is theologically meaningful, indeed, affirming, life-changing, and powerful—an exegesis that honors Christ?

Toward that end, there is one more important point to make, although we need to be brief here, for it is a whole topic unto itself. The conversation that we Protestant evangelicals *must* have is not *simply* with modern biblical scholarship. We must also acknowledge the vital role that the theological traditions of the church have played in providing coherent and relevant readings of Scripture, i.e., systematic theology. Of course, systematic theology means different things to different people, but I mean it to refer specifically to post-Reformation dogmatic formulations of whatever theological tradition you might represent. It is largely through systematic theology, although not necessarily in the full-blown sense of the term, that Christian doctrine has been communicated to the church. Hopefully, such theology is *grounded* in exegesis (without devolving into superficial prooftexting), but the fact remains that most Christians come to the Bible with a theological grid already in place, regardless of how inchoate or developed that grid may be. This must be understood and respected, lest we follow in Spinoza's footsteps.

In a sense, systematic theologies are the culminating statements of both coherence and relevance. But perhaps the greatest source of tension for evangelical *biblical* scholars is that the trajectories set in many of Protestant evangelicalism's theological formulations—be they full-blown systematic theologies, or confessions of faith, or perhaps more brief ten-point doctrinal statements—have largely been set *before* the rise of the modern focus on "Bible in context" (or, sadly, in complete isolation of modern developments). Hence, they are expressed in terms that are not in conversation with the kinds of issues that modern readers of the Bible need to address. Do we just go our separate ways? I say no. Good systematic theology is never a pure abstraction but dependent upon biblical exegesis. But here is the tension put another way: with the advent of modern biblical scholarship, the question now is rightly raised, "What exactly *is* exegesis?" Is it simply paying close attention to Hebrew grammar (maybe giving a nod to text-critical issues)? Or has exegesis developed into a historically conscious discipline that seeks as the first order of business to understand the Bible in its grammatical and *historical* contexts? Is this not the commonly assumed exegetical starting point among evangelicals? So, should such exegesis now be the model upon which older systematic theologies should be *evaluated* and newer ones *based*? Here is the question that many evangelical biblical scholars struggle with: *How can **modern** exegesis be in conversation with theological formulations that have **premodern** roots?* To ask questions such as these is not to answer them. But whatever efforts are expended by biblical interpreters to address matters of coherence and relevance must be in serious conversation with our own systematic theological heritage. But it is hoped that such a conversation would truly be a two-way street.

BIBLICAL MODELS OF COHERENCE AND RELEVANCE

The New Testament's use of the Old is a difficult and widely commented on topic. And for the purposes of theological exegesis, I feel it is an absolutely vital one.[14] My own views on how the church today can read its Bible with coherence and relevance have been deeply influenced by what I see the New Testament writers themselves doing. The

14. I address in more detail the thoughts expressed below in: "Apostolic Hermeneutics and an Evangelical Doctrine of Scripture: Moving beyond the Modernist Impasse," *Westminster Theological Journal* 65 (2003) 263–87; "The 'Moveable Well' in 1 Cor 10:4: An Extra-Biblical Tradition in an Apostolic Text" *Bulletin for Biblical Research* 6 (1996) 23–38; *Inspiration and Incarnation*, 113–65; *Exodus*, NIVAC (Grand Rapids: Zondervan, 2000) 19–32.

New Testament's use of the Old, understood in the context of Second Temple interpretive practices—understood, in other words, as a *historical* phenomenon—should play an important role as we work out hermeneutical practices today.

We cannot dwell here in any detail on the very important issue of the Second Temple context of New Testament hermeneutics. This is a huge, and perhaps somewhat controversial, topic in and of itself—although it is here to stay. I will only remark that a working knowledge of even the basic contours of Second Temple hermeneutics has shed considerable light on explaining the interpretive practices of Jesus and Paul. We are dealing with "Bible in context" yet again. Second Temple literature has had a similar effect as that of ancient Near Eastern parallels. Whereas the *Enuma Elish* has influenced how we understand Genesis, the Dead Sea Scrolls (or Targums, or Jubilees, etc.) have influenced how we understand how *Paul* understood Genesis. So, my hope is that theological exegesis will address this issue with great enthusiasm.

Apart from the Second Temple context, my focus here, in view of our specific topic, is a bit more restricted. As C. H. Dodd noted many years ago, the Old Testament is truly the substructure of New Testament theology.[15] The Old Testament is cited, alluded to, and thanks to the work of Richard Hays, we now understand it to be echoed in, the New Testament.[16] It is as if the New Testament authors cannot say *anything* without bringing the Old Testament into it. In a manner of speaking, the New Testament can rightly be described as a reading of the Old that seeks coherence and relevance *centered around the eschatological fulfillment of Israel's story, the death and resurrection of Christ, and the formation of the church, the new people of God.* In other words, we have again a reading of the ancient texts in light of present realities. And such a hermeneutical attitude—reading the past in view of the present—is presaged in our *own* canon long before we get to the New Testament.

How else can we explain, for example, the Chronicler's history of Israel? Why does a *second* history of the monarchy exist side-by-side with Samuel and Kings? Is it simply the case that these are the "things left over" from Samuel-Kings (reflected in the Greek title of Chronicles,

---

15. C. H. Dodd, *According to the Scripture: The Sub-Structure of New Testament Theology* (London: Fontana, 1965).

16. Richard B. Hays, *Echoes of the Scripture in the Letters of Paul* (New Haven, CT: Yale University Press, 1989).

as seen in the Septuagint, *paraleipomenon*)? But Chronicles is not side-by-side with Samuel-Kings. This is a false impression created by the Septuagint from which our English canonical order is derived. In the Jewish canon, Chronicles is last. Chronicles was not written as a *supplement* to Samuel-Kings, something to skip over in morning devotions because "I just read that." Although certainly interacting with Samuel-Kings, it is nevertheless intended to stand on its own and be read on its own terms. It tells an *alternate* summation of Israel's history, one that differs from Samuel-Kings, not because it is filling in some gaps but because it is told *from a different perspective and for different reasons*— namely from the perspective of those who had returned from captivity in Babylon.

Or better: It is an alternate reading of Israel's history that seeks to communicate the coherence and relevance of the past for the benefit of the present audience. The author is not interested in merely *recounting* past events for the sake of it. Rather he is *recasting* all of Israel's history in the light of postexilic realities—for the benefit of God's people who had returned from exile. We cannot overstate the impact of the exile on Israel's self-identity. Second Samuel 7 makes the emphatic point that a descendent of David will *never* cease sitting on the throne in Jerusalem. Yet Israel went into exile, which meant: no king, no temple, no sacrifice, no land—to the naked eye, the end of God's promises.

And this is where the Chronicler's distinct theology comes into play. He is reminding the people that, despite their difficult present circumstances, they have nevertheless a heritage that is long and honored. The returning exiles were asking whether they were still the people of God, whether his promises to them were still true. How can they still be God's people if all these promises have been dashed? The Chronicler's answer to this question begins with the very first name in the genealogies—the very first word in 1 Chronicles—Adam. Chronicles is an expression of *grand coherence*. The postexilic Israelites are to understand themselves as the people of God, despite appearances, whose pedigree goes back to the very beginning. Moreover, Chronicles presents Israel's history so as to make the lessons of the past *relevant*. We need only mention here, for example, how the Chronicler retells Israel's history so as to emphasize the notion of immediate retribution for the postexilic community: God will deal with *them* according to what *they* do, not previous generations. We also have the well-known issue of David's portrayal as virtually sinless, which reflects the Chronicler's messianic hope for an ideal Davidic ruler.

To bring up Chronicles is not tangential to our topic. *Chronicles is a biblically sanctioned example of theological exegesis*—and one that is put into even starker relief when we turn to the New Testament itself. The apostolic use of the Old Testament likewise constitutes a rereading of Israel's sacred Scripture in light of *the* climactic redemptive event, the event *from* which and *within* which we, standing at the end of the ages, are now to understand Israel's story. Just as we cannot overstate the impact of the exile for Chronicles, we certainly cannot overstate the impact of the cross and resurrection on the Apostles. Christ has died and was raised, and so in light of this climactic event, the New Testament authors provide us with a *new*, grand coherence, which is: *Israel's story is realized in Christ himself.* The Scriptures speak of *him*. And with that coherence we have a *new*, grand relevance, which is: Israel's story is realized *in us*, the in-Christ people of God, the church.

Although these terms may not be very familiar, let me put it this way: the Scripture's *coherence* is *Christotelic*, and its *relevance* is *Ecclesiotelic*. Christ is the end (Greek, *telos*) of Israel's story and so gives the *entire* story its unifying, coherent structure—much as the climax of a well-crafted story puts the pieces of the novel together in wonderful and exciting ways. And that Christotelic coherence is properly embodied only in the *church*, the body of Christ. The proper *application* of Israel's story—its true *relevance*—is in God's newly reconstituted people whose identities are found entirely in their union with Christ and his saving work.

The last thing I want to do—especially at the tail end of an essay—is to come off sounding either simplistic or abstract. This is not a magic key but a hermeneutical paradigm, the church's hermeneutical starting point and its goal. The Scripture's Christotelic coherence is not flat, as if we are trying to "find Jesus" in every corner of the Old Testament. And its Ecclesiotelic relevance is likewise not flat—it touches down on every single corner of our lives, even the most hidden parts, but it is beyond simple moralistic appropriation. An articulation of Christian coherence and relevance is not simple but hard, collective work.

CONCLUSION

I have argued here that it is good to have a clear grasp of where we have been so that we might know better where we are going. Theological exegesis is to be understood in the most recent context of the uneasy relationship between modern study of the Bible and the fundamentalist and evangelical response. But we must also keep before us the broadest of contexts, that within which any Christian exegesis must operate. The present and future of Christian theological exegesis, as it seeks to articulate a model of coherence and relevance, should proceed in self-conscious conversation with the grand hermeneutical trajectories set for us in Scripture itself. To do so is to acknowledge that, however contemporary theological exegesis may be, it is ultimately not so much a new project as an attempt to be faithful in carrying forward an old one.

10

Inerrantist Scholarship on Daniel

A Valid Historical Enterprise?[1]

Stephen Young

THIS CHAPTER ARGUES THAT commitment to inerrancy seals the book of Daniel from legitimate academic and historical analysis.[2] While I would broaden this to encompass all writings considered inerrant by inerrantists, generally those of the Protestant Bible,[3] I focus my analysis on the book of Daniel and associated secondary literature. Daniel has long been recognized as a particularly active site for contestations over inerrancy. This stems from several of its features: numerous issues of historical reference, complexity in composition history, and its more-or-less accurate prophecies (from the standpoint of the sixth-century-BCE literary setting) of Persian and Hellenistic history.[4] After

---

1. All translations come from the ESV unless otherwise indicated. I wish to thank the "(Re)Uniting Fractured Disciplines" Mellon Graduate Workshop at Brown University for the opportunity to present a draft of this paper and for its valuable feedback. In particular I wish to thank Aaron Glaim, Leo Landrey, Brian Rainey, and the seminar organizer, Heidi Wendt, for their candid yet fruitful comments.

2. Compare Lester L. Grabbe, "Fundamentalism and Scholarship: The Case of Daniel," in *Scripture: Meaning and Method, Essays Presented to Anthony Tyrrell Hanson*, ed. Barry P. Thompson (Pickering, North Yorkshire: Hull University, 1987) 133, 148.

3. In this chapter, an unqualified use of "Bible" means the Protestant Bible.

4. For brief overviews see John J. Collins, *A Commentary on the Book of Daniel*, Hermeneia (Minneapolis: Fortress, 1993) 24–38; Grabbe, "Fundamentalism and Scholarship." See also the inerrantist treatments Gleason L. Archer, *A Survey of Old Testament Introduction* (Chicago: Moody, 2007 [1964]) 361–68; Tremper Longman and

outlining what I mean by "inerrantist" as well as "legitimate academic and historical inquiry," I explore inerrantist engagement with issues in the book of Daniel traditionally viewed as problematizing their views, focusing in particular on matters relevant to dating the book. The exploration illustrates both the unacademic character of inerrantist engagement with Daniel and their concern to represent that engagement as legitimate historical analysis.

DEFINING INERRANTIST AND INERRANCY

This chapter works with an etic definition of "inerrantist." It thus will not coincide with the nuances of the particular emic theological views of those discussed. I designate as "inerrantist" those evangelical scholars who explicitly or implicitly consider the Bible to be without error in a notionally historical and true sense. This notion of historically characterized inerrancy is the posited shared or analogous feature that determines inclusion within my category of inerrantist.[5] Those so categorized may differ among themselves in significant and complex ways, even with respect to their very conceptions of inerrancy.[6] All agree that proper historical description of the texts' meanings (exegesis) cannot produce interpretations involving an error in the Bible, whether errors in historical-factual-scientific reference or contradictions between biblical passages.[7]

Raymond B. Dillard, *An Introduction to the Old Testament*, 2nd ed. (Grand Rapids: Zondervan, 2006) 373–92.

5. See the Chicago Statement on Biblical Inerrancy (CSBI) for a widely accepted evangelical articulation of such historically characterized inerrancy.

6. For the importance of reductive generalization theorized by frameworks extrinsic to the data for definition, classification, and comparison in academic study, see E. Thomas Lawson, "Theory and the New Comparativism, Old and New," *Method and Theory in the Study of Religion* 8 (1996) 31–35; E. Thomas Lawson and Robert N. McCauley, "Crisis of Conscience, Riddle of Identity: Making Space for a Cognitive Approach to Religious Phenomena," *Journal of the American Academy of Religion* 61(1993) 201–23; Luther H. Martin, "Comparison," in *Guide to the Study of Religion*, ed. Willi Braun and Russell McCutcheon (New York: Cassell, 2000) 45–55; Fitz John Porter Poole, "Metaphors and Maps: Towards Comparison in the Anthropology of Religion," *JAAR* 54 (1986) 411–57.

7. For examples of inerrantists making this point: L. Russ Bush, "Understanding Biblical Inerrancy," *Southwestern Journal of Theology* 50 (2007) 43–45; D. A. Carson, "Recent Developments in the Doctrine of Scripture," in *Hermeneutics, Authority,*

Inerrancy adds these considerations to historical methodologies for determining relevant evidence and assessing plausible meanings of biblical writings. All writings of the Bible and their "teachings" are considered the most relevant contextual evidence since they share a common essence as God's word. "Lack of error" operates as an overriding standard for assessing plausibility of interpretive options: if a possible interpretation involves an error in the Bible, the interpretation must be wrong.[8] Inerrantists, however, do not consider these added hermeneutical considerations to render their scholarship inaccurate or less historically legitimate, as inerrantist arguments about the date of Daniel clearly illustrate.

DEFINING ACADEMIC AND HISTORICAL SCHOLARSHIP

By "academic" and "historical" I mean research according to the recognized conventions of the modern academy. This means a type of critical inquiry characterized by methodological naturalism where the data sets used, arguments offered, and hypotheses proposed must be critically assessable by the tools of the academy.[9] If historical, sociological, an-

---

and Canon, ed. Carson and John D. Woodbridge (Grand Rapids: Zondervan, 1986) 23–24; John Frame, The Doctrine of the Word of God (Philipsburg, NJ: Presbyterian and Reformed, 2010) 177–78; Richard B. Gaffin, By Faith, Not by Sight: Paul and the Order of Salvation (Waynesboro, GA: Paternoster, 2006) 8–9; James Scott, "Inspiration and Interpretation of God's Word, Part I," Westminster Theological Journal 71 (2009) 129–83; H. Wayne Johnson, "The 'Analogy of Faith' and Exegetical Methodology: A Preliminary Discussion on Relationships," WTJ 31 (1988) 69–70, 73–76, 78–80; J. I. Packer, "Infallible Scripture and the Role of Hermeneutics," in Scripture and Truth, ed. D. A. Carson and John D. Woodbridge (Grand Rapids: Baker, 1992 [1983]) 350; J. Barton Payne, "Higher Criticism and Biblical Inerrancy," in Inerrancy, ed. Norman Geisler (Grand Rapids: Zondervan, 1980) 89–93; Moisés Silva, "Old Princeton, Westminster and Inerrancy," in Inerrancy and Hermeneutic: A Tradition, a Challenge, a Debate, ed. Harvie M. Conn (Grand Rapids: Baker, 1988) 74; CSBI article 18 and "Exposition: Infallibility, Inerrancy, and Interpretation."

8. Variety exists among inerrantists as to the nature of the Bible's coherence and how biblical passages bear on interpreting other passages. See D. A. Carson, "Unity and Diversity in the New Testament: The Possibility of Systematic Theology," in Scripture and Truth, 65–95.

9. For broader discussion of "academic," methodologically naturalist, "critical" inquiry, see Matthew C. Bagger, Religious Experience, Justification, and History (New York: Cambridge University Press, 1999) 6–20, 197–228; Russell T. McCutcheon, Critics Not Caretakers: Redescribing the Public Study of Religion, (Albany, NY: SUNY Press, 2001)

thropological, and scientific approaches cannot access the evidence and adjudicate arguments based on it, then the evidence and arguments in question lack academic validity. Arguments and their undergirding assumptions must operate as articulable and falsifiable entities. One cannot treat a position or its implicated assumptions as self-authenticating or beyond the realm of naturalistic analysis. One cannot refuse to submit them to critical scrutiny and at the same time criticize other positions and assumptions from self-authenticated fortresses.

Participation in academic fields of inquiry also implies *consistent* participation. When historically studying something in the academy one cannot selectively suspend broader methods of historical inquiry and deploy special methods justified by self-authenticating and uncriticizable claims or presuppositions. Assumptions and arguments trading upon supernatural explanations lack academic or historical validity—unless one can introduce these supernatural considerations in ways allowing for their falsification and with a view to submitting them to critical scrutiny as well.[10] This does not entail that supernatural explanations are categorically wrong within any field of discourse. Nor does it involve a metaphysical or ontological claim about the existence or non-existence of the Christian God or other gods or non-obvious beings. Methodological—not ontological—naturalism defines academic and historical inquiry for this chapter.[11] Even if one does not consider naturalistic empirical inquiry to have a natural place, while participating in the academy one must play according to the rules.

4–17, 45–47, 60–62, 85–88, 127–51, 223–30, 239–40; idem., *Manufacturing Religion: The Discourse of Sui Generis Religion and the Politics of Nostalgia*, (New York: Oxford University Press, 1997) x–xii, 5–6, 11–21, 29–31, 61–64, 106–26, 130–39, 147–54, 192–213.

10. In this way I sympathize with Mark Cladis's proposal that religious concerns and positions theoretically have an appropriate place in the academy and classroom so long as people articulate them according to the "virtues of public engagement," not arrogating absolute or privileged authority to them but rather allowing them and their presuppositions to be scrutinized and challenged. See Cladis, "The Place of Religion in the University and in American Public Life," *Soundings* 91 (2008) 389–90, 401–9.

11. While criticizing Russell McCutcheon's work, Michael Slater argues that the kind of methodological naturalism advocated here is implicitly an ontological naturalism. See Slater, "Can One Be a Critical Caretaker?" *MTSR* 19 (2007) 334–35, 338–40.

DANIEL IN THE ACADEMY

This and the following section highlight the historical illegitimacy of inerrantist engagement with the date of Daniel and inerrantist concerns to represent that engagement as legitimate historical study. This section offers a brief overview of basic academic scholarship relevant to the date of Daniel. The following section moves into samplings of inerrantist discussions related to this issue. The focus is primarily on demonstrating that inerrantist scholarship uses kinds of arguments lacking historical validity in contrast to critical scholars, not on arguing in detail for the accuracy of each critical argument.[12] The chapter will expand on some points more than others to acquaint readers who do not specialize in Hellenistic-Roman religions with some basics relating to Daniel.

Modern scholars consider Daniel to be a product of the third–second centuries BCE of the Hellenistic era. Most take its present form to date precisely to 164 BCE, produced in the midst of intense persecution under Antiochus IV before news of his death reached Jerusalem and before the rededication of the temple.[13] The book divides between the wisdom court legends of the first half (Dan 1–6) and the apocalyptic visions of the second half (Dan 7–12). Daniel 1:1—2:4a and 8:1—12:13 are in Hebrew, while 2:4b—7:28 is in Aramaic. While no consensus exists for all the details, it is generally accepted that the legends from Dan 2–6 in Aramaic are older than the visions, likely stemming from the third century BCE and reflecting a provenance of less overt hostility towards Gentile rulers.[14] At some point the tales were collected, with Dan 1 included as introductory material. The second-century producer of the

12. At times I shade into arguing for the accuracy of critical positions to illustrate the broader point. This chapter designates non-inerrantist scholars as "critical scholars," "critics," and "broader scholarship."

13. For a concise overview of this, see Collins, *Daniel*, 60–66.

14. David M. Valeta surveys the recent contestation over genre for the Dan 1–6 tales in Valeta, "The Book of Daniel in Recent Research (Part 1)," *Currents in Biblical Research* 6 (2008) 333–40. He focuses on the increasing number of interpreters favoring "resistance literature" or something similar as an appropriate designation. Such approaches tend to reject the claim that Dan 1–6 reflects a more positive view of Gentile rulers versus Dan 7–12's negative view. Compare Rainer Albertz's questioning of whether the two sections display differing attitudes towards Gentiles, along with positing a fundamental division between Dan 1–6 and 7–12 as opposed to a strict, linguistic division of Daniel into its Hebrew and Aramaic sections. See Albertz, "The Social Setting of the Aramaic and Hebrew Book of Daniel," in *The Book of Daniel: Composition and Reception*, ed. John J. Collins and Peter Flint (Leiden: Brill Academic, 2002) 1:171–204.

Hebrew visions of Dan 8–12 either composed or adapted the vision of Dan 7 in Aramaic and used it, along with numerous editorial strategies, to connect Dan 8–12 with the stories of Dan 2–6. The producer then translated Dan 1:1—2:4a into Hebrew to serve as an overall introduction and to solidify the unity of the book by linguistically linking Dan 1 with the visions of the latter half of the book.[15] The unity of Daniel is editorial and literary, not from a single, original authorship.[16] Scholars almost unanimously consider Daniel a third–second-century pseudepigraphic (forged) Jewish apocalypse.[17]

The reasons for this are manifold. Daniel 11 overviews the Hellenistic history of Palestine as contested by the Seleucids and Ptolemies, culminating in Antiochus IV (175–164 BCE). It does so in the literary form of a vision given to the sixth-century seer Daniel, using cryptic imagery. Scholars identify this as *ex eventu* prophecy, or prophecy after the fact. One finds similar *ex eventu*, often survey-of-history, prophecy in other Hellenistic and Roman period Jewish sources.[18] It was a common strategy among various ancient Mediterranean pseudepigraphal revelatory writings. By textually projecting details of past history—from the standpoint of the actual author and audience of a text—into the mouth or vision of a notionally ancient figure, the producer confers an extra degree of legitimacy on the product. The logic of this aspect of *ex eventu* prophecy is intuitive. If a given ancient figure accurately predicts the future on the basis of divine revelation, inspiration, or other form of divination, then we know the efficacy of the vision, its source, and presumably the rest of the writing recording the vision.[19] This is not simply

---

15. See also the *maskilim* in Dan 1:4 and also 11:33–35 and 12:3. Compare Collins, *Daniel*, 37.

16. H. H. Rowley defends Daniel's original unity as a mid-second-century book. See Rowley, "The Unity of the Book of Daniel," *Hebrew Union College Annual* 23 (1950) 233–73.

17. For concise discussions covering most of the points made in this paragraph, see John J. Collins, *The Apocalyptic Imagination: An Introduction to Jewish Apocalyptic Literature*, 2nd ed. (Grand Rapids: Eerdmans, 1998) 85–90, 114–15; George W. E. Nickelsburg, *Jewish Literature between the Bible and the Mishnah: A Historical and Literary Introduction*, 2nd ed. (Minneapolis: Fortress, 2005) 17–22, 77–83.

18. *Animal Vision* (1 *En.* 83–90) the *Apocalypse of Weeks* (1 *En.* 93:1–10; 91:11–17) *Jubilees, 4 Ezra, 2 Baruch*, and the *Apocalypse of Abraham*, to name a few.

19. "If the 'predictions' are known to have been accurate down to the present, then they are likely to be reliable for the future too" (Collins, *Apocalyptic Imagination*, 111). Compare James C. Vanderkam, "Prophecy and Apocalyptics in the Ancient Near East"

a matter of persuading the audience to trust the reliability of a writing's information about their future, but the generally inextricably linked purpose of urging the audience to accept the writing's authority on other matters as well: how to live, to whom to listen, what to believe, and their place in God's plan. It also bridges the temporal gap between a writing's pseudepigraphic and actual settings (see also Dan 8:26; 12:4, 9 for this purpose).

Daniel 11's *ex eventu* prophecy helps scholars fix a precise date for Daniel. Towards the end of the vision the author attempts an actual prediction, something not uncommon among pseudepigraphic writings with *ex eventu* prophecies.[20] Many of these writings locate their actual audience close to the end or at climactic points of their surveys of history through the retelling of history with details expected to be recognizable by the audience, but given in symbolic-cryptic, prophetic idiom.[21] Audiences thus discern where they are in the "prophesied" (re)telling of history. Such writings often situate the audience in the midst of a period of suffering or chaos, a climactic set-time of distress before relief.[22] This is the point in Daniel when the author tries to make a real prediction. Up until the final events of Antiochus IV's life, the vision of Dan 11 is accurate.[23] Then at 11:40–45 the author shifts from *ex eventu* prophetic

---

[1995], in *From Revelation to Canon: Studies in the Hebrew Bible and Second Temple Literature* (Leiden: Brill Academic, 2002) 272.

20. For discussion of several examples commonly compared with Daniel, see Matthew Neujahr, "When Darius Defeated Alexander: Composition and Redaction in the *Dynastic Prophecy*," *Journal of Near Eastern Studies* 64 (2005) 101–7.

21. A potentially fruitful line of research might be to explore the extent that each writing works to perpetuate social conditions where scribal intellectuals occupy recognized prestigious positions; i.e., where those in the audience who do not know the allusions and meanings of the cryptic images must seek the expertise of intellectuals.

22. The parade comparative example for Daniel of this overall dynamic is the slightly earlier *Apocalypse of Weeks* (1 *En.* 93:1–10; 91:11–17) usually dated around 170 BCE. It divides history into ten "weeks" and represents the eschatological turning point at the transition from the seventh week (period of suffering) to the eighth. Most locate the author's actual time in the seventh week. For a limited overview of climactic periods of distress and suffering in early Jewish literature, see Brant Pitre, *Jesus, the Tribulation, and the End of the Exile: Restoration Eschatology and the Origin of the Atonement* (Grand Rapids: Baker, 2005) 41–130. For discussion of the purposes of these and other literary techniques in eschatologically oriented Hellenistic revelatory writings, see Collins, *Apocalyptic Imagination*, 14–19, 21–23, 37–42, 51–52, 61–65, 70, 110–15.

23. "Now, this is not to say that the content of the *ex eventu* predictions is necessarily 'historically reliable' by modern criteria. . ." The point is that "the author of such

review of history to making an actual prediction, using phraseology from and alluding to earlier Jewish writings.[24] Antiochus, whom the text casts in terms of a decisive eschatological adversary both here and elsewhere,[25] will be attacked by Egypt, continue afflicting the Jews as he passes through their ancestral land, decisively defeat and take control of Egypt (a feat that had eluded him before because Rome intervened), hear news of impending attack, head to the land of Israel for battle, and die in the land of Israel (a traditional site of eschatological battle). The author explicitly casts this as the onset of the "time of the end."[26] He further marks Antiochus's death as the defeat of an eschatological adversary (that precedes or marks the period of a decisive turning point) with the immediately following passage: Dan 12:1–4 depicts the eschatological rescue of faithful Jews after the climactic time of distress. Antiochus IV, however, did not die the way 11:40–45 predicts. Subsequent to the events recounted up through 11:39, ancient sources agree that he died in Persia after having undertaken a military expedition there.[27] Thus scholars plausibly date Daniel after the events of 11:39 and before news of how Antiochus actually died reached the authors: around 164 BCE.

a propagandistic work included events which—whether they happened or not—are recognizable and presumed verified by the intended audience" (Neujahr, "When Darius Defeated Alexander," 107).

24. John Goldingay, *Daniel*, WBC 30 (Nashville: T. Nelson, 1989) 305. Compare Collins, *Daniel*, 388–90. Critical commentaries will indicate a transition to attempted prediction.

25. Compare 8:9–12, 23–25. Antiochus IV also corresponds to the "another horn, a little one" in which "were eyes like the eyes of a man, and a mouth speaking great things" (7:8) of the fourth beast out of the sea in Dan 7. This is the beast killed at the eschatological judgment (7:9–12). Daniel consistently represents Antiochus IV as the final and ultimate adversary who affects cosmic distress and whose death marks the decisive turning point enabling the eschatological deliverance of the righteous. According to Collins, *Daniel*, 389, in Dan 11:40–45 "Antiochus is assimilated to a mythic pattern that underlies later Christian traditions about the Antichrist." Compare Gregory C. Jenks, *The Origins and Early Development of the Antichrist Myth* (New York: de Gruyter, 1991); and L. J. Lietaert Peerbolte, *The Antecedents of Antichrist: A Traditio-Historical Study of the Earliest Christian Views on Eschatological Opponents* (Leiden: Brill, 1996) 224–342.

26. 11:40; compare 11:35. For a discussion of the various meanings of "end" in Daniel, see John J. Collins, "The Meaning of the End in the Book of Daniel" [1990], in *Seers, Sibyls and Sages in Hellenistic-Roman Judaism* (Leiden: Brill, 2001) 157–65. According to Collins, in 11:40 it "has the same meaning as in 11:35: the period when the [Antiochus IV persecution] crisis comes to its resolution" (389).

27. See Collins, *Daniel*, 389–90.

Numerous other aspects of Daniel contribute to the plausibility of the third–second-century identification of its date. In addition to sharing most of the above-mentioned features and even combinations of them with other Jewish sources of the Hellenistic period,[28] the distress of Jews in Palestine under Antiochus IV dominates the visions. The four-kingdom schema, by which (in addition to other editorial and literary strategies) the editors bound the court legends to the visions, reframes the tales such that readers understand them also directly in relation to the distress of the Jews under the Seleucid king Antiochus IV in the second century. The schema appears explicitly in Dan 2 and then again in Dan 7, while references to it and other details relating to it recur throughout each half of the book. This trope, presumably recognizable to Daniel's Hellenistic audience, specifies a succession of kings or kingdoms from the time of the fictional seer Daniel in the sixth century up until the second-century time of composition. In Daniel the sequence goes: Babylon →Media→Persia→Greece; all to be decisively followed by the "kingdom that shall never be destroyed" set up by the God of heaven (2:44–45; compare 7:13–28). The schema structures Daniel such that the legends and the visions move from the earliest point (Babylon) of the fictitious sixth-century literary setting to the second-century Seleucid (Greek) crisis setting.[29] This "Greek" setting dominates the visions, constitutes

---

28. Collins, *Apocalyptic Imagination*; idem, *Daniel*; Esther Eshel, "Possible Sources of the Book of Daniel," in *Book of Daniel*, ed. Collins and Flint, 2:387–94; Martha Himmelfarb, *The Apocalypse: A Brief History* (Malden, MA: Wiley-Blackwell, 2010) 31–48; Michael A. Knibb, "The Book of Daniel in Its Context," in *Book of Daniel*, ed. Collins and Flint, 1:16–35; idem, "'You Are Indeed Wiser than Daniel': Reflections on the Character of the Book of Daniel," in *The Book of Daniel in the Light of New Findings*, ed. A. S. van der Woude, BETL 106 (Leuven: Leuven University Press, 1993) 399–411; Loren T. Stuckenbruck, "Daniel and Early Enoch Traditions in the Dead Sea Scrolls," in *Book of Daniel*, ed. Collins and Flint, 2:368–86; Karel van der Toorn, "Scholars at the Oriental Court: The Figure of Daniel against Its Mesopotamian Background," in *Book of Daniel*, ed. Collins and Flint, 1:37–54; idem, *Scribal Culture and the Making of the Hebrew Bible* (Cambridge, MA: Harvard University Press, 2007) 25, 229–32, 252–64; Vanderkam, "Prophecy and Apocalyptics;" idem, "The Prophetic-Sapiential Origins of Apocalyptic Thought," in *Revelation to Canon*, 241–54.

29. Nebuchadnezzar and Babylon are the setting of Dan 1–4. Daniel 5 transitions from Belshazzar (Babylon) to "Darius the *Mede*" (5:30–31; 6:28) and the Median location on the schema for Dan 6, a chapter that then concludes by referring to "Cyrus the *Persian*" following "Darius the *Mede*" (6:28). The second half of Daniel and its parallel visions repeat this schema, starting with "Belshazzar king of *Babylon*" (7:1; compare 8:1–2) for Dan 7–8, "Darius the *Mede*" (9:1) for Dan 9, and "Cyrus king of *Persia*" (10:1) for Dan 10, which concludes with a reference to "the prince of *Greece* [who] will

the last times immediately preceding the eschatological rescue, and is in fact the actual final compositional setting of Daniel.[30] Numerous other aspects of Daniel coalesce with those discussed above to render the book most plausibly a product of the third–second centuries of the Hellenistic period: in particular linguistic data, manuscript evidence, and what may be termed issues of historical reference (inaccuracy).[31]

INERRANTIST ENGAGEMENT WITH THE BOOK OF DANIEL

Inerrantists reject the consensus Hellenistic dating of Daniel. They instead understand it as a sixth-century-BCE exilic writing from the hands of Daniel or an associated Jew in Babylon.[32] This follows its implied literary setting as well as the visions recounted in the first person by Daniel but set in a third-person frame.[33] Some inerrantists move from these details to asserting a clear textual claim to authorship by Daniel.[34] Though

---

come" (10:20).

30. The vision of Dan 10–11 has the angel mention Darius the Mede again (11:1) before reverting back to Persian kings and then Greek (Alexander the Great and then the Ptolemies and Seleucids). For important studies on the four-kingdom schema in Daniel, see J. W. Swain, "The Theory of the Four Monarchies: Opposition History under the Roman Empire," *Classical Philology* 35 (1940) 1–21; David Flusser, "The Four Empires in the Fourth Sibyl and in the Book of Daniel," *Israel Oriental Society* 2 (1972) 148–75; but see Doron Mendels, "The Five Empires: A Note on a Hellenistic Topos," *American Journal of Philology* 102 (1981) 330–37. Compare Collins, *Apocalyptic*, 92–98; idem, *Daniel*, 166–70; and idem, "The Place of the Fourth Sibyl in the Development of the Jewish Sibyllina," *Journal of Jewish Studies* 25 (1974) 365–80.

31. For more detailed discussion, see Collins, *Daniel*, 1–71; Louis Hartman and Alexander Di Lella, *The Book of Daniel*, AB 23 (Garden City, NY: Doubleday, 1978) 3–110.

32. See, for example, R. K. Harrison, *Introduction to the Old Testament: With a Comprehensive Review of Old Testament Studies and a Special Supplement on the Apocrypha* (Grand Rapids: Eerdmans, 1969) 1127; Andrew E. Hill and John H. Walton, *A Survey of the Old Testament*, 3rd (Grand Rapids: Zondervan, 2009) 571; Stephen R. Miller, *Daniel*, NAC 18 (Nashville: Broadman and Holman, 1994) 23–24, 32–33. Other treatments include Bill Arnold and Bryan Beyer, *Encountering the Old Testament: A Christian Survey*, 2nd ed. (Grand Rapids: Baker, 2008) 427–38; and Arthur Ferch, "The Book of Daniel and the 'Maccabean Thesis,'" *Andrews University Seminary Studies* 21 (1983) 129–41.

33. For a nuanced inerrantist example, see Tremper Longman, *Daniel*, NIVAC (Grand Rapids: Zondervan, 1999) 19, 21–22.

34. See, for example, Gleason L. Archer Jr., *Daniel*, EBC 7 (Grand Rapids: Zondervan, 1985) 4: "The clear testimony of the book itself is that Daniel was the author . . . it is

offering historical arguments for this date, most inerrantists frame the issue in theological terms. For example,

> This issue is of greatest importance for at least three reasons. First, the sovereignty of God in this book is at stake. . . . Second, the divine inspiration of the Bible hangs in the balance. . . . Third, one's understanding of the nature of Jesus Christ depends on the answer to the date of the book.[35]

Similar overt religious framing appears throughout inerrantist writings touching on the date of Daniel: the late date vitiates the value of prophecies, the pseudepigraphic theory renders the writing a fraud and moral failure, the non-traditional position makes Jesus errant or a liar, and so on.[36] For many inerrantists the sixth-century date is the only theologically legitimate option.[37] This maps onto the entailment of inerrancy stipulated in Chicago Statement on Biblical Inerrancy, article 18: "We deny the legitimacy of any treatment of the text or quest for sources lying behind it that leads to relativizing, dehistoricizing, or discounting its teaching, or rejecting its claims to authorship."

Though most inerrantists consider theological constraints to obtain for the issue, they do not envision them negating the historical veracity of their position. Sound and rigorous historical study vindicates the early date of Daniel and its inerrancy. Thus Waltke immediately follows his theological orientation with: "By what accredited methods can the Book of Daniel be dated?"[38] Douglas Fox represents his article as a contribution to broader scholarship. It offers "one more piece of the evidence in

---

conceivable that a close friend or colleague of the prophet might have composed the earlier chapters since they refer to Daniel in the third person. . . . But careful examination shows that the author usually writes about himself in the third person, as was the custom among ancient authors of historical memoirs." Compare Archer, *Survey of Old Testament*, 361.

35. Bruce K. Waltke, "The Date of the Book of Daniel," *Bibiotheca Sacra* 133 (1976) 320.

36. See, for example, Archer, *Daniel*, 4–5; Josh McDowell, *Daniel in the Critics' Den: Historical Evidence for the Authenticity of the Book of Daniel* (San Bernardino, CA: Campus Crusade, 1979) 1–3; Miller, *Daniel*, 34–37; O. P. Robertson, *The Christ of the Prophets* (Philipsburg, NJ: Presbyterian and Reformed, 2004) 326–27, 349–50; George M. Schwab, *Hope in the Midst of a Hostile World: The Gospel according to Daniel* (Philipsburg, NJ: Presbyterian and Reformed, 2006) 8–9.

37. Longman, *Daniel*, 22–23, demurs from representing the situation in stark theological polarities.

38. Waltke, "Date," 320.

a growing body of evidence which should lead to a wider general recognition among scholars that the book of Daniel most certainly deserves to be dated earlier than 165 B.C."[39] Andrew Steinmann makes explicit that he has "scrutinized closely" and offered "a close analysis" of the relevant passages, all in critical conversation with "critical scholars."[40] Stephen Miller represents his discussion of material relevant to the dating of Daniel as "a fair survey of the data" that "seems to indicate that a second-century date for the autograph of Daniel is extremely difficult to maintain."[41] He adduces "strong evidence for the traditional view of authorship and date" in the course of his analysis.[42] Gleason Archer leaves no doubt about whether he conceives himself to be engaging in "intellectually respectable" historical and academic research on Daniel:

> In the preceding paragraphs we have seen that the linguistic evidence from Qumran makes the rationalistic explanation for Daniel no longer tenable. It is difficult to see how any scholar can defend this view and maintain intellectual respectability. We now proceed to two areas of internal evidence that completely rule out the Maccabean hypothesis as a credible explanation for the origin of Daniel.[43]

A primary inerrantist criticism of the Hellenistic dating for Daniel is that it presumes the non-existence of predictive prophecy and uncritically reflects antisupernatural presuppositions. Inerrantists often voice this objection in association with critiques of scholars who both maintain that Daniel contains *ex eventu* prophecy and factor the specific forms of Daniel's *ex eventu* prophecy into their analysis of Daniel's date.[44]

39. "*Ben Sira* on OT Canon Again: The Date of Daniel," *WTJ* 49 (1987) 350: "Perhaps one day still more new evidence will vindicate the champions of an early date for Daniel even more fully."

40. Steinmann, "Is the Antichrist in Daniel 11?" *BSac* 162 (2005) 208–9.

41. Miller, *Daniel*, 39.

42. "Strong evidence for the traditional view of authorship and date comes from the testimony of Jesus Christ himself." See Miller, *Daniel*, 34–35.

43. Archer, *Daniel*, 24. "Yet the fact remains that the objective data, when fairly and impartially considered, provide overwhelming evidence against a second-century date for the composition and strongly favor its authenticity as a genuine work of the sixth-century Daniel" (13).

44. Compare Archer, *Daniel*, 6: "It is axiomatic among critics who rule out supernaturalism that Daniel's successful predictions of events leading up to the reign of Antiochus Epiphanes. . .can be accounted for only by assuming that some unknown pseudepigrapher wrote this book so as to make it seem an authentic sixth-century prophecy."

Some inerrantists articulate the importance of such presuppositions for critical scholars' position on the date but do not represent them as determinative.[45] Many basically boil the matter down to presuppositions.[46]

> In order to avoid the impact of the decisive evidence of supernatural inspiration with which Daniel so notably abounds, it was necessary for rationalistic scholarship to find some later period in Jewish history when all the "predictions" had already been fulfilled, such as the reign of Antiochus Epiphanes (175–164 B.C.), when such a pious fraud could most easily be prepared.[47]

> But the question naturally arises, if the evidence for a sixth-century date of composition is so certain, why do scholars reject it in favor of an unsupportable Maccabean hypothesis? The reason is that most scholars embrace a liberal, naturalistic, and rationalistic philosophy. Naturalism and rationalism are ultimately based on faith rather than on evidence; therefore, this faith will not allow them to accept the supernatural predictions.[48]

For such inerrantists, the antisupernatural assumptions of other scholars determine the issue—and do so in the face of overwhelming evidence. The complex of critical scholarly positions that date Daniel to the Hellenistic era is driven (even invented) by naturalistic and rationalistic convictions. These presuppositions constitute the most basic or only so-

45. See, for example, Hill and Walton, *Survey*, 570; Longman, *Daniel*, 22–23.

46. See Miller, *Daniel*, 33: "One's overall view of Scripture generally and prophecy in particular will dramatically affect the decision concerning the date of the book. . . . Those . . . with . . . antisupernatural presupposition[s] will of course accept the Maccabean thesis."

47. Gleason L. Archer, *New International Encyclopedia of Bible Difficulties* (Grand Rapids: Zondervan, 2001 [1982]) 282. On the charge of "pious fraud," A. J. Droge observes: "It would appear . . . that it is mainly conservative scholars who invoke the label—and then deny it—as a way of discrediting the radical criticism of their opponents. Yet they do so in a fashion that can only be described as disingenuous. By alleging that their opponents dismiss the discovery of the 'Book of the Law' as a 'fraud'—*when they do not*—conservative scholars introduce an incendiary term into the debate designed to discredit a criticism of the Bible that would ostensibly seek to explain human things in human terms" (Droge, "'The Lying Pen of the Scribes': Of Holy Books and Pious Frauds," *MTSR* 15 (2003) 127; emphasis original, concerning Deuteronomy. My sense is that the same holds for Daniel.

48. Waltke, "Date," 329. Compare Robertson, *Christ of the Prophets*, 327n10: "It is difficult to see how Daniel can be established as a pseudonymous second-century document apart from the presupposition that the possibility of predictive prophecy cannot be considered as a valid alternative." See also 325n5 and 350n33.

called evidence for the later date, such that people sharing them "will of course accept the Maccabean thesis." Such inerrantists depict the issue as black and white. According to them the critical consensus lacks any plausibility and does not reflect potentially legitimate engagement with evidence.[49]

Despite inerrantist protestations to the contrary, when scholars assume that a writing postdates a series of events it describes they are not only following ordinary historical methodology but intuitive common sense.[50] Inerrantists do the same when analyzing almost everything outside of various passages in the Bible. This is especially the case if other considerations coalesce to make plausible a date for the writing subsequent to the events it describes. Since inerrantists do not theorize the use of supernatural explanations for Daniel, aside from indicating their theologically determined view of its divine nature, it is difficult to elucidate inerrantists' criteria for conditions of their use. Miller seems to imply that an errant prediction would disqualify a book as true canonical (read: "inspired") prophetic literature and consign it to the category of "pseudoprophetic books."[51] For inerrantists, the distinguishing criteria for acceptability of supernatural explanations are canonical: is a writing part of the Bible or not? If so, its self-claims of authorship, setting, predictive prophecy, and divine revelation are to be accepted. This establishes a place for supernatural explanation during analysis of the writing. If not, inerrantists study the writing the same way scholars study other literature, even highlighting historical inaccuracies, employing

---

49. Inerrantists further reflect this totalizing approach when interacting with critical scholars who address the complaint that their position "rests on a dogmatic, rationalistic denial of the possibility of predictive prophecy" (Collins, *Daniel*, 26). Collins follows this characterization of how "some conservatives have often argued" with, "for the critical scholar, however, the issue is one of probability" (26). He then explicates this in historical terms both on that page and throughout the rest of the commentary. O. P. Robertson, however, rejects Collins's attempt to explain how potentially reasonable engagement with historical data is the more relevant consideration. He instead reduces Collins's argument: "It seems inevitable that on the basis of dogmatic and rationalistic considerations, Collins must reject the repeated claims of divine revelation as the source of Daniel's insight into the course and significance of future events" (Robertson, *Christ of the Prophets*, 350n33).

50. Grabbe correctly points out that most "allow that it is humanly possible to make correct predictions about the future within a limited scope"; he even offers examples. For Grabbe's discussion of inerrantist objections about antisupernaturalism and predictive prophecy, see Grabbe, "Fundamentalism and Scholarship," 136–37, 146–48.

51. Miller, *Daniel*, 37.

their usefulness for dating the writing.[52] Inerrantists thus deploy naturalistic historical methods for analyzing non-biblical writings but deny their sufficiency for studying Daniel. This is the essence of begging the question and making one's position unfalsifiable. Given that inerrantists assume the place of naturalistic methodologies for other data, their protestations about the arbitrariness of excluding supernatural explanations from the study of Daniel are revealed as pretenses for their own arbitrary use of methodologies, at least from the standpoint of the academy.[53]

Even if one allowed inerrantists' arbitrary use of supernatural explanations, how does one identify the correct one for Daniel? By definition they reside beyond the realm of academic adjudication. How do inerrantists demonstrate the plausibility of their supernatural explanation[54] over others? Perhaps another deity, for example, sent the visions to practice tricking people into thinking that a writing comes from earlier than it does?[55] Allowing the legitimacy of supernatural explanations for Daniel does not carry the freight inerrantists imply. Inerrantists advocate their supernatural explanations, which are reinscriptions of the ideologies their interpretations construe from Daniel and other biblical literature.

---

52. See Grabbe, "Fundamentalism and Scholarship," 147–48. Inerrantist arguments against the canonicity or inspiration of the Apocrypha exemplify this. They routinely reject its canonicity and inspiration, and thus the legitimacy of supernatural explanations for it, on the basis of its historical inaccuracies. They instead find such inaccuracies and other details useful for dating its writings long after their implied or claimed settings. Henri Blocher, "Helpful or Harmful?: The 'Apocrypha' and Evangelical Theology," *European Journal of Theology* 13 (2004) 86; Norman Geisler and William Nix, *General Introduction to the Bible*, rev. and exp. (Chicago: Moody, 1986) 271; Harrison, *Introduction*, 1194–278; Josh McDowell, *The New Evidence that Demands a Verdict: Evidence I & II* (Nashville: T. Nelson, 1999) 29; William Webster, *Holy Scripture: The Ground and Pillar of Our Faith*, vol. 2: *An Historical Defense of the Reformation Principle of Sola Scriptura* (Battle Ground, WA: Christian Resources, 2001) 388–89.

53. Grabbe has similar concerns. See Grabbe, "Fundamentalism and Scholarship," 136–37.

54. E.g., the God of Israel revealed and accurately interpreted his own future plans to Daniel, which, for inerrantists, happen to culminate in or at least involve Jesus as Christ and this God's son.

55. This example is chosen simply for illustrative purposes. See Bart Ehrman's similar point in "Is There Historical Evidence for the Resurrection of Jesus?: A Debate between William Lane Craig and Bart D. Ehrman," 31–32. Online: http://commonsenseatheism.com/wp-content/uploads/2010/04/craig-ehrman.pdf.

One way to conceptualize the matter is to observe that the inerrantist claims about scholars' rationalistic presuppositions serve to mask the academic illegitimacy of inerrantist scholarship. By distilling the disagreeable aspects of critical scholarship down to this point and harping on its significance, inerrantists seek to discredit non-traditional scholarship: how could positions driven by such an arbitrary assumption be plausible to a thinking person aware of the data? This strategy turns on and reveals another inerrantist position: they assume the explanatory ultimacy and accuracy of Daniel's self-claims (e.g., claim to authorship, setting, and so on) and represent the matter as though, academically, the burden of proof is on those who would question these claims. This unargued assumption is treated as the obvious correlate of acknowledging the possibility of supernatural explanation, support for why supernatural explanation should apply to Daniel, and evidence for why scholars who question Daniel's self-claims are rationalistic. Inerrantists do not offer falsifiable arguments for this protective strategy of privileging Daniel's self-claims when it comes to analysis.

What do I mean by "protective strategy"? Inerrantists charge that critics fail to approach Daniel (or the Bible) "on its own terms"—as evidenced by rejecting its claims to authorship, date, and supernatural inspiration—and thus fall short of their supposed academic standard. This confuses the distinction/relation between describing what something claims and analyzing it and its claims. Broader scholarship on religion offers an illustrative and fitting comparative example. Numerous scholars have represented the study of religion as the study of something unique and ineffable, requiring special rules and methods for study because religious people claim that religion and their religious experiences are unique and beyond ordinary academic study. Many explicate the inherently unacademic character of such approaches. By privileging informant claims, such approaches collapse the distinction between description and explanation[56] and reinscribe both the claims of religious informants and the (often unarticulated) folk assumptions about religion held by scholars. This blocks analysis in terms of broader

---

56. See Wayne Proudfoot's classic articulation of this criticism, terming them "protective strategies" that confuse the difference between "descriptive reduction" and "explanatory reduction," in *Religious Experience* (Berkeley: University of California Press, 1985) xi–xiv, 2–3, 6, 199–208.

social, scientific, and historical models for examining human practices.[57] Ordinary academic methodology, and even the intuitive common sense by which we all operate,[58] does not analytically privilege self-claims.[59] Neither does it consider them inherently suspicious. Instead, it holds that they too warrant some form of reductive academic-historical analysis.[60] Scholars correctly identify these privileging claims as protective

57. E.g., Bagger, *Religious Experience*; idem, *The Uses of Paradox: Religion, Self-Transformation, and the Absurd* (New York: Columbia University Press, 2007) 26, 30–64, 90–99; McCutcheon, *Critics Not Caretakers*; McCutcheon, *Manufacturing Religion*; Hans Penner, "You Don't Read a Myth for Information," in *Radical Interpretation in Religion*, ed. Nancy Frankenberry (Cambridge: Cambridge University Press, 2002) 153–70; Stanley K. Stowers, "The Concepts of 'Religion', 'Political Religion' and the Study of Nazism," *Journal of Contemporary History* 42.1 (2007) 12–22.

58. E.g., our minds have evolved intuitions and tendencies to detect social cheating, freeloading, others' attempts to manipulate us and our beliefs, and so on, so we can successfully navigate common situations of everyday life. See Brian Boyd, *On the Origin of Stories: Evolution, Cognition, and Fiction* (Cambridge, MA: Harvard University Press, 2009) 57–61, 63–65, 190–99; Leda Cosmides, "The Logic of Social Exchange: Has Natural Selection Shaped How Humans Reason? Studies with the Watson Selection Task," *Cognition* 31 (1989) 187–276; Leda Cosmides and John Tooby, "Cognitive Adaptations for Social Exchange," in *The Adapted Mind: Evolutionary Psychology and the Generation of Culture*, ed. Jerome Barkow et. al. (New York: Oxford University Press, 1992) 163–228; idem, "Neurocognitive Adaptations Designed for Social Exchange," in *The Handbook of Evolutionary Psychology*, ed. David Buss (Hoboken, NJ: Wiley-Blackwell, 2005) 584–627.

59. This would make it impossible, for example, to study propaganda in any meaningful way. More specific analogies abound for how ordinary historical-academic methodology does not privilege informant claims: the study of early-twentieth-century European National Socialism (we do not attempt explanation by assuming all the claims of Nazi leaders and propaganda as an analytic framework), the study of linguistics (scholars do not assume that speakers' folk notions about language and meaning provide the only way to study how languages work), and so on.

60. On the necessity of "reductionism" in the study of religion, see Jeffrey R. Carter, "Description Is Not Explanation: A Methodology of Comparison," *MTSR* 10 (1998) 133–48; Edward Slingerland, "Who's Afraid of Reductionism?: The Study of Religion in the Age of Cognitive Science," *JAAR* 76 (2008) 375–411 (see also the exchange between Slingerland and Francisca Cho/Richard Squier on this matter in the same issue). In this chapter, I operate with a definition of religion that, in contrast to trends in the academy denying its existence or legitimacy as an analytic category, theorizes it in social-ontological terms as something that can be studied academically: e.g., Kevin Schilbrack, "Religions: Are There Any?," *JAAR* 78 (2010) 1117–21; Stanley K. Stowers, "The Ontology of Religion," in *Introducing Religion: Essays in Honor or Jonathan Z. Smith*, ed. Willi Braun and Russell T. McCutcheon (Oakville, CT: Equinox, 2008). "Religion consists of variously linked social practices (involving arrangements of entities at sites) that carry understandings involving the existence and activity of gods, ancestors, and

strategies that place their supposedly unique and religious data beyond academic-historical study. The claims also represent analytic-privileging as legitimate academic study. Inerrantist rhetoric about critics' rejection of supernatural explanations and the self-claims of Daniel involve similar protective strategies that assume the analytic ultimacy of Daniel's self-claims.

Inerrantist scholarship uses this protective strategy to situate scholars who question these assumptions as "critics" driven by assumptions and not evidence. Interpretations that involve positing something about Daniel at odds with its self-claims are inherently less plausible because they "reject" its claims and the possibility of supernatural explanation. By these various unacknowledged moves inerrantists render their positions unfalsifiable, at least in the discursive field in which they operate, making them part of a discourse that is unacademic but nevertheless prizes the notion of academic-historical legitimacy. The characteristics of inerrantist antisupernatural rhetoric and its use against critical scholars, in particular its caricaturing generalities of broader-scholarship, illustrate some specific dynamics of its field of discourse production. Success or prestige does not come so much through actual engagement with broader scholarship. Inerrantist scholarship serves primarily to convince those who already agree and/or remain uninformed of the historical data and landscape of critical arguments about it.[61]

Inerrantists bring several arguments against taking Dan 11:40–45 as a mistaken attempted prediction following *ex eventu* prophecy that helps date the book to 164 BCE. They still understand 11:21–35 to

---

various normally unseen beings, and that shade off into other anthropomorphic interpretations of the world" (Stowers, "Ontology of Religion," 442).

61. It is important to stress that in arguing this point throughout the chapter I do not here question the sincerity of inerrantist scholars and accuse them of nefarious motives. Rather than speculative gauging of deep intentions, I simply try to analyze the actual social interests and effects of discursive practices such as these. What is commonly termed "practice theory" constitutes my theoretical framework here. See Pierre Bourdieu, *The Field of Cultural Production: Essays on Art and Literature*, ed. Randal Johnson (New York: Columbia University Press, 1993) 29–191; Theodore R. Schatzki, *The Site of the Social: A Philosophical Account of the Constitution of Social Life and Change* (University Park: Pennsylvania State University Press, 2002); Joseph Rouse, "Practice Theory," in *Philosophy of Anthropology and Sociology*, ed. Stephen Turner and Mark Risjord (Amsterdam: Elsevier, 2007) 639–81; Pierre Bourdieu, *Outline of a Theory of Practice*, trans. Richard Nice (New York: Cambridge University Press, 1977); idem, *Practical Reason: On the Theory of Action* (Stanford, CA: Stanford University Press, 1998) 75–91.

concern Antiochus IV, while disputing the consensus identification of it as *ex eventu* prophecy.[62] Some then hold that 11:36ff. initially focuses on Antiochus IV but gradually "telescopes," or come to have a dual referent, "so that the more distant event appears to merge with the nearer so as to become indistinguishable from it."[63] This accounts for the seamless flow of the passage with its focus on Antiochus IV and the inclusion of details not fulfilled in him (which would otherwise be errors if the passage is about him). Others argue that 11:36–45 shifts entirely away from Antiochus IV to prophesying the true "antichrist."[64] Various details of 11:36–45, plus the fact that the passage predicts things not historically true of Antiochus IV, are taken to necessitate an interpretive option involving another figure. Specifically, most proceed as though demonstrating that 11:36–45 cannot be adequately mapped onto Antiochus IV's life proves that the passage concerns a subsequent figure.[65] This argument

62. Focusing on one specific inerrantist argument against *ex eventu* prophecy in Dan 11, Ferch, "Book of Daniel," 132–36, argues that Dan 11 lacks the volume and precision of allusions to the Maccabean crisis that would be expected from a writing about it and written in its immediate aftermath. Compare Miller, *Daniel*, 27. However, the point of *ex eventu* prophecy is that its authors produce it in cryptic-symbolic idiom, as though it were not written subsequent to the events. One wonders whether Ferch and Miller would reject *ex eventu* understandings of the *Book of the Watchers* or the *Animal Vision* on these grounds as well, taking this as evidence inclining towards Enochic authorship and authenticity. Some inerrantists insinuate that critics consider the producer of Daniel to be pro-Maccabean (Ferch, "Book of Daniel," 134–36; compare Archer, *Daniel*, 6–7; Miller, *Daniel*, 27). While a few critical scholars may consider Daniel pro-Maccabean, the overwhelming majority understands the book to represent the Maccabeas as "little help" (11:34). They furthermore interpret Daniel as decidedly not calling Jews to join an armed rebellion. See James A. Montgomery, *A Critical and Exegetical Commentary on the Book of Daniel* (Edinburgh: T. & T. Clark, 1927) 458–59; R. H. Charles, *A Critical and Exegetical Commentary on the Book of Daniel* (London: Oxford, 1929) 309; Norman Porteous, *Daniel: A Commentary* (London: SCM, 1965) 168; Hartman and DiLella, *Daniel*, 300; Andre Lacocque, *The Book of Daniel*, trans. David Pellauer (Atlanta: John Knox, 1979 [1976]) 10–11, 230; W. Sibley Towner, *Daniel* (Atlanta: John Knox, 1985) 160–62; Collins, *Daniel*, 386. Surely it is not an indictment against critical scholarship if inerrantists have difficulty imagining a person who advocates intense resistance to a regime without advocating the joining or supporting of a violent rebellion.

63. E.g., Joyce G. Baldwin, *Daniel: An Introduction and Commentary*, TOTC (Downers Grove, IL: InterVarsity, 1978) 199–202; compare Iain M. Duguid, *Daniel* (Philipsburg, NJ: Presbyterian and Reformed, 2008) 203–4; Longman and Dillard, *Introduction*, 374.

64. E.g., Miller, *Daniel*, 306–13; Steinmann, "Is the Antichrist in Daniel 11?"

65. For example, after overviewing "the fact that much of the historical data set forth

trades on a complicating matter: critical scholars locate the switch from *ex eventu* prophecy to attempted prediction at 11:40, with 11:35–39 serving as a distorting polemical sketch of Antiochus.[66] Inerrantists, however, represent critical scholars as "resorting to" the polemical interpretation of 11:36–39 to address "problems."

Critics are said to engage in "special pleading" to "rescue" the passage's discourse of an ultimate blasphemer and all-powerful foe—levels of rebellion and kinds of self-exaltation not imaginable for the historical Antiochus IV—so it can fit Antiochus.[67] This feeds into a broader inerrantist argument about 11:36–45: the passage indicates a shift from Antiochus IV since it depicts a larger and more ultimate figure with heavenly-universal consequences and demonic attributes.[68] Furthermore, 11:36–45 locate this figure at the time of the end, thus after Antiochus IV—since "the end" pictured in Dan 12 did not come with Antiochus's death.[69] Inerrantists offer other arguments as well to show a transition away from Antiochus in 11:36.

Inerrantist treatments of Dan 11:36–45 fall short of academic-historical methodology, particularly because they presume that readings not involving an error in Daniel's text are better interpretive options. But

---

in [11:36–45] is impossible to harmonize with Antiochus' life," Miller (*Daniel*, 305) proceeds to the interpretive conclusion: "Exegetical necessity requires that 11:36–45 be applied to someone other than Antiochus IV." Miller and other inerrantists adduce further reasons for positing this transition, but this consideration is a primary support. See Archer, *Daniel*, 143–49; Duguid, *Daniel*, 204; Ferch, "Book of Daniel," 134–35; Steinmann, "Is the Antichrist in Daniel 11?" 199–204; J. Paul Tanner, "Daniel's 'King of the North': Do We Owe Russia an Apology?" *Journal of the Evangelical Theological Society* 35 (1992) 316–17.

66. Collins, *Daniel*, 386–88. "Verses 36–39 do not continue in chronological sequence but recapitulate the king's behavior during the persecution" (386). See Goldingay, *Daniel*, 304; Hartman and DiLella, *Daniel*, 301–2.

67. Quoted phrases from Steinmann, "Is the Antichrist in Daniel 11?," 201–2.

68. Duguid, *Daniel*, 203–4; Ferch, "Book of Daniel," 134–35. For Steinmann the Antichrist is in view because the passage depicts an intensely "religious figure who stirs up problems of a geopolitical nature." Antiochus serves as a "mirror image" of the Antichrist. See Steinmann, "Is the Antichrist in Daniel 11?," 202–8.

69. This is the implicit inerrantist logic. Consider Miller, *Daniel*, 305: "The context indicates that the ruler now in view will live in the last days, immediately prior to the coming of the Lord . . . the clearest indication that this 'king' will live in the latter days is that the resurrection of the saints will take place immediately after God delivers his people from this evil individual's power. . . . Of course, the resurrection is an eschatological event." Compare Tanner, "Do We Owe Russia," 317.

do critics really think the passage remains accurate up through 11:39? For them, the issue is not actual accuracy but notional or recognized accuracy *on the part of the audience*, which in the case of Daniel's visions also involves numerous cases of historically accurate details in the *ex eventu* prophecy. Moreover, errors in 11:36–45, when compared to what we think we know of Antiochus IV's life, only constitute problems for interpreters who assume the text should be inerrant. Scholars who posit, for example, the polemical distortion reading of 11:36–39 do not "resort to" that reading "to rescue" the passage's inaccurate details.[70] They offer it since it seems most plausible, especially given that other Jewish sources of the Hellenistic-Roman period similarly represent Gentile rulers who oppress Jews.[71] As discussed above, the proposed Hellenistic dating of Daniel in modern scholarship involves precisely the point that Daniel's producers depict Antiochus as an eschatological adversary whose acts of persecution and eventual death are eschatological events.[72] The fact that the resurrection did not happen immediately following his death as Dan 12:1–3 indicates or that this interpretation locates the adversary long before Jesus is irrelevant, unless one presumes that historical readings of Daniel must accord with the theological positions of inerrantists.

Another example involves how inerrantists posit a subject change in the text for 11:36–45, claiming it either has another referent next to Antiochus or a different referent entirely. They posit the shift, however, without offering legitimate evidence for why a reader should detect this transition away from the subject of the immediately preceding sentences and away from how the text has described matters up to this point.[73]

70. See also Ferch's rhetoric about critical scholars and 11:40–45 in Ferch, "Book of Daniel," 135.

71. This includes depicting them with supra-mundane, "universal," and/or mythic valences: e.g., for Antiochus IV: 2 Macc 9:8–10; *T. Mos.* 8; for other Gentile rulers and eschatological adversaries: *Sib. Or.* 3.388–400 (Alexander?); *Sib. Or.* 5:93–107, 137–54, 214–27 (Nero); *4 Ezra* 5:6–12; 11:40–45. See also Isa 14 and Ezek 28.

72. The examples adduced by Steinmann, "Is the Antichrist in Daniel 11?," 203–9, of Daniel representing Antiochus IV as a foreshadowing, mirror image, and parallel of the Antichrist are better understood as Daniel describing Antiochus IV himself as the ultimate eschatological adversary. Far from indicating differentiation in Daniel between Antiochus IV and a subsequent "Antichrist," they demonstrate the mythic framework used for depicting Antiochus.

73. Steinmann offers other arguments for the change in subject. For example, the author uses a structuring "method" involving the introduction to new sections by new keywords. Daniel 11:36 shifts from "the king of the North" (Antiochus IV) to simply

It seems plausible to explain inerrantist arguments about 11:36–45 in terms of them systematically preferring interpretive options that accord with inerrancy and their overall Jesus-involved theology. As with inerrantist claims about antisupernatural presuppositions, their arguments about 11:36–45 operate in a discursive field in which these considerations modify those of historical scholarship. While these concerns may have legitimacy within theological or religious fields of discourse production, they lack historical validity.

Inerrantists also reject the consensus that Greece occupies the fourth spot in the four-kingdom schema in Daniel. For inerrantists the schema does not terminate with Greece and thus testify to the *ex eventu* nature of the book concerned with second-century realities of Jews under Greece (Seleucids). The schema's fourth spot is, instead, Rome.[74] Aside from decrying antisupernatural presuppositions, inerrantists muster a series of arguments that Rome is the fourth kingdom and that the Medes and Persians actually comprise a single empire in Daniel (the "Medo-Persian Empire").[75] This locates the eschatological end in Daniel within the period of Roman hegemony, not Greek—a significant point for those who need Daniel's "end" to involve Jesus. Inerrantists are further troubled by how critics think (wrongly) that Darius the Mede is a fabrication to fit the book's structuring schema. This would witness to the book's fictitious setting since a Jew in the Babylonian court would not likely confuse such significant details

---

"the king" (Antichrist) and remains so focused through 11:45. Problematically for this argument, and not discussed by Steinmann, Dan 11:40 still focuses on "the king of the North" as the subject of the section. See Steinmann, "Is the Antichrist in Daniel 11?," 198–200, 203.

74. Several recent inerrantists interpret the schema as do critical scholars: Babylon, Media, Persia, and Greece. See, for example, R. Gurney, "The Four Kingdoms of Daniel 2 and 7," *Themelios* 2 (1977) 39–45; John H. Walton, "The Four Kingdoms of Daniel," *JETS* 29 (1986) 25–36. Each, however, justifies their interpretations by arguing for the compatibility of their positions with inerrancy and the reality of predictive prophecy.

75. Many of these arguments focus on how Dan 8:3–4, 19–20 pictures the Medes and Persians as dual horns in one animal; they also focus on correlating aspects of the descriptions of various animals in Daniel's visions with the history and supposed characteristics of the empires in history. See Archer, *Daniel*, 24–26; Miller, *Daniel*, 92–99, 194–203; Robertson, *Christ of the Prophets*, 324–28, 331–32; Waltke, "Date," 326–28. This addresses the potential inaccuracy of Daniel treating the Median empire as an entity discrete from Persia that ruled over the Jews. See Baldwin, *Daniel*, 29; Miller, *Daniel*, 94–95; Robertson, *Christ of the Prophets*, 326–27.

about Babylon's downfall.[76] Three main proposals exist:[77] 1) Darius the Mede is Cyrus the Persian in Daniel;[78] 2) Darius the Mede is Cyrus's general Ug/Gubaru, known from the *Nabonidus Chronicle*;[79] or 3) Darius the Mede is Gubaru, the governor of Babylon.[80] Inerrantists argue that these possibilities militate against the view that Darius the Mede is a fabricated character in Daniel.[81]

Inerrantist interpretive choices about the four kingdoms and Darius the Mede stem from their consistent aversion to interpretive options involving an error. It is difficult to imagine interpreters envisioning

76. A common point by modern scholars: whereas Daniel represents the Medes conquering Babylon violently under the leadership of Darius the Mede (e.g., Dan 5:30), the Persians took Babylon peacefully under the leadership of Cyrus and his generals. According to Pierre Briant, it seems likely that Cyrus and his generals met resistance led by Nabonidus when taking the capital. See Briant, *From Cyrus to Alexander: A History of the Persian Empire*, trans. Peter Davids (Winona Lake, IN: Eisenbrauns, 2002 [1996]) 40–44.

77. For overviews, see Lester L. Grabbe, "Another Look at the *Gestalt* of 'Darius the Mede,'" *Catholic Biblical Quarterly* 50 (1988) 199–207; Longman and Dillard, *Introduction*, 377–81.

78. The proposal of D. J. Wiseman, "Some Historical Problems in the Book of Daniel," in *Notes on Some Problems in the Book of Daniel* (London: Tyndale, 1965) 9–16. This position argues that 6:28 could also be translated, "Daniel prospered in the reign of Darius, even [i.e.] the reign of Cyrus the Persian," and that it is possible for an author to designate an individual with different names. Compare Baldwin, *Daniel*, 26–27; Miller, *Daniel*, 174–77 (one of two most probable options); Schwab, *Hope in the Midst*, 7–8.

79. The proposal of W. H. Shea, "An Unrecognized Vassal King of Babylon in the Early Achaemenid Period," *AUSS* 9 (1971) 51–67, 99–128; 10 (1972) 88–117, 147–78; idem, "Darius the Mede: An Update," *AUSS* 20 (1982) 229–47. Shea's argument is complex and revolves around identifying Gubaru and Ugbaru of the *Nabonidus Chronicle* as the same person and dating his death to a year after the fall of Babylon. For summaries of Shea's work, see Grabbe, "Another Look," 199–204; Longman and Dillard, *Introduction*, 379–80.

80. The proposal of John C. Whitcomb, *Darius the Mede: A Study in Historical Identification* (Grand Rapids: Eerdmans, 1959). Whitcomb's argument differentiates Gubaru from Ugbaru. Compare Harrison, *Introduction*, 1121–22; Miller, *Daniel*, 173 (one of two probable options); Waltke, "Date," 327.

81. Indeed, Archer, *Daniel*, 16, declares that "examination of the internal and external evidence shows the hopelessness of this theory." Inerrantists also highlight the archaeological verification of Daniel's accuracy about Belshazzar, treating this as establishing some kind of inerrancy-vindicating momentum in scholarship such that speculative theories about Darius the Mede should receive the benefit of the doubt or that judgment should be suspended. See Arnold and Beyer, *Encountering the Old Testament*, 436; Baldwin, *Daniel*, 24; Robertson, *Christ of the Prophets*, 327–28n11; Schwab, *Hope in the Midst*, 7–8; Waltke, "Date," 328–29.

Daniel's four-kingdom schema ending with Rome apart from the need for Daniel to speak of the Roman period.[82] For example, Dan 8:19–26, the interpretation of the vision in 8:2–14, indicates that the vision concerns "the appointed time of the end" (8:19). It explicitly designates the final kingdom of the vision as Greece (8:21–25). Towards the end of that kingdom "a king of bold face" will enact incredible devastation, even "against the Prince of princes," prior to being "broken—but by no human hand" (8:23–25). The interpretation thus ends in 8:23–25 by explicating the cessation of temple cult and the distress caused by the "little horn" at the end of the vision (8:9–12), cryptically but recognizably in terms of Antiochus IV. It represents his death as the culmination of the 1,150 days until the appointed time of the end when the temple cult would be restored.[83] Just as in the vision of Dan 10–12, this vision represents Antiochus IV and his actions as the period of climactic suffering followed immediately by an event of eschatological import. Since the visions of Dan 7–12 parallel each other and the schema editorially structures the book as a whole, it is difficult to see how Rome could occupy the fourth spot given the overwhelming focus of Daniel on Antiochus IV as the climactic adversary.[84] While inerrantists offer detailed arguments for how elements of the text can be understood to designate Rome as the fourth kingdom, it remains difficult to see how those more speculative interpretations could have greater plausibility apart from the theological presumption that the fourth kingdom must be Rome.

In their attempts to historically identify Darius the Mede, inerrantists consistently prefer interpretive options that either lack evidentiary support or (if Grabbe is wrong[85]) require endorsing an overtly specula-

82. Even the inerrantist Walton makes this point, emphasizing that all extant interpretations of the fourth kingdom as Rome come from the period of the Roman Empire or later. See Walton, "Four Kingdoms of Daniel," 27–28.

83. See Collins, "Meaning of 'The End,'" 159–61, 163–65, for a discussion of the eschatological meaning of "the end" (restoration of temple cult) in Dan 8, and for the 1,150 days calculation as a real attempted prediction that later chapters in Daniel show underwent recalculation and reframing in relation to other eschatological events.

84. Rome does appear in Dan 11:30; a reference to the Roman delegate Popilius Laenas demanding that Antiochus IV withdraw from Egypt (Diodorus Siculus 31.1–3; Polybius 29.26–27). This, however, is not a reference placing them within the schema, whose referents receive explicit designation as the schema progresses in Daniel.

85. Grabbe, "Another Look," 201–4, also offers evidence against the inerrantist proposals, namely that Cambyses was king during the period in question for Darius the Mede, thus invalidating the inerrantist proposals.

tive proposal of the "it is possible" variety. In other words, since other ancient sources mention person *x* (e.g., Gubaru), *it is possible* that this was Daniel's Darius the Mede.[86] If these options prove unsatisfactory, inerrantists suggest withholding judgment until evidence surfaces vindicating the historicity of Darius the Mede.[87] It is true that historical scholarship functions by gauging possibilities and that suspending judgment in the absence of relatively compelling evidence is a virtue. Inerrantists, however, misrepresent the situation. Critical scholars offer positive evidence for analyzing Darius the Mede in Daniel as "a creation from commonplace beliefs about Persian times" in the Hellenistic period; they offer plausible explanations based upon how the producer of Daniel read his sacred writings.[88] This approach configures Darius the Mede in Daniel as notionally derived from the Persian king Darius I of the sixth and fifth centuries BCE.[89] Even though neither Darius I (Persian) nor the Medes conquered Babylon, the book falsely locates him as a Median conqueror of Babylon. The author needs a Median king for his structuring schema; the Medes follow Babylon in the traditional schema used by the author. He also reads his ancestral prophetic literature as predicting a Median conquest of Babylon.[90]

---

86. Inerrantists frequently reframe the lack of evidence for their overtly speculative hypotheses by claiming that only (dubious) arguments from silence militate against them. Compare Miller, *Daniel*, 177: "Such an identification [Gubaru or Cyrus] accords well with the facts, and there is no evidence against it except arguments from silence."

87. Arnold and Beyer, *Encountering the Old Testament*, 436; Hill and Walton, *Survey*, 570.

88. Quote from Grabbe, "Another Look," 211. For several examples, see Collins, *Daniel*, 30–32, 253, 348; Grabbe, "Another Look," 207–12; H. F. D. Sparks, "On the Origin of 'Darius the Mede' at Daniel V.31," *Journal of Theological Studies* 47 (1946) 41–46, referenced in Grabbe, 212n54.

89. Grabbe, "Another Look," 207–12; H. H. Rowley, *Darius the Mede and the Four World Empires in the Book of Daniel* (Cardiff: University of Wales, 1935) 54–61. Designating Xerxes as Darius's father (Dan 9:1) could reflect a confusion on the part of a much later author with only "commonplace" knowledge of Persian history (see Grabbe, "Another Look," 209) or possibly the author thinking Ezra 4 depicts Xerxes (4:6) preceding Darius (4:24). Despite mention of Darius in 4:5, this reading of Ezra 4 is plausible for a Hellenistic Jew.

90. E.g., Isa 13:17; 21:2; Jer 51:11, 28. On the broader use by Daniel's producers of Hebrew "sacred" literature, especially prophetic literature, in writing stories, *ex eventu* prophecies, and attempted prophecies, see Michael Fishbane, *Biblical Interpretation in Ancient Israel* (New York: Oxford University Press, 1988) 482–95; Knibb, "Book of Daniel," 16–19; idem, "'You Are Indeed Wiser than Daniel.'"

These proposals explain the data in relation to broader demonstrable structures of Daniel, how its producers formed their "knowledge" of the past, and characteristics of the legacy of Babylon and Persia within the book.[91] While such speculative proposals about a fictional Darius the Mede in Daniel may prove incorrect, they have more evidentiary plausibility than the more speculative proposals inerrantists have to offer, ones that interpret the data in isolation from this evidence. The choices end up being: 1) opt for soundly critiqued inerrantist proposals or 2) suspend judgment, granting evidentiary consideration to interpretations not involving Daniel in an error. This amounts to special pleading in service of a non-academic, non-historical agenda.[92] It renders one a less accurate historical reader of Daniel since interpretive options accounting for the most data are rejected in favor of options fitting an ideal of how the data should be. Yet again, these inerrantist readings operate in a discursive field where inerrancy-constrained considerations augment and distort historical methodology.

Another common inerrantist argument about the date is that Daniel manuscripts among the Dead Sea Scrolls render the Hellenistic date less likely, or even impossible.[93] Various fragmentary manuscripts of Daniel

91. The nature of different traditions, myths, and remembrances of ancient Mesopotamian cultures in Daniel plausibly situate it in a third–second-century Hellenistic setting. The forms of these "survivals," as they are often called, are best explained in Daniel as "the persistent cultural legacy of Assyria and Babylon in the Hellenistic period," according to Collins, "Current Issues in the Study of Daniel," in *Book of Daniel*, ed. Collins and Flint, 1:6. On this general phenomenon, see *The Heirs of Assyria*, ed. S. Aro and R. M. Whiting, Melammu Symposia 1 (Helsinki: Neo-Assyrian Text Corpus Project, 2000), referenced in Collins, "Current Issues," 6n21. Compare Collins, "Stirring Up the Great Sea: The Religio-Historical Background of Daniel 7" [1993], in *Seers, Sibyls and Sages*, 139–55; John Day, "The Daniel of Ugarit and Ezekiel and the Hero of the Book of Daniel," *Vetus Testamentum* 30 (1980) 180–84; Shalom Paul, "The Mesopotamian Babylonian Background of Daniel 1–6," in *Book of Daniel*, ed. Collins and Flint, 1:55–68; van der Toorn, "Scholars at the Oriental Court;" *pace* Archer, *Daniel*, 19–20; Baldwin, *Daniel*, 37–39; Harrison, *Introduction*, 1122–23; Miller, *Daniel*, 26–27, 150; Schwab, *Hope in the Midst*, 7–8; Waltke, "Date," 328–29. These "survivals" do not attest to a sixth-century compositional setting for Daniel.

92. Longman and Dillard, *Introduction*, 381, concede: "Conservative scholars have erred in presenting their attempted solutions too dogmatically. It must be admitted that there are theological motives at work here." Compare Hill and Walton, *Survey*, 570.

93. Miller *Daniel*, 38–39, approvingly quotes R. K. Harrison: "It would thus appear that, whatever may be thought about the place of prediction in prophecy, the manuscript evidence from Qumran absolutely precludes a date of composition in the Maccabean period."

were discovered among the Dead Sea Scrolls, the earliest of which dates to the late second century BCE.[94] A series of points commonly appear in inerrantist literature. First, given the manuscript and usage-of-Daniel evidence at Qumran, a second-century date for the book does not leave enough time for it to have been accepted as Scripture.[95] Second, other writings previously considered Hellenistic-period compositions have been redated to earlier periods because of similar Qurman manuscript discoveries. Critics treat Daniel differently because of their irrational hang-ups about predictive prophecy.[96] Third, critics allege that Dan 11:40–45 errs in its prediction about Antiochus's death and that the book offers several precise calculations of eschatological events for the late 160s, events that did not transpire. If this is the case, the Qumran evidence makes no sense since Jews would not have accepted an errant prophetic writing as authoritative.[97] Fourth, some appeal to a recent article by Fox arguing that the Hebrew text of *Ben Sira* uses Daniel and thus demonstrates the existence of those parts of Daniel in 190–180 BCE, prior to *Ben Sira*'s composition.[98] Fifth, some inerrantists also argue that a pseudepigraphic (read: deceptive) Daniel would not be accepted as Scripture because "we have no conclusive evidence that literature written under a pen name was ever admitted into the canon." In sum, the Qumran data speaks *against* the critical view.[99]

However, significant problems obtain for all these inerrantist arguments. The claim that the manuscript situation does not leave enough

94. 4QDan[c]; for a concise overview of Daniel manuscripts in the Dead Sea Scrolls, see Collins, *Daniel*, 2–3.

95. See Thomas Finley, "The Book of Daniel in the Canon of Scripture," *BSac* 165 (2008) 208. Compare Arnold and Beyer, *Encountering the Old Testament*, 438; Hill and Walton, *Survey*, 570–71; Miller, *Daniel*, 37–38.

96. E.g., "Equivalent manuscript finds at Qumran of other books where the issue of predictive prophecy is not in question have led scholars to repudiate a Maccabean date for their compositions. . . But critical scholars have refused to draw the same conclusion in the case of Daniel even though the evidence is identical" (Waltke, "Date," 321–22). Compare Douglas E. Fox, "*Ben Sira* on OT Canon Again: The Date of Daniel," *WTJ* 49 (1987) 350; Miller, *Daniel*, 38.

97. E.g., David Gooding, "The Literary Structure of the Book of Daniel and Its Implications," *Tyndale Bulletin* 32 (1981) 72–75; Miller, *Daniel*, 37.

98. Fox, "*Ben Sira* on OT Canon Again," 341–44; similarly Finley: "Daniel in the Canon," 205–6.

99. Quote from Arnold and Beyer, *Encountering the Old Testament*, 438. Compare Finley, "Daniel in the Canon," 208; Ferch, "Book of Daniel," 136–37.

time for acceptance as an authoritative writing is an underexplained generalization. Beyond the confusion that terms like "canon" unnecessarily introduce into the discussion,[100] how do inerrantists know how much time it takes for a writing to obtain authoritative status? This objection furthermore obscures the basic logic of a pseudepigraphic revelatory writing, which is to convince contemporaries to trust the writing immediately. In the critical view, Daniel's producers seek authority for their writing through claims to revelation and via other pseudepigraphic, revelatory strategies such as esoteric claims and (*ex eventu*) prophecy. The idea is not for people to accept Daniel and thereby render its producers successful *after* waiting to verify its universal acceptance by all or most other Jews over an unspecified period of time.[101] Such inerrantist claims illustrate their selectivity in argumentation, for they have no such qualms about the Apostle Paul's letters receiving quick recognition as authoritative writings.[102] Not only this, but critical scholars who, on account of Qumran manuscript finds, redate other writings as earlier but do not do so for Daniel because of predictive prophecy are merely adhering as academics to ordinary historical methodology.[103]

Claims that second-century Jews would reject Daniel if it made incorrect predictions about events in the second century obscure relevant issues. Various ancient Jews did the same thing that various modern people do when the predictions of a perceived sacred writing

100. This relates to the common inerrantist desire to have a full and closed (Protestant) Old Testament canon in existence for all or most Jews by the mid second century BCE. See Roger Beckwith, *The Old Testament Canon of the New Testament Church and Its Background in Early Judaism* (Grand Rapids: Eerdmans, 1986). For a critique of Beckwith, see James Vanderkam, "Revealed Literature in the Second Temple Period," in *From Revelation to Canon*, 11–30.

101. This model lacks a plausibly theorized social context. To the extent a sophisticated writing such as Daniel reaches "ordinary" (non-literate) folks, some of the few literate specialists of its world must mediate it. A more fruitful historical analysis of such a writing's popularity and "authority" would thus start with the scribal social formations first and foremost responsible for its production, transmission, and dissemination. Issues such as the popularity of a writing in scribal curricula or its usefulness in rescribing social conditions serving scribal interests are the most pertinent places to start when asking about what is meant by canonization. See van der Toorn, *Scribal Culture*, 54–55, 63–71, 101–7, 205–33, 244–47; and David M. Carr, *Writing on the Tablet of the Heart: Origins of Scripture and Literature* (New York: Oxford University Press, 2005).

102. Inerrantists see 2 Pet 3:15–16 as evidence for the early acceptance of Paul's letters as Scripture.

103. See above.

or authoritative figure do not come to pass. While some may no longer ascribe authority to the writing or person, others decide that they misread or miscalculated. The text of Daniel itself shows editorial signs of this with its differing calculations of the end.[104] While inerrantists obviously dispute this reading,[105] critical scholars articulate more precisely how they conceive of the nature of these calculations in Daniel, offering specific comparative arguments for their views.[106] Ancient Jews often read their prophetic and oracular literature in various figurative ways, reactualizing or reinterpreting texts in light of their present circumstances,[107] which involved close, detailed, and learned readings of texts. Such readings involved varying exegetical methods dependent upon the interpreter—drawing upon details in a passage's broader

104. Dan 7:25; 8:13–14; 9:2; compare 9:22–27; 12:7, 11, 12. For a discussion of the different meanings of "end" in Daniel and of the different time calculations given along these lines, see Collins, *Daniel*, 357–58, 399–404; idem, "Meaning of 'The End'"; Lars Hartman, "The Functions of Some So-Called Apocalyptic Timetables," *New Testament Studies* 22 (1975) 2–7. Compare Neujahr, "When Darius Defeated Alexander"; and Fishbane, *Biblical Interpretation*, 445, 474–95.

105. Some argue that the apocalyptic-symbolic genre, the varying numbers, and other details indicate that some or all or of the calculations are not to be taken literally but symbolically or theologically. See Baldwin, *Daniel*, 164–68; Duguid, *Daniel*, 132, 166–67, 215–16; Robertson, *Christ of the Prophets*, 342–46. Others reject the critical reading by correlating the calculated periods with Christian and Jesus- (or Antichrist)-involved eschatological events discussed in later Christian sources. See Archer, *Daniel*, 156–57; Miller, *Daniel*, 325–27.

106. For one example, see Hartman, "Functions," 1–14, and his specific points about such calculations in Daniel (2–7). For inerrantist treatments, see Miller, *Daniel*, 193; Robertson, *Christ of the Prophets*, 342, 344–46; and Duguid, *Daniel*, 166–75.

107. *1QpHab* 1.16—2.10 remains a classic example, giving three separate contemporizing and eschatologizing interpretations of Hab 1:5. Many ancient Jews similarly plumbed their prophetic writings as though they were repositories of hidden moral, cosmological, and eschatological wisdom requiring technical and/or inspired unlocking by a skilled interpreter. One finds this phenomenon blossoming in post-exilic prophetic literature and subsequent apocalyptic and other early Jewish revelatory and wisdom literature, displaying the attitude commonly termed revelation-by-interpretation or the scribalization of prophecy. See, for example, Peter Enns, *Exodus Retold: Ancient Exegesis of the Departure from Egypt in Wis 10:15–21 and 19:1–9* (Atlanta: Scholars, 1997); Annette Reed, *Fallen Angels and the History of Judaism and Christianity: The Reception of Enochic Literature* (New York: Cambridge University Press, 2005) 24–83; Michael Stone, "Lists of Revealed Things in the Apocalyptic Literature," in *Magnalia Dei: The Mighty Acts of God*, ed. F. M. Cross (Garden City, NY: Doubleday, 1976) 414–52; van der Toorn, *Scribal Culture*, 203–64; Vanderkam, "Prophetic-Sapiential Origins."

literary context, other times manipulating passages atomistically.[108] In this way the diverse Jewish range of reading strategies resembles broader ancient Mediterranean sensitivities about how to handle texts perceived as prophetic, oracular, or otherwise divinely characterized.[109] We also know that ancient Jews and Christians reinterpreted Daniel, especially the numerological calculating passages, in precisely these ways.[110] It is not at all clear that ancient Jews would have rejected Daniel when its calculated and specific predictions failed to materialize. They figuratively interpreted these aspects of Daniel, particularly if a "problem" of non-fulfillment was perceived, just as do modern inerrantist interpreters who labor to represent Daniel as a book of only true predictions. We lack evidence for the common inerrantist assertion that if Daniel in fact contains failed prophecies about the second century, as critics allege, then ancient Jews would have rejected it. The logic ultimately derives from inerrantist sensitivities about what is appropriate for the biblical canon, not from examinations of ancient data—discussions of which are conspicuously absent from their writings on this issue.

Even Fox's article suffers from numerous problems.[111] The co-occurrence of the two words for "appointed time" and "end" in Daniel and *Ben Sira* that he adduces as evidence is not sufficient for establishing literary dependence (Dan 8:19; 11:27, 35 and *Ben Sira* 36:8; 33:8).[112] He asserts that the frequent co-occurrence of these words in

108. See James Kugel's standard treatment: *Traditions of the Bible: A Guide to the Bible as It Was at the Start of the Common Era* (Cambridge, MA: Harvard University Press, 1999); compare Michael Fishbane, *Biblical Interpretation*, 443–524.

109. Peter Struck's study *Birth of the Symbol: Ancient Readers at the Limits of their Texts* (Princeton, NJ: Princeton University Press, 2004) is the best current treatment of ancient Greek figurative reading techniques, attitudes towards different kinds of texts, and debates about these notions among ancient Greek intellectuals. See also *The Cambridge Companion to Allegory*, ed. Rita Copeland and Peter Struck (New York: Cambridge University Press, 2010); David Dawson, *Allegorical Readers and Cultural Revision in Ancient Alexandria* (Berkeley: University of California Press, 1992); Robert Lamberton, *Homer the Theologian: Neoplatonist Allegorical Reading and the Growth of the Epic Tradition* (Berkeley: University of California Press, 1986).

110. For a discussion of the early Jewish and Christian interpretation of Daniel, see Collins, *Daniel*, 72–122. See also William Adler, "The Apocalyptic Survey of History Adapted by Christians: Daniel's Prophecy of 70 Weeks," in *The Jewish Apocalyptic Heritage in Early Christianity*, ed. James Vanderkam and William Adler, CRINT 3.4 (Minneapolis: Fortress, 1996) 201–38.

111. Fox, "*Ben Sira* on OT Canon," 335–50.

112. Fox, "*Ben Sira* on OT Canon," 341–44. Fox notes two other passages in *Ben*

the Dead Sea Scrolls, for example, is evidence supporting their derivation from Daniel as opposed to their attestation of common practice for second- and first-century Jews writing in Hebrew referring to the time of the end. A generalization about *Ben Sira*'s imitative character versus Daniel's innovative character buttresses the claim that *Ben Sira* must have used Daniel instead of the other way around.[113] This generalization does not shed light on the specific textual situation here. Both *Ben Sira* and Daniel innovate from earlier sources.[114] If one wants to establish the plausibility of *Ben Sira*'s literary dependence on Daniel over the plausibility of the converse or of a reflection of common contemporary scribal phrasing, one must provide a specific exegetical and comparative argument about the specific words and passages in question in each writing. Fox does not do this.

Inerrantist arguments about the impossibility of a pseudepigraphic writing in the canon because the existence of one has never been proven and because they involve deception are not historical-academic positions. They turn on arguments analytically privileging the self-claims of biblical writings and the representations in the canonical Gospels of Jesus' words.[115] None of these assumptions are falsifiable historical claims. Inerrantist arguments accordingly operate in discursive fields whose interests and tacitly accepted methods for engagement involve considerations decidedly different from those of academic-historical arenas of discourse production and consumption.

CONCLUSION

Space considerations unfortunately preclude examination of other relevant inerrantist arguments about the date of Daniel. The above examination, nevertheless, suffices to show that their arguments operate

---

Sira that may refer to Daniel (342–43). For Fox, this constitutes "compelling evidence" that "Daniel [is] to be dated earlier than *Ben Sira*" (342).

113. Fox, "*Ben Sira* on OT Canon," 345: "In addition, it should be recalled . . . that Ben Sira was a conscious imitator, while the author of the Book of Daniel must be seen as a highly creative and original thinker. We expect Ben Sira to rely on others, but not the author of the Book of Daniel."

114. To counter Fox's claim about Daniel, see Collins, *Daniel*, 2–3.

115. See Finley, "Daniel in the Canon," 208; Miller, *Daniel*, 34–36. The claim that the existence of a forgery in the canon has never been proven is tenuous.

in discursive fields whose interests and tacitly accepted methods for engagement involve considerations decidedly different from those of academic-historical arenas of discourse production and consumption. Inerrantists systematically and predictably favor interpretive options not involving the text of Daniel in an error or deviation from their theology. This renders them poor analysts of Daniel by academic-historical standards. However, they energetically represent their inerrancy-vindicating treatments of Daniel as legitimate academic-historical scholarship. In particular, they represent them as such in contrast to critical scholars, whose work they consistently depict as academically illegitimate for its failure to accept Daniel's self-claims and its rejection of the possibility of supernatural explanations. These very discursive moves, however, are inerrantist protective strategies. They analytically privilege Daniel's self-claims and render them and their positions about Daniel beyond adjudication or falsification by historical methods. The specifics of inerrantist scholarship on Daniel reveal engagements with the text and broader scholarship that operate in non-academic fields. They seem designed not for people inhabiting fields of academic-historical inquiry, but for people operating as producers or consumers in fields defined by these inerrantist interests and methods.

11

The Implications of New Testament Pseudonymy for a Doctrine of Scripture

Stanley E. Porter

INTRODUCTION

T HE TOPIC OF PSEUDONYMY continues to be a topic of interest in New Testament studies. As a result, there are a number of standard works on the subject,[1] as well as smaller treatments of some significance.[2] This does not count the usual considerations of the subject

---

1. These include Norbert Brox, ed., *Pseudepigraphie in der heidnischen und jüdisch-christlichen Antike*, Wege der Forschung 484 (Darmstadt: Wissenschaftliche Buchgesellschaft, 1977); David G. Meade, *Pseudonymity and Canon: An Investigation into the Relationship of Authorship and Authority in Jewish and Earliest Christian Tradition*, WUNT 39 (Tübingen: Mohr/Siebeck, 1986); Lewis R. Donelson, *Pseudepigraphy and Ethical Argument in the Pastoral Epistles*, HUT 22 (Tübingen: Mohr/Siebeck, 1986); Mark Kiley, *Colossians as Pseudepigraphy* (Sheffield: JSOT Press, 1986); and Terry L. Wilder, *Pseudonymity, New Testament, and Deception: An Enquiry into Intention and Reception* (Lanham, MD: University Press of America, 2004).

2. These include Kurt Aland, "The Problem of Anonymity and Pseudonymity in Christian Literature of the First Two Centuries," *Journal of Theological Studies* 12 (1961) 39–49, repr. *The Authorship and Integrity of the New Testament*, ed. Kurt Aland (London: SPCK, 1965) 1–13; Donald Guthrie, "The Development of the Idea of Canonical Pseudepigrapha in New Testament Criticism," *Vox Evangelica* 1 (1962) 43–59, repr. *Authorship and Integrity*, 14–39; Bruce M. Metzger, "Literary Forgeries

that occur in books such as introductions to the New Testament and the introductions to commentaries on the books most susceptible to being considered pseudepigraphal.[3] The issue of pseudonymity continues to be an issue that has bearing on a number of different topics within the larger field of New Testament studies. One of these areas is the perpetual issue of determining the authorship of various books in the New Testament, especially but not exclusively the Pauline letters. Another area is the complex issue of canonical formation, and the criteria that were in play as the process of formation of the New Testament canon transpired in the early centuries of the Christian church. Another area is the broader topic of how the books within the New Testament are related to contemporary writings of the time, including Greco-Roman and

---

and Canonical Pseudepigrapha," *Journal of Biblical Literature* 91 (1972) 3–24; Martin Rist, "Pseudepigraphy and the Early Christians," in *Studies in New Testament and Early Christian Literature: Essays in Honor of Allen P. Wikgren*, ed. David E. Aune, NovTSup 33 (Leiden: Brill, 1972) 75–91; E. Earl Ellis, "Pseudonymity and Canonicity of New Testament Documents," in *Worship, Theology and Ministry in the Early Church: Essays in Honor of Ralph P. Martin*, ed. Michael J. Wilkins and Terence Paige, JSNTSup 87 (Sheffield: JSOT Press, 1992) 212–24; Stanley E. Porter, "Pauline Authorship and the Pastoral Epistles: Implications for Canon," *Bulletin of Biblical Research* 5 (1995) 105–23; idem, "Pauline Authorship and the Pastoral Epistles: A Response to R. W. Wall's Response," *BBR* 6 (1996) 133–38 (which two articles by Porter I draw upon below); D. A. Carson, "Pseudonymity and Pseudepigraphy," in *Dictionary of New Testament Background*, ed. Craig A. Evans and Stanley E. Porter (Downers Grove, IL: InterVarsity, 2000) 857–64; Terry L. Wilder, "Pseudonymity and the New Testament," in *Interpreting the New Testament: Essays on Methods and Issues*, ed. David Alan Black and David S. Dockery (Nashville: Broadman & Holman, 2001) 296–335; and Wilder, "Pseudonymity, the New Testament, and the Pastoral Epistles," in *Entrusted with the Gospel: Paul's Theology in the Pastoral Epistles*, ed. Andreas J. Köstenberger and Terry L. Wilder (Nashville: Broadman & Holman, 2010) 28–51. For a popular treatment, see Stanley E. Porter, "Pseudonymity," in *Zondervan Encyclopedia of the Bible*, ed. Merrill C. Tenney and Moisés Silva, 5 vols., rev. ed. (Grand Rapids: Zondervan, 2009) 4:1087–90.

3. In the NT, these books include a number of the Pauline letters, in particular 2 Thessalonians, Ephesians, Colossians, and the Pastoral Epistles (1 and 2 Timothy and Titus); James; the Petrine letters (1 and 2 Peter); and Jude. There is still unfortunate confusion in the secondary literature over anonymous versus pseudepigraphal writings (see Lee Martin McDonald and Stanley E. Porter, *Early Christianity and Its Sacred Literature* [Peabody, MA: Hendrickson, 2000], 388, and discussion below; compare Rist, "Pseudepigraphy"). Anonymous writings are not to be confused with pseudepigraphal ones. In the NT, anonymous writings include all four Gospels (Matthew, Mark, Luke, John) Acts, Hebrews, and the Johannine letters (1, 2, 3 John). The book of Revelation is ambiguous as to authorship, as it refers to its author as John (Rev 1:1, 4, 9; 22:8) who may or may not be the author of the Gospel or John the son of Zebedee, as the name was very common at the time.

Jewish literature that, as we shall see, have the same attendant problems and disputes.[4] Clearly the issue of pseudonymity continues to be a major subject within a set of significant topics at the heart of contemporary New Testament studies. It is difficult, and in some instances virtually impossible, to treat many books of the New Testament without having to raise questions regarding the possibility of pseudonymous authorship. However, one of the questions that is not often addressed is how one's conclusions regarding pseudonymity have a direct bearing upon developing a doctrine of Scripture. In this brief chapter, I wish to raise and focus upon this particular question. As this topic is an extension of previous work that I have done on the topic, I will to some extent assume that discussion, but try to ensure that I have sufficiently introduced the major issues. In this chapter, I will first examine a fairly recent treatment of the issue of pseudonymity, to benefit from its definitions of terms and its framing of the question. Then I will subject this treatment and related treatments to critical scrutiny with an eye toward the issue of how one formulates and conceptualizes a suitably robust doctrine of Scripture in light of the issue of pseudonymity. I then will draw out a number of implications regarding the critical intersection of these topics. I will conclude with some brief comments on how these conclusions relate to the historical-critical enterprise and a doctrine of Scripture.

PSEUDONYMY IN RECENT DISCUSSION: THE BASIC POSITIONS

In a very fine relatively recent discussion, Kent Clarke outlines many, if not most, of the major issues in contemporary discussion of pseudonymy. In distinction to a variety of broader definitions available, Clarke wisely adopts a relatively narrow and succinct definition of pseudonymous literature: "works containing a *clear authorial ascription* determined to have been made by the *actual author* of the literature in question with the *calculated attempt to conceal* his true identity by deliberately endorsing a false author as the real author."[5] I note use of such language in

---

4. McDonald and Porter, *Early Christianity*, 388.

5. Kent D. Clarke, "The Problem of Pseudonymity in Biblical Literature and Its Implications for Canon Formation," in *The Canon Debate*, ed. Lee Martin McDonald and James A. Sanders (Peabody, MA: Hendrickson, 2002) 465. Compare 446–48, where he arrives at the three major elements of this definition in the course of his considering the evidence. This definition eliminates such potentially distracting but not germane

his definition as "calculated," "conceal," "deliberately," and "false," used in juxtaposition to such terms as "clear," "true," and "real." I will return to some of these issues below, but note here that the definition itself enshrines such an opposition.

Clarke then examines the role of pseudonymity in the ancient world as a whole. He begins with the Greco-Roman world, where he chronicles a widespread knowledge, even among ancient times, of pseudepigraphal literature. As he states, offering a conclusion followed by virtually all recent interpreters of the phenomenon of pseudepigraphy: "Pseudonymity was a widespread literary practice in Greco-Roman antiquity."[6] Similarly, the ancient Jewish world "gave birth to a considerable body of pseudonymous literature."[7] Finally, Clarke recognized the same situation within early Christianity: "the history of early Christian literature is full of examples of pseudonymity."[8] Clarke mentions as pseudepigrapha or works falsely attributed to a known author the following writings: the letter by Paul referred to in 2 Thessalonians (2:1–2) if not 2 Thessalonians itself; possibly the *Acts of Paul*; *Gospel of Peter*; a letter defended by Salvian entitled "From Timothy to All the Church"; works mentioned in the Muratorian fragment; *The Apostolic Constitutions*; *The Doctrine of Peter*, mentioned by Origen; a work written in Origen's name; letters attributed to Basil actually written by Eustathius of Sebaste; and works written under the names of Dionysius of Corinth and Jerome, among others.[9]

---

arguments as the role of scribes in composition. See Porter, "Pauline Authorship," 106.

6. Clarke, "Problem," 450. The authors he mentions who had pseudonymous works written under their name or were themselves discovered to be pseudonymous include: Pythagoras and Pythagorean literature; Cynic, Platonist and Aristotelian pseudonomymous authors; Dionysius according to Philostratus; Marcus Aurelius; Numa Pompilius; Epicurus; Anaximenes who used Theopompus's name; Galen; Virgilian poems; *Sibylline Oracles*; Orpheus; Phalaris; Lucian of Samosata; among other possible authors. See Clarke, "Problem," 450–52, who provides references. Most of these are also discussed in many of the surveys noted above. One of the best-known examples that Clarke does not cite is the orator Lysias, as well as the writings of Horace and Hippocrates. See Kiley, *Colossians*, 18 and related notes; K. J. Dover, *Lysias and the Corpus Lysiacum* (Berkeley: University of California Press, 1968).

7. Clarke, "Problem," 452. These include the OT Apocrypha, such as 2 Esdras, Tobit, Ecclesiasticus, and Baruch, as well as possibly others; numerous works within what is called the OT pseudepigrapha, such as the Enoch literature and *Letter of Aristeas*; and Phocylides; among others. See Clarke, "Problem," 452–54.

8. Clarke, "Problem," 454.

9. Clarke, "Problem," 455–57.

In what I think is probably the most important part of the essay, Clarke presents and then compares and contrasts what he isolates as the two major views on pseudonymity: the first views pseudonymity as "acceptable, honorable, or innocent: a licit or permissible convention," to use the subheading of the section; and the second that it is "unacceptable, dishonorable, and deceptive: an illicit or prohibited convention," again to use the subheading of the section.[10]

In the first view, pseudonymity as an acceptable convention, Clarke cites five major proponents: F. C. Baur, Adolf Jülicher, Mark Kiley, Brevard Childs, and David Meade. He notes that Baur set the agenda for subsequent discussion of the issue by being the first to take the position that pseudonymity was "an acceptable literary convention not undertaken with the intent to deceive."[11] Jülicher propounds that conceptions of intellectual property were different in the ancient world than in the modern one.[12] Kiley argues on the basis of a different worldview that ancient pseudepigraphers wanted "to produce a fresh formulation of what was thought to be the renowned individual's thought for a new situation."[13] Childs downplays the significance of the historical author and situation and opts for the "kerygmatic witness of the text and the significance of the portrayed 'canonical' author."[14] Finally, Meade invokes Jewish interpretive conventions whereby a text was made contemporary for a new audience by applying "the prophetic, sapiential, apocalyptic, and apostolic traditions to new situations" that "resulted in the growth of this literature."[15]

In the second view, pseudonymity as an unacceptable convention, Clarke cites four advocates: J. S. Candlish, J. I. Packer, Donald Guthrie, and Stanley E. Porter. Candlish, taking a critical approach to the issue

---

10. Clarke, "Problem," 458, 461. See Carson, "Pseudonymity," 862–63, who distinguishes others, while boiling down the major options to these two.

11. Clarke, "Problem," 459. He cites F. C. Baur, *Paul, the Apostle of Jesus Christ: His Life and Work, His Epistles and His Doctrine*, trans. Alan Menzies, 2 vols., 2nd ed., (London: Williams and Norgate, 1876) 2:110–11.

12. Clarke, "Problem," 459. He cites Adolf Jülicher, *An Introduction to the New Testament*, trans. J. P. Ward (London: Smith, Elder, 1904) 52–54.

13. Clarke, "Problem," 459. He cites Kiley, *Colossians*, 26.

14. Clarke, "Problem," 460. He cites Brevard S. Childs, *The New Testament as Canon: An Introduction* (Valley Forge, PA: Trinity, 1984) esp. 52, 383, 323.

15. Clarke, "Problem," 460–61. He cites Meade, *Pseudonymity and Canon*, esp. 203, 207.

rather than simply theological, draws the conclusion "that no known pseudonymous writing was ever accepted as authoritative in the early church—a conclusion shared by virtually all who regard pseudonymity as an unacceptable practice," along with equating pseudonymous composition with deception and hence the work being unsuitable for the canon.[16] Packer labels pseudonymous works as forgeries and fraudulent, and not suitable to be in the canon, in the same way that their being in the canon guarantees their non-pseudonymity.[17] Guthrie also avers that pseudonymous works were unacceptable to the early church.[18] Finally, Porter notes that the ancients distinguished between genuine and spurious works, and rejects the argument of the noble lie (sometimes used to justify pseudepigrapha) seeing it as still being a lie.[19]

Clarke finishes this section by citing the important monograph of Lewis Donelson, who, while he strongly agrees that pseudepigrapha were written with deceptive intent and were excluded in Christian circles for that reason, argues that the church—because detection of pseudepigraphal writings was so difficult as to be impossible—placed more emphasis upon the doctrinal soundness of a work than on its authorship. As a result, there were pseudepigraphal works included in the canon on the basis of deception.[20]

Clarke concludes by recognizing that pseudonymity was common in the ancient world but generally frowned upon when discovered. However, he also concludes that the canonization process resulted in other criteria being used other than simply authorship, even if these criteria are not entirely clear or were not uniformly applied.[21]

16. Clarke, "Problem," 461. He cites J. S. Candlish, "On the Moral Character of Pseudonymous Books," *Expositor* 4 (1894) 103, 278–79.

17. Clarke, "Problem," 462. He cites J. I. Packer, *"Fundamentalism" and the Word of God: Some Evangelical Principles* (Grand Rapids: Eerdmans, 1958) 183, 184.

18. Clarke, "Problem," 462. He cites Guthrie, "Idea," 38; and Guthrie, *New Testament Introduction*, 3rd ed. (Downers Grove, IL: InterVarsity, 1970) 1012, 1018–20.

19. Clarke, "Problem," 463–64. He cites Porter, "Response," 136, 138; and idem, "Pauline Authorship," 119, 121–22, 123. Reference to the "noble lie" is to Plato's idea that there are circumstances that merit the telling of a lie for a greater purpose (*Rep.* 2.376E—3.392C; 3.414C–414E; 5.459D). See Clark, "Problem," 444 and note 24.

20. Clarke, "Problem," 464–65. He cites Donelson, *Pseudepigraphy and Ethical Argument*, esp. 10, 17–18, 201.

21. Clarke, "Problem," 466.

Despite this fine presentation of the major issues regarding pseude-pigraphy, there clearly are other issues and their implications to consider, and conclusions to draw, when discussing the subject of pseudonymy and a doctrine of Scripture.

PSEUDONYMY RECONSIDERED

This review of Clarke's article provides a suitable foundation and start-ing point for a reconsideration of pseudonymy in relation to the New Testament and how this might have a bearing on a doctrine of Scripture. Since Clarke has presented a fine conspectus of the available evidence, as well as ably presenting the basic arguments of a number of those who have contributed to this discussion, I will for the most part assume this knowledge in pursuing my particular line of reasoning in this chapter.

Rejection of Known Pseudepigrapha by the Ancients

In his conclusion, Clarke states that, though pseudonymity was com-mon in the ancient world and "when discovered, looked upon contemp-tuously," in all probability, "several examples to the contrary do exist."[22] However, he does not state what those examples to the contrary are. As he himself has noted, there is widespread recognition by scholarship concerning Greco-Roman literature, Jewish literature, and Christian lit-erature that pseudepigrapha were present and the phenomenon was rec-ognized in the ancient world, and that such literature poses a problem regarding the place of pseudepigrapha within the Christian canonical literature in particular—hence the two major views that try to address the situation, either as acceptable or unacceptable. Both are attempting to come to terms with a situation in which such literature poses a problem within the context of the nature and development of early Christianity and its canon of authoritative writings. There is also a significant group of scholars—as Clarke notes—who state unequivocally that discovery of such literature led to its being excluded as authoritative. Therefore, it is surprising that he is not more specific regarding what that literature that slipped through the cracks might be.

Clarke's statement itself, however, is ambiguous. He does not clarify whether he is referring to the examples in one or more of the categories

22. Clarke, "Problem," 466.

of Greco-Roman, Jewish, and Christian literature, or to just the Christian literature. Further, he does not indicate whether he means that these "several examples" encompass pseudepigraphal literature being included in the canon, or whether he believes that other pseudepigrapha were accepted within the wider scope of Christian literature. In his discussion of pseudepigraphal Christian literature, Clarke does not in fact cite any New Testament text apart from the possible pseudepigraphal status of 2 Thessalonians with its reference to the apparently pseudepigraphal Pauline letter—although elsewhere he acknowledges discussion of a number of New Testament books as possibly being pseudepigraphal. So far as I can determine—leaving aside possible pseudepigrapha within the New Testament canon, as that is the topic of debate, and we cannot assume the conclusion—Clarke seems to identify only one possible work that was not treated contemptuously when discovered to be pseudepigraphal: *The Apostolic Constitutions* (another might be the *Didache*, which is included within *The Apostolic Constitutions*). However, this third- to fourth-century pseudepigraphon was not included in the canon, even though it was eventually recognized as having authority in both the Eastern and Western church.[23] This hardly seems to be the "several examples" that Clarke intimates.

With no clear evidence to the contrary, I still believe that Donelson's statement is correct: "No one ever seems to have accepted a document as religiously and philosophically prescriptive which was known to be forged. I do not know a single example. We have instead innumerable examples of the opposite." Even with the pressures of library gathering, the ancients strove to maintain the authenticity of their literary collections. Thus, "even though the literary world was inundated by pseudepigrapha, we have no known instance of a pseudepigraphon recognized as such which acquired prescriptive and proscriptive authority as well. If discovered, it was rejected. The same holds true in Christian circles."[24] This process of identification and exclusion includes, but is not confined to, the author of "3 Corinthians" being removed from the office of presbyter (Tertullian, *On Baptism* 17),[25] the rejection of the *Gospel*

23. See Philip Schaff, *A History of the Christian Church*, vol. 2: *Ante-Nicene Christianity* (New York: Scribners, 1884) 185–87.

24. Donelson, *Pseudepigraphy and Ethical Argument*, 11.

25. D. A. Carson, Douglas J. Moo, and Leon Morris, *An Introduction to the New Testament* (Grand Rapids: Zondervan, 1992) 368–69, note rejection of "3 Corinthians"

of Peter by Bishop Serapion in c. 200 (Eusebius, *Hist. eccl.* 6.12.1–6),[26] and the rejection of Salvian's pamphlet written in Timothy's name by Bishop Salonius.[27] Donelson's statement, he believes (and I believe the evidence confirms), applies to the range of ancient literature, but especially includes Christian literature, which I do not believe is actively or convincingly disputed by any discussion since Donelson wrote these statements. If these statements are true, and there is no evidence, especially Christian and more particularly biblical evidence, to dispute them, this forms an important foundation for further analysis.

Assessment of the View that Pseudonymity Was Acceptable

With this position firmly established, it is difficult to know how to respond to the view that pseudepigrapha were nevertheless acceptable in the early church because they were part of an acceptable literary convention. Clarke's definition itself seems to be based upon recognition that pseudepigrapha are conceived and executed on the basis of deception. Even with this position and recognition firmly established, there is still the question raised regarding whether the writing of pseudepigrapha was considered an acceptable practice. As noted above, there are a number of scholars, from Baur to the present, who argue that the writing of pseudepigrapha was an accepted convention of the ancient world. In his presentation of their arguments, Clarke himself assesses the strength—or lack of it—of the arguments of many of those who advo-

---

along with a "Letter to the Laodiceans" and a "Letter to the Alexandrians," both letters mentioned by the Muratorian fragment. The Muratorian fragment says that it accepts two apocalypses, one by John and one by Peter, but then notes that some do not accept the one by Peter to be read in churches—which is the standard that the author uses for authoritative acceptance. See Lee Martin McDonald, *The Biblical Canon: Its Origin, Transmission, and Authority*, 3rd ed. (Peabody, MA: Hendrickson, 2007) 369–78 (371 for reference to the Petrine Apocalypse), though his arguments for a late date of the Muratorian fragment are not convincing.

26. Eusebius states that Serapion, the Bishop of Antioch, wrote to the church at Rhossus in Cilicia about the *Gospel of Peter*, which was being read in the church there: "we receive both Peter and the other apostles as Christ, but the writings which falsely bear their names we reject, as men of experience, knowing that such were not handed down to us" (*Hist. eccl.* 6.12.3 LCL). The process that led to exclusion was a complex one, but it was ultimately excluded, and recognition of its pseudepigraphical authorship was clearly a factor in this decision.

27. Donelson, *Pseudepigraphy and Ethical Argument*, 20–22.

cate for pseudepigraphy as an acceptable convention. These arguments are worth recounting briefly.

Clarke notes that Jülicher's position on intellectual property, though still endorsed by some recent interpreters,[28] has been "debunked" by those who have shown "the presence of such a concept [of intellectual property] in antiquity."[29] This debunking includes a number of major considerations: one is the fact that the ancients made a distinction between authentic and inauthentic writings and hence had a notion of intellectual property associated with authorship, enough so that they could attempt to differentiate between authentic and inauthentic attribution. The ancients also labeled such pseudonymous work with a variety of disparaging terms to mark them as spurious or false.[30] Authors who discovered works written in their own name, when they knew that they did not write the work, were vexed to find such writings, and some took the existence of such works as a personal affront. These authors, such as Galen, did not embrace such works as flattering or continuing in the spirit of their own work, but they clearly recognized the difference between their own intellectual work and the work of others, which they believed should not have been issued in their name. Those involved in the discovery of such pseudepigrapha outright condemned making use of such documents for fraudulent purposes. As Earle Ellis states, the writing of pseudepigrapha was widespread in ancient times, and this fact itself and its detection "presupposes a conception of intellectual property that could be violated."[31]

With a clear concept of intellectual property in place, it makes it much more difficult to accept, with Baur and those who have followed him to the present, that the ancients considered such pseudepigraphic literature venial and part of an accepted and acceptable literary practice. The evidence of those who were involved in the process of discovery of pseudepigrapha is enough to see that the ancients did not consider such practice as innocent. Those authors who expressed their displeasure at authors writing under their names illustrate even more strongly that such work was not regarded as harmless or acceptable. There have been those who have attempted to justify such behavior as honoring

28. E.g. Andrew T. Lincoln, *Ephesians*, WBC 42 (Dallas: Word, 1990) lxxi.

29. Clarke, "Problem," 459n90.

30. Metzger, "Literary Forgeries," 13, who lists a number of the disparaging terms.

31. Ellis, "Pseudonymity," 217.

or continuing the tradition of the person in whose name the work is written. There may well have been some ancients who thought such a thing (although it appears to be modern interpreters who hold to such a position), but it would probably only be those who were not close to the situation and able to judge the works involved (and who hence were in fact deceived by the pseudepigraphon).[32] Those closer to the process had quite a different reaction. The response of those who discovered pseude-pigraphal works shows that the presumption that writing in the name of another was seen to honor and continue the tradition of the author is inaccurate. The hard task of determination of authenticity of writings in the ancient world, such as of the various philosophers or the speeches of Lysias, was not undertaken so that the readers could admire the work of the forger, but to distinguish the false from the genuine writings. As Livy reports (40.29), when books attributed to Nuna were identified as being pseudepigrapha, they were burned.[33] Galen went so far as to write his own book entitled *On His Own Books*, after he himself saw a dispute about the authenticity of his works that involved a person picking up a book in the market with the name Doctor Galen on it but who started to read it and recognized it as not by the author and threw it away with disgust.[34] These are hardly responses of those who accepted pseudepig-raphy as an acceptable convention.

The recent trend, found in such scholars as Childs and his followers,[35] to distinguish between theological and historical analysis and conclusions is also subject to serious question. Childs attempts to deflect the force of the argument against pseudepigraphal works being in the canon by reversing the chronological direction. As a result, the historical and theological arguments are inverted, so that canonical acceptance (theology) precedes authorship (history) in so far as their logic is concerned. The author thereby becomes the object of study, not the subject or creator of the work. In other words, the biblical inter-preter begins from the position of the pseudepigraphon being within the canon and contributing to the picture of the biblical author, rather than

32. Carson, "Pseudonymity," 863.

33. Kiley, *Colossians*, 18.

34. Metzger, "Literary Forgeries," 6.

35. More recent proponents include Robert Wall. See his "Pauline Authorship and the Pastoral Epistles: A Response to S. E. Porter," *BBR* 5 (1995) 125–28; and my "Response."

examining whether and how the pseudepigraphon came to be included in the canon. However, as Clarke rightly says, Childs has "downplayed pseudonymity" by focusing upon the canonical witness rather than its historical basis.[36] Childs's position is, in fact, not a view that argues that pseudepigraphy is an accepted convention, but one that circumvents the discussion by failing to recognize the historical process involved. It further is formulated upon the basis of anonymous rather than pseudonymous literature. Anonymous literature is arguably based upon theology preceding authorship (the book, such as a gospel, is accepted as authoritative and then later attributed to an apostle),[37] but the same is clearly not true of attributed literature, where attribution is part of the work itself. In an earlier essay on this topic, I critiqued such a perspective by using the analogy of developments that had taken place in the art world. It was discovered, after a number of sketches and drawings had been in the Rembrandt canon for quite some time, that many of these were not authentic. There may have been those who wished to defend their remaining in the Rembrandt canon because, after all, they were already in the authoritative collection of Rembrandt's art and deserved to be interpreted on these terms, but this faction—if it existed at all—clearly did not win out. Those works that were determined to be forgeries were identified and henceforth excluded from the Rembrandt canon.[38] However, Childs and his followers do not seem to want to follow this line of thinking. What is overlooked in this formulation is that canonical status is not simply a theological assumption but the result of a historical process—the canonical formation process was a historical event, whatever else it may have been. To neglect it is to compromise the basis for the theological analysis that follows from it. This view of the canon is compromised by failing to accept the implications of pseudonymity.

Lastly, Meade's proposal regarding the development of pseudepigraphal works as a reflection of the changing tradition is also flawed. Of his three major traditions that he uses for comparison with the formation of the New Testament canon (including the wisdom and apocalyptic), only the prophetic tradition seems potentially suitable to the New Testament, and even this proposal is not close enough in at least

36. Clarke, "Problem," 460.

37. I say that this is arguable in light of recent arguments that the names attributed to the Gospels were affixed early on.

38. Porter, "Response," 137–38.

three different ways. Prophetic literature—the major form thought to be pseudepigraphic in the New Testament—is in Meade's analysis different from letters in several ways. The prophetic literature consists of a growing body of writing as material is added directly to the corpus, whereby the pseudepigraphic letters are individual and distinct. Much of the prophetic literature is not written by the prophet but about him, whereas letters are purportedly by the author. A further consideration is the timeframe for pseudepigraphal composition. These timeframes are completely different, with the New Testament writings requiring far less time for the completion of the writing process than Meade posits for the developing Old Testament prophetic traditions. Whereas the developments of the Isaiah tradition may have taken several centuries, the Pastoral Letters, to take a single prominent example, were written within sixty years of the death of Paul (at most, if they are considered non-Pauline). The relative lack of material written about Paul in the second century illustrates that the development of a Pauline apostolic tradition was not at the forefront of the early church's mind, which compresses the timeframe even further.[39] Finally, Meade's notion of growing tradition is not designed to determine which material is pseudepigraphic but to explain material once it has been determined to be pseudepigraphic. Therefore, Meade's analysis is not germane to the issue of pseudepigraphic literature in the New Testament.[40]

If these criticisms stand, and I believe they do, then the defense by the major proponents of the acceptable practice position is significantly eroded. We are left with the view that pseudepigraphy was not an accepted convention in the ancient world.

IMPLICATIONS OF PSEUDONYMITY FOR A DOCTRINE OF SCRIPTURE

The evidence indicates that the ancients realized the difference between genuine and spurious documents, and that there is no firm ancient foundation to justify the position that accepts pseudonymity as

39. On the composition of the Pauline canon, see Stanley E. Porter, "Paul and the Process of Canonization," in *Exploring the Origins of the Bible: Canon Formation in Historical, Literary, and Theological Perspective*, ed. Craig A. Evans and Emanuel Tov, Acadia Studies in Bible and Theology (Grand Rapids: Baker, 2008) 173–202.

40. See Porter, "Pauline Authorship," 116–18.

a normal writing practice in the ancient world. If this is the case, the question becomes what at first appears to be a straightforward one: How does this more limited view of pseudonymity have an effect on a doctrine of Scripture?

Before I tackle this question, however, I wish to return to the view that pseudonymity was an accepted literary convention in the ancient world to tease out its implications further for a doctrine of Scripture. Then I will examine the implications of the view that pseudonymity was an unacceptable convention. This is not the place to present a discussion of views on the doctrine of Scripture and debate their variations here. I wish to perform the relatively more straightforward task of examining in more detail the implications of the several views of pseudonymity for a basic doctrine of Scripture.

A Doctrine of Scripture and the Acceptable Convention Hypothesis

The first position to examine is the acceptable convention hypothesis and its implications for a doctrine of Scripture. If this position were able to be sustained—and it clearly is not, as seen above, but I respond to it here, nevertheless, because it raises some interesting issues for a doctrine of Scripture—the argument would be that within Christian circles pseudonymity is an acceptable convention, with pseudepigrapha created by students and others who desired to honor a venerated person, for constructing and presenting to the church a given piece of theological literature and that doing so does not indicate any deceptive intent by the actual author. The legitimate implications of such a position would be that pseudonymity would constitute a legitimate and undeceptive means of creating and presenting a given work of literature to the church, and that this process would be transparent and clear in order to justify it and to recognize its practice—and even to ensure that the work was not rejected for being overtly deceptive in intent. Thus, one can easily imagine a pseudepigraphon being recognizably written and then being accepted as authoritative Scripture. In fact, so the theory would hold, this is probably what happened.

There are several problems, however, with this position.[41] The first is that this position appears to be self-contradictory, by maintaining, on the one hand, that the writing of pseudepigrapha was an accepted and

41. Compare Wilder, "Pseudonymity, the New Testament," 48–50, who deals more specifically with consequentialist ethical views of pseudonymity.

even conventional literary practice, and, on the other hand, that there was no intent to deceive in performing such a practice. If there were no intent to deceive but simply an intent to follow the acceptable convention, that would imply that the original recipients would recognize and know that the pseudepigraphon was not written by the purported author.[42] The act of writing would be one of honor, piety, or respect, continuing the honorable tradition of the venerated predecessor. Thus, any elements that would appear to be included in order to convince the audience of the letter's authenticity—such as inclusion of personal details of the author, personal references to the original audience, travel details, and the like—are thereby completely unnecessary and themselves potentially deceptive. Such elements cannot be explained as part of a conventionalized or honorable process because they introduce elements extraneous to the simple veneration and continuation of the thought of the honored predecessor. These elements can only be explained as designed to deceive the audience into thinking that the letter was in actual fact written by the original author—as such elements would not otherwise be necessary to convince the audience because they already knew by convention and tradition that the work was a pseudepigraphon. These supposedly unnecessary personal characteristics and details are regularly included in many of the books in the New Testament that are often cited as being pseudepigrapha, such as 2 Thessalonians (2:2, 5; 3:1, 11, 17), the Pastoral Epistles (1 Tim 1:2, 3, 5, 12–13, 18, 20; 2:7; 3:14–15; 4:13; 6:20; 2 Tim 1:2; 2:3, 9–10; 3:11; 4:6, 9–14, 19–21; Titus 1:4, 5; 3:12–13), 1 Peter (5:1, 12), and even Ephesians (3:3–4; 4:25; 6:19–20, 21–22).[43] It is therefore difficult to escape the element of deception, even in this hypothesis, as the basis under which books now found in the New Testament were originally promoted.

Those such as Childs and Wall who accept the results of the canonical process tear the theological conclusion from the historical process. They accept pseudepigraphal authorship, but only by inverting the historical process by placing acceptance into the canon before authorial

---

42. This raises the question of whether pseudonymity was necessary at all, if the convention was transparent and known by the audience. This formulation also contradicts the definition of pseudonymity offered by Clarke above—it may by definition be impossible to have a work that makes a *"calculated attempt to conceal"* the author's "true identity by *deliberately endorsing* a false author as the real author" and not have deception.

43. Carson, "Pseudonymity," 862.

attribution. There are two possible doctrinal consequences of this position. Even if we begin with acceptance of their analysis, we must nevertheless recognize a historical process that led to the canonical process. For Childs, Wall, and others, this involves tacit acceptance of pseudepigraphal authorship. Though they do not necessarily wish to accept an element of deception in this process, as we have seen above it is difficult if not impossible to escape this implication. However, as noted above, the second consequence is that we may well question this entire scenario in which canonical acceptance precedes attribution as one based upon such anonymous literature of the New Testament as the Gospels. The case is completely different for attributed literature such as the epistles, whether it be the Pauline, Jacobean, or Petrine literature. In the case of attributed works, attribution must precede acceptance. If these works are pseudepigraphal yet traditionally attributed, as we have seen above, then the process of acceptance that followed must have involved an element of deception on the basis of the false attribution to the traditional author. Again, we are forced to recognize an element of deception in the acceptance of pseudepigraphal literature.

Donelson recognizes that no pseudepigraphal book was knowingly accepted as authoritative in Greco-Roman, Gentile, or Jewish circles, including the Christian world, but that discovery of a pseudepigraphal work led to its rejection. As noted above, he knows of no such instance, and he discusses all of the cases known to him and that are regularly cited in such discussions. However, as Clarke recognizes, Donelson concludes differently than others on the basis of this evidence.[44] Rather than arguing against pseudepigrapha in the New Testament, he accepts that the writing of pseudepigrapha was widespread in early Christian circles, to the point that there were so many of them that it was impossible to decide which ones were genuine and which ones were forgeries simply on the basis of the documents themselves. As a result, competing forces in early Christianity did not use authorship as the major criterion because they could not in such a climate prove authenticity. Instead, doctrinal conformity formed the basis of acceptance. As Donelson states, "This procedure inevitably led to the theses that there can only be one orthodoxy, that every apostolic document is orthodox, and even that every orthodox document was apostolic."[45] Despite the different path that

44. Clarke, "Problem," 464.
45. Donelson, *Pseudepigraphy and Ethical Argument*, 17.

Donelson takes, he arrives at a conclusion that is inevitably similar to the position described above—that deception is a part of the canonical formation process because pseudepigrapha are within the canon.

We may summarize, therefore, that this position mandates that, whatever view of the finer points of the doctrine of Scripture one takes regarding divine superintendence of the writing, transmission, and canonization of Scripture, an element of deception was part of the process of scriptural development. That is, this view of Scripture accepts deception as a virtually necessary part of the process by which works were written, promoted, and/or accepted as authoritative Scripture. Despite attempts by scholars over a considerable period of time to avoid the implications of such a position, by attempting to minimize the deceptive element and to refashion our understanding of pseudepigraphy so as to exclude any deceptive elements, this position cannot escape this conclusion.

There are at least three major implications of such a view for one's doctrine of Scripture. The most immediate implication for a doctrine of Scripture is that this position mandates that deception occurred at some stage in the process of acceptance of these works as authoritative. This may have been at the time the work was authored or it may have occurred when the work was received by the early church. In any case, deception was a part of the historical process. This means that a doctrine of Scripture that accepts such a scenario deeply embeds the concept of deception in the nature of how Scripture was written, came to be recognized as authoritative, and/or was transmitted. The second major implication of this position is that not just the process of scriptural formation is affected but Scripture itself is therefore open to the charge of being potentially deceptive, as deception is a part of both the canonical process and what constitutes Scripture. Scripture represents itself as one thing—an entirely trustworthy revelation or record of revelation[46]—when in fact it is the product of something else—a process involving deception. The third implication concerns theology and reflects on the nature of the

---

46. I believe that this is both mandated by Scripture as revelation of God and as grounded in his divine character, and the clear witness of Scripture itself. Even if Scripture is seen to be merely a record of or about the revelation of God, it purports to be a true and faithful account. See Wilder, "Pseudonymity, the New Testament," 50. Compare Wayne A. Grudem, "Scripture's Self-Attestation and the Problem of Formulating a Doctrine of Scripture," in *Scripture and Truth*, ed. D. A. Carson and John D. Woodbridge (Grand Rapids: Zondervan, 1983) 19–59; and Roger Nicole, "The Biblical Concept of Truth," in *Scripture and Truth*, 287–98.

God who is in some way involved in such a process. The direct implication is that the God who superintended a process of scriptural formation and transmission also enshrined a process that included deception and, by logical implication, possibly deception within other elements of Scripture. At best, such a God was unable to avoid such a process and, at worst, utilized or endorsed or even instigated such a mechanism. Many will find such a position, with its view of pseudonymity, unacceptable for a doctrine of Scripture. However, as we noted above, there is no substantive proof that pseudepigraphal authorship was considered legitimate practice in the Greco-Roman, Gentile, or Jewish literary worlds, and no text was accepted as authoritative that was a known pseudepigraphon. Instead, when pseudepigraphal authorship was discovered in Christian circles, the pseudepigraphon was rejected as authoritative.

A Doctrine of Scripture and the Unacceptable Convention Hypothesis

I believe that the ancient evidence does not support the position that it was an acceptable convention in the ancient world—including the world of early Christianity—to accept pseudepigraphal authorship as a recognized form of literary tribute to a venerated figure. Furthermore, I believe that such a position, despite its attempts to argue otherwise through various means, inevitably ends up accepting the presence of deception within the process by which a pseudepigraphal work came to be recognized as authoritative. I also think that the ancient evidence is clear that known pseudepigrapha were not accepted or given authoritative status in the Greco-Roman, Jewish, or especially early Christian literature.

There are several implications of such a position for a doctrine of Scripture that must be examined.[47] Because of the implications noted above, I do not believe that it is acceptable to include an element of deception as part of one's doctrine of Scripture with regard to the fundamental process of how Scripture was created and accepted as canonical. I believe that the implications of such a position go far beyond simply one's doctrine of Scripture and have potential and tangible implications regarding one's doctrine of God and possibly other areas of Christian theology in which deception becomes linked to the divine revelation and nature. Therefore, I reject such a position but believe that it is imperative

47. Compare Wilder, "Pseudonymity, the New Testament," 47–48, 50, who deals more specifically with deontological ethical views of pseudonymity.

for us to contemplate some of the other logical implications of such a set of circumstances.

The first major implication is that, by virtue of the fact that the books in the New Testament are within the canon, these books were not thought to be or not recognized as being pseudepigraphal—otherwise they would have been rejected. Donelson contends that there were many such pseudepigraphal books included within the New Testament but that they were not recognized as such. This is, in his view, because doctrine triumphed authorship and their apostolic status assured their acceptance. There are several significant problems with Donelson's position, some already noted above. One is that there is admittedly no ancient evidence of these books being pseudepigrapha; otherwise the books would have been excluded, as Donelson admits. This makes Donelson's contention highly speculative, an argument from silence, and an unacceptable means of moving the argument forward to the conclusion he desires. A second problem is that, if Donelson is right and my analysis above is also right, as already indicated above, in his scenario deception becomes part of the canonical process—a conclusion that I find unacceptable for a doctrine of Scripture. A third problem is his understanding of what it means that doctrine trumped authorship. Donelson treats the issue on a hypothetical local and historical level that cannot be substantiated—although the relationship of doctrine and authorship might well be worth considering on the larger level, as we shall see below.

The second major implication is that, if the books of the New Testament were included in the canon and they were not excluded on the basis of being found to be pseudepigraphal, and if Donelson's hypothesis is rejected (as I have argued it should be above), then the books of the New Testament whose authorship is attributed should be accepted on theological, canonical, and even historical grounds as written by the attributed authors. In other words, there is no reason from a consideration of pseudonymity and its place in the ancient world, as well as how this relates to the canonical process as already discussed, to reject the attributed authorship of these works. I recognize that there are other arguments that are often made regarding authorship of the books of the New Testament, based on such considerations as chronology, epistolary format, style, content, and theology. I have engaged in discussion of these and related topics myself on several occasions.[48] However, this

48. Porter, "Pauline Authorship," 107–13; McDonald and Porter, *Early Christianity*,

evidence, while it may appear clear to those who are arguing one side or the other, is often ambiguous and potentially inconclusive in so far as it goes. For example, one of the major issues often neglected in such discussion is the permissible levels of variation that indicate pseudepigraphal authorship. The argument for pseudonymous authorship of New Testament books is often based on the supposed fact that these books vary in significant ways from other works attributed to the same author; however, they were not thought in the ancient world to vary enough to be rejected as being inauthentic. As we have seen, the books in the canon are all, by virtue of their being in the New Testament, attested as not having been rejected as pseudepigraphal. The issue must, therefore, be solved on other grounds. I believe that the canonical status as recognizably authoritative works, in light of the role deception played within pseudepigraphy in the ancient world and the desire to maintain a robust doctrine of Scripture, compels such a conclusion.

A third major implication—directly related to the one above—is how a doctrine of Scripture might influence how one thinks about authorship of purportedly pseudepigraphal works within the New Testament. I have concluded above that there are good grounds for arguing for authenticity of authorship on the basis of canonical status, what we know about pseudepigraphy and the rejection of pseudepigraphic works as authoritative, and the role of deception. However, I think that it is worth reversing this and considering the implications if we begin with a doctrine of Scripture that excludes the place of deception within the process of authorship, transmission, and canonical formation. If one accepts this stance—and I think that there are good historical and theological reasons for doing so—then I believe that one's theological position compels certain conclusions regarding authorship questions within the New Testament. If one believes that a doctrine of Scripture excludes the role of deception in the process, and that any view of pseudonymity would entail an element of deception, then I believe that one is justified if not compelled to conclude that on the basis of this doctrinal position there is no room for pseudepigraphal authorship within the New Testament.[49]

388–93.

49. I recognize that this position is very similar to those of theologians Candlish ("Moral Character," 103) and especially Packer (*Fundamentalism*, 184), the latter of whom notes that the "position, that their canonicity cannot be affirmed if their authen-

CONCLUSION

I had a colleague tell me once that when it came to theology and historical criticism, if they ever came into conflict then historical criticism won out. I believe that this is a standard position for a number of scholars—and perhaps even an increasing number within the evangelical theological scholarly world. In this chapter, I am raising the question of whether this is the proper stance to take. Evangelicalism has made great strides in the last thirty or so years in gaining academic and intellectual respectability within the world of biblical scholarship. Much of this work is honorable and excellent and deserves the wider recognition that it has gained. However, I fear that at some points such scholarship has come at a price—perhaps the price of elevating particular historical-critical perspectives above theological ones. I would like to think that, in all of the scholarship that we do, our theological conclusions and critical results are in harmony. However, the issue that I have treated above in this chapter—pseudepigraphal authorship of New Testament writings—indicates that such is not always going to be the case—at least for a number of well-intentioned scholars. Rather than opting, as my colleague above did, for the results of historical criticism, I believe that it is worth considering whether our theology—in this case our doctrine of Scripture—should guide, if not dictate, our critical conclusions.

---

ticity is denied, thus seems to be the only one possible; and we may lay it down as a general principle that, when biblical books specify their own authorship, the affirmation of their canonicity involves denial of their pseudonymity. Pseudonymity and canonicity are mutually exclusive" (104). An alternative conclusion—which I earlier suggested as a possibility (Porter, "Pauline Authorship," 123; "Response," 138)—is to reopen the canon and to eliminate those works that are "confirmed" as pseudepigraphal. However, on the basis of what has been said here, as well as what I have found in research on pseudonymity, I do not believe this is a plausible alternative. The canon has been set, and it would now be, in my opinion, impossible to clearly establish that any given book of the NT is undeniably a pseudepigraphon. Compare Wilder, *Pseudonymity*, passim; Wilder, "Pseudonymity, the New Testament," 51.

THEORETICAL PERSPECTIVES

12

Issues in Forming a Doctrine of Inspiration

Craig Allert

INTRODUCTION

THE CANADIAN CHRISTIAN LIBERAL arts university where I teach is, I'm sure, similar in atmosphere to many others in North America that belong in the evangelical tradition. An experience I had a number of years ago will help illustrate what I mean. In a first-year introduction to theology class I was describing how theology has functioned in history. One particular function I entitled, "Theology as an Explanation of Reality." Part of my point was that we need to be careful when we treat the Bible as a science textbook and expect it to provide us with scientific explanations of reality. While this approach is fairly common in some circles, it has sometimes had significant consequences as in the historic condemnation of Galileo.

I continued by relating the example of Galileo to how some people read the creation narratives today. In Gen 1–2, for example, a simple observation can be made: there are two creation accounts, each one ordered differently. In Gen 1, we are told that God first created the animals and finally the human beings, both male and female. But in Gen 2 God first creates the man, then the animals, and finally the woman. I wrapped up by explaining, "Were we to read the narratives of Genesis as scientific descriptions, we would face the need to declare that Genesis contradicts itself." The lesson drawn from this example, I later learned, was met with a bit of dismay by one of my students who passed it on to his father, a pastor. I will spare the details, but my comment was taken as an outright denial of the inspiration and inerrancy of the Bible. I suspect that most of my colleagues who teach theology and biblical studies in Christian liberal arts institutions could give similar accounts.

This experience showed me (once again) that an unfortunate and troubling gap exists between the academy and the church.[1] And this gap can lead to suspicion of those who hold other views of inspiration than that held at the popular level. I have outlined elsewhere how various streams of conservative Christianity converged in evangelicalism, introducing some confusion in its understanding of its core, central doctrines or controlling motifs.[2] Nowhere is this confusion (and gap) more prevalent than in the doctrine of Scripture.

The unfortunate divide between the academy and the church when it comes to the doctrine of scripture is consistent with a biblicism that is endemic to popular evangelical Christianity. Biblicism is closely related to an aberrant understanding of the Reformation *sola scriptura* principle.[3] In this radical appropriation of the Bible alone, Scripture is viewed and used as an isolated authority, independent of the church in which it historically grew. In the words of D. H. Williams, "*sola scriptura* has been construed by many Protestants as if finding the truth of Scripture is an enterprise best done without the church or even in spite of the

---

1. The historical roots of this gap in evangelicalism are detailed by Mark A. Noll, *Between Faith and Criticism: Evangelicals, Scholarship, and the Bible in America*, 2nd ed. (Grand Rapids: Baker, 1991).

2. Craig D. Allert, *A High View of Scripture: The Authority of the Bible and the Formation of the New Testament Canon* (Grand Rapids: Baker, 2007) 17–36.

3. See Craig D. Allert, "What Are We Trying to Conserve?: Evangelicalism and *Sola Scriptura*," *Evangelical Quarterly* 76.4 (2004) 327–48. The argument that the Bible and the Bible alone is the Christian's only source of theology runs deep in popular evangelicalism. Hence, the insistence that a definition or doctrine be biblical is the trump card in any theological discussion. This is well illustrated in an often-reprinted title by an evangelical publisher, Gordon Lewis, *Decide for Yourself: A Theological Workbook* (Downers Grove, IL: InterVarsity, 1970). Lewis exhorts the reader to search the scriptures in order to test the truth of what we hear. With this advice I do not necessarily disagree. However, the book is designed "primarily for individuals who wish to investigate Christian doctrine on their own" (10). The structure of the book makes it abundantly clear that theological reflection requires only the Bible, separated from the rich tradition and traditions in which it lives.

church."[4] The Bible is approached "alone" because it is the very words of God; access to God is through it. Attributes are ascribed to the Bible that belong properly to God. For example, in *Taking a Stand for the Bible,* John Ankerberg and Dillon Burroughs state:

1. God cannot be wrong.
2. The Bible is the Word of God.
3. Therefore, the Bible cannot be wrong.

Immediately after this syllogism the authors attribute perfection to the Bible because "[a]n infinitely perfect, all-knowing God cannot make a mistake."[5] Since God is the Bible's author, the Bible cannot help but share his attributes.[6] Darren Marks has pointed out a troubling legacy associated with this view of the Bible:

> In developing a theology of Scripture . . . we need to avoid two cardinal errors: (1) ascribing to an object what is properly a property of God, and (2) reducing revelation to human insights. The first error leads to bibliolatry—the worship of the Bible because the powers and characters of God are falsely attributed to it. The Bible is perceived to be nearly magical and often is used as a way of manipulating or invoking God.[7]

Another approach that leads to bibliolatry is the widely accepted, indeed cardinal, doctrine of verbal plenary inspiration. David Dockery defines inspiration as "[t]he superintending influence the Holy Spirit exerted on the biblical writers, so that the accent and interpretation of God's revelation have been recorded as God intended so that the Bible actually is the Word of God."[8] Similarly, Bruce Milne explains inspiration as "the way in which God's self-revelation has come to be

---

4. D. H. Williams, *Evangelicals and Tradition: The Formative Influence of the Early Church* Evangelical *Ressourcement* (Grand Rapids: Baker, 2005) 96.

5. John Ankerberg and Dillon Burroughs, *Taking a Stand for the Bible: Today's Leading Experts Answer Critical Questions about God's Word* (Eugene, OR: Harvest House, 2009) 42.

6. Compare also their choice of descriptions for the Bible: "eternal," "perfect and trustworthy," "true," "holy and righteous," and "good." See Ankerberg and Burroughs, *Taking a Stand,* 15–21.

7. Darren C. Marks, *Bringing Theology to Life: Key Doctrines for Christian Faith and Mission* (Downers Grove, IL: InterVarsity, 2009) 108.

8. D. S. Dockery, *Christian Scripture: An Evangelical Perspective on Inspiration, Authority and Interpretation* (Nashville: Broadman & Holman, 1995) 240.

expressed in the words of the Bible. It is the activity of the Spirit of God whereby he superintended the human authors of Scripture so that their writings became a transcript of God's word to man."[9] Thus, concomitant with the definition of inspiration is the idea of divine preservation for both the words and text in order for the Bible to be seen, in fact, as the words of God.

Writing expressly for a popular evangelical audience, Ankerberg and Burroughs explain why this view of inspiration is called "verbal plenary": *verbal* is understood as "extending to the very words, not just the ideas of Scripture," while *plenary* is understood as "extending equally to every part of Scripture."[10] Floyd Barackman takes a further step in definition, claiming not only that the words are inspired but the very choice in wording extending to grammatical forms—whatever is recorded in Scripture—is from God himself.[11] Hence, not only is inspiration *verbal*, it is also *plenary*, it extends to every part of the words and all they teach or imply.[12] According to its proponents, the verbal plenary view is believed to be the view the Bible itself teaches.

So entrenched is this understanding of inspiration that many can scarcely conceive of the "biblical" view of inspiration in any other way than verbal. What generally happens at the popular level is that readers rely on trusted scholars within evangelicalism who are committed to upholding the "biblical" view of inspiration.[13] The problem is these trusted resources are little interested in testing the prevailing evangelical paradigm or re-examining the doctrine of Scripture with regard to the Bible (both its exegesis *and* its phenomena) and theological history. For example, in his *Systematic Theology* Norman Geisler defines theology

9. Bruce Milne, *Know the Truth: A Handbook of Christian Belief* (Downers Grove, IL: InterVarsity, 1982) 34.

10. Ankerberg and Burroughs, *Taking a Stand*, 12.

11. F. H. Barackman, *Practical Christian Theology: Examining the Great Doctrines of the Faith*, 4th ed. (Grand Rapids: Kregel, 2001) 24–26. See also Norman L. Geisler, *Systematic Theology*, 3 vols. (Minneapolis: Bethany, 2002) 1:236.

12. It would certainly be a poor representation of evangelicalism if I claimed that this was necessarily the dominant view of inspiration among evangelicals. My point here is that historically informed approaches to inspiration are rarely represented in the literature written to and read by non-academic evangelical audiences. Thus, their thinking on this topic is dominated by works such as this.

13. That many of these trusted scholars take an apologetic approach (i.e., defense of the faith) is a telling tale about the popular evangelical understanding of theology.

etymologically as "rational discourse about God."[14] However, he also sees the need to qualify *evangelical* theology as:

> . . . a discourse about God that maintains that there are certain essential Christian beliefs. These include, but are not necessarily limited to: the infallibility and inerrancy of the Bible alone, the tri-unity of God, the virgin birth of Christ, the deity of Christ, the all-sufficiency of Christ's atoning sacrifice for sin, the physical and miraculous resurrection of Christ, the necessity of salvation by faith alone through God's grace alone based on the work of Christ alone, the physical bodily return of Christ to earth, the eternal conscious bliss of the saved, and the eternal conscious punishment of the unsaved.[15]

My point here is not that I disagree with Geisler's decision to qualify evangelical theology (it is, after all, a particular theology), but with the implication of the way he qualifies it. Already here on the first pages of the book he sets the stage for how one must approach theology, i.e., with the understanding that evangelicals have certain, non-negotiable beliefs. The implication is that he intends in what follows to provide reasons for these beliefs. This helps explain why under the heading of "Theological Definitions" he includes a definition of "apologetics."[16] In other words, Geisler's is an unabashedly apologetic approach to theology. Any interest in testing the prevailing evangelical paradigm with regard to the Bible or theological history is trumped by apologetic motives.

When this kind of approach is adopted, what can happen is that one view of inspiration is put forth as *the* evangelical view,[17] and this view is read back into the Bible and Christian history by the prevalent method of prooftexting. In these proofs little awareness or care is shown for the context in which the quotes are situated or the broader ecclesial

---

14. Geisler, *Systematic Theology*, 15.

15. Geisler, *Systematic Theology*, 15.

16. Geisler, *Systematic Theology*, 16. "Apologetics deals with the protection of Christian theology from external attacks."

17. See, for example, Jim Hamilton, "Scripture: The Evangelical View, or, The Sixty Six Books of the Protestant Canon Are Inspired and Therefore Inerrant," online: http://jimhamilton.wordpress.com/2009/07/20/the-evangelical-view-of-scripture-66-inerrant-books/. The author states that this essay will be included in a collected volume entitled *The Sacred Text*. No other information is given. Throughout the essay, Hamilton refers consistently to "the" evangelical view with no real acknowledgement of other evangelical views.

settings, both of which are vital for understanding the Bible and our Christian heritage.

For many years now, in books published by evangelical publishing houses, scholars who identify themselves as evangelical have been calling this view into question.[18] Unfortunately, more often than not, these monographs are simply not being read by those most in need of grappling with them. I am compelled to express my concern again and call for frank deliberations on the various issues raised by the popular view of inspiration.

In this chapter I argue that the popular understanding of inspiration (verbal plenary) in evangelicalism is faced with a number of tensions, or what I have less controversially called "issues" in the title of this chapter. Elsewhere I have argued that a precise definition of inspiration goes beyond what the Bible teaches about itself.[19] Herein I will outline some of these tensions with a plea that we not necessarily stop asserting the inspiration of the Bible, rather that we be more realistic about what we can say (and should not say) about inspiration. If inspiration cannot be precisely defined (i.e., *biblically* defined), then we must be aware of the phenomena of the Bible that may help us to approach a doctrine of inspiration that allows us to negotiate the tensions.

THE TENSIONS

The Autographs

Recently Bart Ehrman has brought the complex, yet necessary field of New Testament textual criticism to the attention of popular culture.[20]

18. See, for example, Craig D. Allert, *A High View of Scripture*; Peter Enns, *Inspiration and Incarnation: Evangelicals and the Problem of the Old Testament* (Grand Rapids: Baker, 2005); John Goldingay, *Models for Scripture* (Grand Rapids: Eerdmans, 1994); Kenton L. Sparks, *God's Words in Human Words: An Evangelical Appropriation of Critical Biblical Scholarship* (Grand Rapids: Baker, 2008).

19. Allert, *A High View of Scripture?*, 147–59; idem, "Is a Translation Inspired?: The Problems of Verbal Inspiration for Translation and a Proposed Solution," in *Translating the Bible: Problems and Prospects*, ed. Stanley E. Porter and Richard S. Hess, JSNTSup 173 (Sheffield: Sheffield Academic, 1999) 85–113.

20. See especially Bart Ehrman, *Misquoting Jesus: The Story Behind Who Changed the Bible and Why* (San Francisco: HarperCollins, 2005). Ehrman's exposure in popular culture is astounding given his expertise in a field that would otherwise be of little interest. His website (http://www.bartdehrman.com/index.htm) gives the fol-

In the introduction to his 2005 book, *Misquoting Jesus*, Ehrman relates his own spiritual journey through the fundamentalism of Moody Bible Institute, to the evangelicalism at Wheaton College, and then on to his current self-described agnosticism. The main reason Ehrman gives for his journey into agnosticism is the existence of variants in the numerous manuscripts of the New Testament.

During his years at Moody, Ehrman was in firm agreement with its doctrinal stance that the Bible was verbally inspired—down to its very words. But he was learning things in some of his classes that disturbed him in light of the school's commitment to verbal inspiration.[21] In the words of Ehrman, he knew that ". . . we don't actually have the original writings of the New Testament. What we have are copies of these writings, made years later—in most cases, many years later. Moreover, none of these copies is completely accurate. . . . So rather than actually having the inspired words of the autographs (i.e., the originals) of the Bible, what we have are error-ridden copies of the autographs." For Ehrman, this was a "compelling problem."[22]

The absence of the autographs is, of course, readily acknowledged by holders of a verbal plenary view of inspiration.[23] This is the reason many discussions on the inspiration of the Bible assert that inspiration applies only to the original manuscripts. Usually the assertion is made in a discussion of inerrancy since inerrancy is argued to be the natural

lowing short bio: "Bart D. Ehrman is the author of more than twenty books, including two New York Times bestsellers: *Misquoting Jesus* and *God's Problem*. Ehrman is the James A. Gray Distinguished Professor of Religious Studies at the University of North Carolina, Chapel Hill, and is a leading authority on the New Testament and the history of early Christianity. His work has been featured in *Time*, *The New Yorker*, *The Washington Post* and other print media, and he has appeared on NBC's Dateline, The Daily Show with Jon Stewart, CNN, The History Channel, National Geographic, the Discovery Channel, the BBC, major NPR shows, and other top media outlets. He lives in Durham, North Carolina."

21. Moody's second article in their current statement of faith reads, "The Bible, including both the Old and the New Testaments, is a divine revelation, the original autographs of which were verbally inspired by the Holy Spirit."

22. Ehrman, *Misquoting Jesus*, 4–5.

23. See, for example, Daniel B. Wallace, "Inerrancy and the Text of the New Testament: Assessing the Logic of the Agnostic View," online: http://www.4truth.net/site/apps/nl/content3.asp?c=hiKXLbPNLrF andb=784441 andct=1799301.

outcome of inspiration.[24] Thus, inspiration of the Bible applies only to the *autographa*—only the original manuscripts are inspired.

A good example of this argument is the Chicago Statement on Biblical Inerrancy.[25] Since its initial appearance in 1978 this statement has become a good representation of the stance of many in the evangelical community in North America. Article 10 of the statement makes the following affirmation:

> We affirm that inspiration, strictly speaking, applies only to the autographic texts of Scripture which in the providence of God can be ascertained from available manuscripts with great accuracy. We further affirm that copies and translations of Scripture are the Word of God to the extent that they faithfully represent the original.

J. I. Packer reflects this stance when he states:

> Inspiredness is not a quality attaching to corruptions that intrude in the course of the transmission of the text, but only to the text as originally produced by the inspired writers. The acknowledgement of biblical inspiration thus makes more urgent the task of textual criticism, in order to eliminate such corruptions and ascertain what the original text was.[26]

A recognition of the absence of the autographs is usually made quite early in a student's more formal study of theology and biblical studies, as Ehrman attests. This is what necessitates an awareness and understanding of the field of textual criticism. It is well known that we possess no original manuscript of any Old or New Testament document. Each of the over 5,000 extant New Testament manuscripts are all copies.[27] Further,

24. For example, R. C. Sproul offers the following summary: "1. Inspiration is the process whereby God breathed out His word. 2. God is the ultimate *source* of the Bible. 3. God is the ultimate *superintendent* of the Bible. 4. Only the original manuscripts of the Bible were without error" (Sproul, *Essential Truths of the Christian Faith* [Wheaton: Tyndale House, 1992] 16). In this essay I will deal only with the issue of inspiration.

25. "The Chicago Statement on Biblical Inerrancy," *Journal of the Evangelical Theological Society* 21 (1978) 289–96, also online at http://library.dts.edu/Pages/TL/Special/ICBI_1.pdf.

26. J. I. Packer, "The Inspiration of the Bible," in *The Origin of the Bible*, 2nd ed.; ed. P. W. Comfort (Wheaton: Tyndale, 2004) 36.

27. B. M. Metzger and Bart D. Ehrman list a total of 116 Greek papyri, 310 majuscules, 2,877 miniscules, and 2,432 lectionaries—a total of 5,735 manuscripts. Metzger and Ehrman, *The Text of the New Testament: Its Transmission, Corruption, and*

these copies contain variant readings—differences in spelling, grammar, etc. The job of the New Testament textual critic is to wade through these variant readings and establish a text as close as possible to the original. According to Amphoux and Vaganay, New Testament textual criticism is "any methodological and objective study which aims to retrieve the original form of a text or at least the form closest to the original"[28] from divergent copies. We are indebted to textual critics who undertake this practice every time we open our Bibles.

Textual criticism is not simply a registration of words and phrases to see which one(s) fit in the context. It requires a knowledge of textual recensions, culture, and linguistics, and a measured judgment in choosing between different textual recensions and variants. These choices are extremely important, for they are incorporated in the text that we study as God's word.[29]

A high degree of confidence is placed in the results of textual criticism. It is generally agreed that we have a reliable (i.e., close to the original) Greek text. This is important to the holder of the verbal plenary view because not only do we use this text to translate into other languages, but a reliable text brings us closer to the actual inspired words.

> The original manuscripts have a theopneustic [inspired] quality because of their divinely given rational and verbal content and because of the Spirit's superintendence of the prophets and apostles in the process of writing; copies of the originals, and copies of the copies, on the other hand, share in the theopneustic quality of the originals to the extent that they faithfully reproduce the autographs.[30]

Restoration, 4th ed. (New York: Oxford University Press, 2003) 50.

28. Christian-Bernard Amphoux and Lion Vaganay, *An Introduction to New Testament Textual Criticism* (New York: Cambridge University Press, 1992) 1.

29. Standard works in the area of OT textual criticism include the following: Emanuel Tov, *Textual Criticism of the Bible* (Minneapolis: Fortress, 1992); Ernst Würthwein, *The Text of the Old Testament: An Introduction to the Biblia Hebraica*, 2nd ed. (Grand Rapids: Eerdmans, 1994). Standard works in the area of NT textual criticism include the following: Kurt Aland and Barbara Aland, *The Text of the New Testament*, rev. ed. (Grand Rapids: Eerdmans, 1989); Metzger and Ehrman, *Text of the New Testament*.

30. C. F. H. Henry, *God, Revelation, and Authority*, vol 4: *The God Who Speaks and Shows* (Waco, TX: Word, 1979) 233.

Here Carl Henry acknowledges that we possess only copies of the originals. But because these copies faithfully reproduce the originals, they share in the theopneustic (inspired) quality of the originals. But this assertion raises an important question: From whom does the determination come that the copies faithfully represent the original? This is the point where textual criticism is so important. Textual criticism cannot claim to have an absolute degree of certainty when it chooses one variant or textual recension over another. Since we have no *autographa* the textual critic has nothing to which he or she may compare choices. That is, there exists no original standard against which one may measure the choice.[31]

This lack of certainty is reflected in the letter ratings for the variant readings of the United Bible Society's third edition (corrected) of the Greek New Testament. In the introduction to the Greek text the letter ratings are explained:

> By means of the letters A, B, C, and D, enclosed with "braces" {} at the beginning of each set of textual variants, the Committee has sought to indicate the relative degree of certainty, arrived at on the basis of internal considerations as well as of external evidence, for the reading adopted as the text. The letter A signifies that the text is *virtually* certain, while B indicates that there is *some degree of doubt*. The letter C means that there is *a considerable degree of doubt* whether the text or the apparatus contains the superior reading, while D shows that there is a *very high degree of doubt* concerning the reading for the selected text.[32]

It is true that the "greatest proportion of the text represents what may be called an A degree of certainty,"[33] but even if we ignore the lack of absolute certainty, we may still justifiably ask about those variants that have

31. In "Inerrancy and the Text of the New Testament: Assessing the Logic of the Agnostic View," Daniel Wallace rightly points out that, when it comes to NT textual criticism, we actually have an embarrassment of riches when compared to other fields of textual criticism (3). Because of the significant number of manuscripts available he reasons, "The point in all this is that we have sufficient data in the extant witnesses to construct the original NT in virtually every place" (4). This may be true, but my question is how would we know when we had it? Who makes the determination that we now have the autograph?

32. K. Aland, M. Black, C. Martini, B. M. Metzger and A. Wikgren, eds., *The Greek New Testament*, 3rd ed. corr. (Stuttgart: United Bible Societies, 1983) xii–xiii; emphasis mine.

33. Aland et al., *Greek New Testament*, xiii.

some degree, considerable degree, and a very high degree of doubt—the B, C, and D ratings.

The letter ratings in the UBS Greek New Testament exist, in part, as witness to the lack of certainty as to our eclectic Greek text. None of the letter ratings claims certainty. It is not difficult to see how this could shake a young committed evangelical believer like Bart Ehrman. Consider the assertion of Ankerberg and Burroughs in light of what a young Ehrman was learning about textual variants: "Scripture is 'God-breathed.' This term is translated from a unique word in the Greek New Testament that literally means that the words are of God and therefore an extension of God himself."[34] Later they assert, "What the Bible says, God says (and vice versa)."[35] But, as Ehrman recognized during his time at Moody, this is troublesome, for if the very words were chosen by God and are, indeed, the very words of God, then it follows that they are important. Yet the necessary practice of textual criticism has shown us that we do not have the degree of certainty needed to confirm that these texts are in fact the same as the original. In this sense, Ehrman's concerns are very real: Given the inevitability of copy errors, how can any subsequent text be inspired in the verbal sense?[36]

---

34. Ankerberg and Burroughs, *Taking a Stand*, 28. For a discussion on the uniqueness of this term and its implications see Allert, *High View of Scripture?*, 153–56.

35. Ankerberg and Burroughs, *Taking a Stand*, 30–31. This assertion appears as the heading of a section and a chart illustrating the assertion.

36. Ehrman's position has received able response and critique from competent scholars in the area of textual criticism. See, for example, Craig A. Evans, *Fabricating Jesus: How Modern Scholars Distort the* Gospels (Downers Grove, IL: InterVarsity, 2006); Daniel B. Wallace, "The Gospel according to Bart: A Review Article of *Misquoting Jesus* by Bart Ehrman," *JETS* 49 (2006) 327–49. While it is not my intent here to offer a sustained critique of Ehrman's overall position, I think it necessary to distance myself from some of the conclusions Ehrman reaches as a result of interacting with manuscript textual issues. Timothy Paul Jones (*Misquoting Truth: A Guide to the Fallacies of Bart Ehrman's Misquoting Jesus* [Downers Grove: InterVarsity Press, 2007], 12) correctly recognizes that even though Ehrman is touted as a "new breed of biblical scholar," it is not his findings in the area of textual criticism that are revolutionary—they have been acknowledged by scholars of all stripes for many years. It is, rather, the conclusions Ehrman draws from these long-acknowledged findings. Ehrman is working from "rigid ideas about the verbal inspiration and inerrancy of Scripture" (Evans, *Fabricating Jesus*, 27), and it is by no means necessary that one make the same leap to agnosticism as a result of realizing the well-established findings of textual variants. I happen to agree with Ehrman that textual variants pose a significant problem for certain rigid understandings of inspiration and inerrancy. But this does not necessarily lead one to a rejection of inspiration and the idea that the Bible is God's revelation. In other words,

Despite the lack of certainty in the practice of textual criticism, Benjamin B. Warfield placed a great deal of confidence in it.[37] He asserted that the original text was available among the extant copies and that this could be restored.[38] His complete confidence in the practice of textual criticism is seen in his book on textual criticism:

> The divergence of [the New Testament's] current form from the autograph may shock a modern printer of books; its wonderful approximation to its autograph is the undisguised envy of every modern reader of the ancient books. . . . The great mass of the New Testament, in other words, has been transmitted to us with no, or next to no, variation; and even in the most corrupt form in which it has ever appeared, to use the oft-quoted words of Richard Bentley, "the real text of the sacred writers is completely exact; . . . nor is one article of faith or moral precept either perverted or lost . . . choose as awkwardly as you will, choose the worst by design,

just because a certain theory of inspiration (i.e., verbal) is difficult to hold in light of textual variants does not necessitate the breakdown of inspiration as a model through which the Bible is viewed. There are many within conservative Christianity who are convinced that a rigid understanding of the Bible as God's speech or his very words is not the best way to frame biblical inspiration. For other conservative calls to broaden our understanding of inspiration, see for example, Allert, "Is a Translation Inspired?"; idem, *High View of Scripture?*; Sparks, *God's Words in Human Words*; N. T. Wright, *The Last Word: Beyond the Bible Wars to a New Understanding of the Authority of Scripture* (San Francisco: Harper, 2005).

37. Several decades ago Ernest Sandeen ("The Princeton Theology: One Source of Biblical Literalism in American Protestantism," *Church History* 31 [1962]: 309–21; *The Roots of Fundamentalism: British and American Millenarianism, 1800–1930* [1970, repr. Grand Rapids: Baker, 1978]) argued that Warfield's insistence that inspiration extended only to the autographs was novel for its time—"no such theology existed before 1850" (*Roots of Fundamentalism*, 106). This line of thinking was subsequently accepted and further propagated by Jack B. Rogers and Donald K. McKim, *The Authority and Interpretation of the Bible: An Historical Approach* (San Francisco: Harper and Row, 1979). This thesis, however, was subject to significant scrutiny with the conclusion that it lacks historical support. Randall Balmer, in "The Princetonians and Scripture: A Reconsideration," *WTJ* 44 (1982) 352–65, claims Warfield represents, rather, a shift of emphasis. Balmer shows, quite convincingly I think, the belief that only the autographs are inspired and therefore errorless is found in the writing of Archibald Alexander, Joseph Addison Alexander, Charles Hodge, and Francis Patton, who were all productive before Warfield. For more on the critique of Sandeen, see George M. Marsden, *Fundamentalism and American Culture: The Shaping of Twentieth-Century Evangelicalism, 1870–1925* (Oxford: Oxford University Press, 1980).

38. B. B. Warfield, "Inerrancy of the Original Autographs," in *Selected Shorter Writings of Benjamin B. Warfield*, ed. J. E. Meeter (Nutley, NJ: Presbyterian and Reformed, 1973) 2:583–84.

> out of the whole lump of readings." . . . The autographic text of the
> New Testament is distinctly within the reach of criticism in so
> immensely the greater part of the volume that we cannot despair
> of restoring to ourselves and the Church of God, His book, word
> for word, as He gave it by inspiration to men.[39]

On the one hand Warfield recognizes the existence of variants in the text, but asserts, quite rightly, that, as compared to other ancient literature, the sources for the New Testament far exceed all other ancient literature. But his claim that the great mass of the New Testament has been transmitted to us with no variation, or next to none, is certainly tendentious in view of the nonexistence of the autographs.

Most educated evangelicals since Warfield have had a different response to this dilemma. A typical evangelical response to this is rather that no essential element of the Christian faith is affected by the presence of variants.[40] Arguments are marshaled in this kind of response to show that the important thing in recognizing the reliability of the text is *not* the *words*, but that no copy of the original will destroy the *meaning* of the text so as to render it unable to give its reader "wisdom which leads to salvation through faith in Christ Jesus."[41]

A recent example of this approach is found in Ankerberg and Burroughs. In *Taking a Stand for the Bible* the authors engage in a discussion of inerrancy being the logical implication of inspiration.[42] In recognizing the various manuscript errors that have crept into the text, the authors make what they see as an important qualification with regard to the autographs: "God only inspired the *original* text of Scripture, not the copies."[43] Because of this, they explain, only the original is without error—inspiration only guarantees that the autograph is errorless, not copies. In fact, they state, we should expect that minor errors can occur in the manuscripts. So, we have here the acknowledgement that there are errors in our current Bibles but with the important qualification that

---

39. B. B. Warfield, *An Introduction to the Textual Criticism of the New Testament* (London: Hodder and Stoughton, 1893) 12–15.

40. See, for example, Article 10 of the Chicago Statement on Biblical Inerrancy.

41. 2 Tim 3:15.

42. Ankergberg and Burroughs, *Taking a Stand*, 42. Here the authors employ the typical syllogism discussed above: "1. God cannot be wrong. 2. The Bible is the Word of God [verbally inspired]. 3. Therefore, the Bible cannot be wrong."

43. Ankerberg and Burroughs, *Taking a Stand*, 48–49; emphasis original.

they were not in the original. But after having emphasized the Bible as containing the very words of God (verbal inspiration), Ankerberg and Burroughs recognize the necessity of commenting on the text we have now by asserting that "none of the *minor* errors that have been found in copies change any of the major teachings . . . even when a copyist error occurs, the intended message always comes through."[44] By taking this approach, practically speaking, the importance of the God-chosen words is overshadowed and subordinated to the concept or the meaning of the text because that is what makes the reader wise unto salvation.

This approach appears to involve an inconsistency. We have seen that great emphasis is placed on the particular words as in the original because they are chosen by God himself. Yet through the transmission of the texts variants creep in that matter little to the meaning of the text. The importance of verbal inspiration is lost to the practical value of the text. Even if verbal inspiration could be proven, it matters little to the community that holds the Bible as authoritative.

Further, it is very likely that the New Testament authors did not have the autographs when they made statements about Scripture's origin, nature, and authority. And yet, they make no distinction in kind between copies and originals.[45] Why then do some evangelicals insist on making a distinction between copies and originals when the New Testament writers nowhere make such claims, while even they likely employed copies?[46] Further, the New Testament writers did not argue that the very words were chosen by God. The fact that they make no distinction between the autographs and the copies is good indication of this.

One further inconsistency in evangelical appeals to the autographs should be mentioned. I vividly recall one of my first experiences with the practice of textual criticism during my theological education. One of the assignments in second-year Greek was to choose a textual variant in the Greek New Testament and trace its lineage. I chose one of the best-known variants—Mark 16:9–20 and the so-called longer ending of Mark. My conclusion in that exercise, which also is the conclusion of

44. Ankerberg and Burroughs, *Taking a Stand*, 49.

45. John J. Brogan, "Can I Have Your Autograph?: Uses and Abuses of Textual Criticism in Forming an Evangelical Doctrine of Scripture," in *Evangelicals and Scripture: Tradition, Authority and Hermeneutics*, ed. V. Bacote, L. C. Miguélez, and D. L. Okholm (Downers Grove: InterVarsity, 2004) 107.

46. Dewey Beegle, *Scripture, Tradition, and Infallibility* (Grand Rapids: Eerdmans, 1973) 154–55.

textual critics, was that the final twelve verses of Mark's Gospel were likely not part of the original. Most would come to the same conclusion with the story of the woman caught in adultery in John 7:53—8:11. All the major translations of these texts include these pericopes with a note concerning this point. But it still raises an interesting question: If these texts were not part of the original should we conclude that they are not inspired or inerrant? Should these texts be removed from our Bibles?

The Appeal to History

Broadly speaking, proponents of the verbal plenary view take two lines of presentation. First, and foremost, appeal is made to the biblical data to prove that the Bible itself teaches its own verbal plenary inspiration. This presentation usually ends with a challenge to the effect of, "If you believe the Bible, you will also believe it is verbally inspired because that is what it teaches about itself." The second appeal is to the theological history of the church, and it is this appeal with which I will deal here.[47]

The great Princetonian Benjamin B. Warfield's influence is still felt in evangelical treatments of inspiration. Warfield wrote and taught at a time when the battle between fundamentalism and theological liberalism was at its height—and this battle was waged on the Bible.[48] He is cited often and his writings on inspiration regularly appear in present day bibliographies on evangelical presentations of inspiration.[49] Warfield believed very strongly that the verbal plenary understanding of inspiration and inerrancy had the weight of both the Bible and history behind it. Indeed, he argued that it is historical because it is biblical. Thus, he claimed that any doctrine, on critical grounds, seeking to assault inspiration must do so against the twofold evidence upon which it was based.[50] Warfield believed verbal plenary was the "well-defined church doctrine of inspiration" and the "settled faith of the universal church of God." So

---

47. I have examined the first of these appeals in *High View of Scripture?*, 147–72.

48. Warfield was born in 1851. In 1887 he became president of Princeton Seminary and remained there until his death in 1921.

49. See, for example, the list of recommended sources on inspiration in Geisler, *Systematic Theology*; and Ankerberg and Burroughs, *Taking a Stand*.

50 B. B. Warfield, "The Real Problem of Inspiration," in *The Works of Benjamin B. Warfield*, vol. 1: *Revelation and Inspiration*, ed. E. D. Warfield, W. P. Armstrong, and C. W. Hodge (Grand Rapids: Baker, 2003) 174. Unless otherwise indicated all references to Warfield are from this volume.

certain was he that that this is correct, he claimed that one could actually take this "church doctrine" as a starting point and find the truth.[51] In this rendering the dual weight of the Bible and historical theology is apparently against any who dare deviate from this well-established truth.[52]

This line of argument continues in some contemporary evangelical treatments of inspiration. In them the verbal plenary view is usually read back into Christian history—the church fathers are approached to discern their understanding of inspiration but they end up looking suspiciously evangelical in their approach to Scripture.[53]

Norman Geisler's 2002 *Systematic Theology*, which has been described as "the most extensive defense of the consistent evangelical view of Holy Scripture available," illustrates this tendency.[54] Generally speaking, apologist Geisler's presentation suffers from two foundational presuppositions that subsequently distort the literature he examines. First, the evidence cited is extremely selective. The lack of a sustained engagement with any church father he cites betrays a rather simplistic presentation that is unconcerned with the context in which the Scriptures functioned for the particular father being discussed.[55] Second, Geisler assumes that any reference to inspiration or truth indicates a "widespread acceptance of the New Testament claim for inspiration."[56] What this really means, however, is that it agrees with Geisler's understanding of inspiration—the verbal plenary view. Despite the fact that no church father he cites gives a detailed account or even a broad theory of inspiration and inerrancy, he still insists that these texts show a verbal plenary understanding.

51. Warfield, "Inspiration of the Bible," 52.

52. See Allert, *High View of Scripture?*, 68–75.

53. On the one had, I applaud the few evangelicals who do think it important that the fathers be consulted. Too many evangelicals have little concern for our Christian heritage. But, on the other hand, an apologetic motive too often accompanies those that do practice historical theology. It is apologetic in that it attempts to *prove* verbal inspiration is in the fathers rather than letting the fathers themselves speak.

54. Back cover of Geisler, *Systematic Theology*.

55. Even the data he cites sometimes is simply wrong. For example, on p. 283 Geisler implies that when Clement "chapter 2" quotes Mat 9:13, Mark 2:7, and Luke 5:32 "as Scripture" he is also calling them "canon." But chapter 2 of 1 *Clement* neither quotes these passages nor does it even employ the term "Scripture." Further, Geisler appeals to the first chapter of Clement's epistle as quoting Jeremiah with the introductory formula, "For the Holy Spirit saith . . ." when the quotation is actually from chapter 13.

56. Geisler, *Systematic Theology*, 282.

For example, in a chapter entitled, "The Church Fathers and the Bible," Geisler states, "The history of the Christian church is in overwhelming support of what the Bible claims for itself, namely that it is the divinely inspired, infallible, and inerrant word of God [the verbal plenary view]. This is true of the earliest fathers after the time of Christ, as well as down through the centuries following them up to modern times."[57] He then proceeds to prooftext selected church fathers who flourished during 150–350 CE.

In reference to Origen of Alexandria's (ca. 185–254) understanding of inspiration, he conflates statements from the same passage in the preface of *De principiis*: "the Scriptures were written by the Spirit of God, and have a meaning . . . not known to all, but to those only on whom the grace of the Holy Spirit is bestowed in the word of wisdom and knowledge."[58] Not only does Geisler here claim that this statement proves Origen's acceptance of verbal inspiration, his conflation of the passage significantly downplays Origen's argument for reading the Scriptures allegorically—something with which I suspect Geisler would be uncomfortable. The full quotation reads as follows:[59]

> *Then, finally,* that the Scriptures were written by the Spirit of God, and have a meaning, *not such only as is apparent at first sight, but also another, which escapes the notice of most. For those (words) which are written are the forms of certain mysteries, and the images of divine things. Respecting which there is one opinion throughout the whole Church, that the whole law is indeed spiritual; but that the spiritual meaning which the law conveys is* not known to all, but to those only on whom the grace of the Holy Spirit is bestowed in the word of wisdom and knowledge.[60]

Because the Bible is inspired by God, argues Origen, most Christians cannot see beyond the literal to the spiritual meaning of the text. This ought, at least, give pause to what Origen means here, as he is setting the stage for the necessity of allegorical interpretation.

There is certainly no doubt that Origen repeatedly affirms his belief that Scripture is divinely inspired. But, even though this affirmation is

---

57. Geisler, *Systematic Theology*, 282.

58. Geisler, *Systematic Theology*, 286. The translation employed by Geisler is from Phillip Schaff, ed., *Ante-Nicene Fathers*, vol. 4 (Grand Rapids: Eerdmans, 1950).

59. I have placed the words that Geisler omits in *italics*.

60. Origen, *De princ.* preface 8.

clear, it is not clear that it is of the verbal plenary variety. For Origen, the divinely inspired text contained things that historically did not occur.[61] These are included in divinely inspired Scripture so that the reader will look beyond these historical impossibilities and inconsistencies and learn the "divine element."

In commenting on the different creation accounts of Gen 1 and 2, Origen states, "Now what man of intelligence will believe that the first and the second and the third day, and the evening and the morning existed without the sun and moon and stars?" Then, after listing similar inconsistencies in the creation account, he adds, "I do not think that anyone will doubt that these are figurative expressions which indicate certain mysteries through a semblance of history and not through actual events."[62] Similar in argument is Origen's *Homily on Numbers* 16.4, where he comments on Prophetic speech:

> . . . and the things which are spoken through a prophet are not always to be taken as spoken by God. And even though through Moses God spoke many things, nevertheless Moses commanded other things by his own authority. . . . And Paul also shows things in his letters, when he says concerning some things: "The Lord says and not I," and concerning others, "These things moreover I say, not the Lord" [1 Cor. 7].

Geisler's claim that "what the Bible says, God says"[63] certainly does not appear to have the support of Origen. In fact, his is a view of inspiration that Geisler would clearly not endorse as evangelical. Yet he claims Origen is consistent with the evangelical view.

Clement of Alexandria is described by Geisler as holding to a "strict doctrine of inspiration,"[64] by which he means a verbal plenary

---

61. Origen, *De princ.* 4.2.9. One could cite the entire section here, but note these short statements: ". . . the Word of God has arranged for certain stumbling-blocks, as it were, and hindrances and impossibilities to be inserted in the midst of the law and the history . . ." and ". . . God has dealt in like manner with the gospels and the writings of the apostles. For the history even of these is not everywhere pure, events being woven together in the bodily sense without having actually happened; nor do the law and commandments contained therein entirely declare what is reasonable." The translation employed here is G. W. Butterworth, *Origen: On First Principles* (Gloucester, MA; Peter Smith, 1979).

62. Origen, *De princ.* 4.3.1.

63. Geisler, *Systematic Theology*, 233–36.

64. Geisler, *Systematic Theology*, 285.

doctrine. But for Clement the writings of philosophers like Plato who declare the only true God "are recorded by God's inspiration."[65] Further, the thoughts of virtuous men are said by Clement to have been produced through the inspiration of God.[66] I doubt that a strict doctrine of inspiration for Geisler includes Plato and the thoughts of virtuous men.

Consider also Geisler's presentation of Eusebius of Caesarea's doctrine of Scripture:

> As the great early-church historian, Eusebius is an important witness to the views of Scripture in the nascent Christian church. He held to the inspiration of the Old and New Testaments and wrote much about God's Word in his *Ecclesiastical History*. It was Eusebius who was commissioned to make fifty copies of the Scriptures following the Council of Nicea (325). Eusebius was a tremendous defender of Scripture, writing extensively on the topic. Related works include . . . [here Geisler simply lists the works written by Eusebius]. Add to this his treatise on *Easter* and his *On the Names and Places in the Holy Scriptures* (*Onomastica Sacra*) to round out his massive defense of the Bible as the divinely inspired Word of God.[67]

This is all Geisler says about Eusebius. In all this "massive defense of the Bible" not a single example from Eusebius is given to show how he conceived of this inspiration or even the canon that Eusebius apparently held as authoritative. There is not even a mention or discussion of the passage in *Ecclesiastical History* 3.25.1–7 where Eusebius gives his famous list of canonical Scripture.[68]

There are actually two problems here. The first problem is what I sought to illustrate above: when many hear the word "inspiration" they immediately think verbal, in the technical sense, as the only understanding. This understanding is then read back into Christian history.[69] But, at

---

65. Clement of Alexandria, *Exhortation to the Greeks* 6.

66. Clement of Alexandria, *Stromata* 6.17.157.

67. Geisler, *Systematic Theology*, 287.

68. See Allert, *High View of Scripture?*, 132–39.

69. Other evangelicals claiming verbal plenary to be the position of the historic church include Clarence H. Benson and Robert J. Morgan, *Exploring Theology: A Guide for Systematic Theology and Apologetics* (Wheaton, IL: Crossway, 2004) 127, 131; Louis Igou Hodges, "New Dimensions in Scripture," in *New Dimensions in Evangelical Thought: Essays in Honor of Millard J. Erickson*, ed. David S. Dockery (Downers Grove, IL: InterVarsity, 1998) 217.

least in the cases of Origen, Clement, and Eusebius, it appears that Geisler has not responsibly represented their doctrines of inspiration. The second problem relates to the readers of evangelical works like Geisler's *Systematic Theology* and his more popular works on Scripture where similar claims are made.[70] As a speaker and writer on the evangelical "circuit," his influence is quite substantial.[71] In other words, Geisler is viewed as a trusted scholar who has already studied this difficult field for us, why shouldn't we rely on his research?

But, as I have briefly shown, there is good reason to doubt that Geisler's presentation of the church fathers and the Bible shows the broader picture of a formative period in the Christian history. Contrary to Warfield and Geisler, the fathers did not have a verbal plenary view of inspiration.

The Model of God Speaking

A very common way of attempting to understand inspiration has been through the Old Testament concept in which the very words of God are said to be expressed. That is, because the Old Testament often expresses the very words of God, this model is subsequently used as the overarching model for understanding inspiration. A somewhat extreme example of equating the words of God with inspiration is found in an article by Leon Morris. Morris explains that over 3,808 times in the Old Testament some kind of formula is employed to show that God is speaking (usually in the Prophets). This he presents as evidence that God has chosen to put his words into writing: "The prophet does not regard himself as originating a tract for the times. Rather he passes on a message which he understands to have been divinely given. *So with other writers.*"[72]

70. Norman L. Geisler, *Decide for Yourself: How History Views the Bible* (Grand Rapids: Zondervan, 1982); Norman L. Geisler and William E. Nix, *From God to Us: How We Got Our Bible* (Chicago: Moody, 1974).

71. Geisler's website (http://www.normangeisler.net) includes this introduction: "Dr. Norman Geisler is the author or co-author of some 70 books and hundreds of articles. He has taught theology, philosophy, and apologetics at the college or graduate level for 50 years. He has spoken or debated in some 26 countries on six continents. He has a B.A, M.A., Th.B., and Ph.D (in philosophy). He has taught at some of the top Seminaries in the United States, including Trinity Evangelical and Dallas Seminary and currently he is Distinguished Professor of Apologetics at Veritas Evangelical Seminary in Murrieta, CA (www.veritasseminary.com). He maintains an active writing, speaking, and lecturing ministry across the country."

72. L. Morris, "Biblical Authority and the Concept of Inerrancy," *Churchman* 81

Similarly, when asking, "What Makes [the Bible] So Special?," Ankerberg and Burroughs point to its verbal plenary inspiration.[73] To show this, they cite several passages that have God speaking at the forefront.[74] As mentioned above, when explaining the meaning of the term "inspired," the same authors state, "This term is translated from a unique word in the Greek New Testament that literally means that the words are of God and therefore an extension of God."[75]

While Millard Erickson does not insist on the prophetic model as heavily as Morris, he does insist on the importance of seeing Scripture as "actually being the Word of God" and the "actual speech of the Lord."[76] In his chapter on bibliology, Floyd Barackman states that the Scriptures are God's breath and that they record God's words.[77] In a section entitled "The Origin and Inspiration of the Bible" in his *Systematic Theology*, Norman Geisler states that all biblical writers were "channels through which God conveyed his message to humankind." We have already seen that for Geisler, "what the Bible says, God says."[78] The understanding is that inspiration is to be equated with God's speech. Thus, if the Bible is inspired it must, therefore, be seen as God's very words.

Many have pointed out shortcomings in such a facile equation. William Abraham, for example, believes this to be a conceptual mistake. Rather than reflecting on divine inspiration, evangelical theologians, he says, have built their ideas around the idea of divine speaking.[79] The shortcoming can be illustrated from the book of Jeremiah and also Paul's Second Epistle to the Corinthians. For example, while it is

(1967) 23; emphasis mine.

73. This is the subtitle of the first chapter in Ankerberg and Burroughs, *Taking a Stand*, 11.

74. Ankerberg and Burroughs, *Taking a Stand*, 13–14. Passages cited include: Jer 36:1–2; 2 Pet 1:21; John 12:49–50; Rev 1:1; Heb 1:1; Hosea 1:1; Exod 24:4, 31:24; 2 Pet 3:2, 15–16.

75. Ankerberg and Burroughs, *Taking a Stand*, 28. Criticism could also be made here on the author's knowing the definition of this unique word. If it is unique (indeed, this is the only time it is used in the entire Bible) how can the authors claim to know the definition? See Allert, *High View of Scripture?*, 153–56.

76. Millard Erickson, *Christian Theology*, 2nd ed. (Grand Rapids: Baker, 1998) 225–26.

77. Barackman, *Practical Christian Theology*, 25.

78. Geisler, *Systematic Theology*, 232–33.

79. W. J. Abraham, *The Divine Inspiration of Holy Scripture* (Oxford: Oxford University Press, 1981) 58.

true that the book of Jeremiah contains words that God spoke, it also contains words that Jeremiah spoke to God as well as stories about Jeremiah. The latter are sometimes told in the first person while at other times in the third person. The book contains a mixture of various material—it is not simply a report of the very words of God. Likewise, in 2 Cor 12:9 Paul records his own actions and words as well as God's reply to his prayer. Just as in Jeremiah, we can distinguish between the words of God and the words of the author, the latter actually constituting the bulk of Paul's letters.

The point need not be pressed—strictly speaking, the Bible contains more than the actual speech and words of God. It contains human interactions with God as well as human interactions with other men and women. The Old Testament model of God speaking as comprising our *total* definition of inspiration thus appears inadequate. This model fails to do justice to large portions of Scripture since the multi-faceted dynamic of Scripture is much larger than God speaking.

John Goldingay also understands this shortcoming as generating difficulties for understanding the nature of Scripture.[80] In discussing the model of inspiration as God speaking, he illustrates his point with an example from Anglican liturgy:

> Our problem is that "word of the Lord" suggests a category mistake; it needs to be replaced by some statement such as "this is part of God's story" or "isn't it amazing the things you can say to God?" To either of these statements the congregational response "thanks be to God" would be entirely appropriate. That is more than can be said regarding the other common situation when these phrases bring a wry smile to one's lips, when listeners on autopilot respond gratefully to some prophetic oracle or dominical saying which may indeed be the word of the Lord but which brings some exceedingly bad news to its hearers and to which some response other than "thanks be to God" is surely required.[81]

Models—such as God speaking, or prophecy—are important, but one model cannot do justice to the nature of the whole Bible. The models used to understand the nature of Scripture have been used or stretched

---

80. See J. Goldingay, *Models for Scripture*; idem, "Models for Scripture," *Scottish Journal of Theology* 44 (1991) 19–37; idem, "Inspiration, Infallibility and Criticism," *Churchman* 90 (1976) 6–23.

81. Goldingay, "Models for Scripture," 30.

so as to provide answers to different and broader questions than the ones they originally addressed. For Goldingay, the traditional model of God speaking will not do because, while it does make a necessary contribution to a particular understanding of Scripture, it is simply too narrow to serve as an overarching model:[82]

> We must not "generalize in univocal fashion the concept of inspiration derived from the prophetic genre and assume that God spoke to the redactors of the sacred books just as he spoke to the prophets," (Ricoeur) any more than we should flatten the notion of inspiration so that the way it applies to such redactors determines the way it applies to prophets. The experience of evangelists and psalmists was unlike that of the prophets. Their words are just as much God's words, just as effective and relevant, but they did not come to and through their writers in the same way.[83]

Human Authors and the Divine Author

Generally speaking, an affirmation of inspiration means "that in some way the Bible comes from God, that he has in some sense a part in its origin, that there is a linkage between the basic mode through which he communicated with man and the coming into existence of this body of literature."[84] This statement is, of course, quite broad and many would want to add to it certain limitations. The task for theologians has been to attempt an explanation of how God has had a part in Scripture's origin, process, and development. Tensions immediately arise, however, when we try to explain this link between the human and the divine in Scripture. Did God dictate what he wanted written to the writers of Scripture? Did the writers record what they saw fit? Did God later use this product for his purposes? Every proposed solution runs the risk of emphasizing one aspect to the detriment of another.

In dealing with the phenomena of Scripture we are forced to admit that God respects the human element because Scripture shows this to be the case.[85] In other words, the Bible shows that human beings had a significant part in its origin, which therefore must mean that God uses this

82. Goldingay, "Models for Scripture," 30.

83. Goldingay, *Models for Scripture*, 254.

84. J. Barr, *The Bible in the Modern World* (London: SCM, 1983) 17.

85. T. Forestell, "The Limitations of Inerrancy," *Catholic Biblical Quarterly* 20 (1958) 11.

human element. Apart from this we can say, with certainty, precious little else about how this dual aspect of Scripture *actually* functions. Often the analogy of the incarnation is brought out to help explain the way the human and the divine elements in Scripture function.[86] The pre-existent Jesus took on flesh such that he came to be described at Chalcedon as "at once complete in Godhead and complete in manhood, truly God and truly man." As true and essential as this is, it does not really clear up the tension. As the various theories of *kenosis* attest, we are far from understanding the mystery of the hypostatic union. So while an analogy does exist here, it does not really help us clear the tension of the relation between the human and the divine in Scripture. If the former qualifies as a mystery of the faith, perhaps the latter should follow suit.

Since the latter half of the eighteenth century Christianity has endured battles with scientists, philosophers, historians, exegetes, and theologians who have approached the Bible in a way that has caused many Christians to react defensively. For this reason the Enlightenment has become a very important backdrop in understanding the evangelical view of the Bible. Historian Mark Noll believes that virtually every aspect of evangelical attachment to the Bible was shaped by the Enlightenment.[87] Evangelicals came to believe that the Bible needed to be reasserted as first and foremost a divine book with supernatural origins—often at the expense of the Bible as a human book, with real flesh-and-blood authors writing within and for communities of faith. In the battle against the perceived dangers of Enlightenment thinking, evangelicals "fashioned the weapon of unassailable supernaturalism which attested to the divine origins of the sacred Scriptures and to the divine assistance necessary for infallibly interpreting them."[88] This reactive stance against the Enlightenment is an example of what I have identified elsewhere as a spirit of protest that runs deep in evangelicalism.[89]

---

86. See, for example, Hodges, "New Dimensions in Scripture," 214.

87. M. A. Noll, *The Scandal of the Evangelical Mind* (Grand Rapids: Eerdmans, 1994) 97. See also D. W. Bebbington, "Evangelical Christianity and the Enlightenment," *Crux* 25 (1989) 29–36; idem, "Evangelical Christianity and Modernism," *Crux* 26 (1990) 2–9; G. M. Marsden, *Fundamentalism and American Culture*; and Noll, *Between Faith and Criticism*.

88. D. A. Milavec, "The Bible, the Holy Spirit and Human Powers," *Scottish Journal of Theology* 29 (1976) 215.

89. Allert, *High View of Scripture?*, 26–29.

In protesting against Enlightenment-driven biblical criticism, a wall was built around the Bible in order to protect it.

Consider again Warfield's examination of inspiration. In it, he begins with a discussion on the nature, process, and mode of revelation. The fundamental fact that Warfield emphasizes is that revelation is from God. He states, ". . . the completely supernatural character of revelation is in no way lessened by the circumstances that it has been given through the instrumentality of men. They affirm, indeed, with the greatest possible emphasis that the Divine Word delivered through men is the pure word of God, diluted with no human admixture whatever."[90] In spite of Warfield's positive recognition of the human element in Scripture that immediately precedes this statement, his absolute stress on its divinity subsequently makes it all but moot. It appears that Warfield's presupposition about what revelation must be has already informed and taken over his doctrine of inspiration.

The danger here has been called a "docetic" view of Scripture. Docetism was an early christological view that derived its name from the Greek verb *dokein*, which means "to seem." Docetists treated Jesus as a purely divine being who only had the appearance of being human. To call a certain understanding of the Bible "docetic" is to decry the way the divine aspect is being emphasized to the detriment and practical exclusion of the human. When the text is seen as the direct product of God with "no human admixture," it becomes all that matters. The Bible is understood as the unmediated link between God and humanity because the text is wholly divine. As such, there is no need to trifle with history or tradition—all we need to study the Bible properly is the Bible itself. The desire to maintain and strongly assert the divine nature of the Bible is certainly laudable. But the tradeoff that occurs when its supernatural character is emphasized at the expense of the human is not always positive. Further, it does not always provide the bulwark against "liberalism" that so many evangelicals seem to be counting on.

Examples of what can happen if this attitude is adopted are provided by theologians who were on the front lines of battle against biblical criticism. For instance, former president of Dallas Theological Seminary Lewis Sperry Chafer remains one of dispensationalism's best-known theologians. In his *Systematic Theology*, Chafer makes the following statement: "The very fact that I did not study a prescribed

90. Warfield, "Biblical Idea of Revelation," 18.

course in theology made it possible for me to approach the subject with an unprejudiced mind and to be concerned only with what the Bible actually teaches."[91] For Chafer and the dispensationalists, the Bible was the sole source for theology and anything brought to the table whenever interpreting it would only serve to contaminate and sever the unmediated link between God (i.e., the Bible) and the Spirit-filled interpreter. Proper study and interpretation of the Bible required humility "without any other guide than the Bible itself."[92] The assumption in this kind of appropriation of Scripture is that although interpretation may require deep study and hard work, all the student really needs is the facts of the Bible to achieve proper interpretation. The Bible itself serves as its only ground. The interpreter is exhorted to let the text speak for itself bringing nothing to the text that might otherwise color one's interpretation. The Bible is all that matters.

James K. A. Smith provides us with a more contemporary example.[93] Smith writes about an advertisement for a Bible he saw in a leading evangelical periodical. The dust cover proclaimed, "God's Word. Today's Bible translation that says what it means." Underneath the photograph, in large bold letters the publishers added, "NO INTERPRETATION NEEDED." Implicit in this example is the perceived necessity of surmounting our situatedness, our humanness, in order to attain a pure reading of the text, a reading that delivers the "explicit teaching of God" in an unmediated form. The desire here is to escape into the divine world of the text all the while suppressing any human connection whatsoever. This, I think, is the natural outcome of the overemphasis on the divinity of the text. Human admixture in the text serves to undermine its authority, and just as human admixture must be taken out of the text itself, we also must approach the text in an unmediated way, with no presuppositions whatsoever that may cloud an otherwise pure reading. Bring nothing to the divine text so that we may ascertain what it *really* says.

But there is a problem with reading the Bible this naively—differing interpretations. Even those who claimed to approach the Bible this

91. L. S. Chafer, *Systematic Theology* (Dallas: Dallas Seminary Press, 1948) 8:5–6.

92. A. T. Pierson, *Knowing the Scriptures* (New York: Gospel Publishing, 1910) 2–3, cited in T. P. Weber, "The Two-Edged Sword: The Fundamentalist Use of the Bible," in *The Bible in America: Essays in Cultural History*, ed. N. O. Hatch and M. A. Noll (New York: Oxford University Press, 1980) 111.

93. J. K. A. Smith, *The Fall of Interpretation: Philosophical Foundations for a Creational Hermeneutic* (Downers Grove, IL: InterVarsity, 2000) 39.

way came up with radically different interpretations of what it said. The problem here is well illustrated by William Newton Clarke (1840–1912).[94] As a twenty-three-year-old Baptist, Clarke was a firm biblicist who believed that the Bible was "so inspired by God that its writers were not capable of error."[95] But through a series of events surrounding education and years in ministry, by 1880 he had come to deny his previously held view of the Bible. Essentially, Clarke had come to deny the view that Warfield and Chafer would come to affirm—verbal plenary inspiration. The rub here is that Clarke had come to deny this doctrine by appealing to the same immediacy of the text that was described above—he claimed to have no presuppositions.[96]

There are other examples of this throughout church history.[97] In the fourth century, Arius used a host of scriptural passages along with biblical terminology to explain and affirm his denial of the eternality of the Son, which led to the subordination of his deity. In doing this, Arius sincerely believed he was reading the Scriptures correctly. Another example comes from the sixteenth century when a Reformed priest, Sebastian Franck (who subsequently turned Anabaptist), wrote a letter to John Campanus. In his letter, he advised Campanus to be sensitive to "the spirit" of the text whenever approaching Scripture. Yet in Franck's own sensitivity—which involved listening to the divine text alone—he ended up denying the cardinal doctrine of the holy Trinity.[98]

94. Example taken from Weber, "Two-Edged Sword," 104–7.

95. W. N. Clarke, *Sixty Years with the Bible* (New York: Scribner's, 1909) 42.

96. W. N. Clarke, *The Use of Scripture in Theology* (Edinburgh: T. & T. Clark, 1907) 25–26. Cited in Weber, "Two-Edged Sword," 106–7.

97. The following two examples are more fully explained in Craig D. Allert, "What Are We Trying to Conserve?: Evangelicalism and *Sola Scriptura*," *EvQ* 76 (2004) 339–43.

98. Franck believed that immediately after the death of the Apostles the external church of Christ ascended into heaven. The church is thus spiritual. This caused Franck to lay great stress upon the Spirit of God—it is only the Spirit, through the Scriptures, who can teach what is divine. Scripture needs to be interpreted "spiritually" and the interpreter's aim is to not become addicted to the "letter" of Scripture because this draws away from the teaching of the Spirit. Franck encourages Campanus, therefore, to interpret according to conscience. This way Scripture testifies to the heart. The culmination of this exhortation to Campanus occurs when Franck states, "Now the Spaniard [Michael Servetus] of whom the bearer of this letter, thy brother, will speak postulates in his little book a single Person of the Godhead, namely, the Father, whom he calls most truly *the* Spirit or most properly the Spirit and says that neither of the [other] two is a Person. The Roman Church postulates three persons in one essence. I should rather agree with the Spaniard." Franck, "A Letter to John Campanus," in *Spiritual and*

Appeals to the Bible to deny orthodox doctrines continued to be widespread in the wake of the Enlightenment, often in language disturbingly similar to that of Chafer quoted above.[99] For example, in the late eighteenth century one minister of a more liberal persuasion, Simeon Howard, urged other ministers to "keep close to the Bible" and "lay aside all attachment to human systems, all partiality to names, councils and churches, and honestly inquire, 'what saith the Scriptures?'" Even though Howard heeded his own advice, he still came to conclusions about what the Bible said that were at odds with conservative Christians, both during his time and ours.

Charles Chauncy (1727–87) was a Boston pastor who sought to free himself from all human systems, devoting himself to the study of Scripture for an extended period of time. After two whole years of "impartial" study of the Bible, Chauncy wrote to a friend, "I have made the Scriptures my sole study for about two years; and I think I have attained a clearer understanding of them than I ever had before." His conclusions, based on this impartial study of the Bible alone, included a rejection of eternal punishment and an acceptance of universalism. The fact is that "rational Christians" were prone to appeal to the Bible alone to argue against evangelical orthodoxy, an all-too-common scenario enduring well into the nineteenth century.[100]

The issue here is one of presuppositions. Both "camps" may claim to approach the Bible on its own terms but it becomes quite clear that this is never really the case. For on the one hand, *the strict emphasis on the divine nature of the Bible* is built on an assumption that inspiration is prophetic inspiration ("I have put my words in your mouth").[101] This virtually forces one to a dictation theory of inspiration because Scripture says what God says. Despite denials to the contrary, this is where this foundation leads: from this fundamental presupposition all the others flow. Yet on the other hand, *the strict emphasis on the human nature of the Bible* is built on an assumption of naturalism—that the only explanations to be accepted are natural explanations. This virtually forces

Anabaptist Writers, ed. G. H. Williams and A. M. Hergal, LCC (Philadelphia, 1957) 145–59, esp. 158–59.

99. The following examples are from N. O. Hatch, "*Sola Scriptura* and *Novus Ordo Seclorum*," in *Bible in America*, 62–63.

100. Hatch, "*Sola Scriptura*," 63.

101. C. H. Pinnock, "A Response to Rex A. Koivisto," *JETS* 24 (1981) 155.

one to a non-supernatural understanding of the Bible, bereft of a God accommodating and breaking into the natural realm via things like miracles. Thus, the Bible could not possibly be a divine book.

Everyone brings presuppositions to the text—this is an inescapable part of being human.[102] The person who emphasizes the supernatural origin of the text has as much of a presupposition as the person who emphasizes the human origin of the text. Thus, the accusation that presuppositions cloud a pure reading cuts both ways.[103]

SUMMARY AND CONCLUSION

To point out issues and tensions such as these in "the" evangelical doctrine of inspiration will likely elicit some backlash, particularly from those who hold the verbal plenary view. My desire is not that we further entrench ourselves into "the" evangelical view of inspiration, but rather that we recognize the complexity of the issues and honestly deal with them without fear of being labeled a liberal.

As stated above, the issues I have raised here are by no means new. They have been asked by many evangelicals before me and will continue to be raised by others. What I find troubling is *how* these issues have been dealt with when they are raised. What I mean here is illustrated by the way Richard Gaffin, Emeritus Professor of Biblical and Systematic Theology at Westminster Theological Seminary, critiques Peter Enns's *Inspiration and Incarnation*.[104] One of the bulwarks in Gaffin's argument against Enns's position is Gaffin's own conviction that it does not agree with the Westminster Confession of Faith. In that same essay, Gaffin criticizes my book, *A High View of Scripture?* (which Enns recommends), by stating, "but the inspiration he [Allert] affirms explicitly rejects plenary verbal inspiration, as held, e.g., by Warfield." What appears to be happening here is that, as with Geisler above, the prevailing paradigm has become so equated with biblical truth that it rarely undergoes examination. Thus, in this case, the Westminster

102. See Smith, *Fall of Interpretation.*

103. An excellent example of this is the dispensationalist use of the Bible as shown in Weber, "Two-Edged Sword," 101–20, esp. 113–17.

104. "A Word From Dr. Richard B. Gaffin, Jr.," on the blog Green Baggins, June 25, 2008, online: http://greenbaggins.wordpress.com/2008/06/25/a-word-from-dr-richard-b-gaffin-jr/.

Confession and the writings of Warfield become the standard against which all evangelical doctrines of inspiration are measured. By raising these issues we do not intend to attack the inspiration of the Bible, nor do we mean to undermine confidence in it. Rather, we are posing a criticism of a particular *theory* of biblical inspiration that is coming under scrutiny by many other evangelicals.

Jaroslav Pelikan once remarked, "Tradition is the living faith of the dead, traditionalism is the dead faith of the living."[105] When a *theory* is raised to the level of essential Christian belief and accepted as the litmus test of true Christianity, traditionalism has certainly managed to take over.[106]

---

105. Jaroslav Pelikan, *The Christian Tradition: A History of the Development of Doctrine*, (Chicago: University of Chicago Press, 1971) 1:5.

106. See Allert, *High View of Scripture?*, 17–36.

13

How Evangelicals Became Overcommitted to the Bible and What Can Be Done about It

J. P. Moreland

SINCE MY CONVERSION IN 1968, the inerrancy of the Bible has been an important and strong belief of mine. In 1986, I published a piece that sought to clarify the precise sense of what I meant by inerrancy, and defended the idea that it is rational to believe inerrancy.[1] While at seminary in the late 1970s, I wrote a paper responding to a book by Dewey Beegle, which sought to undermine the doctrine of inerrancy I had come to embrace.[2] I was appalled at Beegle's claim that in accepting inerrancy, certain Evangelicals were actually guilty of "bibliolatry."

Today, I am more convinced of inerrancy than at any time in my Christian life, but the charge of bibliolatry, or at least a near, if not a kissing cousin, is one I fear is hard to rebut. To be more specific, in the actual practices of the Evangelical community in North America, there is an overcommitment to Scripture in a way that is false, irrational, and harmful to the cause of Christ. And it has produced a mean-spiritedness among the overcommitted that is a grotesque and often ignorant distortion of discipleship unto the Lord Jesus. In this chapter, I shall (1) clarify

---

1. J. P. Moreland, "The Rationality of Belief in Inerrancy," *Trinity Journal NS* 7 (Spring 1986) 75–86.

2. Dewey M. Beegle, *Scripture, Tradition, and Infallibility* (Grand Rapids: Eerdmans, 1973).

what I mean by this overcommitment, (2) explain why I believe it is ubiquitous among North American evangelicals, (3) present three areas in which it has brought great harm to the church, and (4) provide two suggestions for correcting the problem. If I am correct, it falls to the intellectuals, teachers, pastors, and leaders of our community to be more aggressive in solving this problem among our people.

AMERICAN EVANGELICAL OVERCOMMITMENT TO THE BIBLE.

The very idea that one could be overcommitted to the Bible may strike one as irreligious. In a sense, this judgment is just. For one could never be too committed to loving, obeying, and promoting Holy Scripture. In another sense, however, such overcommitment is ubiquitous and harmful. The sense I have in mind is the idea that the Bible is the *sole* source of knowledge of God, morality, and a host of supplemental yet important items. Accordingly, evangelicals typically take the Bible to be the *sole* source of authority for faith and practice. Applied to inerrancy, the notion is that the Bible is the *sole source of such knowledge and authority*.

But the Protestant principle of *sola scriptura* does not entail this claim. For example, the Westminster Confession of Faith (1646) says:

> The Supreme Judge, by which all controversies of religion are to be determined, and all decrees of councils, opinions of ancient writers, doctrines of men, and private spirits, are to be examined, and in whose sentence we are to rest, can be no other but the Holy Spirit speaking in the Scripture.[3]

Similarly, the Chicago Statement on Biblical Inerrancy (1978) states:

> We affirm that the Holy Scriptures are to be received as the authoritative Word of God. We deny that the Scriptures receive their authority from the Church, tradition, or any other human source. We affirm that the Scriptures are the supreme written norm by which God binds the conscience, and that the authority of the Church is subordinate to that of Scripture. We deny that Church, creeds, councils, or declarations have authority greater than or equal to the authority of the Bible.[4]

3. John H. Leith, ed., *Creeds of the Churches*, 3rd ed. (Louisville: Westminster John Knox, 1982) 196.

4. Norman Geisler, ed., *Inerrancy* (Grand Rapids: Zondervan, 1980) 494.

Clearly, the idea that from within the Christian point of view Scripture is the *ultimate* authority, the *ultimate* source of relevant knowledge, does not entail that it is the *sole* authority or source. But this fact has a severe public relations problem and, as I will illustrate below, many in our community make this entailment, or at least accept the consequent, and act as though a challenge to the entailment is a denial of Scripture's ultimate authority. Right reason, experience, the creeds, and tradition have all been recognized as subordinate sources of knowledge and authority within the Christian point of view, subject to the supreme and final authority of Scripture.[5]

The idea that Scripture is the sole source of knowledge is often widespread among pastors, parachurch staff, and parishioners. And while evangelical scholars may not admit to accepting the idea, far too often it informs their work. To cite one example that observes this egregious problem, J. Budziszewski, in concluding his study of the social and political thought of Carl Henry, Abraham Kuyper, Francis Schaeffer, and John Howard Yoder, observes:

> All four thinkers are ambivalent about the enduring structures of creation and about the reality of general revelation. Although Henry vigorously affirms general revelation, he undermines it just as vigorously. Although Kuyper unfolds his theory mainly from the order observable in creation, he insists on hiding this fact from himself, regarding his theory of creational spheres as a direct inference from Scripture. Although Schaeffer acknowledges the importance of general revelation, he makes little use of any part of it except the principle of non-contradiction. No sooner does Yoder affirm God's good creation than he declares that we have no access to it.[6]

5. A helpful evangelical theology text that appropriately integrates relevant sources of knowledge is, in my estimation, Gordon Lewis and Bruce Demarest's *Integrative Theology* (Grand Rapids: Zondervan, 1996).

6. J. Budziszewski, "Four Shapers of Evangelical Political Thought," in Budziszewski, *Evangelicals in the Public Square* (Grand Rapids: Baker, 2006) 120.

HOW CONTEMPORARY AMERICAN EVANGELICALS MAY HAVE BECOME OVERCOMMITTED TO THE BIBLE

Whatever the reason—e.g., an aversion to anything that smacks of Catholicism, a commitment to a certain view of human depravity—Budziszewski's observation above could be insightfully applied to analyzing why there is a dearth of sophisticated evangelical political thought and an aversion among white evangelicals to serious political reflection and engagement, along with appropriation of natural moral law in evangelical moral/political dialog in the public square. The sparse landscape of evangelical political thought stands in stark contrast to the overflowing garden both of evangelical biblical scholarship and Catholic reflection on reason, general revelation, and cultural and political engagement. In my view, this dearth of political thought, and the absence of natural moral law reasoning in evangelical cultural engagement, cannot be explained biblically.

Years ago Alan Johnson wrote what I believe to be a definitive defense of natural moral law reasoning in the Bible,[7] even if it cannot be adequately explained theologically. One may think that an aversion to natural moral law is a consequence of strong Calvinist views of human depravity, but Stephen Grabill has shown that there has always been a robust respect for natural moral law in the Reformed tradition.[8]

How did evangelicals come to be "overcommitted" to the Bible? To answer that would seem to require more of a historical and sociological explanation; an account of individual and institutional habits and practices that were responsive to historical and sociological tendencies and currents in American culture, especially within American university and intellectual culture. In her authoritative work *The Making of the Modern University*, Harvard professor of education and historian Julie Reuben describes in painstaking and, for Christians, painful detail the transition from the American liberal arts college to the modern research university from 1880 to 1930.[9] Reuben divides this time of upheaval into three overlapping periods: the Religious Stage (1880–1910), the Scientific Stage

7. See Alan F. Johnson, "Is There a Biblical Warrant for Natural-Law Theories?" *Journal of the Evangelical Theological Society* 25 (1982) 185–99.

8. Stephen Grabill, *Recovering the Natural Law in Reformed Theological Ethics* (Grand Rapids: Eerdmans, 2006).

9. Julie A. Reuben, *The Making of the Modern University* (Chicago: University of Chicago Press, 1996).

(1900–1920), and the Humanities and Extracurricular Stage (1915–30). During the first years of the period, colleges took themselves to have two mandates: the impartation of wisdom and knowledge and the tools needed to discover them, and the development of spiritually, morally, and politically virtuous graduates who could serve God, the state, and the church well.

Note carefully that the college's purpose was filled with material content and was normative: *people should be taught how to live well and knowledge was available to give content to what this should look like.* Because the Christian God was understood to be (at the very least) a single, unified mind and the source of all truths, the curriculum was unified so that every discipline shed light on and harmonized with every other discipline. College faculty and administrators were confident that knowledge existed in all the fields of study. In particular, spiritual, ethical, aesthetic, and political truth and knowledge were real and on a par with truth and knowledge in other disciplines, including science. Front and center in the educational endeavor were the importance of teaching, gaining a breadth of knowledge, and fostering spiritual and moral virtue.

However, due to several factors (for example, the need to develop technology for industry and defense, the increased specialization occurring in the sciences in particular), this perspective changed. As time went on, in the cultural mental environment of many institutions, a fact/value distinction arose according to which truth and facts, along with the knowledge thereof, were considered the sole domain of empirical science. Religious and ethical claims were reduced to private feelings, individual attitudes, and personal perspectives. The realm of religion and values became non-cognitive—knowledge was not possible in these domains—and non-factual, religious and ethical claims were considered neither true nor false; their function was to simply help people live better lives.

A shift in what counted as knowledge also meant a shift in education's desiderata. Traditionally, educational institutions were known for their desire to pass on to students a received body of knowledge and wisdom. But that aim changed to the ideal of merely conveying dynamic research and information. The idea that there exists a stable body of knowable truths gave way to the notion that truth changes constantly, that progress, not wisdom, is what matters, and that university education should focus on method and "learning how to think" rather than trying to impart knowledge and wisdom to students, especially outside the empirical sciences. Academic freedom, "open" inquiry, a spirit of skepticism, and specialized research became the central values of American universities.

The abandonment of Christian monotheism from the cognitive domain meant that there was no longer a ground for a unified curriculum. Without a single, rational God, why think that there is a unity to truth, that one discipline should have anything at all to do with another discipline? Thus, uni-versities gave way to plural-versities, and we have lived with fragmentation in our schools ever since the 1930s. No longer did possession of a body of knowledge distinguish college graduates from those without such an education. Instead, the main gift of a college education, besides helping one get a job, was the impartation of a vague "scientific attitude," of the mental discipline to "think for oneself," of a spirit of open inquiry, and of an attitude of tolerance for various viewpoints. Great hostility arose to natural and revealed theology and their claim to provide knowledge of God and related matters and, instead, religion was tolerated as long as it did not claim to be cognitive or factual. As the fact/value distinction prevailed, scientism won the day, and along with it, the widespread view that there is no such thing as non-empirical knowledge. Because it is difficult to sustain the notion that in a domain of life, such as the religious and ethical domains, there are truths but no one can know what they are, the denial of non-empirical knowledge resulted in the denial of truth outside the empirical sciences.

So far we have noted two important, related shifts: 1) from a unified curriculum, grounded in a monotheistic God, and in which knowledge and truth was present in all areas of study, to plural-versities with a fragmented curriculum in which electives and specialization proliferated, and in which knowledge was limited to the empirical sciences; 2) from a cognitivist view of theological and ethical claims according to which these claims are often both true and items of knowledge, to a fact/value distinction according to which empirical science is the sole domain of facts and knowledge, and non-empirical fields, especially religion and ethics, study the realm of "values," that is, non-factual, private feelings, attitudes, and behaviors, which are not topics for which knowledge is available.

These shifts left university presidents and administrators in a pickle, and the pathetic way they tried to address the problem should be a lesson to all who would seek to remove theology and ethics from the domain of objective knowledge. Remember the two purposes of college/ university education? The first one about acquiring knowledge and the tools necessary to obtain it was retained, though in a modified form. The new goal was not the discovery of truth, but to facilitate research that could provide useful information against a background of changing truth. This was easy to accomplish in the sciences and, as a result, the better scientific scholars were increasingly rewarded with not having to teach. The humanities were left with shuffling paradigms and teaching students new and different language games. If science is the sole domain that studies reality, then the humanities are the domain that studies how we talk about reality and other things.

The second purpose was simply impossible to achieve—the development of spiritually, morally, and politically virtuous graduates who could serve God, the state, and the church well. For a moment, forget about spirituality, God, and the church. The development of morally and politically virtuous graduates who could serve their culture requires an assumption—the existence of a body of moral knowledge—that is inconsistent with the modern university, which eschews any sort of dogmatism and values diversity, tolerance, academic freedom.

Given the fact/value distinction and the non-cognitivist attitude towards religion and morality, the universities did the best they could, I suppose, but the history of their attempt to satisfy this second goal is pretty pathetic. At the beginning of the period, all fields of study were understood to be relevant to religious and moral knowledge and training, so this second mandate was integrated throughout the curriculum. This is as it should be if the domains are cognitive ones. But along the way, the scientists wanted to get rid of religious and ethical ideas in their fields and, along with them, the need to teach students how to live. So the responsibility for moral and religious development fell to the humanities. Administrators looked to professors in literature, art, history, language, and philosophy to unify the lives of students and teach values for university life in general, and the curriculum in particular.

There was just one problem: professors in the humanities had accepted the non-cognitivist view of these domains and, thus, they could not find any basis for agreement about whose values, whose justice, whose religion should be taught. The attempt to teach character was inconsistent with the other values of the university, viz., tolerance, academic freedom, a spirit of non-dogmatic and free inquiry. So humanities professors could not mount a robust common vision of moral and religious truth and knowledge apt for fulfilling this mandate. As a result, ethical and religious training was punted to extracurricular activities.

Universities sought to provide a unifying, distinct university experience that would convey a sense of community and spiritual/moral values by developing these extracurricular structures: (1) faculty advising, which was to go beyond academic aid and include personal mentoring; (2) the expansion of dorms and an emphasis on living in dorms as vehicles for creating a sense of community in which students from various fields could enrich each other and learn spiritual and moral lessons in a community atmosphere; (3) the office of Dean of Students arose at Yale in 1919, and the dean's job was to facilitate spiritual and ethical community among students; (4) freshman orientation was instituted as a means of socializing new students into the university community and orienting freshmen to important spiritual and moral values. Again, these efforts failed because no one could agree on exactly what spiritual and moral values these programs should aim to foster. More importantly, by shifting moral and spiritual training from classroom to extracurricular venues, the non-cognitivist, non-factual, purely private nature of religion and ethics was underscored.

All of this signifies the development away from the conviction that there is truth and knowledge in religion and ethics to the view that spiritual and moral guidance is so subjective that it is best left for extracurricular specialists like the Dean of Students. The university's second mandate, to impart moral and spiritual knowledge to its students, devolved into the vague aim of developing a rich student life as part of the college experience. Given the scientism that filled the atmosphere, morality soon became morale or school spirit, and the goal of making a college education a distinct experience turned out to revolve around athletic teams and the school spirit associated with supporting them. As scientism permeated American universities, the second mandate went out with a whimper. The moral and spiritual wisdom of Plato, Aristotle, Moses, Solomon, and Jesus was replaced with football and school spirit.

By and large, evangelicals responded during this shift by withdrawing from the broader world of ideas, developing a view of faith that was detached from knowledge and reason, and limiting truth and belief about God, theology, and morality to the inerrant Word of God, the Bible.[10] If I am right about this, could American evangelical overcommitment to the Bible significantly result from the influence of secularization on the church, and not as a consequence of biblical or theological reflection? Could it be a reactionary epistemic posture and not the result of scriptural teaching?

THREE AREAS WHERE OVERCOMMITMENT TO THE BIBLE IS HARMING AMERICAN EVANGELICALS.

Consider the following. Suppose that an archeologist, on the basis of biblical texts, sought and found some previously undiscovered city, temple, or some such thing. To make matters easy, let's suppose he/she discovered a portion of the ancient city of Jerusalem that was fairly specifically described in the Old Testament. Now, could the archeologist have discovered that site without the use of the Old Testament? Once discovered, could the archeologist learn things about the site that went beyond what was in the Old Testament? Clearly, the answer is "yes" to both questions. Why? Because the site actually exists in the real world. It does not exist in the Bible. It is only described in the Bible, and the biblical description is partial. If the archeologist claimed to discover something at the site that contradicted the Old Testament description, one would engage in various activities to avoid falsification of the Old Testament text. Without getting into issues of whether or under what conditions the Old Testament description could or would be falsified, such harmonization efforts could easily be epistemically and theologically permissible and even obligatory. But there would be no such obligation to reject further information about the site that did not contravene Old Testament assertions.

This is so commonsensical that it seems hardly worth mentioning. Unfortunately, what seems obvious about an ancient site has implications to three areas where many evangelicals fail to disproportionately engage in parity of approach, especially given the number of evangelical scholars (especially philosophers and theologians) that exist today: 1)

10. See J. P. Moreland, *Love Your God with All Your Mind* (Colorado Springs, CO: NavPress, 1997) ch. 1.

natural theology and moral law, 2) the realm of spirits/souls, 3) and divine guidance, prophetic revelation, words of knowledge, and wisdom.

I have already made reference to natural moral law above, and in regard to it (and natural theology), we evangelicals could learn a lesson or two from our Catholic friends, for example, Pope John Paul II. In contradistinction to the evangelical political/cultural reflection by Carl Henry and the others mentioned earlier, when Pope John Paul II reflected on Christian engagement with the political, cultural climate of the West to foster a culture of life and a plausibility structure for the gospel, even though he made frequent reference to scriptural texts he grounded Christian engagement on natural theology and moral law, an ontological analysis of the human person and human moral action, and a theological/metaphysical analysis of reason, freedom, human dignity and flourishing.[11] And Benedict XVI has deployed the same strategy.[12]

By way of application, we must teach our people two things: 1) it is appropriate, proper, and obligatory to reason for God's existence from general revelation and to use the natural moral law in moral debate; and 2) how to engage in such reasoning regarding the important issues of our day. In my experience, laypersons typically have never been exposed to a course on ethics or moral reasoning. This must be remedied.

Second, because the human soul/spirit and demons/angels are real, it is possible and, in fact, actual that extrabiblical knowledge can be gained about these spiritual entities. Regarding the human soul, on the reasonable assumptions that it is real and that its properties, parts, and relations lie within the epistemic bounds of human noetic faculties, there is no good reason to think that psychology, neuroscience, and studies in spiritual theology and discipleship could not gain true, helpful information about the soul and its functioning. However, since the early 1970s, thinkers in the "biblical counseling" movement have eschewed these sources of knowledge to varying degrees, ranging from substantial distrust to almost total disregard for them.[13] According to

---

11. John Paul II, *The Splendor of Truth* (Boston: Pauline Books & Media, 2003).

12. Joseph Ratzinger and Marcella Pera, *Without Roots: The West, Relativism, Christianity, Islam*, trans. M. Moore (New York: Basic, 2006).

13. See John Coe, "Why Biblical Counseling Is Unbiblical, or, Speaking Psychology Gently into the Church," delivered at the Western Division meeting of the Evangelical Theological Society, 1991. Available upon request from the Institute for Spiritual Formation, Talbot School of Theology, Biola University.

these thinkers, the Bible is "the *sole* source for authority concerning human nature, values, and prescriptions of healthy behavior."[14]

Typical in this regard is the following—and in light of our dialectic, ironic—statement by John F. MacArthur Jr.:

> True psychology ("the study of the soul") can be done only by Christians, since only Christians have the resources for understanding the transformation of the soul. Since the secular discipline of psychology is based on godless assumptions and evolutionary foundations, it is capable of dealing with people only superficially and only on the temporal level. . . . Scripture is the manual for all "soul work" . . .[15]

Interpreted modestly, there is a grain of truth in MacArthur's statement. Obviously, one should be wise in evaluating any claim in any field by its comportment with the Bible. And while now is not the time to discuss the role of assumptions in knowing reality, nor to defend adequately the claim that MacArthur paints with too broad of a brush in identifying the assumptions of secular psychology or in characterizing their ubiquity, I simply note that he fails to tease out the implications of the ontological reality of the soul. Given its reality and even partial availability to human investigation, it is hard to see why the Bible is the *sole* source of information for it anymore than for an archeological site.

Regarding demons and angels, on the reasonable assumptions that they are real and their natures and activities lie within the epistemic bounds of human noetic faculties, there is no good reason to think that extrabiblical knowledge about demons and angels cannot be vouchsafed. For example, Charles Kraft has studied the realm of the demonic for years, and, correctly in my view, made the following methodological observation:

> Regularities, rules and principles in the relationships between the human world and the spirit world exist and can be studied scientifically. Some do not believe we can approach the spiritual realm scientifically, but I firmly believe we can. The research tools we have learned to use in the behavioral sciences also can be used to discover regularities in the interactions between the human and spiritual realms. We cannot expect the kind of certainty, of course, that we are supposed to have in the physical ("hard")

14. Coe, "Why Biblical Counseling," 1; emphasis original.
15. John F. MacArthur Jr., *Our Sufficiency in Christ* (Dallas: Word, 1991) 58.

sciences. But we have learned a lot in psychology, anthropology, sociology and each of the other behavioral sciences through discovering *correlations* that may indicate causality. . . . Such methodology can be just as applicable to the results of spiritual interventions as to psychological interventions.[16]

Yea, verily, and amen! Since the spiritual realm is real, one should be able to learn about it in appropriate ways outside the biblical text.

Again, the Bible is the *ultimate* and not the *sole* source of knowledge or justified beliefs in this area. The importance of this point seems to be missed by Priest, Campbell, and Mullen in their criticism of the proffered insights about the demonic realm from anthropologists and missiologists like Charles Kraft, Peter Wagner, and others:

> Our concern about the new doctrines . . . [is that they] are theories about spiritual realities not given in Scripture. . . . We do not cast doubt on contemporary accounts of the supernatural which are congruent with what we know about the supernatural from Scripture (as in many account of demonic possession). We believe in the supernatural—within the framework of biblical teaching. It is only when such accounts imply ideas about demonic power not given in Scripture . . . that we are interested in submitting such accounts and doctrines to careful scrutiny.[17]

By "submitting such accounts and doctrines to careful scrutiny," Priest et al. mean "rejecting them." Moreover, the charge of developing extrabiblical doctrine is both a straw man and a red herring. "Doctrine" rightly carries an authority in our community only reserved for the explicit or rationally inferred teachings of Scripture. But Kraft and others never refer to their inductively derived principles as "doctrines." More to the point, from what I can tell, Priest et al. do not take into account adequately the fact that this domain is real and, without grounds for embracing noetic closure here, capable of being studied. Demons do not

16. Charles Kraft, *Confronting Powerless Christianity* (Grand Rapids: Baker, 2002) 61. Compare idem, *The Rules of Engagement* (Colorado Springs, CO: Wagner, 2000).

17. Robert J. Priest, Thomas Campbell, and Bradford A. Mullen, "Missiological Syncretism: The New Animistic Paradigm," in *Spiritual Powers and Missions: Raising the Issues*, ed. E. Rommen (Pascadena, CA: William Carey Library, 1995) 25. In response, Kraft, *Confronting Powerless Christianity*, 113, correctly notes that Priest et al. are wrongly assuming that truth in the spiritual area must be derived from Scripture, instead of correctly assuming that we are free to follow the evidence as long as our views do not contradict Scripture.

exist in the Bible. They exist in reality. Information—ultimately authoritative information—about demons exists in the Bible, but knowledge can also be gleaned from studying the relevant aspects of reality as well. Imagine the same argument advanced about an archeological discovery. Presumably, one would only be allowed to discover information about, say, an ancient biblical city that was already contained in the Bible!

The third and final area where overcommitment to the Bible is harming the church is in the rejection of divine guidance, revelation, and so forth from God through impressions, dreams, visions, prophetic words, words of knowledge and wisdom. If "revelation" is defined as the divine communication of information that was not or could not have been known at the time otherwise, then God is constantly giving revelation to his people. Not revelation of theology and ethics, not revelation for the universal church, and not revelation on an authoritative par with Scripture. But when the elders of the church return from a planning retreat to announce—correctly, let us assume—that God has lead them to emphasize the family this year and not, say, evangelism, this is extrabiblical revelation in the sense just mentioned. On the reasonable assumptions that God is real, that he continues to speak to and guide his children in various ways, and that all this lies within the epistemic boundaries of human faculties, there is no good reason to reject this sort of thing out of hand. But those who are overcommitted to Scripture do this all the time.[18]

TWO SUGGESTIONS FOR CORRECTING THE PROBLEM

Space forbids me from presenting anything but a cursory glance at two points of practical application. First, in dispatching our pastoral and teaching duties, we must teach people how to avail themselves appropriately of the extrabiblical knowledge available in these areas. Great harm has been done to the cause of Christ by overcommitment to the Bible here. To correct this problem, we must instruct those under our care about the availability of this knowledge and helpful ways to use it. Second, in dispatching our scholarly duties as Christian intellectuals, we

18. Fairly typical in this regard is Richard B. Gaffin Jr., "A Cessationist View," in *Are Miraculous Gifts for Today?: Four Views*, ed. Wayne Grudem (Grand Rapids: Zondervan, 1996) 25–64. Compare Sam Storms, *Convergence: Spiritual Journeys of a Charismatic Calvinist* (Kansas City: Enjoying God Ministries, 2005).

need to develop biblical, theological, and philosophical justifications for such knowledge along with guidance for its use.[19] In particular, we need to direct our efforts in developing epistemological reflections about non-empirical knowledge.

In sum, we evangelicals rightly confess the ultimate authority of God's inerrant Word. But we can no longer afford the luxury of evangelical overcommitment to the Bible. In this chapter, I have tried to say why this price is too high and why it is an expense that does not need to be paid.

---

19. For perhaps a further development of this suggestion, see my comments from a recent reception at the annual meeting of the Evangelical Philosophical Society, online at http://blog.epsociety.org/2009_11_01_archive.html. I would also encourage interested readers to consider these suggestions in light of the helpful and inspiring book by Dallas Willard, *Knowing Christ Today* (San Francisco: HarperOne, 2009), especially his last chapter, "Pastors as Teachers of the Nations."

14

Biblical Authority

A Social Scientist's Perspective

Brian Malley

INTRODUCTION

T HIS CHAPTER IS MUNDANE in the sense of being concerned with earthly affairs, the affairs of human beings as opposed to those of God. In this chapter I describe biblical authority, not as idealized by theologians and their critics, but as it exists among the people in an evangelical institution. This account is thus descriptive rather than pre-scriptive, and anthropological rather than theological.

This description is worthwhile because the facts of evangelical bib-licism are rather badly misunderstood by both evangelicals and their critics. Consider the following facts:

1. The doctrine of biblical authority is justified by appeal to the Bible itself. The circularity of this argument is apparent to most evan-gelicals but does not perturb them.

2. Evangelicals are very selective about which biblical commands they obey—but they don't obey the Bible only when doing so is convenient, either. Their actual practice is neither one of doing what the Bible says nor one of carrying out only those biblical injunctions they like.

3. In establishing a relevant connection between the Bible and their lives, evangelicals are much more concerned with the *fact* of a connection than with the *nature* of the connection.

Those who view Christian doctrines only in the abstract tend to over-look these facts, to dismiss them as human weakness, or to pounce upon them as evidence of hypocrisy. From an anthropological and psychological viewpoint, these phenomena are clues: they point to *structural* features of evangelical biblicism, revealing tensions that are inherent in the social and psychological complex that is biblical authority.

The concern of this volume is with biblical inerrancy, and by the end of this chapter I will discuss what inerrancy means in practice. But the bulk of the discussion will be devoted to the broader topic of biblical authority, for only when we see what biblical authority amounts to *in practice* will we be able to appreciate what the doctrine of biblical inerrancy *does*, its *function* in evangelical communities.

The model advanced here is based on my ethnographic research from 1997 to 2001 at Creekside Baptist, an evangelical church in Ann Arbor, Michigan.[1] Creekside Baptist is a predominantly white, middle-class church with 350–450 attendees on an average fall or winter Sunday. Although nominally Baptist, its doctrine, liturgy, ethics, and ethos are not distinctively Baptist. It is affiliated with a loose federation of churches but, like most Baptist churches, it makes decisions in-house. My research consisted of a Sunday morning survey, interviews, and participant observation. The present chapter draws heavily from my ethnography, *How the Bible Works: An Anthropological Study of Evangelical Biblicism*, the conclusions of which have largely been sustained by subsequent research.[2] The reader is referred to my ethnography for a more extensive and more rigorous discussion of most of the points presented here.

---

1. The names of the church and all informants are pseudonyms. I must emphasize that the description given here pertains to Creekside Baptist only during the period of my fieldwork. Following a change of leadership shortly after my fieldwork ended, Creekside Baptist appears to have shed much of its emphasis on the Bible.

2. B. Malley, *How the Bible Works: An Anthropological Study of Evangelical Biblicism*, Cognitive Science of Religion Series (Walnut Creek, CA: AltaMira, 2004). See J. S. Bielo, *Words upon the Word: An Ethnography of Evangelical Group Bible Study* (New York: New York University Press, 2009); J. S. Bielo, ed., *The Social Life of Scriptures: Cross-Cultural Perspectives on Biblicism* (New Brunswick, NJ: Rutgers University Press, 2009); E. Keller, *The Road to Clarity: Seventh-Day Adventism in Madagascar* (New York: Palgrave Macmillan, 2005).

My interpretations have been shaped also by my childhood experiences. I grew up in a northern fundamentalist church formed in 1929 as part of the first wave of fundamentalist churches. Although I no longer think of myself as a fundamentalist, and probably not even as an evangelical, I respect fundamentalists and evangelicals for their intellectual courage and I laud their sincere devotion to God. I hope that my work brings them some small bit of self-understanding and a heightened appreciation of their tradition.

Although I describe biblicism as a set of psychological and social processes, I do not deny that God speaks to individuals or institutions through the Bible—please do not understand this omission as a tacit denial. But here I am discussing just the human side of things.

DOCTRINAL STATEMENT

Creekside Baptist was formed in 1964 and has always identified itself as an evangelical Christian church in which the Bible is regarded as inspired, inerrant, and authoritative. The following is from the church constitution, the first item in the Affirmation of Faith:

> We believe that the Bible is the Word of God, fully inspired and without error in the original manuscripts, written under the inspiration of the Holy Spirit, and that it has supreme authority in all matters of faith and conduct (II Timothy 3:15–17; II Peter 1:16–21; 3:14–18; Luke 24: 36–49).

The statement on the Bible is thus a mixture of conservative doctrine about the high status of Scripture and a somewhat more liberal limitation of its authority to "matters of faith and conduct."

In prioritizing its statement on the Bible, Creekside Baptist is similar to many other evangelical institutions. The historian Mark A. Noll reviewed statements of faith by three denominations in the American evangelical tradition, six evangelical parachurch organizations, and documents from the 1974 and 1989 International Congresses on World Evangelization:

> Convergence in these evangelical statements of faith begins with the *Bible*. Eight of the ten begin with a statement on Scripture (for the other two—Wheaton and Lausanne—Scripture comes second). All of them speak in unison by affirming that the Bible

is infallible (it does not let people down) and inspired (its writing reflects the direct influence of God). They are equally in agreement that Scripture is the ultimate authority for beliefs and practices. The InterVarsity statement puts it most economically in affirming belief in "the unique divine inspiration, entire trustworthiness and authority of the Bible." The Lausanne Covenant expands matters considerably, but much along the lines of the other statements: "We affirm the divine inspiration, truthfulness and authority of both Old and New Testament Scriptures in their entirety as the only written word of God, without error in all that it affirms, and the only infallible rule of faith and practice. We also affirm the power of God's word to accomplish his purpose of salvation. . . . Through it [Scripture] the Holy Spirit still speaks today. He illumines the minds of God's people in every culture to perceive its truth freshly through their own eyes and thus discloses to the whole Church ever more of the many colored wisdom of God."[3]

Clearly, evangelical institutions like Creekside Baptist emphasize their view of Scripture, at least in their doctrinal statements.

Why such an emphasis? Belief in the special status of the Bible is not part of the Christian gospel; it is not required for salvation. If the special status of the Bible is the *result* of its divine inspiration, then it would seem that the statement on the Bible should *follow* rather than *precede* statements on God and God's revelatory activity in the world. So why foreground the institution's view of the Bible? There are three related reasons, I think, that evangelical institutions emphasize their doctrine of the Bible: epistemology, distinctiveness, and discursive structure. I will consider these in turn, along the way making some observations about what they mean in practice.

Epistemology

Part of the epistemology of evangelical institutions is biblical foundationalism: the expectation that their beliefs are ultimately to be derived from the Bible. The people of Creekside Baptist sought to hold *biblical* views, make *biblical* choices, and lead *biblical* lives. Ideally, the Bible was the rule for their lives. In light of this shared epistemology, it makes

---

3. Mark Noll, *American Evangelical Christianity: An Introduction* (Malden, MA: Blackwell, 2001) 59–60.

sense for an institution to state the foundation before explicating the beliefs that are derived from it.

This statement involves narrowly circular reasoning: Creekside Baptist grounds its doctrine of biblical authority in the Bible itself. Interestingly, the patent circularity of this line of reasoning did not disturb the people of Creekside Baptist. This is particularly striking because the people of Creekside Baptist were unusually well educated—64 percent had done postgraduate work—and because it was not uncommon for them to examine intellectual arguments during Sunday school classes or Bible studies. Obviously, these people were not *blind* to the problems of circular argumentation nor had they *failed to notice* that this argument is circular. Rather, there are two possibilities here:

1. They found this circular argument, but not most others, compelling.
2. They recognized that this argument was circular but did not find this a compelling criticism in this case.

These are genuinely distinct possibilities: 1) allows that the argument is persuasive and that there is some formal difference that they detected between this circular argument and others; 2) suggests that although the statement has the form of an argument, its persuasiveness derives not from the argument but from some other source. My discussions with the people of Creekside Baptist strongly favored the latter option: they recognized that the argument is circular—they did not suggest that it was somehow different from other circular arguments—but they did not seem perturbed by its admitted circularity. Rather, it was very much as if they felt the charge of circularity were of limited interest—*valid* but not really *relevant*. We will see why it was largely irrelevant later.

Distinctiveness

In terms of institutional distinctiveness, evangelical institutions distinguish themselves from the less "traditional," mainline Christian churches by their high view of the Bible. A high view of the Bible is part of evangelical identity. So it makes sense for evangelical institutions to foreground their view of the Bible because this is an evangelical distinctive.

It is important to note that this distinction is *self-perceived*; it is part of evangelicals' normative self-concept. In my research, I asked people how they identified themselves religiously. Specifically, I asked a standard series of six questions:

1. "Do you consider yourself a Christian?," followed by, "And what do you mean by *Christian*?"

2. "Do you consider yourself an evangelical?," followed by, "And what do you mean by *evangelical*?"; and

3. "Do you consider yourself a fundamentalist?," followed by, "And what do you mean by *fundamentalist*?"

I posed the questions in this way so as to gather information about people's religious identities without forcing upon them one or another definition of the categories *Christian, evangelical,* and *fundamentalist.* All of my informants identified themselves as Christians, and none of them included belief in the Bible as part of what made them Christian. Almost all of my informants identified themselves as evangelicals, and all who did picked out their belief in the Bible as the primary (and often only) thing that identified them as evangelical. Thus belief in the Bible was perceived as a necessary (and often sufficient) condition for being an evangelical.

Thus biblical authority is tied in with individuals' sense of identity. It was also a primary criterion by which they select a church. In response to the question, "What do you look for in a church?," most informants mentioned belief in the Bible:

> Well, I think the most important thing is doctrine; that they believe that Jesus Christ is the only way to God. Something I don't think I mentioned in my definition of Christian—maybe it was implied—but just that Jesus is the only way [and] the Bible is the word of God. . . . But a church should definitely hold to the Bible as the word of God, [and] Jesus [as] the only way—I think those are kind of the first things you can check up on.

Another informant responded similarly:

> Flat off, the assumption that they believe in the Bible. . . . Those type of things. So it would have to be a Christian church, it would have to believe that the Bible is the word of God, and seek to do that evangelism we spoke of. But are you looking for . . . what are some more peripheral type of things? In more detail, I would look for the preaching, programs for kids, the type of participants and what do they do with their kids, things like that.

In general, I found that the people who attended Creekside Baptist were attracted to the church in part by its biblicism. So biblical authority is part not only of how evangelicals define themselves but also how some individuals select churches. Given that the American religious landscape is pluralistic and voluntary, it is *good marketing* for evangelical churches, as evangelical churches, to advertise their view of the Bible.

The link between biblical authority and both individual and institutional identity is a potent one. Psychologically, there is good reason to believe that individuals are strongly motivated by their identities. Sociologically, it is necessary for institutions, if they are to survive, to reproduce their defining features.[4] We should expect, therefore, for evangelicals, both individually and institutionally, to be particularly concerned with biblical authority.

Discursive Structure

Finally, it is useful for evangelical institutions to foreground their view of the Bible because doing so communicates something about the predominant discursive structure in such institutions. Reference to the Bible was a common feature of discourse at Creekside Baptist. Expository sermons took a Bible passage as their point of departure, but also returned to the passage regularly and also referenced other biblical texts. Most Sunday school classes and small group meetings were structured as Bible studies in which people either read a text together and then talked about what it meant or started with a topic and interrogated the Bible for its teaching thereon. In both cases, the focus was on identifying the Bible's teaching. This assumption of biblical authority is part of the ground of evangelical discourse, and therefore it is practical for evangelical institutions to advertise this fact up front.

On the other hand, they seemed almost completely unconcerned with the *nature* of the connection to the Bible. For instance, men were discouraged from ogling women by appeal to Jesus' saying in Matt 5:27–28: "You have heard that it was said, 'Do not commit adultery.' But I tell you that anyone who looks at a woman lustfully has already committed adultery with her in his heart." Looking at a woman to admire her—"the second look," as one fellow put it—was (ostensibly) equated with adultery. This saying of Jesus was taken at face value, and the context in

---

4. See D. Sperber, "Anthropology and Psychology: Towards an Epidemiology of Representations," *Man* 20 (1985) 73–89.

which it occurred—the hyperbolic Sermon on the Mount—was ignored
. . . unless discussion proceeded to the next verse.

In Matt 5:29–30, Jesus himself offered a rather straightforward and,
I should think, effective solution to the problem of ophthalmological
adultery:

> If your right eye causes you to sin, gouge it out and throw it away.
> It is better for you to lose one part of your body than for your
> whole body to be thrown into hell. And if your right hand causes
> you to sin, cut it off and throw it away. It is better for you to lose
> one part of your body than for your whole body to go into hell.

The straightforward interpretation of this solution—though contextually relevant and well reasoned—was never even considered. It was
regarded either as an allegory in which the parts of one's body stood
for friendships and associations or—more often and, I think, more accurately—as hyperbole.

To be more precise: Matt 5:27–28 was taken at face value, automatically, without discussion; Matt 5:29–30 was taken as hyperbole,
automatically, without discussion.[5] When, in individual discussions
with evangelicals, I have suggested either that both be treated hyperboli-
cally or that both be taken at face value, discussants have regarded this
suggestion as if it were obviously unreasonable. I take this as an honest
and forthright response; I am sure that when they read Matt 5:27–30
their inferential processes are following rules that preclude such interpretations. Specifically, I think that they dismiss the lopping off of body
parts as *unwarranted* and the permissibility of lustful looking *irrelevant*.
There is compelling psychological evidence that we have a moral inference system, one function of which is to reckon proportionality between
offenses and punishments. Jesus' solution, though theologically sound,
violates those intuitions, and its face-value reading is thus almost immediately dismissed because the belief that Jesus was *just*—that is, acted
in accordance with the intuitions produced by this moral inference system—precludes him intending for us to violate those intuitions. Largely
preconscious inferences cause evangelicals to think that Jesus *just cannot*
have intended for that solution to be taken at face value.[6]

5. I have also witnessed interactions where Matt 5.31–32 were taken at face value,
automatically, without discussion—but not at Creekside Baptist.

6. Psychologically, this is an issue of relevance. The inference that Jesus intended
what he actually said—that it was intended to be taken at face value—does not receive

The converse possibility, that Jesus really did not mean for men to abstain from looking lustfully at women, is considered *irrelevant*.[7] Surely Jesus meant *something* by what he said, and if he did *not* mean that men should not look at women lustfully, it is difficult to see what that would be. Thus the presumption that Jesus' statement is relevant virtually ensures that it will be taken at face value.

Except, I predict, for the *adultery* part. I have not tested this, even hypothetically, so it is merely a prediction, but I predict that our moral inference system would generate the intuition that it would be *unjust* to apply the full penalty for actual adultery to a lustful look. If we lived in a society where the punishment for adultery were, say, castration, I predict that evangelicals would not advocate castration as punishment for lustful looking. I predict that they would regard that as *unwarranted* by exactly the same psychological mechanism that causes them to regard lopping off body parts as unwarranted. We do not see this in practice because there are no practical consequences for calling a lustful look *adultery*.[8]

The point I am making is that evangelicals, even though they assign great importance to establishing connections between their beliefs and the Bible, are inconsistent in the kinds of connections they establish and—importantly—are not much concerned by this inconsistency per se. So long as all *particular* interpretations seem reasonable to them, they are not concerned with consistency in their *method* of interpretation. They are concerned when interpretive inconsistency creates some theological or practical problem, but they do not much worry about interpretive consistency *in its own right*.

It is not that they fail to see the problem with inconsistent interpretative methods. Rather, they see the problem but it just does not bother them very much. Mostly they just shrug it off and do not change their

---

enough support from other inferences to achieve relevance. See D. Sperber and D. Wilson, *Relevance: Communication and Cognition*, 2nd ed. (Malden, MA: Blackwell, 1995).

7. On the cognitive principle of relevance, see Sperber and Wilson, *Relevance*.

8. This might more realistically be tested as follows. Find a community where adultery is considered legitimate grounds for divorce and pose the following scenario: "A woman wants to divorce her husband because he has committed adultery: by his own admission, he looked lustfully at another woman. Is this legitimate grounds for a divorce?" I predict that most people in this community will say *no*, even if they have been primed by affirming that adultery is a legitimate ground for divorce.

interpretations at all. Looking at women is still adultery, and they are not cutting anything off. It is very much as if the inconsistency is *irrelevant*—a point to which we will return.

Limitations of the Formal Statement

Thus far I have suggested that evangelical institutions emphasize their doctrine of the Bible because doing so reflects their epistemology, distinctiveness, and discursive structure. Along the way, I have hinted that evangelicals' practice of biblical authority—in particular their circular justification of it and their inconsistency in applying it—suggests that there is more going on in practice than the doctrinal statement would indicate.

I have not spent much time unpacking the doctrinal statement itself, however, and this is because the doctrinal statement is of very limited value in understanding how the people of Creekside Baptist think about biblical authority and inerrancy. First, the constitution of Creekside Baptist, while available in printed form, in practice gets cited only to define issues of official procedure: never did I hear the Affirmation of Faith quoted in a sermon, Sunday school, or Bible study. Rather, the constitution is distributed to new members when they join the church, and they are given to understand that this document defines church polity and procedure. Once part of the church, they use the constitution seldom, if at all. Below we will consider why this might be.

Second, the doctrinal statement is not an accurate representation of people's actual beliefs. For example, it leaves out an assumption critical to biblical foundationalism. In the doctrinal statement, the Bible's inerrancy is limited to *the original manuscripts*. By *original manuscripts* is meant the parchments and papyri upon which the biblical authors (or their secretaries) first wrote the biblical texts—documents that are usually referred to as the *autographs*. This declaration allows that all manner of errors may have crept into the Bible in the process of copying. By itself this is completely irrelevant: the attribution of inerrancy to the original manuscripts is of little interest if that inerrancy has not been preserved. The doctrinal statement leaves out the assumption—necessary for confidence in actual Bibles—that the transmission process was largely faithful. If we are to understand what people actually think about biblical authority, we cannot trust the formal statement of doctrine but must look to more direct evidence.

LAY BELIEF AND PRACTICE

I will treat lay belief in and practice of biblical authority first in terms of ideation and then with regard to institutional and private practice. These approaches are not distinct so much in their subject matter as in their approach. All data are behavioral: in my discussion of ideation the behaviors are verbal responses to survey and interview questions; in my discussion of practice the behaviors are activities carried out in more natural contexts. And in both cases the theoretical object is what the people of Creekside Baptist—and by extension, other evangelicals—think. In this section, the distinction between ideation and practice is merely methodological. In the next section I will draw a different distinction, between two different sorts of biblical authority, each of which has its associated motivations, ideas, and practices.

Authority, Inspiration, and Inerrancy

Biblical authority is closely connected in people's minds with the beliefs about the Bible's divine inspiration. The following is from my discussion with Chris, a middle-aged man who had attended Creekside Baptist for almost ten years.

> BRIAN: Is the Bible the word of God?
>
> CHRIS: Boy, you're asking a lot of . . . now if we define what is the word of God . . .
>
> BRIAN: I'll let you define it however you like.
>
> CHRIS: You know, for me it is the word of God, it's the inspired word of God. Is it affected by who wrote it? Yeah, I think it is. I think . . . but it is the inspired word of God. I believe, you know. And it is inerrant, in things spiritual.
>
> BRIAN: What does it mean to say the Bible is inspired by God?
>
> CHRIS: Well to me it means that the person who wrote it is basically—I don't know how to say this—is mentally stimulated through a spiritual force, the Holy Spirit, that is in them, and they are attuned so much when they are writing this, or God has them attuned so much, that it would be as if he were writing it. That's what I think the inspiration of the Holy Scriptures is, is that they sat down to write this, and they could do nothing else but write what they wrote. It was inspired by God.

Chris's answers were among the most explicit that I received and reflect his independent study of his faith. His rhetorical question, "Is it affected by who wrote it?" shows that, somewhere in his study, he had come across the objection—usually posed rhetorically in discussions of inspiration, just as Chris does here—that the biblical writings vary considerably in vocabulary, grammar, and style. He did not say where he ran across this objection, but it was probably not at Creekside Baptist. The doctrine of inspiration was seldom mentioned, let alone discussed, at Creekside Baptist.

Chris's ideas about inspiration were as well developed as those of any other layperson whom I interviewed. He gave an almost physical description of how God, acting through a "spiritual force," determined what the biblical writers would write. Other informants described inspiration with phrases like "God guided their thoughts" or "impressed their minds." But they were clearly reaching for words, and freely admitted that they were very uncertain about how inspiration might have worked.

When informants said that they did not know exactly how inspiration worked, I followed up with questions about the *implications* of the belief in biblical inspiration: Does it entail that God is the author of the Bible? Does it entail that the Bible is true? Does it entail that the Bible is authoritative? Each of these questions received an unequivocal "yes" from all interviewees. Whatever the inspiration of the Bible might be exactly, the people of Creekside Baptist believed that it entailed that the Bible is authoritative, true, and authored by God.

The Sunday morning survey I gave had two items related to inerrancy, to which respondents had the options to agree, disagree, or choose not to say. The first item, which received 100 percent affirmation, was that the Bible is authoritative in spiritual matters. The second item, that the Bible is authoritative even in matters of science and history, received 69.5 percent affirmation. These sorts of conscious reflections are essential to understanding what people think about the Bible, but they give us a very incomplete picture. They must be complemented by observations of what people actually do with Bibles.

Discourse about the Bible

Bibles were ubiquitous at Creekside Baptist. Many people—even children who could not yet read—brought Bibles to church. When the Bible was read aloud during the Sunday morning worship service, it was common for people to follow along in their own Bibles. People also consulted their own Bibles during Sunday school classes and in Bible studies.

At Creekside Baptist, the order of worship on Sunday mornings involved a reading from the Bible. Sometimes the church followed the lectionary, other times not. Often the Bible reading was preceded by the invitation, "Listen to the word of the Lord," and closed with the statement, "This is the word of the Lord." Sermons at Creekside Baptist were expository: they took a Bible passage as their point of departure and usually framed their exhortations as exegesis or application of what the passage said. Sermon series were sometimes topical and sometimes systematic studies of a book of the Bible. Sunday school meetings, Wednesday evening meetings, and small group meetings during the week usually took the form of Bible studies in which some passage was interrogated for its instruction for the readers.

In all these contexts was evidenced the discursive convention of tying assertions about faith and practice to one or another biblical passage. The consistency and pervasiveness of this discursive pattern was such that one *could not help* but infer 1) that the people of Creekside Baptist regarded the Bible as authoritative and 2) that they assumed that other people at Creekside Baptist did too. I do not mean merely that their discursive behavior was compelling evidence that they regarded the Bible as authoritative: I mean rather that the attribution of this belief to them was *conversationally necessary*, that one *could not understand* their conversation, much less actively participate in it, if one did not assume that they regarded the Bible as authoritative. In this way, biblical authority was woven into the discourse of the institution.

I never heard anyone suggest, for any important practical question, that the Bible simply did not address it, nor did I ever hear anyone challenge biblical teaching on any point. People were perfectly willing to admit that the Bible left some things mysterious or that its overall teaching on a point might be complex enough that different passages could seem contradictory (e.g., regarding free will and determinism), but I never heard anyone suggest that the Bible was inadequate, whether by omission or error, as a guide to faith and practice. Most likely, the people of Creekside Baptist never entertained these possibilities. The Sunday morning survey showed that the people of Creekside Baptist regarded the Bible as both infallible and inerrant in matters of faith and practice, so it is not surprising that they never suggested fallibility or error in conversation.

Devotional Reading

Biblical authority was not, however, just an institutional affair: the people of Creekside Baptist practiced biblical authority independently, as individuals and families. The strongest evidence of biblical authority in people's lives was their independent devotional reading of the Bible.

Their devotional Bible reading was motivated and framed, psychologically, by an expectation of profound relevance. Evangelicals expect the Bible to be profoundly relevant to them in their individual circumstances. They expect it to say especially important things about their contemporary needs and concerns. In response to the question, "Does your Bible reading differ from other reading you do?," one of my informants told me:

> Yeah, I read the Bible differently. It's to understand the significance of what it says and how it relates to me today. And that's why it's so fascinating, 'cause it's so relevant, it's just so profoundly relevant. So yeah, I read it differently. I mean I can read other stuff about the Bible and learn from it . . . but I take the Bible also as authoritative, so I don't take the other stuff as being authoritative.

The Bible need not say something evangelical readers necessarily *like*, but they believe it should be highly relevant to them, and they try reading it in different ways to see how it might be.

In talking with people about their devotional reading habits, I inquired how they decided to stop reading for the day. How did they decide that they had read enough? I found that devotional reading is often brought to a close by mundane external factors such as the clock or by convenient divisions in the text, but people also stop reading when something strikes them, when they come across something especially meaningful. This latter sort of voluntary, motivated cessation suggests that devotional reading is at least partly a goal-directed process that is terminated when its objective is achieved. Its objective is an interpretation that achieves a high degree of relevance. When you suddenly see the importance of a passage for your life, it means God has spoken to you.

Close questioning indicated a slight asymmetry in the sort of relevance sought. I posed the following question: "Suppose you set down to read your Bible for fifteen minutes. And you're reading along, and after ten minutes you encounter a verse that strongly convicts you of some sin in your life. Would you stop reading or continue?" Most informants responded that they would stop reading and pray about whatever they had been convicted about. I then posed a variant of the question in which, instead of being convicted of sin, they were strongly reminded of God's love for them. Again, they said they would stop reading. I then asked the convicted-of-sin version again, but this time the conviction came after only three minutes of Bible reading. They seemed less certain of their answers this time, but they generally said they would stop reading and pray. Finally, I posed a version in which they were impressed with God's love, but after only three minutes of reading. All agreed that in this last scenario they would keep reading. Conviction stops reading, even after only three minutes, because it calls for a response—it is an actionable outcome. The reader then has something to do and has no need to read further; full relevance has been achieved.

Contrary to a common assumption, the people of Creekside Baptist were *not* finding in the Bible only what they wanted to find. But the fact that they were looking for relevant connections between the Bible and their lives and that, in particular, they were looking for some actionable item is evidence of their belief that the Bible is authoritative. This interpretation is strengthened by their reports that they then tried to make choices in conformity with what they understood God to be saying to them.

AN ANTHROPOLOGICAL MODEL OF BIBLICAL AUTHORITY

It is now time to explicate an anthropological and psychological model of biblical authority, one that makes sense of the preceding observations.

The Principle of Biblical Authority

The *principle* of biblical authority is evangelicals' self-conscious belief that the Bible is the inspired Word of God and thus authoritative. This belief has particular importance for self-identified evangelicals because it is linked to their identity. The link to identity provides this belief with its primary motivation. This is why the circularity of the doctrine of biblical authority—the citation of the Bible in support of its own authority—is recognized by evangelicals but does not bother them. Because the principle is *categorically* linked with identity—"I believe the Bible is inspired and authoritative because I am an evangelical"—the weakness of its justification is simply irrelevant. They see the weakness, but it does not count against the belief's real motivation.

The principle of biblical authority is precisely a *principle*: people express their belief in what the Bible says in advance of knowing what exactly that might be. It is an abstract principle that defines an individual's relationship to the Bible and stipulates an ideal: belief that the Bible is authoritative in principle creates a situation in which actual practice may be compared to the text. The abstract nature of this principle contributes to a dynamic of renewal and reformation.

On an institutional level, the principle of biblical authority is part of an evangelical community's self-definition in a pluralist, voluntaristic religious environment. Statements of biblical authority occur mainly on institutional borders, where the institution is being defined and marketed. Thus such statements are seldom used *within* the institution.

The Practice of Biblical Authority

Evangelicals' *practice* of biblical authority consists in the establishment of connections between the Bible and their lives. Whether conducted institutionally or privately, evangelicals search for relevant connections between the Bible and their lives.

This search is guided by the cognitive principle of relevance.[9] The operation of this principle, modified by the genre-specific expectations, leads evangelicals to slip from one interpretive approach to another largely without conscious awareness. Their hermeneutic is consistent not in its assumptions about language but in its assumption that the text will be highly relevant to them today.

This is why most evangelicals are more concerned with the *fact* of a connection between the Bible and their lives than with the *nature* of that connection, and also why they find the charge of interpretive inconsistency to be of limited interest. The practice of biblical authority is motivated by its productivity in their lives: the Bible is for them a source—a fountain—of highly relevant inferences. This utility alone justifies the practice. The *practice* of biblical authority is not motivated

9. See Sperber and Wilson, *Relevance*.

by the *principle* of biblical authority, and so concerns relevant to the principle are not necessarily relevant to the practice: evangelicals see the problems that interpretive inconsistency poses for biblical foundationalism, but they are not greatly concerned by them.

Evangelicals' selectivity in the biblical injunctions they obey requires some further explanation. First, in the face of ambiguity, people often look to others to see how they are interpreting the situation, a process called *informational social influence*. This sort of social influence also impacts the ways evangelicals understand the Bible: they look to other people to see what they think the Bible says, or what they think it means to live a *biblical* life. So from the time a person first begins to develop an evangelical identity, his or her ideas about what the Bible teaches are informed by what others practice. (This is in the nature of a working assumption and may later be overturned with regard to specific issues.)

Second, part of evangelicals' practice of biblical authority is the assumption that the meaning of a particular passage is never exhausted: there is always more to understand. In my experience, this belief is occasionally articulated, but the strongest evidence for it is that evangelicals are always open to re-examining any particular passage. They might reach a point where they feel the returns for further study are diminishing, but they never seem to claim that there is no more for them to learn from a passage.

Principle vs. Practice

I have drawn a sharp distinction between the principle of biblical authority and the practice of biblical authority because they are different psychological and social processes. People commonly assume that the principle of biblical authority *motivates* the practice of biblical authority, but the evidence does not support this interpretation. In fact, it is curiously easy to find examples of perfectly clear biblical injunctions that are uniformly ignored by large communities of people who claim to believe the Bible.

I have in mind texts like Rom 16:16, "Greet one another with a holy kiss" (repeated in 1 Cor 16:20, 2 Cor 13:12, 1 Thess 5:26, and in another form in 1 Pet 5:14). When I inquired about this command of a few people at Creekside Baptist, informants concurred 1) that its meaning is quite clear, 2) that it is in the Bible, and 3) that they are not going to do it. My informants' explanation was that this particular command is "cultural." In the words of one woman: "Well, in their culture that was how people greeted each other, you know, a kiss on each cheek. It would be weird if you went to church and just started doing it." But of course, this rationale could be used to get one out of nearly any biblical command, and my informants were unconvinced by the parallel argument that what was objectionable about homosexuality was the particular way it was practiced in biblical times. Conversely, *weirdness* is not considered a barrier to obeying other biblical commands. The "cultural" rationalization is an ad hoc argument widely endorsed because it has the convenient consequence of exempting evangelicals from a socially awkward command.

Ad hoc explanations develop when the results of the practice of biblical authority conflict with the principle of biblical authority. In principle, the whole Bible is authoritative, but in practice, in a community like Creekside Baptist, commands like "Greet one another with a holy kiss" are not because unrelated Midwesterners just do not walk up and kiss each other. The "cultural" rationalization finds an audience because it defers the conflict and changes it into an abstract hermeneutic one. The audience is susceptible to it because they are caught between the principle and the practice of biblical authority.

I would suggest that the real reason that evangelicals do not find the kiss-one-another command binding has to do with informational social influence. Informational social influence is a social process whereby an individual, faced with an ambiguous situation, looks to others to see how they are interpreting the situation. In this case, the fact that the Bible says "Greet one another with a holy kiss" is ambiguous in the sense that the *importance* of this command is not clear from the Bible. According to the principle of biblical authority, all such commands should be authoritative, but remember, the principle does not guide the practice. The practice is driven by relevance, and not all biblical injunctions are *equally* relevant or relevant *in the same way*. Thus it is not surprising that individuals observe the community to see *in what way* this injunction is relevant. They can observe that others are not taking this injunction at face value, so they do not do so either. They do not see themselves as rejecting the command; rather, they see themselves as taking its point without implementing it in its face-value form. By the process of informational social influence, communities shape their participants' interpretations.

INERRANCY

As this volume is concerned with the doctrine of inerrancy, I should like to close with predictions about the implications of changing this doctrine.

The *practice* of biblical authority would, I think, be unaffected. The practice of biblical authority is driven by cognitive relevance but may produce relevant inferences that are either consistent or inconsistent with the reader's other motivations. A conflict arises only if the inferences are inconsistent with other motivations. In such a case, the reader must resolve the conflict by repentance (overriding the other motivations) or by reinterpreting the passage (finding a different relevant inference) so that there is no conflict. There are many forms that this reinterpretation can take, and I do not see how adding the possibility that the passage is in error will really change anything. In the practice of biblical authority, the issues are relevance and motivation, not verity.

The *principle* of biblical authority would be affected by the allowance of errors in the Bible. For most evangelicals, the doctrine of biblical inerrancy amounts to *confidence* that the most popular Bibles—the major translations—are reliably true. The allowance of unspecified errors would, I think, effectively dissolve this confidence. It would probably create a market for a new Bible with only the true parts, perhaps something along the lines of the one created by Thomas Jefferson.

I think that evangelicals would have to give up their epistemology of biblical foundationalism. Evangelical epistemology is analogous to scientific epistemology in that both accept something as given and then build knowledge upon it.[10] For scientists, the basis is reality (as revealed by observation, direct and indirect); for evangelicals, it is the Bible. Evangelicals generally find this a plausible and intuitive epistemology. If the Bible were not reliable, however, I am doubtful that this epistemology would have the same popular appeal.

If an institution gave up the doctrine of inerrancy, it would no longer attract people who identify themselves as evangelicals. Because biblical authority is tied to identity, and inerrancy is at the crux of the principle of biblical authority, I think many evangelicals would react strongly against this change.

10. See E. Keller, *Road to Clarity.*

It was clear from my interviews that the doctrine of inerrancy was psychologically grounded in people's confidence in God's loving nature. I think that some evangelicals would have a difficult time reconciling an error-prone Bible with a loving and involved God, at least so long as they still subscribed to biblical foundationalism.

In short, my analysis suggests that inerrancy is critical to the principle of biblical authority, but not to its practice, and that dropping inerrancy would force a reconception of evangelicalism, but not necessarily many changes in practice.

15

Authority Redux

Epistemology, Philosophy of Science, and Theology

Christian Early

INTRODUCTION

ONE OF THE CENTRAL questions of philosophical theology is the status of knowledge claims that come into being from within a relationship characterized by the functional presence of authority (community and adherent, master practitioner and apprentice, and formative text and reader). The question is startlingly simple: is following authority rational? But perhaps it is better to rephrase it as: under what conditions would following authority (aesthetically, ethically, and epistemologically) be rational? The rational status of Christianity, with its emphasis on the adherence to a community of faith, the discipleship after Jesus of Nazareth, and the reading of sacred Scripture, is implicated in the way in which the question is answered.

Jeffrey Stout's classic text in philosophy of religion, The Flight From Authority: Religion, Morality, and the Quest for Autonomy,[1] argued persuasively that in the age of scientific (probable) reasoning following authority could no longer be understood as a rational activity. To put

1. Jeffrey Stout, *The Flight from Authority: Religion, Morality, and the Quest for Autonomy* (Notre Dame: University of Notre Dame Press, 1981).

the point bluntly: given the shift in our conception of rationality, there could no longer be a positive epistemological role for authority. I will argue, against Stout, that there is a way that is open.[2] That way is the turn, initiated by Michael Polanyi and later extended by Thomas Kuhn and expanded by Alasdair MacIntyre, to the craft tradition in philosophy of science specifically but also philosophy in general, a turn that Stout overlooked. According to the craft tradition, following after authority is rational since it is the only way to acquire the know-how necessary to practice one's trade. If Christianity is understood as a craft, then initiation into and practice of Christianity can be understood as a rational activity.[3]

THE FLIGHT FROM AUTHORITY

Jeffrey Stout chronicles some of the more recent history of "authority." Here is his take on its theme:

> The unifying historical theme is this: that modern thought was born in a crisis of authority, took shape in flight from authority, and aspired from the start to autonomy from all traditional influences whatsoever; that the quest for autonomy was also an attempt to deny the historical reality of having been influenced by tradition; and that this quest therefore could not but fail. But there is more to the story than this.[4]

There is indeed more to the story—much more, in fact, and a fuller story needs to be told because it impacts how we view our current epistemological options. To get a sense of those options, it may be helpful to pick up the story of authority, modern thought, and our historical situatedness again.

---

2. Stout's own arguments have been met head on by Nancey Murphy in her *Theology in the Age of Scientific Reasoning* (Ithaca, NY: Cornell University Press, 1990). Murphy argues, in brief, that theological research programs (as defined by Imre Lakatos) are precisely like scientific research programs and that consequently theology need not shy away from scientific reasoning. My argument here, however, is that both science and theology are crafts and that because practicing a craft is a rational activity doing science and doing theology are rational activities.

3. It should be mentioned for sake of clarity that understanding the practice of Christianity as a rational activity does not, of course, entail any demonstration that the claims of Christianity are true.

4. Stout, *Flight from Authority*, 2–3.

In the midst of the crisis of authority, brought about by the adoption of a mechanical cosmology and the breakup (breakdown?) of Christendom, it occurred to René Descartes that knowledge could be seen as a building. If the structure was unsafe for human habitation, as it was in his day, we could tear it down and build a new one from scratch on a sure foundation. Most importantly for the stability of the structure of knowledge, we would need not to combine scientia (demonstrated knowledge) and opinio (wisdom of authorities) since this combination was the source of instability.[5]

It turned out, however, that discovering sure (stable) foundations—the existence of an "I" that thinks or the experience of being appeared to "greenly"—is a mixed blessing; sure foundations do not uncontroversially allow for additional layers to be built with the same initial sense of certainty. There seems to be a trade-off between certainty and usefulness: the more certain the knowledge is, the less useful it is for getting around in a world of objects and persons; the more useful the knowledge is for getting around, the less certain it is. Navigating physical and social space, so it seems, requires accepting a measure of epistemological vulnerability: in moving about, we make mistakes. "We have got onto slippery ice," says Wittgenstein, "where there is no friction and so in a certain sense the conditions are ideal, but also, just because of that, we are unable to walk."[6] Wittgenstein's point is that we can only walk in a world that has friction, but conditions will no longer be ideal and in an un-ideal world we risk misjudging things; we stub our toes and get disappointed with others and ourselves.

Opinio, with its emphasis on discernment and weighing evidence or testimony that is short of proof, seemed a better bet for epistemological traction, but it needed to be unhinged from authority and attached instead to the calculations of probability. (What is often missed here is that although the advocates of the new probability were not foundationalists, they were equally committed to severing the connection between probability and authority and thus just as "modern" as Descartes in their response to the crisis of authority). As the new probability began to make an impact on the understanding of theological doctrines, it caused

5. The distinction between *scientia* and *opinio* goes back at least to Plato. Plato distinguished between *scientia* and *opinio* by means of demonstration in conversation.

6. Ludwig Wittgenstein, *Philosophical Investigations*, ed. P. M. S. Hacker and J. Schulte, 4th ed. (Malden, MA: Wiley-Blackwell, 2009), § 107.

a shift in emphasis and perception of those doctrines that made them seem problematic.

A doctrine such as the two natures of Jesus Christ or a miraculous event such as a saint's healing are, according to the old probability, likely to be true because of a long tradition of authorities having held them. According to the new probability, however, beliefs and events are evaluated on their own regardless of who held them, and consequently they became improbable. "A large collection of dogmas," says Stout, "some utterly mysterious and some relatively straightforward, came to seem improbable. Mysteries became mere paradoxes. Many historical claims simply became questionable—hypotheses to be tested in light of all available evidence."[7] In short, the new probability pushed religious convictions from the mysterious to the paradoxical, from humble acceptance to irrational obstacle. Faith became mere faith, and the circular reasoning begs the question.

It is easy to see how the new probability spells trouble for biblical authority once its calculative mode of reasoning is applied to the Bible. Before the late seventeenth century, the Bible is among the privileged sphere of authoritative texts. It may be difficult to interpret, its sayings and the stories of characters and events that it tells may be mysterious, but ultimately it is authored by God and therefore not submitted to critical investigation. That attitude changes with the arrival of the new probability in biblical studies; suddenly it becomes possible to evaluate the credibility of the biblical texts on their own merit, and even to evaluate their credibility in light of what else we know about the world and its history. The transition from precritical to critical attitudes towards the biblical texts, says Hans Frei, is like "a voyage from one world to another. The logical, hermeneutical difference bespeaks a chasm between worlds of thought and imagination."[8] The biblical description of events was detached from the "real" historical world, which was considered as an independent and autonomous framework that could verify (or falsify) the biblical description. "The point," says Frei, "is that the direction of interpretation now became the reverse of earlier days."[9]

7. Stout, *Flight from Authority*, 9.

8. Hans Frei, *The Eclipse of Biblical Narrative: A Study in Eighteenth and Nineteenth Century Hermeneutics* (New Haven, CT: Yale University Press, 1980) 90.

9. Frei, *Eclipse of Biblical Narrative*, 5.

Following Quine, Donald Davidson, and Larry Laudan, Stout makes an important historicist move: he argues that we do not need a theory of rationality as such. A theory of rationality relies on the notion of a conceptual scheme, which he calls the third dogma of empiricism. Once the third dogma of empiricism is rejected, rationality can then be defined functionally—without having an essence—as making good sense in context such that "the rationality of a given person's beliefs or actions is relative to the reasons or reasoning available to that person."[10] This is not conceptual relativism because the reasons and reasoning that are available today are so precisely because of the evolving story of rationality in which other modes have died out. So while Aquinas was rational in believing in divine mysteries, Hume was equally rational in rejecting them because the new probability mode of reasoning was alive to him.[11] (Hume, of course, did not argue that miracles were impossible, he only argued that they could not serve as foundations for religious belief). And, according to Stout's historicism, it no longer works to hold a Thomistic position because it relies on a dead conception of authority.[12]

There is, then, a contrast between traditional thought and modern thought on the role of authority. In traditional thought, the opinions of an authority or many authorities (and ultimately the authority was, in theological writings, God) rendered mysteries and anomalies probable (even, as with God, certain). It may not make sense, but if the word of God says so, then it must be true; it is a mystery. In modern thought, however, the connection between authority and probability or legitimacy is broken, and mysteries are consequently calculated in terms of whether they make intrinsic sense. In the final historicist move, rationality becomes defined functionally as an ability to make sense—having sound reasons for thinking and acting in a particular way—but this is no relief for traditional thought since it cannot afford to transition through the stages of rationality and make its appeal in the current environment of the new probability.[13]

10. Stout, *Flight from Authority*, 168.

11. Stout says that he has "tried to show that the reasons available to Aquinas differ from those available to Hume and that the evolution of this difference has contributed heavily to the secularization of thought. [. . . A]ny adequate distinction between traditional and modern modes of thought will highlight differences in the status of authority" (Stout, *Flight from Authority*, 173).

12. Stout thinks that Barth, to his credit, realized this.

13. Stout argues that "[d]istinctively Christian thought and experience may still be

RETURN TO AUTHORITY

Stout's narrative of authority is a three-part narrative: a precritical conception of authority in which authority is accepted and things that do not make sense are left as mysteries, a critical conception of authority in which authority is not inherently accepted and things that do not make sense become paradoxes and obstacles to belief, and finally a historicist move in which the idea of a conceptual scheme is rejected such that the intellectual ghetto walls of traditional communities no longer provide any refuge against modern thought. The hinge of the narrative is the new probability, the new *opinio* of the Port-Royal Logic. The consequences of the new probability and the critical approach to authority in biblical studies have been seen in the broad spectrum of critical approaches to the biblical texts. But the story is neither as simple as Stout makes it appear nor is it unproblematic in the way that it is told. It is at least possible to narrate the story of authority differently such that new possibilities may be discerned.

There are, to be specific, two problems with Stout's story of authority. The first is that it relies on a progress conception of intellectual history inherited from the Enlightenment. On this view, "history" is one-directional and progress is cumulative. There are very good reasons to reject this view, one of which I will discuss later (namely that intellectual narratives have the a-teleological shape characteristic of evolution rather than the teleological shape of cumulative progress towards enlightenment), but here I simply wish to register a "Protestant" disagreement with this notion of progress: there is always the possibility of protesting the current mode of things and to call for a going back to a time at which a possible mistake was made in order to explore whether other options might now be available. Stout does not consider the possibility of a protesting return that would constitute a new path of thought extending the current range of options.[14]

---

possible in an age largely shaped by social differentiation and the new probability, but only at the margins of public life and in the recesses of private existence" (Stout, *Flight from Authority*, 147).

14. Henri Bergson's conception of time is particularly helpful here in the way that it pays attention to the possibilities in the present that open up as a result of memories from the past. See H. Bergson, *Creative Evolution*, trans Arthur Mitchell (Charleston, VA: BiblioLife, 2010).

The second problem is that Davidson is quite simply wrong in his arguments against the notion of a conceptual scheme because he fails to consider the lived experience and epistemological position of someone inhabiting more than one language and culture. Such a person is in the position of being able to identify areas of conceptual incommensurability and linguistic untranslatability, which are the phenomena caused by alternative conceptual schemes and intellectual traditions.[15] Because Davidson does not place himself empathically in the position of a bicultural person, he cannot imagine a scenario in which the notion of a conceptual scheme makes sense and consequently that which cannot be translated must not be a language at all.

This leaves us with a question: Is a new return possible? Is there a way forward with respect to the epistemological role of authority that is equally historicist as Stout's way but does not make the dual mistakes of accepting the Enlightenment notion of progress and the Davidsonian rejection of the notion of a conceptual scheme? I believe there is: it is the rediscovery of the craft tradition in philosophy of science.

Michael Polanyi's *Personal Knowledge: Towards a Post-Critical Philosophy* is a good place to begin picking up a different conception of knowledge that, if carried forward, is neither a precritical acceptance of authority nor is it a critical dismissal of authority but a crossing (not necessarily a synthesis) of the two.[16] The title heralds this neither-nor-but structure of the book. "Personal Knowledge. The two words may

15. See Alasdair MacIntyre, "Moral Relativism, Truth, and Justification," in *The Tasks of Philosophy: Selected Essays*, vol. 1 (Cambridge University Press, 2006). MacIntyre developed a very specific conception of tradition and tradition-constituted rationality in his *After Virtue: A Study in Moral Theory*, 3rd ed. (Notre Dame: University of Notre Dame Press, 2007); *Whose Justice? Which Rationality?* (Notre Dame: University of Notre Dame Press, 1988); and *Three Rival Versions of Moral Enquiry: Encyclopedia, Genealogy, and Tradition* (Notre Dame: University of Notre Dame Press, 1990). For MacIntyre, there is a distinction between craft and tradition in the sense that a craft is a discipline and a tradition is what gives you resources of argumentation and narrative sense-making. Sometimes he uses the terms in combination, such as when he asks, "What then is this kind of tradition-constituted, craft-constituted enquiry?" (*Three Rival Versions*, 81), but in terms of the argument of the book what ultimately distinguishes "tradition" from "encyclopedia" and "genealogy" is that "tradition" has as its central claim that a discipline such as philosophy is a craft. That position can be traced back to Plato.

16. Michael Polanyi, *Personal Knowledge: Towards a Post-Critical Philosophy*, corr. ed. (Chicago: University of Chicago Press, 1974).

seem to contradict each other," he acknowledges.[17] In common usage, anything that is personal (opinions are personal) cannot be counted as being knowledge, and anything that is knowledge cannot be personal. Knowledge, if it is going to count as knowledge, must be objective not subjective. "But the seeming contradiction is resolved by modifying the conception of knowing."[18] For Polanyi, knowing is an act of comprehending. Knowing, since it is an act, is a matter of skillful performance using particulars as clues and as tools.

> Such is the personal participation of the knower in all acts of understanding. But this does not make our understanding subjective. Comprehension is neither an arbitrary act nor a passive experience, but a responsible act claiming universal validity. Such knowing is indeed objective in the sense of establishing contact with a hidden reality; a contact that is defined as the condition for anticipating an indeterminate range of yet unknown (and perhaps yet inconceivable) true implications. It seems reasonable to describe this fusion of the personal and the objective as Personal Knowledge.[19]

Knowing is, for Polanyi, a personal act and achievement. The personal aspect of the act of knowing is not an imperfection but a vital (necessary?) component of knowledge. That said, because it is personal, the act of knowing is "inherently hazardous" or vulnerable to being mistaken.

All knowledge constitutes a human perspective on the world; knowledge is anthropocentric. "The new Copernican system was as anthropocentric as the Ptolemaic view, the difference being merely that it preferred to satisfy a different human affection."[20] If the Ptolemaic and the Copernican systems are both anthropocentric, then how is one more objective than the other? Polanyi argues that the more a form of knowledge relies on theory than on immediate sensory experience the more objective the form of knowledge is. To claim greater objectivity for a theory is to imply that its excellence is more than mere taste and that it deserves universal acceptance, that it can "speak for itself," and that we can accredit it with prophetic powers: "We accept [a theory] in the hope of making contact with reality; so that, being really true, our theory may

17. Polanyi, *Personal Knowledge*, vii.

18. Polanyi, *Personal Knowledge*, vii.

19. Polanyi, *Personal Knowledge*, vii–viii.

20. Polanyi, *Personal Knowledge*, 4.

yet show forth its truth through future centuries in ways undreamed of by its authors."[21] Objectivity is an inspiration to conceive "a rational idea of the universe which can authoritatively speak for itself."[22] Discovery of anthropocentric-objective truth uses the experiences of our senses as clues but transcends these experiences "by embracing the vision of a reality beyond the impressions of our senses, a vision which speaks for itself in guiding us to an ever deeper understanding of reality."[23]

If anthropocentric knowledge does not entail a letting go of objectivity, then what does it mean? For Polanyi, to say that knowledge is anthropocentric is to say that it relies "on skills and connoisseurship"; at all points, shaping all factual knowledge, "the act of knowing includes an appraisal."[24] What is interesting is that the skilful act of knowing relies on observing "rules which are not known as such to the person following them."[25] The skilful act of riding a bicycle is like that and so is the skilful act of laboratory work. "Even in the modern industries the indefinable knowledge is still an essential part of technology."[26] That is to say, the skilful act of knowing is a scientific art or a human craft. Knowing, then, is a craft, which cannot be specified in detail and therefore cannot be transmitted by painstaking articulation of prescriptive rules; "it can be passed on only by example from master to apprentice."[27] Consequently, while the content of science may be taught in universities, "the unspecifiable art of scientific research has not yet penetrated to many of these."[28]

The importance of this insight into science is, of course, the epistemological role of authority:

> To learn by example is to submit to authority. You follow your master because you trust his manner of doing things even when you cannot analyse and account in detail for its effectiveness. By watching the master and emulating his efforts in the presence of his example, the apprentice unconsciously picks up the rules of the art, including those which are not explicitly known to the

21. Polanyi, *Personal Knowledge*, 5.
22. Polanyi, *Personal Knowledge*, 5.
23. Polanyi, *Personal Knowledge*, 5–6.
24. Polanyi, *Personal Knowledge*, 17.
25. Polanyi, *Personal Knowledge*, 49.
26. Polanyi, *Personal Knowledge*, 52.
27. Polanyi, *Personal Knowledge*, 53.
28. Polanyi, *Personal Knowledge*, 53.

master himself. These hidden rules can be assimilated only by a person who surrenders himself to that extent uncritically to the imitation of another. A society which wants to preserve a fund of personal knowledge must submit to tradition.[29]

Here is a point of departure for a different conception of authority than the one told by Stout: the reappearance of the craft tradition in philosophy of science. It proposes, quite simply, that knowing is a craft—and scientific knowing, or research, is no exception but rather a quintessential example—and that it therefore is characterized by a learning-by-example within a dyadic, asymmetrical relationship between apprentice and master in which the apprentice picks up the implicit know-how of the art in order to go on.

It is important to notice that in the two conceptions of authority—the one being the new probability highlighted by Stout and the other being the craft tradition—there are also two conceptions of philosophical anthropology at work in the background. (Blaise Pascal is an interesting exception to this because he can be read in both ways. Stout does not see that ambiguity and consequently misreads him at crucial points, namely, that for Pascal moments of decision are not best characterized by calculations but by intuitions. As he says, "Mathematical formalizers wish to treat matters of intuition mathematically, and make themselves ridiculous. . . . The mind . . . does it tacitly, naturally, and without technical rules," and elsewhere, "the heart has its reasons that reason does not know."[30]) The two conceptions of authority, and of philosophical anthropology, begin from a very similar—if not the same—recognition about probable knowledge: it relies on human judgment. From that recognition, however, they go in different directions. One kind of philosophical anthropology and vision of things attempts to secure the judgment objectively, ideally by removing the human element altogether. The other kind of philosophical anthropology and vision of things attempts to deepen the judgment by opening it up for revision through critical reflection. One understands humans as computers that learn to judge by crunching the numbers; the other understands humans as animals that

29. Polanyi, *Personal Knowledge*, 53.

30. Blaise Pascal, *Pensées* (1670), as quoted in Dreyfus and Dreyfus, *Mind over Machine: The Power of Human Intuition and Expertise in the Era of the Computer* (New York: Free Press, 1986) 16 and 3.

learn to judge by imitating others navigating the surrounding landscape. The former has no rational room for authority; the latter does.

Here is Leibniz articulating the project of the human-as-computer view of things:

> The most important observations and turns of skill in all sorts of trades and professions are as yet unwritten. This fact is proved by experience when, passing from theory to practice, we desire to accomplish something. Of course, we can also write up this practice, since it is at bottom just another theory more complex and particular . . .[31]

Notice that for Leibniz all practice is at bottom theory and skills are not yet written or as yet unwritten, and consequently what can eventually be eliminated is the authority of the master practitioner.

Dreyfus and Dreyfus, in their *Mind over Machine: The Power of Human Intuition and Expertise in the Era of the Computer*, argue that this vision of things is simply mistaken. In describing the philosophical project of describing everyday experience, thinkers such as Heidegger, Merleau-Ponty, and Wittgenstein "came to the conclusion that perception could not be explained by the application of rules to basic features. Human understanding was a skill akin to knowing how to find one's way about in the world, rather than knowing a lot of facts and rules for relating them."[32] Human understanding, on this view, is fundamentally a matter of knowing how (implicit procedures) rather than a knowing that (explicit rules and facts); it is based in our capacity for picking up flexible styles of behavior and forms of life.

Dreyfus and Dreyfus studied the skill-acquisition process of a broad range of crafts (pilots, chess players, drivers, adult learners of a second language, etc.) and identified five stages in skill development from novice to expert.[33] What is noteworthy is that as a practitioner moves through the stages of skill development, he or she relies less and less on formalized rules and more and more on the implicit "sense" of the situation, or "judgment." To be specific, as the practitioner moves from novice to expert, he or she begins to see the situation from an involved perspective as a landscape to navigate rather than from a detached

31. G. W. Leibniz, *Selections*, ed. Philip Wiener (New York: Scribner, 1951), 48.

32. Dreyfus and Dreyfus, *Mind over Machine*, 4.

33. Compare Patricia Benner, *From Novice to Expert: Excellence and Power in Clinical Nursing Practice*, comm. ed. (New Jersey: Prentice Hall, 2000).

manner as a problem to solve. This sense of the situation—or intuition—will highlight or foreground some features and gloss over or background other features of the landscape. "Because of the performer's perspective, certain features of the situation will stand out as salient and others will recede into the background and be ignored. As events modify the salient features, plans, expectations, and even the relative salience of features will gradually change. No detached choice or deliberation occurs."[34] In fact, the involvement with the situation is so deep that experts talk about "becoming one" with a car or ball or fishing rod.

This particular point is important because the transition occurs also in handling a tool or instrument. A novice can identify a thing as a tool or instrument, which is to say that the object is understood to be useful for achieving a certain purpose. (Outside the craft, the object remains merely an object with little actual use; inside the craft, it becomes part of the life-world). At this beginning stage, the tool is used pragmatically, which is to say merely instrumentally. Something happens, however, when with experience and development of skill the tool becomes absorbed into the whole and one's senses and feelings are transposed, for example, "from the palm to the tip of the probe;"[35] and a bit later, as Polanyi suggests, "we pour ourselves into them and assimilate them as parts of our own existence. We accept them existentially by dwelling in them."[36] And once we indwell them, they are no longer functioning "pragmatically" or "instrumentally" any more than our body or our language functions pragmatically or instrumentally; we simply navigate our landscape with them. This does not mean that we do not submit our bodies, language, and instruments to critical reflection, revising them and so on; but, when we reflect on them critically, we do so from the perspective of indwelling them. Pragmatism, then, is characteristic of the stage of the novice who has not yet had sufficient experience with a tool to trust it and to indwell it; there is nothing superior about its detached, ironic stance. The truth about the navigated landscape is never lost from sight; it matters greatly what the landscape is really like but the knowledge of that landscape will always be personal.[37]

34. Dreyfus and Dreyfus, *Mind over Machine*, 28.

35. Polanyi, *Personal Knowledge*, 57.

36. Polanyi, *Personal Knowledge*, 59.

37. The hard Kantian distinction between things-as-they-appear and things-as-they-really-are also does not apply to the immersed perspective. This does not mean

Intuition, or know-how, is the fluid performance of a bodily skill. It is developed through experience; it is the understanding that arises as one begins to notice similarities with previous experiences. It is a product of deep situational involvement. It is neither a guess nor irrational conformity. It is also very common; it is "the sort of ability we all use all the time as we go about our everyday tasks."[38] This does not mean that mistakes cannot be made or that detached decision making ceases. Often, the spell of involvement in the situation is broken, and careful conscious deliberation momentarily takes over. But even when careful conscious deliberation takes over, it does not require the detached perspective of calculative problem solving, but rather involves critically reflecting on one's intuitions.

Since intuition is largely an implicit sense of the situation, trouble often comes when asked to provide reasons for action. (Why do you think that? Why do you feel that? Why did you do that?) According to Dreyfus and Dreyfus, rationalization for the expert often "amounts to the invention of reasons," in fact experts act "arationally" if by "rational" we mean calculative reasoning. We can therefore distinguish between the reasoning of a novice and the reasoning of an expert by saying that a novice relies on detached calculative rationality whereas the expert relies on situation-immersed judgment. Judgment, to be clear, is regularly submitted to critical reflection.

THE CRAFT TRADITION AND AN A-TELEOLOGICAL CONCEPTION OF TRUTH

Thomas Kuhn, in his seminal *The Structure of Scientific Revolutions*, introduced the term "paradigm" to describe a particular way of doing science and to highlight the fact that the history of science has not developed continuously but that there have been periods and ruptures (even revolutions) along the way.[39] As Kuhn says:

that we don't make mistakes. But the important thing to emphasize here is precisely that we do discover mistakes and we do have ways of restoring our sense of what the landscape is really like.

38. Dreyfus and Dreyfus, *Mind over Machine*, 29.

39. Thomas Kuhn, *The Structure of Scientific Revolutions*, 2nd enl. ed. (Chicago: University of Chicago Press, 1970). Kuhn was almost immediately criticized for using the term "paradigm" in too many ways. Stout is, of course, aware of Kuhn's work, but

Close historical investigation of a given specialty at a given time discloses a set of recurrent and quasi-standard illustrations of various theories in their conceptual, observational, and instrumental applications. These are the community's paradigms, revealed in its textbooks, lectures and laboratory exercises. By studying them and by practicing with them, the members of the corresponding community learn their trade.[40]

Notice that Kuhn is repeating Polanyi's understanding of science as a craft by stating that becoming a scientist is a matter of learning by exercises how to practice the trade. "Normal science" is conducted within a particular paradigm, and it consists largely of puzzle solving "mop-up work" and attempting "to force nature into the preformed and relatively inflexible box that the paradigm supplies . . . [and] those that will not fit the box are often not seen at all."[41] That which will not fit the box is an anomaly, and when attention is focused on that which does not fit the box, then another paradigm (a production of extraordinary science) that accounts for the anomaly and that is often incommensurable with the paradigm which has gone before may arise. A revolution from one paradigm to the next may occur.[42] Kuhn's argument is that because science is a craft, and scientists learn to practice their trade through practicing a paradigm, in particular discarding anomalies initially and then focusing on them almost exclusively if they remain recalcitrant, science develops through periods of cumulative progress (normal science) and periods of revolution (extraordinary).

The history of science, then, is ruptured by successive paradigms because it is a craft. Kuhn talks about the transition from one paradigm to another as a conversion, using (like Polanyi) the language of gestalt.[43] This raises a particularly important question: are we getting better at

---

his focus is on Kuhn's historicism and reading him in a way that is congruent with a rejection of the idea of a hard conceptual scheme. He does not see the important notion of the craft tradition and therefore misreads him.

40. Kuhn, *Structure of Scientific Revolutions*, 43.

41. Kuhn, *Structure of Scientific Revolutions*, 24.

42. Sometimes the new paradigm emerges out of a creative thought in the middle of night. See Kuhn, *Structure of Scientific Revolutions*, 90.

43. Science, on the craft analysis, is a human activity and converting is one of the things that humans do. Kuhn says, "Though a generation is sometimes required to effect the change, scientific communities have again and again been converted to new paradigms. Furthermore, these conversions occur not despite the fact that scientists are human but because they are" (Kuhn, *Structure of Scientific Revolutions*, 152).

understanding what the world is really like? Or, to put it more generally, what conception of truth is on offer here if we accept that the production of knowledge is a craft? Kuhn says that we have to relinquish the notion that changes in paradigm carry scientists "closer and closer to the truth."[44] The developmental process described is a "process of evolution from primitive beginnings . . . [b]ut nothing that has been or will be said makes it a process of evolution toward anything."[45] Kuhn recognizes that this may be disturbing because we are deeply accustomed to science as drawing nearer a goal set by nature in advance, fine-tuning the correspondence. The abolition of a teleological kind of evolution is perhaps "the most significant and least palatable of Darwin's suggestions," and yet Kuhn thinks that a number of vexing problems may vanish if we "learn to substitute evolution-from-what-we-do-know for evolution-toward-what-we-wish-to-know."[46]

Some problems may certainly vanish, but surely other problems immediately become acute, such as how an "evolution-from" conception of intellectual progress can avoid a pragmatic instrumentalism according to which paradigms are reduced to "mere" instruments but do not themselves tell us anything about what the world is really like. The craft tradition would then be self-referentially inconsistent because while it resists instrumentalism at the practical level it cannot avoid instrumentalism at the theoretical level. Is it possible to give a non-instrumentalist reading of an "evolution-from" conception of intellectual progress? Is a craft-defined, non-pragmatist, a-teleological theory of truth even possible? There is good reason to think that it is, but it will take some teasing out.

Alasdair MacIntyre argues that dramatic narrative is the crucial form for the understanding of human action, and that consequently "science can be a rational form of enquiry, if and only if the writings of a true dramatic narrative—that is of history understood in a particular way—can be a rational activity. Scientific reason turns out to

---

44. Kuhn, Structure of Scientific Revolutions, 170.

45. Kuhn, Structure of Scientific Revolutions, 170–71; emphasis original.

46. Kuhn, *Structure of Scientific Revolutions*, 171. Kuhn mentions the problem of induction as one such vexing problem. It is not clear to me at all, however, how the problem of induction (reasoning to conclusions about the whole from a knowledge of the parts on the basis that the whole is like the part) would vanish if we substitute evolution-from for evolution-toward.

be subordinate to, and intelligible only in terms of, historical reason."[47] Later, he says that "it matters enormously that our histories should be true, just as it matters that our scientific theorizing makes truth one of its goals."[48] And finally, he says that a disregard for ontological truth neglects "the way in which the progress toward truth in different sciences is such that they have to converge."[49] This, of course, is the teleological conception of truth, which Kuhn says will no longer do, but I wish to argue that we can unhook the teleological conception of truth from MacIntyre's point that science is rational if dramatic narrative is rational, or to put his point differently, that scientific reasoning is intelligible in terms of historical reasoning.

The crucial question is whether a transition from one paradigm to another paradigm is rational, which is to say whether it can make narrative sense. In fact, many transitions—but not any and all!—make narrative sense.[50] To be specific, the transition from Aristotelian physics to Galilean physics makes sense whereas a transition from Galilean physics to Aristotelian physics does not make sense: the transition is not bidirectional. This is to say that there is an asymmetry between the two paradigms of doing physics. As MacIntyre says, "It is more rational to accept one theory or paradigm and to reject its predecessor when the later theory of paradigm provides a standpoint from which the acceptance, the life-story, and the rejection of the previous theory or paradigm can be recounted in more intelligible narrative than previously."[51] Note, however, that there is nothing inherently teleological about this transition; going from Aristotelian physics to Galilean physics does not entail anything about where one goes next or where one will ultimately end up. The transition is a transition-from and thus an example of evolution-from.

47. Alasdair MacIntyre, *Tasks of Philosophy*, 15; emphasis mine. MacIntyre argues this in the essay "Epistemological Crises, Dramatic Narrative, and the Philosophy of Science," which was first published in *The Monist* 60 (1977) 453–72.

48. MacIntyre, *Tasks of Philosophy*, 20.

49. MacIntyre, *Tasks of Philosophy*, 21.

50. Not only can they make sense, they are also very common. "I used to think *this*, but now I think *that* because of such and such," is one of the most commonly articulated personal intellectual narratives. It is the pattern displayed in a minor change of mind as well as a major conversion.

51. MacIntyre, *Tasks of Philosophy*, 18.

We can do more with this (a-teleological, transition-from) narrative conception of rationality and truth. MacIntyre says that science has shown that some existence claims such as humors and phlogiston are false (they are not really there "whatever any theory may say") whereas other existence claims such as molecules and cells have survived exceptionally well (although our beliefs about them "are by no means what they once were"). Note two things: first, that the existence claims still in use have "survived," which is evolution language; and second, that scientists have discovered that it was a mistake to think that there are humors and phlogiston. There is a distinction between "that which has been shown to be false" and "that which has survived." To identify a mistake as a mistake is inherently a non-relativist, narratively-shaped intellectual move because it rules something out as false and it inserts a distinction between past and present such that it is possible to tell the intellectual story, "I once thought there were humors, but now I see that that was false." The progress here is, again, progress-from and does not require an ultimate intellectual resting place. It is, however, progress with respect to truth because that which is false has been identified and ruled out.

It is possible, then, to understand transition-from as progress with respect to truth without requiring a teleological conception of truth on the basis of our ability to identify mistakes as mistakes. This is more than a mere recognition of fallibilism; it is the ability to rule things out as false. MacIntyre concludes his article saying that

> Kuhn's view may, of course, seem attractive simply because it seems consistent with a fallibilism which we have every reason to accept. Perhaps Einsteinian physics will one day be overthrown just as Newtonian was; perhaps, as Lakatos in his more colorful rhetorical moments used to suggest, all our scientific beliefs are, always have been, and always will be false. But it seems to be a presupposition of the way we do natural science that fallibilism has to be made consistent with the regulative ideal of an approach to a true account of the fundamental order of things and not vice versa.[52]

Against MacIntyre, I am arguing that it is entirely consistent to have an a-teleological conception of truth, which is grounded in our ability to discover mistakes as mistakes and not grounded in a mere fallibilism. The conception of truth being proposed here is consistent at all

---

52. MacIntyre, *Tasks of Philosophy*, 22.

levels since it is able to say that a transition from Aristotelian physics to Galilean physics is of the mistake-identifying type and consequently progress with respect to truth is being made without the need for the logic of an ultimate goal. Moreover, this conception of truth is not instrumentalist or pragmatic because it inhabits the current concepts in use. It indwells them precisely the same way we indwell everything else. We inhabit our convictions just as we inhabit our bodies; in fact, we are our bodies and we are our convictions—there is nothing pragmatic about it.[53]

A CRAFT PROPOSAL: AUTHORITY, SCRIPTURE, AND TRUTH

I will now sketch some of the consequences of the craft tradition for the discussion concerning authority, Scripture, and truth. The first and most obvious consequence is that Stout's narrative of authority is quite simply inadequate. Stout's narrative, to repeat, is that theism could not survive the arrival of the new probability (either in its modern or in its historicist phase) according to which events or doctrines were to be evaluated on their own merits instead of being inherently believable because authorities held them to be true. With the re-emergence of the craft tradition in philosophy of science, however, that narrative no longer holds because authority can now again be understood to play an ineliminable epistemological function.

On the craft view, a novice learns a skill through practice (trial and error) with an instrument guided by imitation of those more proficient until the novice becomes an expert, at which point the instrument has become an extension of the body and situations are intuitively navigated from the inside with the help of critical reflection. I am suggesting that from a craft perspective we can understand the community and its exemplars as authoritative guides, Scripture as the instrument of the craft, and theology (broadly understood as incorporating biblical studies, church history, and systematic theology) as a discipline of critical reflection. What is noteworthy about this suggestion is that Scripture itself is not authoritative as such; the community and its saints are.

53. See James Wm. McClendon and James Smith, *Convictions: Defusing Religious Relativism*, rev. ed. (Valley Forge, PA: Trinity, 1994).

A novice disciple of Jesus, then, learns to indwell Scripture in much the same way that a surgeon learns to indwell a scalpel: by practice and imitation. The focus here is on the learning to live life as a disciple of Jesus by watching the community and by engaging in its practices. That life becomes less and less about following formal rules and more and more about relying on the embodied intuitive know-how as the novice becomes increasingly competent, proficient, and finally an expert. Life as a disciple becomes more fluid, rapid, and involved; it starts to look "natural," which is not to say that mistakes do not happen or are not identified but that they are addressed with the resources of the craft such that mistakes get folded into the involved perspective. On this view, theology serves a critical function but from an involved perspective.

Scripture is, as mentioned, not itself authoritative and can be submitted to criticism just as any instrument of any craft is submitted to criticism by its practitioners. This means that we are free to engage in critical reflection: free to discover everything there is to know about the stories told in Scripture and everything there is to know about the story of Scripture itself (traditionally known as lower and higher criticism), free to discuss what should and should not be canonical within the Bible,[54] free to prioritize certain texts and events over others, and free even to reject certain cosmologies and images of God as false. Such freedom is risky, and we may come to the conclusion that being a disciple of Jesus and living towards his vision of the kingdom of God is no longer a living possibility, that it is a fantasy, or that its costs are too high. We fool and disfigure ourselves, however, if we think that we can protect ourselves entirely from those risks. Every form of life faces the possibility of irreparable breakdown, and the shared life of discipleship after the way of Jesus is no exception.[55]

James Sanders argues that the canon functions properly as an identity-forming document rather than as a source book for the history of Israel, early Judaism, Jesus of Nazareth, and the early church. The canon is a

> mirror for the identity of the believing community which in any
> era turns to it to ask who it is and what it is to do, even today. The

54. G. Ernest Wright has been arguing for the recognition of a canon within the Bible, or a canon within the canon.

55. See Jonathan Lear, *Radical Hope: Ethics in the Face of Cultural Devastation* (Cambridge, MA: Harvard University Press, 2008).

believing community, whether synagogue or church, can find out both what it is and what it ought to be by employing the herme- neutic rules when reading the Bible. The believing community abuses the Bible whenever it seeks in it models for its morality but reads it with validity when it finds in the Bible mirrors for its identity. By dynamic analogy the community sees its current ten- sions, between what it is and what it ought to be, in the tensions which Israel and the early church also experienced. By reading the Bible correctly the believing community sees itself on the pilgrimage that Israel too was making from the one to the other, from its enslavements to its freedom.[56]

The point that Sanders is making here is that the believing community reads the Bible well when it navigates the current tensions of the world in the understanding (or gestalt-like vision) that its pilgrimage is the pilgrimage of Israel and the pilgrimage of the early church: from its en- slavements to its freedoms. This is what it means to belong to the com- munity of the disciples of Jesus of Nazareth.

The understanding of Scripture proposed here is not necessar- ily incompatible with a "high" view of Scripture as the Word of God. Practitioners of a craft trust implicitly the instruments and tools of their craft, and the same is true of disciples of Jesus. When we lose confidence in our ability to navigate the world by indwelling Scripture, we revise and discuss and reflect on what we might need to or be able to change in order to re-establish traction in the world (our contact with the road, so to speak). Nothing about that is incompatible with our treating Scripture as the Word of God. By contrast, the fact that Scripture is able upon revi- sion to re-establish traction serves to deepen our indwelling of it and to confirm its status in our lives.

CONCLUSION

Stout's narrative of the flight from authority and modern scientific (prob- able) reasoning, while persuasive in its simplicity, needs to be problema- tized at two critical points: first, it assumes that the new probability, once it arrives on the epistemological scene, constitutes an irreversible ratio- nal progression. Second, it rejects the notion of a conceptual scheme on the basis of arguments concerning translatability and untranslatability

56. James Sanders, *Torah and Canon*, 2nd ed. (Eugene, OR: Cascade, 2005) xv–xvii.

between two incommensurable schemes, but those arguments have been undermined by paying attention to the unique position and ability of a bilingual (bischematic) who not only can identify what cannot be translated but who can also creatively extend the resources of either language such that it is possible to say that which could not previously be said.

Moreover, the rediscovery of the craft tradition in philosophy of science provides a new possibility for conceiving of a positive epistemological function of authority. In fact, if the craft tradition is correct, which I believe it to be, then any account of knowledge that does not make space for authority will at best be inadequate and at worst misleading. "Following after" is simply woven into the way in which human animals come to know about their world.

This conclusion is particularly important as it relates to the function of the Bible in the believing community. If we adopt a craft-tradition conception of science specifically and of knowledge in general, Christians would then be in a position to argue that it is the lived experience of Israel, of the early church, and of Jesus of Nazareth that is authoritative for us today. But note that, on this view, Scripture is not authoritative any more than a person's body or a community's language and culture is authoritative. For Christians, Scripture is indwelt and trusted in the same way that bodies, languages, and cultures are trusted.

Scripture and Prayer

Participating in God

Harriet A. Harris

EVANGELICAL LOVE OF SCRIPTURE is rooted in the experience of receiving guidance, comfort, edification and challenges through reading the Bible. Much of our relationship with God is mediated through Scripture. The Bible's inerrancy, or, at least, a belief in the Bible's inerrancy, may be thought to be necessary to this experience. But let us speak of this experience without reference to that doctrine, and see how far we get.

WORD AND PRESENCE

Before a service of Holy Communion I often pray this prayer:

> Be present, be present Lord Jesus Christ. Be our companion in
> the way. Kindle our hearts and awaken faith, that we may know
> you as you are revealed in Scripture and the breaking of bread.
> Amen.

This prayer draws on the story of the road to Emmaus, in which the risen Lord is made known to the two disciples at the point where he breaks bread with them (Luke 24:13–35). They then reflect that their hearts had burned within them on the way, when he had opened the Scriptures to them.

When we celebrate Communion, the expectation is that Christ will be made known to us both through the Scriptures and through the breaking of the bread. This expectation shapes the pattern of worship. A Communion service in my tradition (Episcopalian), as in many others, falls into two parts. In the first part of the service, "the liturgy of the Word," the highest point is the reading of the Gospel; in the second half, "the liturgy of the sacrament," the focal point is indeed the breaking of the bread.

When we meet and break bread together we do so in the faith that Christ is present among us (the manner of which is then debated amongst the denominations). There is also anticipation that Christ will be present to us when we read the Bible and will convict, guide, comfort, and shape us as his disciples—for to be a disciple is to be one who is disciplined; one who follows and is formed by one's teacher. We are people in the process of being transformed more and more into the likeness of Christ.

How does the Bible contribute to that transformation? It is not that the Bible is a "sacrament" in the way that Communion is held to be within the historic churches; as a visible sign of an invisible grace. The Bible has not been considered a sacrament in any branch of Christian teaching. In a significant way, Christianity is not a "religion of the book," as it is described in the Qur'an, but a religion of the Body. It is the Body of Christ that signifies God's presence: perfectly in the person of Jesus, and derivatively at Communion (in ways debated between the denominations) and in the generations of Christ's disciples who, since Christ himself ascended, have been called to be his body now on earth. Nonetheless, while the Bible is not a sacrament—it is not in itself a visible sign of an invisible grace—it can have sacramental qualities. If God so chooses, God becomes present to us as we read it, and we frequently anticipate this presence.

INGESTING THE SCRIPTURES

We are transformed by Scripture, and the image of eating, which is heightened at a service of Holy Communion, helps to make this point. Of course, at Communion what we eat literally is the bread, which is typically received with the words "the body of Christ," however that is then understood within the different denominations. And since we are what we eat—the things that we ingest constitute us—if we eat the body of Christ, we are constituted as the body of Christ. It is Christ who is the Word of God, the Word become flesh. The relationship between the Word of God and the words of Scripture is one for further thought,[1] but it is not pushing the parallel between Word and sacrament too far to say that we ingest the Scriptures.

We do not eat the Bible literally, but we have in our language many metaphors that link words and food. A term used in *lectio divina* (divine reading) is that of "ruminating" on the Scriptures, that is, a returning to them so that we can digest them again. We speak of "digesting a novel," "savouring a good book," "chewing over an idea," having "food for thought." "Book worms" are those who eat their way through, or perhaps "devour" books. The practice of memorizing Scripture is not for the sake of committing verses to memory as an end in itself. It is done because when we commit words to memory they become part of us. We internalize them, and they start to change us from the inside out. While we do not literally eat Scripture, we are nourished by it. We take in its words and are shaped by them.

PRAYERFUL READING

An anticipation of divine presence is behind many, although not all, methods of reading Scripture, including when we read or hear it in worship, and when we read it more privately, such as when reading it meditatively as with *lectio divina*, or spiritual exercises, or in quiet times. However, I will qualify that term "privately" shortly.

When engaging in *lectio divina*, we are encouraged to listen very attentively to the text, and perhaps to mirror those times when we know ourselves to have been listened to well and to have been really heard. Having listened carefully, we are then invited to ruminate upon what we have "heard"—the expectation being that God has something to say to us through the passage of Scripture. The expectation is very

---

1. Kevin Vanhoozer helpfully explores this distinction, especially in terms of the essential link between God and ourselves as communicative agents, in his *Is There a Meaning in This Text?: The Bible, the Reader and the Morality of Literary Knowledge*, 2nd ed. (Grand Rapids: Zondervan, 2008). I will comment later in this reflection on a radical discontinuity between Christ or God as Word and the words we humans produce.

personal—God has something to say to me. If we read Scripture in this way, we read it in the context of prayer; praying before we begin that we would be open to what God may have to say, and praying afterwards that the word we have heard will take root in us.

Moreover, the very method of reading is itself prayerful; it involves a dismantling of ourselves as we make room for God's Spirit to dwell in us. This is to say, *lectio* and similar ways of reading Scripture are very close to prayer itself. Prayer is not a means we have of laying a path to heaven, but the way God has of making a home in us. Prayer involves an opening up of ourselves. When we pray, we open ourselves to God in the realization that, first, God is already there, second, God knows us better than we know ourselves, and third, God has a goal in mind and is transforming us to that end. "When we cry, 'Abba! Father!' it is that very Spirit bearing witness with our spirit that we are children of God" (Rom 8:15–16). Eventually we realize that it is not we who pray, but God's Spirit who prays through us:

> Likewise the Spirit helps us in our weakness; for we do not know how to pray as we ought, but that very Spirit intercedes with sighs too deep for words. And God, who searches the heart, knows what is the mind of the Spirit, because the Spirit intercedes for the saints according to the will of God. (Rom 8:26–27)

When we read the Scriptures prayerfully, we are opening ourselves up to the same dynamic; the dynamism of God breathing through us. We are participating in the life of the Triune God. In doing so, we are joined to the communion of God's people down the ages, for we are asking God to breathe through us as God breathed through those who wrote and compiled the Scriptures.

LEVELS OF READING

The ways of reading Scripture that anticipate God's presence are not the only ways to read it. The Bible is like any other literature in the sense that it can be read on many levels. It can be analysed critically and from that we gain insights, for example, into the history of the texts and the communities for which they were written. What we learn from critical readings may inform prayerful readings. For example, appreciating that the community for which the Gospel of Matthew was written was one struggling with the synagogue can help us draw parallels between the narrative of that community and the narratives of our own lives. Historical insights can render the text all the more pertinent to situations in which we find ourselves. Critical readings are not the same as prayerful readings, but nor are they radically discontinuous with prayerful readings. They are simply on a different level, and it is in the nature of all literature that it can be read on multiple levels.

For example, we can read *The Crucible* and be interested in the composition of the text and the histories behind it—both the Salem witchcraft trials and the McCarthy "witch-hunts." We can engage with it according to its genre as a play to be performed on stage. We can think about how it might have been received by its original audience and by subsequent audiences as directors choose particular moments to restage it. And we can also engage with it at a level where deep speaks to deep: where the human anguish, emotion and dilemmas of the characters in the play touch our innermost souls. Our thoughts regarding those other levels are not irrelevant to this deeper level of reading and may influence it. But nor are they necessary to our being able to read deeply.

The Crucible can be read on many levels because it has been spoken on many levels, and the deepest of those levels is where Arthur Miller opened up his inmost self to communicate truths that we recognize in our inmost selves (whether or not he himself was aware of or intended all that he communicated—that is irrelevant). It is tempting to call deeper levels of reading more "private," but they are not more private. They are just less instantly accessible. They are deeper, but arguably more communal. When we communicate from the depths within us, what we find are truths shared by all of humanity.[2]

The Bible can be read on many levels, like other literature. However, the Bible is unlike other literature in that when we engage it at the depths, we are being engaged in our innermost being not only or primarily by the human author, but by the Author of our being. That God inspires the Scriptures means something so much deeper than an assurance that the human authors got their facts right. And it means something for the present and not only for the past act of writing down. It means that when we read Scripture we can be drawn in to the activity of God. The dynamics are Trinitarian: God is in the speaking, and in the hearing, and

---

2. These two paragraphs are much influenced by Herbert McCabe, OP, *God Matters* (New York: Mowbray, 1987) 172–73.

is that to which the speaking and the hearing point. This is why reading the Bible can have the same dynamic as prayer: God's Spirit within us speaks to God in order to move us closer to God.

AUTHENTICITY

Since prayer is at source an act of God, and on our part an opening up of ourselves to God, honesty is fundamental to it. When there is a lack of honesty in prayer, we feel dissatisfied; we have not really brought ourselves before God, therefore a significant meeting has not really happened. A lack of honesty in the prayerful reading of Scripture is similarly dissatisfying. A number of post-evangelical groups emerged in the 1990s in the United Kingdom, as they did also in the United States. The overriding common feature of these groups was a burning concern for authenticity, having felt that they had lived with a level of dishonesty and disillusionment with quiet-time spirituality. Members of such groups spoke about feeling "like a fraud," or "faking it" when asked to "share" what they had heard God saying to them. Their consequent quest for authenticity was most overtly expressed in the name of the alternative worship community called Be Real, which was attached to St. John's Church in Long Eaton, England.

What happens when we become so frustrated? We have not trusted God's action in our reading of Scripture. We have tried to make the encounter happen. We have tried to build ourselves up, perhaps into the spiritual greats that we think we see in one another. We have tried to lay our path to heaven. We may indeed have striven really hard. Not surprisingly we have got burned out and disillusioned. The effort has been spent in the wrong direction, putting on layer upon layer of spiritual demeanor, rather than peeling back the layers of pretense behind which we protect ourselves. Prayerful reading of Scripture has the dynamics of prayer. Prayer is a peeling back; it is the process of letting God in to forgive and heal us. It is the process of being disarmed by God until we no longer want to pretend and no longer seek to take credit. Indeed, the reason why prayer is necessary for God to act is because all prayer is a surrender of the self and a making room for God.

DO NOT BE ANXIOUS

I have tried to convey how the reading and hearing of Scripture draws us in to relationship with God or, to put it better, draws us into the life of God without recourse to the doctrine of inerrancy. I took leave of that doctrine not only or primarily because I found it unsustainable, but because I found it unimportant. For, within an inerrantist apologetic, God is depicted as backing up the human authors in order to ensure they got their facts right (or some other matter right, depending on what form the particular doctrine of inerrancy is taking), so that when we read the Scriptures we can be sure we have an accurate record for carrying out our scrutiny before we decide to commit to God. This is very different from a theology in which God is continually active, drawing us into the divine life by breathing through the speaking and the hearing and enabling our response.

We sometimes do apologetics as though we have got to get right about Scripture first before we can come to Jesus to have life;[3] as though we have to know that everything the New Testament says about Jesus is accurate before we can have faith in Jesus. If we have got ourselves into this way of thinking, then logically, or epistemologically, Scripture needs to come first; hence all the ink and blood that has been spilt in trying to address seeming inconsistencies in the biblical witness.

And yet, when we read Scripture, and especially when we do so below the surface level of numerical, or geographical, or chronological data, and engage at the depths, we are already participating in the life of God. Reciting the Psalms has formed the daily practice of prayer of Jews and Christians down the centuries. Eventually we realise that we are giving back to God the words God has given us. For the Christian this reaches its zenith when we pray the Lord's Prayer; giving back to God the words that God has given us through the person of Jesus. God is our beginning and our ending; the circle is begun and completed in God.

While an inerrantist fear raises its head and says, how can we know that these words in the prayer Jesus taught us are precisely or adequately close to the ones Jesus used, we can only and happily say, these are the words handed down to us. In our practice, that is sufficient for us: they are words that most of us learn first of all in community before we read

---

3. "You search the scriptures because you think that in them you have eternal life. . . .Yet you refuse to come to me to have life" (John 5:39-40).

them for ourselves off the pages of the Bible. And we can be glad that we have been taught by people who were taught by people who were taught by people . . . who were taught by Jesus. When we do read for ourselves the words of the Lord's Prayer in Scripture, we find that, in whatever version of Scripture we use, they are not exactly the same as the prayer we have learned and ingested. But I have not known this to cause concern. What we have ingested has already taken root in us and brings us life.

FIXED AND UNFIXED MEANING

One advantage that a doctrine of inerrancy might be felt to confer is in fixing the meaning of biblical texts and so avoiding interpretative anarchy. Of course, the doctrine itself does not do this. Ten different interpreters may subscribe to the doctrine of inerrancy and differ in ten ways over how they interpret the text, as we know happens in practice. Yet adherence to inerrancy does incline one towards the prospect of fixing the meaning of texts because it encourages interpreters to place meaning in a particular place, such as in the author's intention. Yet again, the efforts are not successful because authorial intention is elusive. I do not wish here to rehearse the difficulties of fixing meaning. Kevin Vanhoozer has done a good job of debating the multiple issues around this problem.[4] Rather, I would like to end with a few words about why I do not wish to fix meaning and thereby to show where I differ from Vanhoozer.

I share Vanhoozer's Trinitarian conception of biblical writing and reading and also his contentment with "adequate interpretation," which is a middle path between absolute knowledge and interpretative anarchy. I would place adequate interpretation within the context of specific situations so that what a text "means"—its communicative action in relation to us—is context relative: a text can actively communicate quite different things in different settings. This I see as part of God's ongoing agency in respect of Scripture. Herein lies one of my main differences with Vanhoozer and my reluctance to want to fix meaning.

A central question in the metaphysics of meaning is whether meaning needs to be fixed. Do we cease to have meaning if that which we call meaning is not fixed? Vanhoozer accepts Roland Barthes's line that "to refuse to halt meaning is finally to refuse God." I question that. The

4. Vanhoozer, *Is There a Meaning in This Text?*.

refusal to halt meaning can be a matter of humility, an acknowledgement that God cannot be grasped, though it can also be a matter of pride. Vanhoozer voices the justifiable concern that we will not halt meaning when we do not wish to be challenged by the text. But sometimes we halt meaning because we want to use the text in a particular way, perhaps as a rod with which to beat others, and we do not render ourselves open to correction. One folly that is always with us is the folly of making God too small, of thinking we have got our minds around God. Vanhoozer makes himself vulnerable to this folly when he rejects negative theology.[5]

When thinking of the inspiration of Scripture and of all our acts of communicating, it is helpful to follow Vanhoozer, who makes a Platonic link between God and ourselves as communicative agents. But there is also a significant Platonic discontinuity, for only God can *be* Word: "In the beginning was the Word, and the Word was with God and the Word was God" (John 1:1). Only God can be so undivided, so pure, so non-diabolical as actually to be Word. The rest of us are divided, complex creatures whose words, intentions, and actions are not one (for a host of moral, social, and psychological reasons). Our communication is therefore in significant ways not like God's. And Jesus, as Word, chose not to put pen to papyrus so far as we know. He wrote in dust on the ground; his letters were sure to be quickly changed and lost. He wrote nothing down for posterity and instead trusted an unstable process of change, transmission, misunderstanding, and multiple interpretations in the carrying of his message. So I am brought again to reflect on the significance of Christianity not being a religion of the book. In the same vein, I find it skewed when Christians wish to call themselves "Bible Christians," for it is sufficient and theologically correct to be a "Christ Christian," that is, simply a Christian. Ours is the religion of the Word made flesh. With this Vanhoozer would concur, but he then goes further than his theology would seem to require in wanting to fix the meaning of the accompanying text.

The pragmatist Richard Rorty holds that there is nothing deep down inside us except what we have put there ourselves. Vanhoozer, deeply influenced by Augustine, combats this anthropocentric-anarchic outlook with faith in a God who knows us better than we know ourselves. Augustine can say something positive to both Vanhoozer and Rorty about our lack of self-knowledge. Sometimes we do not know what we

---

5. Vanhoozer, *Is There a Meaning in This Text?*, 310.

mean, even as authors, preachers, and speakers. Sometimes we know that we do not know what we mean. Sometimes we are glad that our words have a life beyond what we have given them and that they have been received as bringing life in ways we had not envisaged or intended. What is true of our words is true of the words of Scripture too, in terms of their relation to their human authors. If we try to fix their meaning in the author's intention or at some other point in the writing-reading process, we do not recognize the extent to which God is both sovereign and continually active in communicating to us through the Scriptures.

God is in the speaking and in the reading/hearing and is that to which the speaking and the hearing point. God's presence to us as we read Scripture is really our being brought in to the activity of the Triune God, and—thank God—God will not be bound by any meanings we try to fix.

I opened this reflection with the thought that much of our relationship with God is mediated through Scripture, and I wondered how far this could be explored without reference to the doctrine of inerrancy. At the point I have now reached, I have come to think that belief in inerrancy is irrelevant, and potentially a hindrance, to the life of God in us, or, rather, to us in the life of God.

17

"A Certain Similarity to the Devil"

Historical Criticism and Christian Faith

Gregory Dawes

A T A CERTAIN POINT in the history of European thought, a revolution occurred in the understanding of the Bible. In a move that
was and remains controversial, an increasing number of scholars, both
Jewish and Christian, began interpreting the Scriptures "like any other
book."[1] This is sometimes referred to as the emergence of the "historical-
critical method" of interpretation. It *was* historical in character, insofar as it regarded the Bible as a product of human history rather than
a work transcending history. But it was not so much a new *method* of
interpretation, since historical critics could and did employ a variety of
methods. These differing methods were, in due course, given a variety
of names–such as form criticism and redaction criticism–and there was
a lively debate as to the fruitfulness of each. There was never just one
historical-critical method. What the emergence of historical criticism
signaled was a changed *attitude* towards the Bible. No longer was the
Bible regarded as different in kind from any other book, a work of divine
rather than merely human origin. No longer was it regarded as a reliable

---

1. The phrase is used repeatedly by Benjamin Jowett in his essay, "On the
Interpretation of Scripture," in *Essays and Reviews*, 7th ed. (London: Longman, Green,
1861). This essay was first published in 1860.

source of knowledge on any matters about which it happened to speak.[2] Historical critics now came to regard the Bible as a human work, sharing in the fallibility of all human productions, even while (many believed) it bore witness to a gradual divine revelation.

The last point is an important one. The first historical critics were not, on the whole, skeptics or nonbelievers. They continued to maintain that the Bible contained essential religious truths, revealed by the Spirit of God. The difference was that they no longer took the revelatory character of the Bible for granted. It was something that needed to be demonstrated—and, they believed, something that *could* be demonstrated—from a study of the biblical message. As Benjamin Jowett wrote in *Essays and Reviews* (1860), "when interpreted like any other book, by the same rules of evidence and the same canons of criticism, the Bible will still remain unlike any other book."[3] The difference between their attitude and that of their predecessors is that this uniqueness was now regarded as a contingent fact about the biblical writings, which had to be demonstrated in the process of interpretation. It was, in other words, conceivable the Bible might *not* contain such religious truths; it just happens to be the case, Jowett and others believed, that it did.

One could ask what historical influences led to this changed attitude to the Bible. I have addressed this question elsewhere.[4] The question I wish to address here is a different one: it has to do with what this changed attitude entails. What does a historical attitude to the Bible involve and what implications does it have for Christian faith? Is historical criticism a neutral tool that can be put at the service of traditional Christian belief? Or does it embody assumptions that are somehow antithetical to belief? If the latter is true, can those assumptions be set aside without abandoning historical criticism altogether? How should an orthodox Christian regard the historical criticism of the Bible? Should she avoid it altogether as a danger to her faith? Should she embrace it unconditionally? Or should she employ it only in some carefully modified form?

2. Arthur McCalla, *The Creationist Debate: The Encounter between the Bible and the Historical Mind* (London: Continuum, 2006) 28.

3. Jowett, "On the Interpretation of Scripture," 375.

4. Gregory W. Dawes, *The Historical Jesus Question: The Challenge of History to Biblical Authority* (Louisville: Westminster John Knox, 2001) 1–38. Arthur McCalla's excellent recent study, *The Creationist Debate*, covers some of the same ground, while adding more detail.

All three responses are evident in the history of modern Christian thought. Firstly, rejection: there are many believers (and, for that matter, non-believers) who feel that historical criticism undermines belief. The publication of *Essays and Reviews* caused enormous controversy and many of its first readers felt their faith to be under threat. As one undergraduate at Oxford wrote, upon reading Jowett's essay, "I had always, it seemed, held the same, only without knowing. But at the end of the essay, where was my orthodox Christian faith? Overturned in irretrievable ruin, never to be rebuilt on the old foundations."[5]

In our own day, at least one distinguished biblical scholar, Eta Linnemann, has turned her back on historical criticism. She has come to believe that its assumptions were incompatible with her newly discovered evangelical faith.[6] Linnemann represents an extreme position in this respect, rejecting the historical-critical project in its entirety.[7] Other theological critics are not prepared to go this far: they admit that at least some of the questions asked by historical critics are legitimate. Yet they insist that the Christian can accept historical criticism of the Bible only in some modified form, once it has been "chastened" by its subordination to the demands of faith.[8]

But alongside those theologians who consider historical criticism a danger, there are others who appear to embrace it unconditionally. The Jesuit scholar Joseph Fitzmyer, for instance, accepts that in the hands of many of its practitioners historical criticism has been coupled with presuppositions that are hostile to orthodox belief.[9] But he also argues that these assumptions are a result of the prejudices of the interpreters; they are not inherent in the method. The same methods of criticism, Fitzmyer argues, can be employed with very different assumptions. Catholic exegetes approach the interpretation of a biblical book assuming that it

5. Martin Geldart, cited in Jude V. Nixon, "'Kill[ing] our Souls with Literalism': Reading *Essays and Reviews*," *Religion and the Arts* 5 (2001) 35.

6. Eta Linnemann, *Historical Criticism of the Bible: Methodology or Ideology?— Reflections of a Bultmannian Turned Evangelical*, trans. Robert W. Yarbrough (Grand Rapids: Baker, 1990) 17.

7. Linnemann, *Historical Criticism*, 20.

8. S. A. Cummins , "The Theological Interpretation of Scripture: Recent Contributions by Stephen E. Fowl, Christopher R. Seitz and Francis Watson," *Currents in Biblical Research* 2 (2004) 182, 184.

9. Joseph A. Fitzmyer, "Historical Criticism: Its Role in Biblical Interpretation and Church Life," *Theological Studies* 50 (1989) 252–54.

contains God's Word set forth in human words of long ago; that it has been composed under the guidance of the Spirit and has authority for the people of the Jewish-Christian heritage; that it is part of a restricted collection of sacred, authoritative writings (part of a canon); that it has been given by God to His people for their edification and salvation; and that it is properly expounded only in relation to the Tradition that has grown out of it within the communal faith-life of that people.[10]

Fitzmyer writes as though the presuppositions that matter in this context are the religious (or anti-religious) assumptions that the interpreter brings to his work. These will certainly make a difference to how the methods of historical criticism are used. But one could argue that there are presuppositions inherent in the very use of historical criticism. It is these presuppositions upon which the opponents of historical criticism focus. Fitzmyer, it must be said, fails to examine these presuppositions, remarking only that they are "neutral" with regard to faith.[11]

So who is right, the religious defenders of historical criticism or their theological critics? In an effort to answer this question, I shall reexamine a key essay by the German philosopher and theologian Ernst Troeltsch (1865–1923). In the early twentieth century, Troeltsch was among the best-known defenders of a historical approach to the biblical text. He certainly recognized the theological challenges posed by the historical criticism of the Bible. He himself remarked that "from a strictly orthodox standpoint" historical criticism "seems to bear a certain similarity to the devil."[12] But he also believed that this first impression was deceptive: a historical understanding of the Scriptures was not necessarily a threat to the Christian faith. In the course of his essay "On Historical and Dogmatic Method in Theology," Troeltsch sets out what he sees as the assumptions that underlie a historical understanding of any phenomenon. At least one of these assumptions—that the historian must employ a principle of analogy—has been, to put it mildly, controversial. So Troeltsch's essay has become somthing of a *locus classicus* for this discussion, one that deserves continual rereading. My aim here is to

10. Fitzmyer, "Historical Criticism," 254–55.

11. Fitzmyer, "Historical Criticism," 255.

12. Ernst Troeltsch, "Historical and Dogmatic Method in Theology (1898)," trans.E. Fischoff, rev. W. Bense in *Religion in History—Ernst Troeltsch: Essays*, trans. J. L. Adams and W. F. Bense (Edinburgh: T. & T. Clark, 1991), 16.

re-examine Troeltsch's principles, to see to what extent they are defensible and what implications they might have for the believer.[13]

TROELTSCH'S THREE PRINCIPLES

Troeltsch begins his essay by noting that contemporary theology has not yet come to terms with the implications of the new, historical consciousness of our time. Theologians do grapple with some of the *particular* issues raised by the historical criticism of the Bible. But when they come to treat Christianity in a systematic fashion, Troeltsch writes, they merely seize hold of whatever aspects of modern thought will enable them to shore up "the old, authoritarian concept of revelation."[14] In this way they do manage to create what seems to them "a tolerable dogmatic system," while leaving exegetes and historians to grapple with the strictly historical issues. The problem is that the exegetes and historians fail to deal with the larger theological problems raised by their research. So neither historians nor theologians have yet undertaken a systematic reworking of theology on the basis of our new historical mode of thought.

What is this new mode of thought so characteristic of the modern world? Troeltsch summarizes the historical viewpoint of our time under three principles. The first is the principle of "criticism," which holds that the source materials of the historian's work must be subject to evaluation. What this means is that the historian must take a critical attitude towards his sources, recognizing that they may be mistaken or deceptive. The results of this critical scrutiny can never be more than a matter of probability: we can never enjoy certainty in any assertion that we make about the past. Troeltsch's second principle is that of "analogy." This principle comes into play both in the task of evaluating historical sources and in the task of constructing an account of what actually occurred. In the task of evaluating his sources, the principle of analogy means that a historian should make use of his own experience of the ways in which accounts can become distorted. This can help him to recognize similar distortions in the material we are studying. In constructing his own account, the historian should assess the likelihood that certain events did actually

13. Section 1 of this essay follows closely my treatment of Troeltsch's seminal work in Dawes, *Historical Jesus Question*, 163–64.

14. Troeltsch, "Historical and Dogmatic Method," 12.

occur by the standards of the present.[15] If we regard an event as highly improbable in our own time, then we must also regard it as unlikely that it occurred then. So what the principle of analogy assumes is that all historical occurrences are (in some sense) essentially similar. And this means that the history of early Christianity is comparable to early history of other religious traditions.

In practice, Troeltsch writes, modern theologians do recognize these similarities when dealing with most aspects of the Christian phenomenon. But they make certain key exceptions, in order to maintain what they view as the uniqueness of Christianity. In particular, Troeltsch writes, theologians cease to employ the principle of analogy when dealing with "Jesus' moral character and the resurrection,"[16] both of which they regard as without historical parallel. But a consistently historical approach to the Bible would not allow such exceptions to be made. Even Jesus' moral character and the accounts of what happened after his death must be assessed by reference to similar events and claims in the history of other religions.

The third principle underlying the historical method, Troeltsch argues, is that of "correlation." Correlation suggests that any historical event, however novel, must also be understood as a product of the context in which it occurs. This means, for instance, that the emergence of Christianity cannot be understood without a careful study of "the general political, social, and intellectual history of antiquity."[17] In other words, Christianity may be of divine origin, as in a certain sense even Troeltsch wishes to affirm. But it did not fall from heaven ready-made: it emerged only within a particular historical context and was decisively shaped by that context. It follows that Christianity must be understood as a product of factors such as "the political movements and apocalyptic ideas" of late Second Temple Judaism.[18]

15. Troeltsch, "Historical and Dogmatic Method," 13–14.

16. Troeltsch, "Historical and Dogmatic Method," 14. Troeltsch deals briefly with the resurrection appearances in his work of systematic theology, *The Christian Faith* (1925), trans. G. E. Paul (Minneapolis: Fortress Press, 1991) §18 (219). He expresses a preference for the view that these are explicable psychologically, as "visions" (an idea first put forward in the nineteenth century by D. F. Strauss and popularized in our own time by Gerd Lüdemann). In this way he brings the resurrection *appearances*, at least, under the principle of analogy.

17. Troeltsch, "Historical and Dogmatic Method," 15.

18. Troeltsch, "Historical and Dogmatic Method," 15.

AN EVALUATION

What are we to make of these three principles so briefly described in Troeltsch's essay? Are they defensible as principles of historical research? And what implications do they have for the believer?

The Principle of Criticism

Troeltsch's principle of criticism closely resembles a point made by a later writer about historical method, R. G. Collingwood (1889–1943). In *The Idea of History*, Collingwood criticized what he called "scissors and paste" as opposed to "critical" history writing.[19] It is not enough, he writes, for historians to paste together the material they find in their sources to form a coherent narrative. They need to treat those sources critically. Collingwood's analogy here is that of a detective interviewing witnesses to a crime. A good detective will not simply take at face value what the witnesses are saying, for they may be deceiving or deceived. Even eyewitness testimony, after all, is not always reliable. He must treat the witnesses' testimonies critically, creating his own, plausible narrative, which may not correspond to what any of the witnesses have told him.

A traditional Christian believer may, perhaps, wish to reject this analogy when it comes to the Bible. He may insist that the biblical writers, being inspired by God, could not be deceiving or deceived. They are reliable witnesses. But a distinction is required here. Troeltsch's principle of criticism, interpreted in the light of Collingwood's remarks, does not require the Christian to believe that the biblical writers are deceiving or deceived. All it requires is that we not assume from the outset that they are not. It demands that we approach the question of their reliability with an open mind. If indeed they were inspired by God, then the believer will have nothing to fear from such an openminded examination, for there will be no reason to call their testimony into question. It is true that this spirit of free enquiry is not the way in which Christians have traditionally approached the biblical text. But it does not seem incompatible with a traditional Christian faith. It simply leaves the believer with some work to do if his confidence in the reliability of the biblical testimony is to be justified.

---

19. R. G. Collingwood, *The Idea of History* (1946; repr. Oxford: Oxford University Press, 1961) 257–61, 274–82, etc.

The Principle of Correlation

At least at first sight, there does not seem to be anything incompatible with traditional belief in Troeltsch's second principle, that of correlation. There are features of Troeltsch's discussion that seem questionable. He notes, for instance, that "all historical happening is knit together in a permanent relationship of correlation, inevitably forming a current in which everything is interconnected and each single event is related to all others."[20] But while this may be true, it hardly seems necessary for the historian to understand the interconnection of all events in order to make sense of a particular historical phenomenon.[21] So let me understand Troeltsch's principle of correlation in a more restricted sense. I shall understand it as the claim that all historical events are the products of a particular historical context and can (in principle) be understood by reference to that context. And that entails a further claim: that all historical events are naturally explicable. Applied to Christianity, the principle of correlation suggests that the origins of this particular religious movement, like all others, can be explained by reference to natural causes. Both the Bible itself and the events to which it bears witness can be explained naturally.

In many cases, this will not seem problematic—even to the most traditional of believers. Let me take a famous example, one central to the narrative of the Hebrew Bible. The Babylonian exile of 536 BCE is depicted by the prophets and the editors of the Deuteronomic history as the act by which God punished Israel for its failure to keep the Torah. But the same event is also explicable in geopolitical terms, as the act by which the Babylonians asserted their claim to the land of Canaan over against the rival claims of Egypt. The first explanation is a theological one, but it is compatible with the second, natural explanation. Indeed the prophets themselves seem well aware of the natural causes that brought about the exile: they endorse a natural explanation, even while offering a theological account. Jeremiah, for instance, counsels the king of Judah against his reliance on Egypt and defiance of the Babylonians, seeing the likely consequences of such a policy.

What about the events to which the New Testament bears witness? Can they also be naturally explained without undermining the Christian

---

20. Troeltsch, "Historical and Dogmatic Method," 14.
21. Dawes, *Historical Jesus Question*, 343–44.

faith? In many cases, it seems that they can. To take an example that is central to the New Testament, the execution of Jesus may have been part of God's plan to redeem humanity. But it is also perfectly explicable as a response of the Roman (and perhaps Jewish) authorities to one whom they regarded as a dangerous messianic pretender. Once again, the biblical writers themselves appear to sense no contradiction between a theological and a natural explanation of the events about which they are writing. The author of the Fourth Gospel, for instance, describes what he alleges were the motives of the high priest as he plotted to bring about Jesus' death. This natural explanation seems entirely compatible with the idea that these events occurred as part of a divine plan of salvation.

So at least some of the events to which the Bible bears witness can be naturally explained in ways that are compatible with the Christian faith. But what about the Bible itself? Can its origins be naturally explained without undermining its authority? It is important to note, in this context, that Jews and Christians have always recognized that the biblical books had human authors. (Muslims, by way of contrast, are much less willing to recognize that the Qur'an has a human author.) The words of Saint Paul may have been inspired by God, but they also reflect the thinking of the apostle. And Saint Paul does not deny that these are his words, even if he believes that he speaks with an authority given by God. The Christian theologian might even want to invoke a certain analogy here with what she believes about the incarnation. Just as, in Chalcedonian Christology, Jesus was wholly human as well as wholly divine, so (it might be argued) the Bible is wholly a human work as well as wholly a divine one. Indeed precisely this analogy was appealed to by the Second Vatican Council in its statement on the interpretation of Scripture, *Dei Verbum*. "The words of God," the Council fathers write, "expressed in human language, have been made like human discourse, just as of old the Word of the eternal Father, when He took to Himself the weak flesh of humanity, became like other men."[22]

Yet this very analogy highlights the difficulties inherent in Troeltsch's principle of correlation. For in traditional Christian belief Jesus' origins are not entirely explicable in natural terms since he is believed to have been virginally conceived. It follows that for most Christians, recognition of the full humanity of Jesus does not entail a belief that every aspect

---

22. "Dogmatic Constitution on Divine Revelation" (*Dei Verbum*) ,§13 in *The Documents of Vatican II*, ed. W. M. Abbott (London: G. Chapman, 1966) 121.

of his life can be naturally explained. Is the same true of the Bible? Even if Christians recognize the Bible as in some sense a human work, can they hold that the origins and characteristics of biblical writings can be exhaustively explained without reference to God? It may be that such an idea is not necessarily incompatible with Christian belief, for it is at least possible that those who wrote the Bible were also guided by God. The idea that God works through secondary causes, which are themselves naturally explicable, is hardly a new one. Yet acceptance of this idea does raise two problems: the problem of explanatory redundancy and the problem of miracles.

The Problem of Explanatory Redundancy

The first difficulty can be simply expressed. If we can explain the origins and characteristics of the biblical writings without reference to God, then what reason do we have to speak of a providential divine guidance? Talk of divine action in connection with the Scriptures seems to be redundant. Why is this a problem? Well, it is a problem if one accepts the principle of economy in explanation: that we should posit only those entities that are required for a successful explanation.[23] This principle is often attributed to William of Ockham (1288–1347), being known as "Ockham's razor": the principle that "entities should not be multiplied without necessity." But in fact it long predates Ockham's work, being implicitly acknowledged by Thomas Aquinas (1225–74)[24] and perhaps first enunciated by Aristotle (384–322 BCE).[25] It has played an important role in the practice of the modern sciences, being employed by early scientists such as Galileo Galilei (1564–1642), Isaac Newton (1643–1727), and Antoine Lavoisier (1743–94), and in our own day by no less a figure than Albert Einstein (1879–1955).[26] This principle may or may not be

23. As E. C. Barnes points out, this is best thought of as an "anti-superfluity principle" (ASP), which aims to eliminate *unnecessary* theoretical components, rather than an "anti-quantity principle" (AQP), which seeks to minimize the mere *number* of theoretical components. While AQP entails ASP, they might require a different justification. See E. C. Barnes, "Ockham's Razor and the Anti-Superfluity Principle," *Erkenntnis* 53 (2000) 354.

24. Aquinas, *Summa Theologiae* 1a 2.3.

25. Aristotle, *Posterior Analytics* 1.86a.

26. For a helpful discussion of this principle and its various justifications, see Alan Baker, "Simplicity," in *The Stanford Encyclopedia of Philosophy*, ed. E. N. Zalta (Winter 2004), online: http://plato.stanford.edu/archives/win-2004/entries/simplicity. As Barnes points out, some versions (such as Newton's) are expressions of the "anti-

contestable, but it is not normally part of the dispute between theists and atheists. Many Christian thinkers have accepted it.

Given such a principle, one should not invoke divine agency when reference to human agency is sufficient to explain the phenomenon. If there is no feature of the biblical writings that cannot be explained without reference to divine agency, then a principle of economy in explanation would suggest that we should cease to claim divine inspiration. At least, we should cease to do so unless we have some other reason—one that does not involve an explanatory claim—that can be offered in support of this belief. Christians, it is true, have often claimed to have other reasons for asserting the Bible's divine origin. While John Calvin, for instance, believed there are "external evidences" in support of the divine origin of the Bible, he ultimately considered the "internal testimony" of the Holy Spirit to be decisive.[27] Critics such as David Friedrich Strauss[28] have pointed out that Calvin's appeal to the internal testimony of the Spirit is question-begging: it is viciously circular in its appeal to the authority of Scripture in support of the authority of Scripture. But let me leave that criticism aside here. The fact remains that, given the success of natural explanations of the biblical writings, we would need to find some other reason to affirm that these naturally explicable works are anything more than what they appear to be: yet another collection of ancient writings.

This line of reasoning has an interesting implication. Twentieth-century theologians often wrote against what they called the "God of the gaps": the practice of invoking divine agency to explain some feature of the world for which we do not (yet) have a natural explanation. But if one accepts a principle of explanatory economy, akin to Ockham's razor, then the believer needs to have a gap in the network of natural explanations in order to be justified in speaking about divine action. Such a gap could be a fact that currently lacks an adequate natural explanation, even though such an explanation is at least conceivable.[29] (An example might be the

quantity principle" (AQP) rather than the "anti-superfluity principle" (ASP), but few if any of these thinkers made this distinction. See Barnes, "Ockham's Razor," 355–56.

27. John Calvin, *Institutes of the Christian Religion*, trans. F. L. Battles, LCC 20 (London: SCM, 1961) I vii 4, 78–80.

28. David Friedrich Strauss, *Die christliche Glaubenslehre in ihrer geschichtliche Entwicklung und im Kampfe mit der modernen Wissenschaft dargestellt* (Tübingen: C. F. Osiander, 1840) 1:131–36 (§12).

29. Gregory W. Dawes, *Theism and Explanation*, Routledge Studies in the Philosophy

experiences of the young people in Bosnia-Herzegovina, who since 1981 have reported visions of the Virgin Mary. Aspects of their experiences do seem difficult to explain naturally,[30] although such an explanation is surely conceivable.) Or—perhaps preferably from the believer's point of view—the gap could be a fact for which we cannot conceive that a natural explanation is even possible.[31] (Richard Swinburne, for instance, argues that the existence of both the universe itself and laws of nature are facts of this kind.[32]) But in the absence of any other reason to affirm divine action, a "God of the gaps" is precisely what the theologian needs.

The Problem of Miracles

But the theological problems raised by Troeltsch's principle of correlation do not end here. I have interpreted this principle to entail that all historical events are susceptible to natural explanations. But the Bible itself speaks of events that lack natural causes, namely miracles. In fact, some of these events—in particular the virginal conception and resurrection of Jesus—are events that the New Testament writers regard as foundational to the Christian faith. A thoroughgoing employment of the principle of correlation (as I have interpreted it) would seek to "explain away" these events, assuming that they, too, have natural causes.

As it happens, this assumption is a characteristic feature of the modern sciences and of history. Science and history are both characterized by a "methodological naturalism," an assumption that even if at present we have no natural explanation for some fact, one could in principle be found.[33] I have argued elsewhere that this assumption should be regarded as nothing more than a defeasible presumption. There is no reason, in principle, why the historian or scientist might not suggest a supernatural explanation, if all attempts at natural explanation had failed.[34] It is true that historians and scientists would normally exclude talk of miraculous divine action from their work. But are they necessarily bound to do so?

of Religion (New York: Routledge, 2009) 66–67.

30. René Laurentin and Henri Joyeux, *Scientific and Medical Studies on the Apparitions at Medjugorje*, trans. L. Griffin (Dublin: Veritas, 1987) 35–36.

31. Dawes, *Theism and Explanation*, 67.

32. Richard Swinburne, *The Existence of God*, 2nd ed. (Oxford: Clarendon, 2004) 75, 140–43, 160.

33. Neal C. Gillespie, *Charles Darwin and the Problem of Creation* (Chicago: University of Chicago Press, 1979) 115.

34. Dawes, *Theism and Explanation*, 144–46.

Not even if all attempts at natural explanation have failed and the proposed supernatural explanation meets our usual standards of explanatory adequacy? The issues raised here are complex and relate to matters customarily discussed under the heading of Troeltsch's third principle, that of analogy. So let me approach them by way of a consideration of that principle.

The Principle of Analogy

One reason sometimes given why the historian should not posit a miraculous divine action is that such an action would lack analogy. Let me take an obvious and apparently straightforward example. In every other case of which we are aware, when a person dies, he remains dead. He does not come back to life. So what are we to do, as historians, when faced with a report such as we find in the New Testament regarding the resurrection of Jesus? Our prior experience of the way the world works, it might be argued, makes the antecedent probability of Jesus' return to life exceedingly small.[35] And our prior experience of human credulity in matters religious lends some support to the idea that the reports of his resurrection are mistaken. In any case, the probability that the reports are mistaken will always be greater than the probability that the event occurred. It follows that the historian should not accept such reports.

This is nothing more than a restatement of a famous argument first put forward by David Hume (1711–76). While Hume is remembered primarily as a philosopher, in his own day he was at least equally well known as a historian. And it is a question close to the historian's heart with which he is dealing here: How are we to evaluate reports of what occurred in the past? Hume's argument is of interest to us here because it makes essentially the same point that Troeltsch makes when discussing the principle of analogy. As Troeltsch puts it, "the illusions, distortions, deceptions, myths, and partisanships we see with our own eyes enable us to recognize similar features in the materials of tradition."[36] And it is "agreement with normal, customary, or at least frequently attested happenings and conditions" that renders a historical report probable.[37]

---

35. I appreciate that in Christian belief the resurrection of Jesus is not *merely* a return to life. But it is, nonetheless, a return to life, albeit to a transformed mode of life.

36. Troeltsch, "Historical and Dogmatic Method," 13.

37. Troeltsch, "Historical and Dogmatic Method," 13–14.

But is this correct? I have cited R. G. Collingwood in order to explicate Troeltsch's principle of criticism, but Collingwood famously disagreed with Troeltsch's principle of analogy. He argued that our own, inevitably limited experience of the way the world works should not be used as a basis for assessing the accuracy of historical reports. As he writes, "that the Greeks and Romans exposed their new-born children in order to control the numbers of their population is no less true for being unlike anything that happens in the experience of contributors to the *Cambridge Ancient History*."[38]

It is not clear that Collingwood's example is decisive. It may be true that there is no *precise* parallel to infanticide in the experience of modern historians. But there are sufficient parallels to enable us to see the Greek and Roman reports as credible. We can readily imagine, on the basis of our own experience, the circumstances under which infanticide may be practiced. Indeed loosely analogous decisions (such as those regarding abortion or euthanasia) *do* fall within the experience of at least today's Cambridge historians. In addition to this, Collingwood's remark overlooks the fact that Troeltsch's principle of analogy refers not just to the correspondence of past events with present experience, but also to the correspondence of past events with each other. We certainly have records of infanticide outside of the Greek and Roman world, records that, once again, make the Greek and Roman reports credible.

However, even if Collingwood's example is not a good one, he may still have a point. A better argument against Hume's appeal to past experience (and Troeltsch's appeal to analogy) is offered by the philosopher John Earman. Scientists, he writes, "not uncommonly spend many hours and many dollars searching for events of a type that past experience tells us have never occurred (e.g., proton decay)."[39] If the probability of success were measured by past experience, then it would be zero, which would render this scientific activity entirely irrational. But scientists are rightly unperturbed by the fact that the event they are searching for has never hitherto been witnessed, if they have a promising theory that predicts that this event will at some time occur. As I write, scientists have just switched on the Large Hadron Collider near Geneva, in the hope of discovering, among other things, the Higgs boson. But this is a hitherto

38. Collingwood, *Idea of History*, 240.
39. John Earman, "Bayes, Hume, and Miracles," *Faith and Philosophy* 10 (1993) 297.

undiscovered particle: we have no direct evidence of its existence, which is merely predicted by the standard model of particle physics.

What lesson can we draw from this example, assuming, that is, that these scientists are acting rationally? It seems that we can legitimately posit some hitherto unknown entity or event *if* we have a promising theory that supports this posit. And positing such an entity or event would be acceptable if it represents the best available explanation of the fact to be explained. It follows that the secular historian should have no objection to the theologian positing a divine action, if the theologian can show that such a posit represents the best available explanation, not merely of this event but of a whole range of phenomena. A successful demonstration of this fact would certainly revolutionize the way in which scientists and historians customarily think. It would overturn the naturalistic presumption that underlies much modern science and would pave the way for a scientific demonstration of the truth of religious claims.

Of course, this is precisely what many Christian philosophers have attempted to do. Richard Swinburne, for instance, in a series of publications, has tried to show that the probability of God's existence can be demonstrated in the same manner as any scientific hypothesis.[40] And "intelligent design" theorists, such as Stephen Meyer, have attempted to overturn the methodological naturalism of the modern sciences by showing that the existence of a designer is the best, or perhaps only, explanation of the specified complexity of biological organisms.[41] None of these attempts has been, in my judgment, entirely successful.[42] But there is certainly nothing objectionable about making such an attempt.

40. Swinburne, *Existence of God*.

41. Stephen C. Meyer, "The Return of the God Hypothesis," *Journal of Interdisciplinary Studies* 11 (1999) 1–38. Other intelligent design theorists include William Dembski, from whom comes the phrase "specified complexity," and Michael Behe, who uses the similar phrase "irreducible complexity." But Meyer's work is of particular interest insofar as he presents the design hypothesis as an "inference to the best explanation."

42. For an evaluation of Swinburne's work, see Dawes, *Theism and Explanation*, 102–3, 118–19; for an evaluation of the intelligent design arguments, see Dawes, "What Is Wrong with Intelligent Design?" *International Journal for Philosophy of Religion* 61 (2007) 69–81.

THE DEFENSE OF A GOD HYPOTHESIS

So it does seem that Troeltsch's principle of analogy is problematic. What it overlooks is the possibility of positing a hitherto unknown cause, and demonstrating that this represents the best available explanation of the fact to be explained. It follows that there is no *in-principle* objection to positing even a miraculous divine action[43] if a posit of this kind could be shown to have sufficient explanatory force. If this could be done with regard to a range of phenomena, then theism would represent a successful research tradition of the kind already represented by the natural explanations of modern science.

It is true that this claim is, as philosophers say, a counterfactual: there is, at present, no successful theistic research tradition that is comparable to that of the modern, secular sciences.[44] Indeed, the last four hundred years of human thought have seen a progressive retreat from theological explanation in favor of natural explanations. Nonetheless, it would be a regrettable case of naturalistic prejudice if we were to forbid the Christian historian from attempting to (re-)establish such a tradition by showing that his theistic hypothesis has explanatory power.

But this also imposes a certain obligation on the theologian. Confessions of faith in this context are not sufficient. It is not enough for a Christian historian or theologian to affirm that *because he is a Christian* he should be permitted to invoke divine agency when writing history. Rather, he needs to show that his invocation of divine agency has explanatory power. More precisely, he needs to show that his God hypothesis has some explanatory force: that it would explain the phenomena, if it were true. He also needs to show that it exhibits, to a satisfactory extent and to a greater degree than any competitor, certain explanatory virtues: that it is simpler, more economical and more informative than any competing hypothesis, that it is consistent with the rest of our knowledge and that it has survived independent tests. (Other lists of explanatory virtues are possible, but these particular ones are relatively uncontroversial.) My own view, for which I have argued elsewhere,[45] is that a theistic hypothesis is unlikely to meet these standards. But to say this is not to forbid the theologian from making the attempt.

43. For a fuller discussion of the particular issues involved in positing a miraculous divine action, see Dawes, *Theism and Explanation*, 71–75.

44. Dawes, *Theism and Explanation*, 131–32.

45. Dawes, *Theism and Explanation*, 115–42.

It seems, then, that Troeltsch's principles of criticism and correlation are both defensible and not, in themselves, incompatible with Christian faith. It is true that they leave some work for the theologian to do. He needs to offer some evidence that the biblical writers are reliable witnesses, and he needs to find some fact that would justify talking of divine action in place of offering a natural explanation. But if he can do this, he has nothing to fear from historical criticism. Troeltsch's principle of analogy, on the other hand, seems less defensible, at least in the form in which he articulates it. It overlooks the possibility of positing a hitherto unknown cause and demonstrating this to be the best available explanation of a range of phenomena. Given this possibility, there is no feature of the historical criticism of the Bible that is *necessarily* antagonistic to the Christian faith.

Yet my argument leaves no room for theological complacency. I have argued that the theologian (or Christian historian) is *free* to posit divine action and argue that this is the best available explanation of some phenomenon. But it is far from clear that any theologian could marshal the kind of evidence that would force us to take that claim seriously. For it is not enough, in this context, to rely on confessions of faith or *a priori* commitments to a Christian position. If he wishes his claims to be taken seriously, the theologian needs show that his Christian faith is capable of doing some explanatory work. He needs to show that there is some feature of the biblical writings that requires us to regard them as a divine as well as a human work. And he needs to show that his accounts of divine action, perhaps drawn from the Bible, are in fact the best available explanations of a range of phenomena.

Is this asking too much? Surely not! To make these demands of the theologian or Christian historian is to demand no more than is required by any serious historical or scientific research. There is no substitute for the hard work of offering evidence or constructing arguments. That theologians are now expected to offer such arguments is an indication of the changed status of Christian faith in the modern world. It no longer enjoys the taken-for-granted authority that it once enjoyed in Western culture. It has been reduced to the status of merely one story among others. But surely here there are no legitimate grounds for complaint. And if the Christian story is indeed true, would it not be odd if there existed no evidence in its support?

18

Critical Dislocation and Missional Relocation

Scripture's Evangelical Homecoming

Telford Work

THE CRITICAL BIBLE

I WAS IN MY SECOND year of a master's program at Fuller Seminary. My research project for my Old Testament Theology course was an analysis of Gerhard von Rad's *Old Testament Theology*.[1] I was somewhere in volume 2 when something just snapped. I threw the book across the room in frustration and cursed. I had had enough of German biblical criticism.

On every page were claims that seemed to come out of nowhere. They treated passages and whole books of the Bible in ways I could not predict or verify, according to some kind of esoteric knowledge I had never seen before. *This* passage of Paul's was authentic; *that* was not. One bit of Israelite prophecy came from centuries after the fact, and the one next to it came from generations later. I think what frustrated me most was the *attitude*. These claims were all made with such serene confidence

---

1. Gerhard von Rad, *Old Testament Theology*, 2 vols. (Louisville: Westminster John Knox, 2001).

371

that they sounded unassailable. Yet they turned the Bible into something shockingly unlike what I had always taken it to be.

Was this just a passing storm during my seminary years? Not exactly. My faith did survive those trials, and today I have the truly delightful job of teaching the Christian faith to hundreds of wonderful undergraduates every year. Moreover, many of the claims of biblical criticism no longer trouble me. Sometimes this is because I accept them as unproblematic; sometimes it is because I reject them as disproven, unlikely, or overly speculative; sometimes it is because they seem irrelevant. Yet my years in the academy have impressed upon me a stubborn picture of Holy Scripture that is at least somewhat alien to the historic Christian faith and even more alien to most of my fellow believers. And while I do love the Bible and regard the improved understanding as a genuine blessing, my grad school legacy is still a mixed one. My exposure to biblical criticism subdued the enthusiasm that had brought me to seminary in the first place and has left me more distanced from Scripture's voice than I had been or needed to be. And I have colleagues whose ministries and even faith did not survive their exposure to biblical criticism. Their stories still weigh on me.

Some readers will take liberal theology as the villain here and conservative apologetics the hero who unfortunately arrived too late to save me. However, I was already well versed in conservative evangelical apologetics, having found people from Cliff Kenechtle to Josh McDowell to C. S. Lewis exceedingly helpful in breaking through my late adolescent skepticism and protecting my maturing evangelical faith. Some other readers will see shoddy conservative evangelicalism as the villain, or at least the dupe, and liberal theology the emancipator of my reason and my intellectual authenticity. However, I was raised on liberal theology, and I have never found reason to alter my early impressions that contemporary liberal Christianity is anemic, ideologically in-grown, and intellectually hollow. This story does not follow the usual scripts.

What role, then, does my exposure to German biblical criticism play in my story? It is neither villain nor hero, but only an especially heavy straw on this camel's back. Under it were already many others. Or, to change metaphors, biblical criticism is like an old schoolmate of my wife's who shows up with friends at a school reunion. As they exchange stories about her, a past opens up that I had sometimes heard about but never taken seriously. And as I listen, the one I live with and thought I knew suddenly seems like a stranger. It's quiet as we drive home and get ready for bed, my mind tired and racing with unwelcome thoughts.

A lone voice would not have had the same effect on me. So who are those other friends of his?

Well, since early adolescence I had absorbed our culture's folk skepticism about the Bible, repeating the usual canards that it is the product of a backward ancient culture, that it is just "a translation of a translation of a translation," and that "you can make the Bible say anything" anyway. In a high school "great books" course I had read passages in Genesis and Matthew not as holy writ but as literary foundations of Western culture. And I had long placed the Bible mentally alongside the canons of other world religions, from Mormonism to Islam, relativizing all of them as rival scriptures.

The legacy of the Enlightenment is peeking through here. Yet many of the forces shaping my relativism and skepticism are older. The conviction that one can make the Bible say anything arises out of the bitter experience of a whole Western world seeming to do just that in the Reformation, not disingenuously but in full conviction. It is tempting to climb above the fray with skeptics and sociologists of "religion," declare the whole game to be about something else than the players themselves think, and treat the Bible as other than what Christians believe.

Other factors are older than Protestantism. The Reformation did not explode out of nothing, but reflected pent-up frustrations with medieval biblical interpretations that found obscure meanings (or imposed unpersuasive theological interpretations) on the texts. Clear and intuitive senses of Scripture might have been widely available through iconography, hymnody, and other liturgical channels, but other senses were within reach of ecclesiastical experts alone. Technical, mystical, and simply implausible exegesis—some dating all the way back to the patristic and subapostolic eras—had already distanced common European Christians from the Bible enough to precipitate radical fourteenth-century reactions from the likes of Wycliffe and Hus. Now a new set of experts was making surprisingly similar arguments that the Bible was something other than a collection of texts whose meanings were intuitively clear.

Yet these experts, in every era from the apostles' to von Rad's, were reacting to genuine ambiguities, complexities, contradictions, and mysteries in the texts that could not be dispelled by assertions that the Bible was perspicuous (an obscure word ironically meaning "clear").

These were among the burdens I was already carrying when I enrolled in seminary, the voices that seemed to give my wife's old acquaintances so much sudden credibility.

CONTESTED BIBLES

The "critical Bible," so to speak, that these voices narrate contrasts with another picture I will call the "ecclesial." This is my wife as my friends and I know her, the Bible whose life is the life of our churches. For all the distinctions between Roman Catholic ecclesial Bibles, Lutheran ecclesial Bibles, and all the others, in each of these locations the Bible is at home. I have been a part of an Episcopal church, several Presbyterian churches, a Congregational church, a Willow Creek-inspired nondenominational church plant, a Foursquare Pentecostal church, a Covenant church, and a Baptist church. Some embraced inerrancy, some infallibility, some neither, but each one's ecclesial Bible seemed to live more or less unproblematically at or near the center of its life and worship.

In such places, the Bible was and is *holy* scripture: sharing somehow in God's strange sanctity and sharing its holiness graciously with us. It was and is *powerful*: it operates in ways so manifold that none of our traditions has fully articulated the scope of its work, not merely as words but in the Spirit (cf. 1 Thess 1:5). It was and is *ours*: not as a possession, let alone a monopoly, but as formally and supernaturally directed to all who assemble in Christ's name.

These two pictures of the Bible are not held apart by details such as positions on the authorship of the Pentateuch or the authenticity of 2 Peter. Both the critical and the ecclesial picture can accommodate any number of positions on those questions. But the two remain distinct, and what distinguishes them above all is the stance of the reader, who reads each from very different stances for very different purposes. The critical Bible is scrutinized and judged, however respectfully; the ecclesial Bible is received and heard, however interactively.

The critical Bible has long weighed on many ecclesial Bible readers. It weighed on me before and after my conversion in college to conservative inerrantist evangelicalism. It still weighed on me when I temporarily traded biblical inerrancy for biblical infallibility while at Fuller Seminary and Duke University.[2] Yet it was not some Enlightenment skeptic or partisan Protestant or medieval allegorist who got to me; it was von Rad. And it is von Rad's guild of modern biblical scholars that seems to get to so many other seminary students. I never hurled assigned readings from systematic theologians, philosophers, apologists, or historians; after all, however much their arguments might have disturbed me, they always stood further removed from the holy book at the heart of the apostolic tradition. None haunt students' imaginations the way historical critics do.

Alasdair MacIntyre and Michael Polanyi show that rationality is constituted within traditions. The Bible is ecclesial shorthand for a set of traditions—"the set of canonical textual, oral, practical practices created by and constitutive of the community of God's chosen people."[3] Yet the term's simplicity is deceiving. The Bible is also what Walter Bryce Gallie called an "essentially contested concept."[4] We manage to use the word in conversation with others who still radically disagree with us because both our agreements and our disagreements go to the core of what the Bible is and how it works.

The Bible's essentially contested character is especially visible in the contemporary academy. Consider its places in the fields of literature, philosophy, history, gender studies, biology, sociology, comparative religion, psychology, and physics! All these "Bibles" and more intersect at the crossroads of contemporary biblical studies.

Academic biblical scholarship has accumulated a considerable list of achievements. However, both it and its disciplinary sibling, academic theology, have done so at a growing distance from the *specific* traditions that have been the Bible in the lives of Christian churches. These academic disciplines have in effect become traditions of their own in which the Bible lives differently than "at home," so to speak, in its original communities of faith.

2. This was in part due to my disappointment with accounts of biblical inerrancy such as Norman L. Geisler's edited volume *Inerrancy* (Grand Rapids: Zondervan, 1980).

3. Telford Work, *Living and Active: Scripture in the Economy of Salvation* (Grand Rapids: Eerdmans, 2002) 319.

4. See W. B. Gallie, "Essentially Contested Concepts," *Proceedings of the Aristotelian Society* 56 (1956) 167–98.

I am not at all against the critical stance as such. It has yielded in-valuable knowledge about God and God's people that can serve Christ's mission and church. We have nothing to fear from honest, accurate in-vestigation. Students and leaders should learn everything from original languages to basic exegesis to historical background to the histories of the biblical texts. However, we cannot go on living with the dissonance between these two stances. We need to turn these two different pictures back plausibly into one. We need to learn and pass along the skills and findings of biblical scholarship in ways that are not a burden on the faithful. Indeed, critical reading of the Bible should be a tradition that invigorates and strengthens ecclesial reading and vice versa. Relocating biblical scholarship in the missional life of the church that is the Bible's home promises to strengthen the church's own doctrines of Scripture as well as offer a congenial setting for fruitful biblical scholarship. After all, if Jesus really is Lord of all, then each stance ought to express and serve, or at least respect the primacy of, the mission out of which the Bible emerged in the first place. A school reunion ought to be fun.

TRADITION AS REVOLUTION AND REACTION

John O'Keefe and R. R. Reno show that the theological academy treats the Christian Bible at a similar distance from its first generations of readers:

> We tend to think that the Bible is important because of the x that it represents: historical events, ancient religious sensibilities, ideas, doctrines, and so forth. For this reason, we adopt disci-plines that help us get from Scripture to the x. For example, if we think that the book of Leviticus represents the taboo system of ancient Israelite religion, then we might use a sociological theory of taboo to organize our reading of the text. We discipline our reading in order to bring out what we imagine to be the proper subject matter of the text. The same holds if we are convinced that the gospel of Luke reveals the truth about Jesus Christ as a report on the events that occurred. We then adopt historical methods to weigh the evidence that the story represents, trying to bring what actually happened into focus by screening out the obvious ways in which the author's faith colors the telling of the story. In each instance, the exegetical discipline flows from a

perceived need to focus and concentrate attention on the subject matter of the text . . .

For the fathers, the scripture text itself is the subject matter of interpretation; it is not the means to that subject matter. . . . The scriptures are the *x*, and the interpreter's job is to adopt the disciplines and methods suitable to drawing ever closer to the "language of God," for the mind that conforms to the specificity of the scriptures is shaped in a divine fashion. To think in and through the scriptures is to have a sanctified vision.[5]

Much critical interpretation has aimed at getting something *out* of the Bible like ore from a mine. The ore is then delivered to others—theologians, preachers, philosophers, and ethicists—to refine.

This approach seems to have been pioneered in the church rather than the academy—not least in Martin Luther, who found the Bible's power to lie in the law and gospel it *contains* rather in the canon as such. It is probably not coincidental that the research university was born among Germans, who had acquired habits of scrutinizing the Scriptures for the treasures that lay within. Even so, and with all due respect to Luther's faith and devotion to the Scriptures, the Bible is not a mine. It is communication that arises from the people of God being the people of God. It so profoundly represents them that when we practice it—all of it—then we are practicing being God's people, and through God's grace that is who we become. By contrast, judging and mining both turn the Bible into something else, and they turn both the judge and the miner into someone else.[6]

David Kelsey's analysis of modern Christian theological education describes a similar irreducible tension between two dominant traditional models of the Christian theological school. The first is education as *paideia* that emphasizes moral training in order "to know God by *gnosis*, an immediate intellectual intuition."[7] It aims at a better understanding of God through the divinely assisted conversion of the

5. J. O'Keefe and R. R. Reno, *Sanctified Vision: An Introduction to Early Christian Interpretation of the Bible* (Baltimore: Johns Hopkins University Press, 2005) 116.

6. In *After Virtue* (Notre Dame, IL: Notre Dame University Press, 1984), Alasdair MacIntyre makes the similar complaint that modern ethicists have used prooftexts and technical terms of classical ethics selectively, from a great conceptual distance, and without a real understanding of the roles they played in their original worlds.

7. David Kelsey, *To Understand God Truly: What's Theological about a Theological School* (Louisville, KY Westminster, 1992) 72.

learner through exposure to publicly available material. It conceives of the teacher as "midwife" (since knowledge of God cannot be given directly), and focuses on the student as personally shaped by the subject. Following Werner Jaeger, Kelsey claims that *paideia* was the original model for excellence in schooling, and the most influential one from the patristic age through the Renaissance and Reformation.[8] The second model is education according to the agenda of the modern European research university, emphasizing *Wissenschaft* or orderly and disciplined critical research.[9] Faculty produce professionals who are taught critical historical research methods and trained in the scientific use of reason as the final arbiter of all questions about truth. These disciples then join their *Doktorvatern*—their academic parents—in the shared enterprise of original research protected by traditions of academic freedom, which subject all other authorities to reason.[10] The goal is transformation of the character "upon the basis of the unity of human civilization and scientific work, the unity based on the modern ideal of humanity."[11]

Kelsey sees theological education as shifting from "Athens" toward "Berlin," rather as O'Keefe and Reno see the Bible's contemporary readers engaged in fundamentally different pursuits than the Bible's original readers. And he reports that theological educators live in some confusion over whether and how we can arrive at Athens's conclusions through Berlin's techniques. Our theological schools' curricula generally center on teaching material content (what O'Keefe and Reno would call "an *x*" that stands in for Kelsey's "Athens" but is really one sector of "Berlin"—biblical, historical, theological, and practical information that emerges from assured results of scientific research) and then interpretive techniques (Berlin's various ways toward that *x*). What's wrong with that? It still treats the Bible as a repository of some "content" that is distinguishable from the Bible itself and recoverable through scientific methods. It treats biblical writings as something other than subapostolic readers and even the New Testament writers did, so it imposes a distance between the holy Bible and its true ecclesial context.

---

8. Kelsey, *To Understand God Truly*, 72–75.

9. Kelsey, *To Understand God Truly*, 83.

10. Kelsey, *To Understand God Truly*, 78–81.

11. Friedrich Paulsen, quoted in Kelsey, *To Understand God Truly*, 81; see T. Work, "Education as Mission: The Course as Sign of the Kingdom," *Journal of Education and Christian Belief* 11 (2007) 35–47.

By relying on modern academies for pastors' formative theological education and professional knowledge base, we train leaders to prefer academic biblical traditions to ecclesial biblical traditions. These efforts amount to catechizing them in still another confession and culture that asserts primacy over all others. We take some of our churches' most promising Athenians and tell them that faith only happens in German. Our churches *have* found uses for all the ore that critics produce and academics refine. However, many of those uses distort both the Bible's voices and our churches' life.

For instance, we are already divided confessionally and we are increasingly marginal culturally, so our various camps are protective of our past exegetical judgments. Defensive situations like these tempt us either to give in to anti-intellectualism or to "play it safe" with scholarship, using academic theology and hermeneutical technique to reproduce predictable moral, experiential, or theological results that are congenial to our traditions. William F. Abraham argues that over the centuries the desire to justify doctrinal positions over against other positions has driven Christian communities to treating their canons, including the canon of Scripture, "epistemologically"—as mere means and objects of rational justification. They no longer function as canons in the earlier and proper sense, but as mines from which we extract the materials we want to defend ourselves.[12] So, across our confessions and all along our modern liberal-to-conservative ideological spectrum, our supposedly ecclesial Bibles are actually quite critical and reactionary. We use them for our own maintenance, replication, and protection.

Meanwhile, the incentive structures of the research university system reinforce a culture in academic theology and biblical studies of what Peter Berger calls "the heretical imperative."[13] It fosters the academy's familiar proliferation of new proposals, idiosyncratic syntheses, and fashionably revisionist readings. These in turn raise armies of traditionalists to respond to the latest controversies. Reactionaries and revolutionaries have thus become cottage industries that depend on one another's provocations as much as their own constituencies.

12. William F. Abraham, *Canon and Criterion in Christian Theology: From the Fathers to Feminism* (New York: Clarendon, 1998).

13. See Peter L. Berger, *The Heretical Imperative: Contemporary Possibilities of Religious Affirmation* (New York: Doubleday, 1979).

As a frustrated student, I think I was reacting more to the debilitating social dynamics of this endless cycle as to von Rad's actual argument—to the overall context rather than just the specific text. These dynamics have confused, isolated, and demoralized our churches and the church leaders that the Christian academy trains. Moreover, they have distorted and degraded the Bible in both ecclesial and academic settings.

This is what we have inherited, and what has shaped us into who we are, so it can seem impossible to imagine any other way. Yet there is one, and always has been.

TRADITION AS APOSTLESHIP

Heretical imperatives and rearguard reactionism distract us from apostolic mission. The letters and gospels of the New Testament are the fruit of such mission and only explicable as such. So if we want to recover a healthy and true appreciation of the Bible, reviewing the mission of Jesus' apostles is a good place to start.

In an age when our instincts have been formed so profoundly by critical biblical scholarship, it is worth mentioning what the New Testament writings are not, in order to get a better idea of what they are. They are not an authorized history of Jesus and his movement. They are not a recipe or instruction manual of directions on how to be the church. They are not minutes of executive meetings or canons of councils. They are not a prayer book or hymnal. Instead, they are a *collection*, and a rather haphazard one at that. The New Testament collects writings that arose from the church of Jesus Christ *being* the church, in some of the crucial ways that reflect just how it *was* that church.

Namely: in a short while after its founder's departure, Jesus' church was a network of small communities that had sprung up in towns across the eastern Roman Empire. This happened because disciples and leaders had quite consciously brought Jesus' good news there. The apostles whom Jesus had designated were key figures in this network, both as the missionaries who fostered new churches and as the guardians of Jesus' traditions who catechized and oversaw them.

We have the letters of the New Testament because of the ways these figures and communities communicated and because audiences prized these communications and held onto them, copied them, and distributed them around their far-flung network. We also have four stories of Jesus, which most likely arose within this apostolic network as his eyewitnesses preserved the most significant details of his life and teaching to aid the church's mission and catechesis.[14] The book of Acts straddles and organically connects these two eras and families of writings. It is significant that the New Testament writings that remained longest at the canon's margin, Hebrews and Revelation, also departed the most from these two. Yet Acts shows that they too represent common Christian activities from the church's first generation: preaching and prophecy. Only by being the church in these ways could the New Testament's writers, readers, and collectors have brought anything like it into being. Only the apostolic mission, lived out imperfectly but faithfully, explains it.

And what about the Old Testament? The Scriptures of Israel that become the church's Old Testament resemble these writings even while they reflect different moments in the life of God's people. The Gospels' predecessors are the histories in the Torah, Joshua-Kings, Chronicles, and a few others that recount the story of God's people in ways that remind them mainly of God's steadfastness and their own stubborn rebelliousness. The Prophets reveal the terrible and wonderful apocalyptic outcomes of that collision, in order to kindle repentance and hope in Israel's hardened heart. And, like the New Testament letters, the Torah's rules and the Writings' wisdom literature pass along the traditions that maintain Israel's identity over all those troubled generations and beyond. The apostolic mission is the Messiah's eschatological extension and fulfillment of *Israel's* mission, which alone accounts for the existence and content of the Old Testament. Israel's Scriptures arise as Israel becomes aware of what God has been making it. The process is itself a compelling argument for each testament's divine inspiration. "Who knew the Lord's mind?" (Isa 40:13 LXX, in Rom 11:34).

So: mission, church life, preaching, prophecy, all focused on Jesus as Israel's Christ and the church's past, present, and eternal Lord—all these activities were the lifeblood of the church that generated and kept the canonical writings by which we know we remain in it and in him.[15] They

14. Richard Bauckham, ed., *The Gospels for All Christians: Rethinking the Gospel Audiences* (Grand Rapids: Eerdmans, 1997); idem, *Jesus and the Eyewitnesses: The Gospels as Eyewitness Testimony* (Grand Rapids: Eerdmans, 2008).

15. I am often struck by how new this information is to many of my students. They regard the Bible devotionally, or critically, but not really ecclesially or missionally. It comes as something of a revelation for them to see what the composition and content

remain so today. "The ecclesial Bible" is demonstrably primary because the Bible's ecclesial setting is the context from which the Bible arose and in which it lived and lives; and any "critical Bible" that abstracts the Bible from its ecclesial settings has already unmoored it and artificially distanced it from the context in which it makes sense. Restoring the church's appreciation of Scripture to health involves reintroducing and reconciling it to its own ecclesial Bible—and to the sovereign, advocating Holy Spirit who is ultimately responsible for it.

THE BIBLE AT HOME

From Israel's beginnings through the career of its messiah to the past and present life of the church, God's people are distinguished by their dependence upon the grace of the Holy Spirit. Their being, life, purposes, gifts, and fruitful work are the Spirit's work and must be understood as such. As Israel's Scriptures are Israel being the people of God in its origins, memory, and life, so the New Testament is the apostolic church being the church of Jesus Christ in its own commissioned witness and life. While the church's rhetoric and reasoning drew from Jewish and Greco-Roman structures of its day, its true power lies not in those cultural and epistemological powers and principalities of the present age but in the missional power of the Spirit.

So far we have concentrated on problems. What might evangelical faith look like when it honors and rehabilitates classic evangelical convictions, centers in the Bible's true ecclesial context, and obeys the Spirit's missional power rather than the destructive dynamics of our age? The following sketch is not of an idealized "dream church" or future Christianity, but of a present reality. It draws on churches and believers I already know, doing what they do (sometimes unreflectively) with the Bible as they follow Jesus in word and deed. In fact, it describes the tradition that had shaped me well enough to make my seminary immersion in criticism so discouraging.

---

of the Bible actually is and what this suggests about the Bible's origins and character.

INERRANCY AS TRUTHFULNESS

Ecclesially rather than critically focused evangelical faith knows the Bible to be *true*, and *worthy* of its trust. After all, the Bible *is* true: Jesus trusted the Scriptures of Israel, though he did not always trust his contemporaries to interpret it correctly. Indeed, like nothing else, his life, death, and resurrection fulfilled them in plain as well as subtle ways. Jesus' followers stayed true to his traditions, conveying eyewitness testimonies in their lives and ministries and eventually in written accounts, and testifying to him in their work and worship. We see all this in writings that follow the oral and literary habits of their day. They do not always resemble ours, but they do not compromise the integrity or clarity or power of their apostolic tradition, and they honor the indwelling Spirit who was working and speaking through them. So the Bible gives a clear picture of the fundamental shape of Christian knowledge and faithfulness. We stand under every book and every verse because we stand in the holy tradition that it norms.

Awareness of the Bible's truthfulness animates many a church and many a disciple I know. It also moves beyond the classic understanding of biblical inerrancy. A weakness of that doctrine is that it opposes a flawed critical stance with what is another essentially critical stance. It thus concedes too much to the errantists it opposes. Modernist biblical critics have been guilty of two errors: reducing the Bible's value to modern epistemological categories of factuality and judging it to have fallen short there. Fundamentalists have addressed the latter shortcoming in a way that tends to reinforce the former one, abstracting the concept of Scripture from the Bible's many useful and colorful forms of discourse.[16]

Disciples who really know the Bible's truthfulness will be less interested in battles over accuracy—"Is this detail really right?" or "What really happened?" or "What explains this passage?"—and more willing to take the writers on their own terms: "What is this writer saying?"

---

16. Inerrancy can also lead to a distorted picture of divine action, by either refocusing God's power on making the Bible true through inspiration and keeping the text intact through providential preservation, or by divorcing the Bible's textuality from God's supernatural power in ways that leave believers vulnerable to spiritualism and liberalism. Strategies like these tend to pull churches into the orbits of liberal and conservative critical Bibles and the epistemologies that created them rather than the other way around in which the church, displaying the kingdom of God in its life, words and deeds like light shining in darkness, shows its Lord to the world.

Evangelical theologians who treat the Bible as truthful rather than simply accurate will be less prone to continue treating the Bible *merely* as Charles Hodge's "storehouse of facts"—as a collection of propositions for them to isolate and string together into theological generalizations, then arrange into theological systems.[17] Since these systems often just reproduce the arrangers' own assumptions, when they invariably clash with one another they perpetuate the cycle of critical reaction and revolution so debilitating to our institutions and imaginations.[18] They also take on a rather sterile tone that many fellow evangelicals have long found off-putting and alienating. Regarding the Bible as truthful and transformative rather than merely accurate and informative will yield different kinds of theological readings that will shape a different kind of debate than the battles so familiar to evangelical theology. Its different hermeneutics will lead readers to make more appropriate inferences and ask better questions, shaping theologies that describe the apostolic faith less artificially. It will help readers appreciate the humanity and cultures of the biblical writers less as problems and more as something we share with them as common objects of God's justifying and sanctifying grace.[19] Kevin Vanhoozer is one of the evangelical theologians whose work respects the Scriptures in these ways.[20]

Readers who treat the Bible as wholly truthful rather than merely accurate will be less troubled by the biblical oddities that drive liberals to artificial demythologization and arrogant dismissal and conservatives to strained apologetics. Indeed, as experience gives them a sense of the whole of the Bible's riches, they will rejoice in these oddities as in the quirks of a beloved and respected family member. They can also come to appreciate that quirkiness is an aspect of the human condition that they

17. This is not to imply that propositional claims and inferences, which are among the many legitimate uses of language, are inappropriate to theology! They have always been necessary aspects of articulating the gospel and its implications—just not in the ways they came to dominate and be understood in much of the modern era.

18. This common (though not ubiquitous) structural feature in evangelical theological proposals can be identified by examining, for instance, the various positions catalogued in Gregory A. Boyd and Paul R. Eddy, *Across the Spectrum: Understanding Issues in Evangelical Theology*, 2nd ed. (Grand Rapids: Baker, 2009).

19. I have tried to develop an account of Scripture that respects these aspects of its character and life. See Work, *Living and Active*.

20. See Kevin Vanhoozer, *The Drama of Doctrine: A Canonical Linguistic Approach to Christian Theology* (Philadelphia: Westminster, 2005).

themselves share; it is not something to be excised or even bracketed, only disciplined by God's reign. They will treat the cultural distances between biblical writers and themselves more as liturgists and cross-cultural missionary Bible translators do: not as insurmountable ditches or irreversible restoration and modernization projects, but as messages that apply in all local contexts, though requiring careful attention to each of those contexts when being communicated, because the church of Jesus Christ is an eschatological work of God that transcends and connects those contexts without eradicating them.

The Spirit's truthfulness is more profound and more penetrating than mere freedom from error. After all, accuracy alone is no guarantee of reliability. Adam's protest to God that "the woman you gave me—she gave me of the tree, and I ate" (Gen 3:12) is both a string of technically accurate statements and a monstrously sinful abuse of language that cannot be called true without doing violence to the term. It is a world away from the *honesty* that the Spirit has inspired in the Bible's voices. Israel's extraordinary self-criticism in the Old Testament and the disciples' New Testament counterpart are wonders of supernatural truth-telling whose candor sometimes even discomforts the pious. The gift of the Spirit has given God's prophets and apostles an *awareness* borne of divine revelation that knows what no logic itself can deduce and no intuition can anticipate.

As it sinks into our own consciousness, the Spirit cultivates biblical honesty and self-awareness in ourselves. This comes not by putting biblical language on a modern pedestal of inerrancy or putting ourselves on a critical pedestal of modern superiority, but by identifying *with* the canonical writings: its Spirit and Lord as ours, its figures as our progenitors, its legacy as our inheritance, and its good news as addressed to our needy souls. The Bible is unique in its canonicity and its place in the church's life; however, that does not distance it from us and turn it into some esoteric or exotic thing. Quite the opposite! This is what it means that the Holy Spirit has come alongside us all as our advocate, judge, and Lord. This is the grace of God that lets unworthies like us benefit from God's magnificent work of redemption and even share in that work as Christ's representatives.

Inerrancy sought to defend the Bible's integrity against liberal assumptions that its observations were so deeply conditioned by the limited cultural horizons of its original audiences that recovering its truth required radical criticism, retranslation, and even theological revision. This depended on the classic theological claim of the Scriptures' inspiration, while moving in a somewhat different direction from John Calvin's doctrine that God accommodates his word adequately to limited human categories and mysteriously illuminates human understanding.[21] Each of these three approaches—accommodation, revision, and inerrancy— has its strengths; yet none adequately honors the redemptive logic of God's engagement with human life in the word of truth. In *The Open Secret*, Lesslie Newbigin describes this as a three-way exchange between the acculturated missionary, the cultural mission field, and Scripture.[22] As they interact, all three are susceptible to the kingdom's transformation as the Spirit guides the Son's disciples into all the truth, showing the church and ultimately the world that all the Father has belongs to the Son (John 16:12–15). The Spirit's power converts both the gospel's herald and its audience to bigger and better visions of God and God's new creation that show Scripture in their new light (1 Thess 1).[23] God does not merely accommodate or yield to human limitation, nor does God surpass it. Instead God engages it, judges its sin, affirms its original goodness, and transforms it into the likeness of the risen Son. As the faith spreads across the world, the Bible is becoming a shared heritage of redeemed peoples: a Spirit-authored universal memory of God's fulfilled promises to save us and make us one body though the cross. In the end, a better category for honoring the particular and universal humanity of Scripture's words from and to our Lord might be *catholicity*. No critic or civilization stands above it or outside its scope.

Have you seen the Bible's catholicity at work in churches, families, and ministries? I have.[24] What distinguishes these contexts from poorer ones is the assumption of the common ecclesiality of the Bible's original

---

21. Kenton L. Sparks, *God's Word in Human Words: An Evangelical Appropriation of Critical Biblical Scholarship* (Grand Rapids: Baker, 2008), 230–47.

22. Lesslie Newbigin, *The Open Secret: An Introduction to the Theology of Mission*, rev. ed. (Grand Rapids: Eerdmans, 1995).

23. Telford Work, "Converting God's Friends: From Jonah to Jesus," *Word & World* 27 (2007) 165–73.

24. Often these communities still claim biblical inerrancy. Inerrancy as a doctrine does not need to be abandoned. Compare Work, *Living and Active*, 318–19. My own college and many of my past and present churches have embraced it and even benefited from it. However, how it *functions* in these healthy communities tends to be determined more by these sorts of ecclesiological qualities than by strictly philosophical ones.

communities and its current ones. The Bible is truly at home in every church that knows it shares essentially the same ecclesial setting as audiences in other times and places, including the Bible's original ones.

BIBLICAL INFALLIBILITY AS TRUSTWORTHINESS

Truthfulness is an inherently personal quality. A watch may be accurate, but it is not truthful. So we respond to the Bible's equally personal discourse not with mere recognition or assent but with suspicion or trust, resistance or reliance, doubt or assurance. This response brings up another honored evangelical conviction, a corollary of inerrancy (and sometimes an alternative to it): the evangelical doctrine of biblical infallibility. Infallibility holds that the Bible cannot fail or mislead its readers, particularly in the matters of faith and practice that are its focus.

Infallibility guards against the stance of critical suspicion and even skepticism that characterizes much mainstream biblical scholarship. Yet, like inerrancy, it begs bad questions. Defenders end up debating alleged failures on the part of biblical writers. Is Paul sexist? Are the psalmists triumphalists? Is the Fourth Evangelist anti-Semitic? If so, are these failings really incidental to the faith and practice they are teaching? The doctrine of infallibility thus turns readers into evaluators—in this case, juries of the apostles' and prophets' character—and trains us to hear the writers' voices only against the backdrop of some other moral standard to which they should measure up. That moral standard, which is invariably our own, then becomes the real canon of infallibilists and their opponents.

Like inerrancy, infallibility casts our accounts of the Bible's truthfulness in modern terms of radical certainty over against radical doubt.[25] Either the Bible is infallible or it is not; and what if it is not? Some fundamentalist churches argue in just this way—"if this or that detail isn't accurate, then why believe the Bible on anything else, such as Jesus' divinity or resurrection?"—in effect holding their congregations' respect for the Bible hostage to their fear of abandoning their core convictions. If we become convinced that the Bible is errant or fallible, then we are left seeking some other source that is not, or else left in a sea of uncertainty

---

25. Lesslie Newbigin, *Proper Confidence: Faith, Doubt, and Certainty in Christian Discipleship* (Grand Rapids: Eerdmans, 1995).

and relativism. We have departed from the Christian way of knowing and turned the Bible into something it is not.

A better framework for situating readers in the apostolic tradition is simply to honor, in word and deed, the *trustworthiness* of the Bible and its authors. This takes us out of the jury box and sets us at our teachers' feet. It is hardly a novel approach; in fact, it is a common assumption behind the way evangelical churches usually preach the Bible. A sermon that honors the Bible's trustworthiness does not criticize the Scripture, nor spend much time defending its veracity either rhetorically or apologetically, nor distance the congregation from its voice by emphasizing cultural or historical differences. Instead, it demonstrates the Scripture's trustworthiness by reading the text attentively and respectfully and by focusing on conveying its meaning and implications for a trusting congregation to hear.

Imagine a mother at the dinner table, reading a letter from a traveling relative to an attentive family. She might gloss sentences or simplify the language, answer curious children's questions, allow for authorial style and tendencies, and fill in details and background. But in a healthy family she would not be defending, deconstructing, or discounting the letter. This simple stance is what I have usually encountered in evangelical sermons, Bible studies, and devotions. It is intuitive, available evidence warrants it, and it expresses the right relationships we are graced to have with God and God's representatives. It is probably the church's most powerful hermeneutic.

It can look naive, but there is no reason it has to be. Affirming trustworthiness is not an *anti*-critical stance, for it calls us to determine whether we ought to place our trust in the Bible's authorities. The Christian tradition supplies such grounds, outside as well as inside the canon. Do these texts seem to be faithful witnesses to what God has done in Israel, Jesus, and the church? If so,[26] then we should heed them, as disciples; for we and they are all disciples of a trustworthy God.

There are still degrees of trustworthiness among evangelicals. Many of us are bothered by the Bible's rough edges, its contrasts and discrepancies, its silences and approvals on matters we find morally outrageous, and its many passages that startle us and puzzle us and fail to convince. Some respond to these difficult passages in ways that remind me of Paul's

---

26. This is not the place to argue the point, but no critical results I have seen have finally indicated otherwise to me.

description of the "weak" or "powerless" (Rom 14–15): they avoid what they find troublesome by either sticking to familiar passages or finding refuge in safe interpretations that seem to explain away the difficulties. There is trust there, but fear too, with which the trust is guarded and supported. Others respond in "stronger" ways, eager to hear the Bible's unfiltered voices and engage its irksome passages without scandalizing congregations or forfeiting the apostolic faith. The trust here can be mixed with the arrogance that Paul warned about, which might bring the powerless to ruin.

The best evangelical preaching and teaching carries a tone of grateful, confident humility and maintains a fruitful dialectic of support and challenge that honors both our trustworthy Bible and our own universal depravity. One happy example of the exegetical fruits of trust is N. T. Wright's work with the biblical traditions on hell and the intermediate state.[27] Wright never fails to honor even the most difficult and least attractive texts for our culture, even while setting them in an affirmative conversation with the cultural challenges and convictions that make them so.

AUTHORIAL INTENT AND THE WHOLE SENSE OF SCRIPTURE

Scholars in seminaries complain endlessly that churches are hermeneutically negligent when they interpret Bible passages: Pastors practice eisegesis rather than exegesis. They prooftext, disregard literary and historical context, spiritualize what is straightforwardly literal, and cherry-pick Bible translations to get the Bible to say what they want. Rather than conveying the sense of a text when they teach and preach, they merely reproduce the vast set of assumptions and conventional interpretations of evangelical folk religion. It does not take much time traveling in evangelical circles to see how right they are.

To counter this plague of biblical misinterpretation, evangelical scholars have insisted on giving priority, and even determinative meaning, to the biblical authors' original intentions. To recover these, scholars tend to restrict their readings to those of grammatical-historical method. This approach has the considerable virtue of linking present audiences

27. N. T. Wright, *Surprised by Hope: Rethinking Heaven, the Resurrection, and the Mission of the Church* (San Francisco: Harper, 2008).

and the Bible's originators. It also trains interpreters in habits of modest, sober judgment that beat both the inaccuracy of some folk interpretation and the recklessness and sheer audacity of much contemporary revisionist interpretation. However, this restriction can cultivate a spirit of caution that ironically distances contemporary readers from the biblical writers' interpretive boldness, prophetic vision, and hermeneutical imagination. Suddenly the New Testament looks like it is mishandling the Old. Such a restrictive hermeneutic also fosters an uncharitable attitude towards popular interpretation that senses some of the synthetic and allegorical potential of biblical material that beloved hymnody, respected literature, and influential folk evangelicalism have all long drawn on. Seminary grads can end up acting like dour and self-righteous Pharisees nattering about messianic parties and Sabbath healings. The result is yet another critical gap—between a solid but too narrowly disciplined approach to the Bible and the deeper sensibilities of the Bible's own writers, original audiences, and contemporary audiences.

A better way seeks to share "the mind of Christ" that the Old Testament anticipates, the New Testament exemplifies, and healthy churches absorb. It cultivates apostolic judgment that can appreciate both the original senses of biblical texts and their fuller resonances in light of the gospel's fullness of time. It prizes the theological interpretation of Luther, Calvin, Simons, and Wesley, of Anselm and Thomas Aquinas and the Middle Ages' other brilliant interpreters, of Augustine, Athanasius, Irenaeus, and their fellow church fathers who explicated and developed the orthodoxy of the apostles—and of the contemporary readers among us who follow in their footsteps. It is open to revisiting prior conclusions where responsible scholarship and tradition call them into question or develop them in new ways—not out of some grander commitment to revisionism or a radicalized principle of *semper reformanda*, but out of confidence that Scripture's clarity, coherence, and fullness are actually discernable, even if they can never be exhaustively or flawlessly expounded.

An enriched evangelical academic hermeneutic should not involve *fanciful* exegesis that turns the Scriptures into playthings of our own imaginations. That would impose another unhealthy distance, now a postmodern one, from the ecclesial Bible. Instead, it can be accurate interpretation that is disciplined by the unchanging apostolic faith, the Spirit's work to renew minds in the living church (Rom 12:2), the explosion of knowledge that has happened over the last five centuries, and the common *hope* that the first generation of Christians shares with all of its predecessors and successors (Heb 11:39—12:2).[28] Examples of such good work abound. One fine example is Tim Keller's spiritual exegesis of the parable of the prodigal son.[29] Drawing not only on careful exegesis but the tradition's theological wisdom, Keller's own pastoral experience, and insights from the behavioral sciences, it translates and develops the whole gospel brilliantly. Another is "In Christ Alone" from Irish hymn writers Keith and Kristyn Getty, a lyrical and powerful synthesis of biblical and theological themes that precious few contemporary hymns achieve.[30] All go beyond original intent to what Jeannine K. Brown nicely calls the wider *implications* and *effects* of the text.[31]

"THE BIBLE ALONE" AS THE CHURCH'S CANON

In the Reformation, disillusionment over Catholic and Orthodox overconfidence in tradition became the backdrop for a new regard for the Bible's canonicity, clarity, and especially its sufficiency as a source of knowledge of God and God's good news. This has driven the steady evangelical conviction that the Bible alone—*sola scriptura*—is the final authority on Christian faith.

This "Scripture Principle" can deteriorate into a popular attitude that the church is incidental to the Bible's real work, which is mediating God's truth to individual consciences. That attitude deposes the ecclesial Bible, which is the church's common inheritance and teaching task, and sets up the individualist as Scripture's private critic. Life experience, academic qualifications, urban legends and conspiracy theories, and even personal preferences all tend to override even the wisest of the church's

28. A helpful examination of how discipline functions in figural biblical interpretation is O'Keefe and Reno, *Sanctified Vision*, ch. 6.

29. Incidentally, Timothy Keller affirms the Bible's infallibility in his *The Prodigal God: Recovering the Heart of the Christian Faith* (New York: Dutton, 2008) xiv.

30. "What we sing affects how we think, how we feel and ultimately how we live," Keith Kelly says, "so it's important that we sing *the whole scope of truth the Bible has given us*." See "Keith and Kristyn Getty," online: http://www.gettymusic.com/about. aspx. Emphasis mine.

31. Jeannine K. Brown, *Scripture as Communication: Introducing Biblical Hermeneutics* (Grand Rapids: Baker, 2007).

other interpreters. We are all too familiar with the resulting jumble, as well as the cliché that one can make the Bible say anything. Weariness with this biblicistic chaos has spawned flights from orthodoxy, such as the journey of a disenchanted seeker from New York's "Burned Over District" named Joseph Smith. At the same time it has spurred flights to tradition among former biblicists who find order, stability, harmony, and beauty in Roman Catholicism and Eastern Orthodoxy.

Yet *sola scriptura* contains within it the antidotes to these problems. No theological proposal will resolve our chronic conflict of interpretations or banish idiosyncratic biblical interpretation. The New Testament writers foresaw this. However, what *sola scriptura* means is that the Bible is *canonical,* and that involves respect for Scripture's intrinsic ecclesiality.[32] The Bible is *ta biblia,* "the books," a collection of believers' writings that did not come from a newspaper or a bookstore for indiscriminate public consumption, but from Israel's and the church's leaders communicating with one another and with God in the course of their life of shared covenantal faith. The biblical canon carries to us the full force of their words. In fact, as a collection it intensifies that force, as the Holy Spirit indwells Christ's communion of saints and numbers us among them.

An inerrant or infallible Bible implies, in some sense, an inerrant or infallible church—if only in its role in the Bible's origin. That strains the Scripture Principle. Why should Israel and the church not have erred *only* in these roles—in factual recall and authorial intent? Our alternative categories of truthfulness, trustworthiness, and whole sense are friendlier to the spirit of *sola scriptura* because they are better at honoring the relationship between the Bible and the church in each case. An inerrant Bible can only be contrasted with its errant apostles and prophets and their errant successors, maintaining *sola scriptura* only on the basis of that artificial and not terribly plausible difference. However, a collection of true and trustworthy testimonies reflects the truthful and trustworthy figures whom we do and must depend on for their Spirit-driven roles in bringing the kingdom's good news to us. That these writings are

---

32. William F. Abraham points out that canonicity in the early church referred to a cluster of traditions rather than one collection of scriptures treated as epistemically unique. See W. Abraham, *Canon and Criterion.* Even so, within that canonical cluster of traditions the Bible held a unique place as God-inspired words that were not to be contradicted or relativized by any church tradition, but only interpreted through, alongside, *and* over them—a true "canon within the canon."

canonical does not diminish these people's reliability or authority in any way. Instead, it honors precisely that reliability and authority by judging all things according to their standard (which is Christ's standard), even these people's other works. Because they are the people of God doing what they have been doing, the Bible is the incomparable and reliable canon that it is.

I see evangelical canonicity in action in churches where the Bible is treated as the living voice of God's agents to every local gathering of believers, to outside observers among them, and to the whole church in all times and places.[33] Not as a political blueprint for Constantinian restoration or national Christian reconstructionism. Not as a personal spiritual medium whose authenticity contrasts with "organized religion." Not as just one of the church's many treasures. Not as a cryptic or esoteric document whose meaning can only be unlocked by elite scholarly or clerical custodians. Not as the only trusted source of truth in an otherwise dark world or a corrupt church. Not as a wild and dangerous thing that must be tamed by orthodoxy or sensible thinking.

Perhaps the healthiest contemporary combination of canonical respect and critical savvy is found within "postcritical" circles. The biblical interpretation and theology of Richard Hays and the constructive and interdisciplinary theology of Miroslav Volf—two of my own teachers—have exemplified to me the practice of postcritical biblical canonicity. Neither restricts his research or intellectual respect to the canon, nor even the Christian tradition. However, both submit every authority and every proposal to the Bible, including the church traditions and the biblical- and theological-critical methods that have made them who they are. They embody a canonical rather than critical spirit.[34]

33. Canonicity can function in a way that is magisterial, but it need not, as Free Church traditions have learned. At any rate, it is certainly not civil, individualistic, or idiosyncratic except where we force it to be.

34. However, in congregational preaching and life I have found the happiest results in charismatic and evangelical churches where a lived-out respect for canonical biblical primacy informs church-centered preaching, teaching, and discipline and where there is a greater (but *qualified*) suspicion of critical methods, less intellectualism, and lower acculturation to academic habits.

POWER RECEIVED RATHER THAN HARNESSED

The same Reformation history, followed by centuries of revivals and awakenings that have crossed the globe, has taught evangelicals to appreciate the Bible's power. It is not only the power of truth, but the very power of salvation (1 Thess 1:5). Evangelicals have historically centered our preaching and study on Scripture. Bible translation is a focal point in cross-cultural mission. The Gideons distribute Bibles and New Testaments that (except for a few introductory pages) speak for themselves.

Yet some uses of Scripture cross the line between honoring its power and redirecting it. Apologists can treat biblical information as "ammunition" to use against skeptics and antagonists. Activists press biblical themes into service to promote contemporary causes of political freedom, social justice, and personal prosperity. Pastors develop campaigns for church growth or personal progress, then underwrite them with supporting material culled from Scripture. Civil authorities turn ethical codes into policies that govern the willing and unwilling alike. These seek to *harness* the Bible's power as a resource for some other project, however related or similar it is to the original apostolic mission. This moves the reader from an ecclesial stance to a critical one because it inevitably involves gauging which of the Bible's many diverse materials are best suited to that project. And that turns the reader into a miner and a judge.

What these exercises sacrifice is the wholeness of the gospel's power. The word of God does more than just remake aspects of our present age; it closes the age and ushers in the next. It changes not just aspects of a world but the world itself. Such a transformation is not harnessed or coerced. It can only be *received* with the patience that comes from trust.

What is received is forgiveness of sins, which brings about the whole new life of shared anticipation and celebration that the creeds call the fellowship of saints. Participants in this life do not approach the Bible selectively—as, say, a blueprint of a just society, a manual for family harmony, or a roadmap of our geopolitical near future—but holistically: as a gift whose mysterious power never lies in our grasp.

An influential evangelical tradition that expects to receive rather than harness the Bible's power is inductive Bible study: close reading of biblical passages to observe their details, interpret their significance, and apply findings in readers' lives. Inductive Bible studies are happening among graduate students at Chinese and American research universities, among imams in mosques and madrasas, in parliaments and headquarters of international businesses and among homeschooling parents, in prisons in Australia and brothels in Southeast Asia. Their participants might not be expecting God to work powerfully. However, God does just that, and the spread of inductive Bible study technique to such an extraordinarily broad range of contexts worldwide has spawned the expectation among its promoters of even greater things to come.

Critics point out that the questions and assumptions readers bring to the texts set their expectations for what they will find and that in some circles those can be loaded. Even so, the governing assumption of inductive Bible study is that the Bible's authors *have* voices, and that God *does* speak and act through them when we approach Scripture humbly and attentively, and that we *should* be open to being surprised and even remade by encountering God there. Those of us who have tried it have ended up trading stories of prior assumptions upset, not just confirmed. This does not mean inevitably revisionist interpretations. At the dissertation stage in my graduate education, I was so inured to critical suspicion that it shocked me to discover how *orthodox* the New Testament was![35] Much fine inductive biblical reading happens among scholars who find greater support for traditional conclusions. A rewarding recent example is Richard Bauckham's work on the Gospels, whose own internal evidence and historical horizons better support the subapostolic accounts of their authorship, purpose, and message than the form-critical consensus, whose rise and dominance owed more to the plausibility of modern social theory than to the Gospels' actual suitability to its approach.[36] His thesis, that the Gospels are largely eyewitness testimony after all, is a critical insight that can return critical and postcritical readers to our earlier receptivity to the power of that apostolic testimony, which arose not because of flesh and blood but by our heavenly Father, and on which rests Christ's whole church (Matt 16:17–18).

---

35. Sharing this observation at my dissertation defense provoked round and merry laughter from my committee, who were glad I had *finally* stumbled into what was obvious.

36. See Bauckham, ed., *Gospels for All Christians*; idem, *Jesus and Eyewitnesses*.

CONCLUSION: A MISSIONAL RELOCATION

Framing classic features of evangelical (and, often, more broadly Christian) affirmations about the Bible from an ecclesial rather than primarily critical stance consolidates the strengths of each one. When Christians locate our understanding and use of the Bible more truly in the ecclesial setting in which it arose and naturally operates, we become better readers of Scripture, better practitioners of the faith, even better critics. Relocating inerrancy in truthfulness, infallibility in trustworthiness, authorial intent in the whole sense of Scripture, the Scripture Principle in canonicity, and power in reception of God's sovereign initiating grace do not amount to an ambitious proposal for "reconstructing evangelical biblical practice" or some such. They merely contrast the critically shaped approaches and convictions in some areas of the evangelical imagination with the more ecclesially shaped practices and sensibilities of other areas of the same imagination. This is already what we are doing in our living out of biblical faith.

If there is one word for summing up this whole relocation, it is *missional*. The distortions of the critical stance spring from two mistakes: either a failure to recognize and properly characterize the missional nature of the church and its holy Scriptures, or a refusal to take that mission at face value and a tendency instead to interpret it as something else. Any approach to the Bible that falls short in either of these ways cannot help but be artificial and ultimately alienating. However, we need not reject the techniques that inspired the contemporary critical perspective, especially because those techniques predate it, often going back at least to careful patristic practitioners such as Origen, Augustine, and Jerome. Properly reoriented in the Bible's true missional context, scholarly study and characterization of the texts themselves, their historical backgrounds, their likely prehistories, their genres and grammatical particulars, and their interrelationships is instrumental for the church's healthy understanding of Scripture.[37]

---

37. Contemporary scholarship is blessed with a number of scholars who have a good sense of the Bible's character. Among my personal favorites are Richard Bauckham, Richard Hays, Marianne Meye Thompson, N. T. Wright, Markus Bockmuehl, and Robert Alter. In their work one senses how natural the compatibilities are between the Jewish and apostolic faith, the generations of believers whose words comprise the Scriptures, the church that carries on their traditions, and careful research in the various disciplines within the field of biblical studies.

Contributors

Craig Allert is Associate Professor and Chair of Religious Studies at Trinity Western University, Langley, British Columbia. He is author of *Revelation, Truth, Canon, and Interpretation: Studies in Justin Martyr's* Dialogue with Trypho, and *A High View of Scripture: Biblical Authority and the Formation of the New Testament Canon.*

Carlos R. Bovell is an independent scholar. He is author of *Inerrancy and the Spiritual Formation of Younger Evangelicals, By Good and Necessary Consequence: A Preliminary Genealogy of Biblicist Foundationalism*, and *Rehabilitating Inerrancy in a Culture of Fear.*

Gregory Dawes is Associate Professor of Philosophy and Religion at the University of Otago, New Zealand. He is the author of *The Body in Question: Metaphor and Meaning in the Interpretation of Ephesians 5:21–33, The Historical Jesus Question: The Challenge of History to Religious Authority*, and *Theism and Explanation*, in addition to articles in biblical studies and philosophy.

Stephen Dawes is Canon Theologian of Truro Cathedral, England, and a retired Methodist minister. He has spent much of his ministry in theological education in both church and university contexts, and his latest book is *The Psalms: SCM Studyguide.*

Seth Dowland is assistant professor of Religion at Pacific Lutheran University, Tacoma, Washington. His book *Family Values: Gender, Authority, and the Rise of the Christian Right* is forthcoming from the

University of Pennsylvania Press. He has authored several articles about evangelicalism, gender, and politics in contemporary America.

Christian Early is Professor of Philosophy and Theology at Eastern Mennonite University, Harrisonburg, Virginia. He is coeditor with Ted Grimsrud of *A Pacifist Way of Knowing: John Howard Yoder's Non-Violent Epistemology*.

Peter Enns is Senior Fellow of Biblical Studies at The BioLogos Foundation. He is the author of *Inspiration and Incarnation: Evangelicals and the Problem of the Old Testament*.

Harriet A. Harris is Chaplain at the University of Edinburgh. She is author of *Fundamentalism and Evangelicals* and numerous publications in philosophical theology.

D. G. Hart is visiting Professor of History at Hillsdale College, Michigan. He is the author of numerous books on Christianity in the United States, including biographies of J. Gresham Machen and John Williamson Nevin, studies of evangelicalism and Presbyterianism, and works on religion and politics. He is currently writing a global history of Calvinism for Yale University Press.

J. Daniel Hays is Professor of Old Testament and Dean of the Pruet School of Christian Studies at Ouachita Baptist University, Arkadelphia, Arkansas. He is the author of *The Message of the Prophets* and *From Every People and Nation: A Biblical Theology of Race*. He has also co-authored *Grasping God's Word*, *Journey into God's Word*, and *Preaching God's Word*.

Brian Malley lectures in psychology at the University of Michigan. His ethnography, *How the Bible Works*, was one of the first systematic, empirical studies of how Christians think about and use Bibles. He has authored other articles on Christian Biblicism, the dynamics of religious systems, and the interaction of individual minds with broader cultural systems.

Todd Mangum is Associate Professor of Theology and Dean of the Faculty at Biblical Theological Seminary, Hatfield, Pennsylvania. He is the author of *The Dispensational-Covenantal Rift: The Fissuring of American Evangelical Theology from 1936 to 1944* and *The Scofield Reference Bible: Its History and Impact on the Evangelical Church.*

J. P. Moreland is Distinguished Professor of Philosophy at Biola University, La Mirada, California. His many publications include *The Kingdom Triangle*, *The Blackwell Companion to Natural Theology*, *Consciousness and the Existence of God* and *The God Question.*

Stanley E. Porter is President and Dean, and Professor of New Testament at McMaster Divinity College, Hamilton, Ontario. His many publications include *Verbal Aspect in the Greek of the New Testament*, *The Paul of Acts*, *The Criteria for Authenticity in Historical-Jesus Research* (with Wendy J. Porter), *New Testament Greek Papyri and Parchments: New Editions* (with Jeffrey T. Reed and Matthew Brook O'Donnell), *Fundamentals of New Testament Greek*, and *Inking the Deal*, a guide for successful academic publishing.

Richard Schultz is Carl Armerding and Hudson T. Armerding Professor of Biblical Studies and Professor of Old Testament at Wheaton College. He is the author of *The Search for Quotation: Verbal Parallels in the Prophets.*

Paul Seely is President of Evangelical Reform. He is author of *Inerrant Wisdom* and has published articles on science and the Bible in *Perspectives on Science and Christian Faith* and *Westminster Theological Journal.*

Telford Work is Associate Professor of Theology and Chair of Religious Studies at Westmont College, Santa Barbara, California. He is the author of *The Brazos Theological Commentary on the Bible: Deuteronomy* and *Living and Active: Scripture in the Economy of Salvation.*

Stephen Young is a doctoral student in Brown University's Department of Religious Studies (Religion in the Ancient Mediterranean). His research analyzes early Christian and Judean sources and their producers alongside broader religious, philosophical, and other kinds of specialists.